Write of Way

Essay Strategies and Readings

Douglas B. Rogers

Niagara College

Prentice Hall Allyn and Bacon Canada
Scarborough, Ontario

Canadian Cataloguing in Publication Data

Rogers, Douglas B. (Douglas Bays)
  Write of way : essay strategies and readings

Includes index.
ISBN 0-13-020907-4

1. English language – Rhetoric. 2. Essay. I. Title.

PE1471.R633 1999   808.4   C99-932674-8

Prentice-Hall, Inc., Upper Saddle River, New Jersey
Prentice-Hall International (UK) Limited, London
Prentice-Hall of Australia, Pty. Limited, Sydney
Prentice-Hall Hispanoamericana, S.A., Mexico City
Prentice-Hall of India Private Limited, New Delhi
Prentice-Hall of Japan, Inc., Tokyo
Simon & Schuster Asia Private Limited, Singapore
Editora Prentice-Hall do Brasil, Ltda., Rio de Janeiro

ISBN 0-13-020907-4

Vice President, Editorial Director: Laura Pearson
Acquisitions Editor: David Stover
Art Direction: Julia Hall
Associate Editor: Susan Ratkaj
Production Editor: Matthew Christian
Copy Editor: Kelli Howey
Production Coordinator: Peggy Brown
Marketing Manager: Sophia Fortier
Cover Design: Carole Knox
Cover Image: Tony Stone Images/David Arky
Page Layout: Janette Thompson (Jansom)

1 2 3 4 5 03 02 01 00 99

Printed and bound in Canada.

Visit the Prentice Hall Canada web site! Send us your comments, browse our catalogues, and more
at **www.phcanada.com**. Or reach us through e-mail at **phabinfo_pubcanada@prenhall.com**.

Contents

Our Community

Appendix: Fundamentals of Grammar 455

Readings Listed by Method of Developing Ideas

Explaining Causes and Effects

Comparing and Contrasting

Arguing and Persuading

Student/Example Essays
Listed by Theme

Write of Way Web Pages

www.prenticehall.ca/rogers

Need to write a resume? Want to issue a press release? Wish you could take minutes at a meeting? Visit the Web pages to apply what you learned in *Write of Way* to the documents listed below.

Taking Care of Business

1. Business Letters
2. Memos
3. Job Applications and Résumés

Acing Written Tests

1. Writing Essay Answers for Tests

Writing for Your Life

1. Agendas and Minutes for Meetings
2. Letters to the Editor
3. Newsletter Articles
4. News Releases
5. Notices and Posters
6. Petitions
7. Proposals and Grant Applications
8. Social Communication (toasts, invitations, thank-you's)

To the Student

Worker, family member, citizen—in all your roles, it is more important than ever to write well. To get even an entry-level job, you must write a résumé. To create your own job, you may write a job proposal or grant application, or—like a student I collaborated with recently—sales letters to promote a small home-office business (in this case, selling perfume). You may fax messages to order lunch. You may write e-mail and send it via the Internet to family members half a world away. As a volunteer, you may keep minutes for the minor hockey league.

Your intelligence—your worth—is judged every time you write. One year, when the members of a service club had grown too old and too few to run the Santa Claus Parade, a young man stepped in and saved it. The next year, when Darrin wrote to say he'd like to continue to run the parade, a city councillor displayed his letter and ridiculed Darrin's writing as semi-literate and said his teachers should be fired. Imagine how embarrassed he must have felt to be centred out that way. Consider the effect: citizens with good ideas, but unsure of their writing ability, might remain silent rather than risk public embarrassment by writing to the newspapers or their politicians.

Writing is judged against four standards. The moment readers set eyes on a document you've written, the judging begins. Readers form a favourable or unfavourable first impression based on the appearance of your document. After they begin to read, they begin to evaluate the content—do you make sense? Next, readers will be pleased by well-organized writing and frustrated by badly organized documents. Finally, readers will be distracted by any deviations from Standard English—the language they expect of other educated people.

You are among the most diverse group of students who have ever attended college. Seated with you are students who have written letters to the editor, people who have submitted grant applications for bingo funds to buy books for the school library, citizens who have started petitions. *Write of Way* shows you how to write brief essays and research essays; then, via the *Write of Way* Web pages (www.prenticehall.ca/rogers) it continues by helping you with all these other kinds of writing, and more. It teaches you to write documents with good content (C), efficient organization (O), Standard English expression (S), and a pleasing appearance (A)—the components of the COSA formula for excellent writing—and the foundation of *Write of Way*, a textbook specifically written for Canadian students.

How do you know whether this is the right book to help you write better? Well, have you understood this introduction? You read well enough to learn everything else in this book. Have you left a note to tell a family member where to reach you? Have you written answers to teachers' test questions? If you can already write that well, you are ready for *Write of Way.* Are you confident that you can write an MLA-style research essay? Do your pronouns always agree in number with their antecedents? If you answered "no" to either of these questions, then *Write of Way* can help you write better.

Write of Way presents the COSA formula as an orderly, logical procedure for improving writing. Do you want to improve your writing in the fastest, most efficient way possible? Get help from a teacher who will coach you and critique your writing, and use *Write of Way* to study topics indicated by your teacher. Study precisely how to write better by improving the content, organization, Standard English, and appearance of your writing.

Employers want workers who take charge of their own professional development. College teachers want to help students learn to teach themselves. *Write of Way* makes it easy to take over some of the job of transforming yourself into a better writer. You will find many exercises to practise what you study. Try to answer each question. Then, see how your answer compares to the text. (If you see a star beside an activity number, you know you can find the answers in chapter 15.) You can study precisely what you need to know, test yourself, and assess your current understanding by correcting your own work.

Beginning with the introduction, *Write of Way* shows you specific ways to improve your writing. Use the book *to learn to write better.* Use it as *a reference manual* when you need to remind yourself about how to use the comma or how to write a research essay. Use your new knowledge and skills *to help someone else learn to write well*, perhaps a nephew or daughter. As you plan your career—and your life—in the age of the information revolution, you will need to write proficiently, or yield the right of way to others more skilled.

To the Instructor

Write of Way, Essay Strategies with Readings is one result of thirty years of trying to understand how we human beings learn to read and write. My apprenticeship has included stints tutoring adult illiterates, teaching our own three children—while they were babies—to read and write, tutoring reading and writing in elementary schools, teaching reading education courses to teachers and teachers-in-training, and teaching English composition to college students studying everything from engineering technology to nursing to culinary skills.

I believe passionately that the lives of working men and women are enriched by the ability to read and write well.

Write of Way is a work-in-progress by someone who believes that English teachers do valuable—no, make that *invaluable*—work, and that all of us must continue to learn how to teach better. *Write of Way's* Instructor's Resource Kit, designed to help overburdened composition teachers save time, suggests ideas to help our students write well. The *Write of Way* Web pages will permit the publishing of contributions from you and your students: more essays that showcase Canada, more grammar tests, and other activities that tell your stories about the people and places in this wonderful, fragile country. *Write of Way* could be an interactive composition textbook: tell me what you want, and I'll try to respond via e-mail (douglasb.rogers@sympatico.ca) or the Web pages (www.prenticehall.ca/rogers). I hope that *Write of Way* is an exciting new stage in my continuing efforts to find effective ways to help students write better. I hope that when you read over this list of features, you'll decide *Write of Way* is a good choice for a text to help *your* students improve as writers.

* ★ *Write of Way* **is a Canadian college composition text.** Students are spurred to talk about their own experiences of our country because the text is suffused with stories of ordinary and extraordinary Canadian people and events, from studying hospitality at Holland College in PEI, to visiting the Lennoxville Campus of Champlain Regional College in Quebec, to sipping cappuccino in the Annex near the University of Toronto, to celebrating Harriet Tubman and the Underground Railway, to watching ferruginous hawks in Alberta, to reviewing the art of Mary Pratt at the Emily Carr Institute of Art and Design in Vancouver.

* ★ *Write of Way* **is flexible.** *Write of Way* makes it easy for teachers to jump-start student writing by beginning with the hands-on overview of essay writing in the

first chapter or by studying the details of essay writing in chapters 2-5 and reviewing the writing process by studying chapter 1 just before writing the first essay.
Some teachers will use the text to help their students study how to write more
proficiently in each rhetorical mode. Other teachers will take a thematic approach
since both the published essays and the student/example essays explore three
themes: ourselves, our stories, and our communities.

★ ***Write of Way* is based on contemporary teaching methods.** Under the
guidance of a more experienced writer, students write better than when they work
alone. Vygotsky, the cleverest educational psychologist of the twentieth century,
noted that we learn more quickly when we work collaboratively. With other textbooks, my students *studied* writing for four to six weeks before they *did* any writing.
With *Write of Way*, students are engaged in writing from the beginning of the course.

Write of Way promotes activity-based, student-centred teaching. You can use the text
and the Instructor's Resource Kit to engage students in activities—individual and
group—to study researching, notetaking, outlining, and grammar. The tone of the book
conveys to students that their author and their instructor are colleague writers. *Write of
Way* shows that we are all in this together: we all have to write, and we all want to do
it well and quickly.

Students learn faster when they have an understanding of the overall goal of the
individual learning tasks. The COSA formula shows students the big picture: good writing results when great content (C) is effectively organized (O), expressed in Standard
English (S), and presented with a pleasing appearance (A). This easy-to-remember
formula helps students understand the need to learn the details of narrowing a topic,
creating outlines, controlling the semicolon, and learning MLA style.

Each chapter is written to stand alone, but *Write of Way* is also based on a spiral
curriculum. Often, a topic is introduced in a general, global way. Later the topic is revis-
ited, but the second look is more detailed because the student is now ready for that
detail. The instruction about brief essays shows students how the skills they are learning
empower them to write better research essays, memos, press releases, and job applications. Essays analyzed in the first chapter are referred to throughout the book, making
it easier for students to understand—and remember—the guidance about how to write
better. Excerpts from press releases and letters to the editor are used to make points
about essay writing, too. The focus is on using the writing of brief essays as a lead-in to
writing research essays and the other kinds of documents students will write later in
their undergraduate courses. The brief essays—like our students—vary in sophistication,
allowing all learners to find papers they can emulate. There is also a section of readings,
published essays, mostly Canadian.

Write of Way encourages students to show the initiative that employers tell us they want in college graduates. A student needs to study how to preview the thesis? Assign that student to read that particular section of text. There's text that explains previewing main points and an activity—with answers—to test the new understanding. Problems with Standard English? Instructors who like to directly teach the grammar conventions most typically violated by college students will find these conventions conveniently grouped in chapter 11. Teachers can guide students to other sections of the text for both remediation or enrichment because *Write of Way* has a huge grammar section so that composition teachers can comment on virtually every error students make—as employers do. To encourage students to read the particular advice they need, the conventions are presented in small sections. Students can teach themselves, once their teachers pinpoint what must be learned.

★ *Write of Way* **saves instructors time.** As colleges reduce the number of hours in programs and reduce the amount of time students participate in college English courses, conscientious instructors are constantly searching for ways to give their students the most bang for their educational bucks. Teachers can use the editor's feedback system—printed in the Instructor's Resource Kit, which is available on computer disk so that you can customize it for lecture notes, acetate transparencies or PowerPoint presentations—to write students coded comments, comments that show students exactly what and where to study in the text. Handout 1 describes a system for motivating students to do this follow-up work for marks. Time-stressed teachers can encourage their students to read the text by testing them with the multiple-choice tests provided for each chapter. While students can mark some of their own work because the answers are given in the text, the answers for other activities appear only in the *Instructor's Manual*, and some activities *and* answers appear only in the *Instructor's Manual* so that teachers can present new material for group activities, lecture examples, or tests; for example, the material about writing research essays includes a nine-activity handout that presents individual and group activities for in-class and homework assignments, activities that ensure students learn concrete skills such as how to take notes while researching, how to outline essays, and how to format their bibliographies and essay covers in MLA and APA style.

★ *Write of Way* **is designed to facilitate writing across the curriculum.** When teaching content area courses, teachers can hand out the editor's response forms for research essays and as much as they are comfortable with of the response form for Standard English—with its simple system for coding errors—to reinforce the writing skills taught in the generic skills composition courses. The easy-to-learn, easy-to-use editor's response forms—which can be customized—provide a fast way for a teacher of a program course to show students writing errors that lead their readers to lower their opinion of the student's competence. Content-area teachers will know their students can find in their composition textbook a lesson for each code on the forms. Think of the greater power of our literacy instruction if writing skills were reinforced when students studied their content-area courses!

★ *Write of Way* **teaches writing for the real world.** *Write of Way* teaches the usual: writing for school—brief and research essays—but it goes well past that. It aims to be a textbook and a reference book for writing for the real world. It treats post-secondary students as the rounded people they are, as parents, spouses, and citizens. On the *Write of Way* Web pages, students can see how to write grant proposals to get lottery funds to re-roof the arena their kids skate in. They can learn how to write résumés and job application letters—and how to write for their company or service club newsletter. Web documents show them how to petition their local or provincial government for more child-care services. The concepts of *Write of Way* are applied in all the examples on the Web pages. Readers will see that adults who learn to write better can be more helpful to the children in their lives—their sons and daughters, their nieces and nephews. When students see the relevance of writing to their lives, they work harder in first-year composition courses.

Write of Way shows students that they can live better lives if they learn to write better. Can we do less for our students in this new information era?

Introduction

"Some essays are descriptive, narrative, or argumentative; some are whimsical, humorous, or satiric; some are biographical, critical, or historical; some are objective, some subjective."
—*Dictionary of Literary Terms*

"Great writers leave us not just their works, but a way of looking at things."
—*Elizabeth Janeway*

Essays are all around you. You'd find an essay if you wrote down the words Don Cherry speaks when he looks into the television camera and rants about how the game of hockey is going downhill. Columnists—some earn six-figure incomes—write essays that are among the most popular parts of daily newspapers. Sometimes distinguished speeches, such as the Massey Lectures at the University of Toronto, are published as a series of essays. Listen to a politician give a speech. Write out the speech, and you'd probably find an essay with a simple thesis: You should vote for me. And effective politicians always detail the reasons you should give your support.

The skills you use to write essays—asserting a point and supporting it with details—are all around you, too. Your job application contends that an employer should hire *you*, and you include details about your qualities and experiences to try to prove you're the right choice. Learn to write essays well, and you're also on your way to writing effectively other documents that will be important in your life. Need a summer job? Perhaps you should write a grant proposal. Want schools to be funded more generously? Write a letter to the editor or your member of the legislature. Need a faster modem? That persuasive memo you'll write has a lot in common with a persuasive essay.

Chapter 1 reviews what you already know about essay writing and previews what *Write of Way* teaches to help you write better essays.

Introduction to the COSA Formula for Good Writing

"Writing is no trouble: you just jot down ideas as they occur to you. The jotting is simplicity itself—it is the occurring which is difficult."
—Stephen Leacock

CHAPTER OBJECTIVE

After you've worked your way through the introductory chapter—reviewing and previewing important concepts about writing—you will have a solid understanding of how to write a brief essay.

Write of Way shows you how to write brief essays and adapt them to any length you need to express your thoughts and feelings. Essays—brief pieces of writing—are usually non-fiction (although some humorous essays may stray from literal truth). They are written for many different purposes. The essays presented in *Write of Way* show effects, such as the ways the lives of citizens change when the police use photo radar to enforce speed limits. Essays explore comparisons, such as how young and adult offenders are treated when they break the law. Many essays are written to persuade readers; essays may advocate outlawing spanking or banning nicknames.

As different as essays are from one another, all have something in common: each essay adds to what human beings know. Essays are not simply reports or summaries of what is already known; when you write an essay you contribute to human knowledge by presenting new perspectives, making new points, and supporting them with additional information. As you create essays, you analyze your audience and tailor your message to meet their needs. When you can write effective essays, you have developed the thinking skills that characterize highly educated people.

You'll write better essays if you remember the COSA formula: Excellent writing is the product of good content (C) that you effectively organize (O), express in Standard English (S), and format with an attractive appearance (A). As you learn to write essays, *Write of*

Way also shows you how to apply the COSA formula to write the other documents important in your life: you can visit the *Write of Way* pages on the Prentice Hall Web site (www.prenticehall.ca/rogers) to study models and specific suggestions for how to write job applications, research essays, letters to the editor, résumés, memos, and more. Start by learning to write powerful essays.

1.1 IMPROVE YOUR WRITING BY STUDYING MODELS

A good way to improve your writing is to study a document similar to what you want to write. Read "It Takes a Whole Village to Raise a Child," an example of a narrative essay. (It's the first essay in chapter 6.) As you read the essay, think about to whom the author was writing and for what purpose.

Experienced readers hold in their memories prototypes—models—of different types of writing, including essays. As educated readers begin reading "It Takes a Whole Village to Raise a Child," they identify it as an essay and expect it to conform to their idea of an essay. They expect the writer to assert a viewpoint, to state a *thesis*. What does the author contend in "It Takes a Whole Village to Raise a Child"? He says that "we really must take better care of all our children." The content of the essay also includes three main ways we must improve our care of children: share our culture, our food, and our schools. The writer speaks directly to his audience of college students and the general public to urge them to work to improve the lives of our poorer children.

Readers also expect writers to support each main point they make. Did the writer add convincing detail to support, for example, the point that we should take better care of our children by ensuring that they have enough food? The anecdotes that showed poor children were shorter as preschool and junior-high students may convince readers that some children don't grow normally because they don't get enough to eat.

"It Takes a Whole Village to Raise a Child" has the essentials of an essay: a thesis, main points that support the thesis, and convincing, specific details to support the main points. You may have to write similar brief essays on job applications—Why do you want to work for our company?—and to answer questions on tests.

As you read the essay, you may have wondered: How did the writer create the content of the essay? How did he organize it? How did he write the five paragraphs that it comprises? Read the rest of chapter 1 for a review of what you already know about writing essays and a preview of what *Write of Way* teaches in more detail in the next several chapters. Follow the discussion of how to build essays paragraph by paragraph.

Begin to write better essays by considering what educated readers expect of your paragraphs. Take a look at Donovan Cutler's paragraph, "Down-Home Cooking" (figure 1–1).

FIGURE 1–1

Sample Paragraph, "Down-Home Cooking"

> Where I grew up on Ramea Island, my mother ran a traditional Newfoundland home, including planning evening meals that were different every night of the week, but the same from week to week. On Sundays, we sat down to a big baked chicken dinner with boiled carrots, cabbage, potatoes, and gravy. Such a big meal meant Mondays were leftover days. Tuesday was soup day; usually the soup stock was made from wild game—moose, caribou, or rabbit. If it was a Wednesday, we counted on a boiled dinner, maybe veggies and fish or veggies and salt beef. On Thursdays, meat and mashed potatoes with gravy were the centre of our main meal of the day. The meals on Fridays and Saturdays were even more traditionally Newfoundland. Fridays were fish days; the fish was often battered and fried in oil. For religious reasons, there was never any meat on Fridays. On Saturdays we ate pea soup. There was always salt beef in the soup, and Mom often served pork cakes (ground pork and flour—no rising agent—fried). Although the food changed a little with the seasons—September might mean a partridgeberry pie—there was a reassuring rhythm to these evening meals, which were planned a week in advance, all year long.

As educated readers begin reading Cutler's document, they will expect it to conform to their idea of a paragraph. They expect, for example, that the writer will express the main point of the paragraph in the first sentence, the topic sentence. What does Cutler contend? What is his main point? He says that his mother planned the family meals so that they were different every day of the week and then repeated that pattern all year round.

ACTIVITY 1–1*

Making a Balloon Outline of a Paragraph

Test your own ability to recognize the topic sentence in the paragraph in Figure 1–1 by encircling it with a balloon, like the speech balloons around the dialogue in newspaper comic strips. Write the label *topic sentence* beside the balloon.

Readers also expect writers to support the point they make in the first sentence. Did Cutler show that the meals were organized around the days of the week? Yes. Most often he wrote one sentence to show the pattern of meals for each day of the week. Sometimes he provided more detail, as he did when he told us that the family ate fish every Friday because of religious beliefs. Draw a balloon around the sentences Cutler wrote to support his point that his mom followed a pattern in her meal planning. Label this balloon *support sentences*.

Experienced readers may also expect that at the end of a paragraph the writer will remind readers of the point; there will be a concluding sentence. Balloon and label Cutler's concluding sentence, in which he restates, or recaps, the point he made in his topic sentence. You can check your work by looking at figure 15–1 in chapter 15. (Chapter 15 includes the answers for every activity marked with an asterisk.)

"Down-Home Cooking" is very short, a single paragraph. Writers create a separate paragraph for each main idea in a document. They also leave white space on a page—either blank lines between paragraphs or five-space indentations at the start of each paragraph—so that readers can easily distinguish paragraphs. Experienced readers hold such similar conceptions of paragraphs that you can actually outline a paragraph. Figure 1–2, "Outline of a Simple Paragraph," shows the organization readers expect essay writers to conform to, the kind of organization you'll want to create for most of your paragraphs.

FIGURE 1–2

Outline of a Simple Paragraph

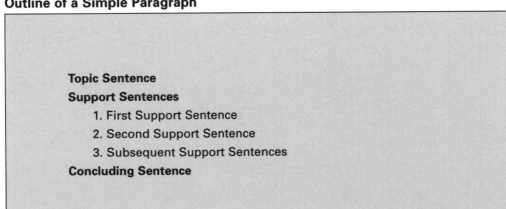

Topic Sentence
Support Sentences
    1. First Support Sentence
    2. Second Support Sentence
    3. Subsequent Support Sentences
Concluding Sentence

Keep this outline in mind when you need to write a paragraph; your effective organization will make a good impression on your readers.

It takes lots of practice to write as well as the newspaper columnists who earn six-figure salaries for writing two or three essays a week, but in the next section you can read about the fundamentals of their craft. Begin by studying simple and concrete essays, and you'll be on your way to developing skill at one of the most remarkable achievements of our species: creating new knowledge by writing essays.

1.2 IMPROVE YOUR WRITING BY COLLABORATIVE COMPOSING

Collaborate in the writing of a paragraph and an essay, and you will consolidate your vision of the process of composing essays. Start by reading this description of a group of students creating a slightly more complex paragraph. Complete the activity yourself. That way you, too, can get a little ink on your hands. Focus on an important fundamental of writing: how writers create the support for a point. The topic is supplied; you create the support.

▶ ACTIVITY 1-2*

Brainstorming Ideas for How to Enjoy a Blizzard

Imagine that on a cold, grey, snowy winter day you decide to write a paragraph to share ideas with other college students about how to enjoy a Canadian blizzard. What's one way you could enjoy a blizzard? Another? Write down several ideas. Compare your ideas to the list of ideas brainstormed by other students (figure 15–2). It shows the support the students created for the assertion in the topic sentence that you can enjoy a blizzard if you prepare for it.

When you read figure 15–2, you may notice two distinct themes, main points, or ideas about how to respond to a blizzard. Some of the details are about *surviving* a blizzard, but most of the details support the idea that you can actually *enjoy* a blizzard if you prepare for it.

To improve your ability to move from writing notes to creating a sound paragraph, examine an outline of another kind of paragraph (figure 1–3), the type of outline needed for a paragraph more complex than Cutler's. This is the type of outline you could refer to to complete a paragraph called "How to Enjoy a Blizzard."

FIGURE 1–3

Outline of a Complex Paragraph

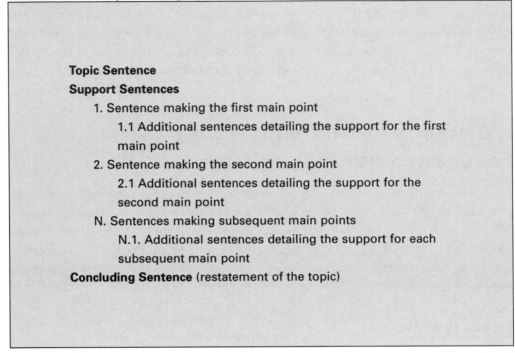

Topic Sentence
Support Sentences
   1. Sentence making the first main point
      1.1 Additional sentences detailing the support for the first
      main point
   2. Sentence making the second main point
      2.1 Additional sentences detailing the support for the
      second main point
   N. Sentences making subsequent main points
      N.1. Additional sentences detailing the support for each
      subsequent main point
Concluding Sentence (restatement of the topic)

Perhaps some of the details and examples of ways to enjoy a blizzard can be combined into main points. That way your paragraph won't be just a long, disorganized list of ideas. If you ignore the ideas for just surviving blizzards, you may find three patterns or groups of ideas—main ways you can enjoy being snowed in. You might first notice this main idea: you can enjoy a blizzard by being prepared with the right food. Make sure you've got food you really enjoy. Notice how this main point can be supported by several suggestions:

First Main Point:
You can enjoy a blizzard if you make sure you've got great food.
Supporting Details:
   be sure to have enough food
   buy your favourite snacks
   get the ingredients to cook a gourmet meal while you're snowed in

Can you identify two other main points about how to enjoy a blizzard? Jot them down along with the details that support them, then look at the suggestions below.

Second Main Point:

Enjoy a blizzard by arranging for good entertainment.

Supporting Details:

    rent good videos

    find your favourite games

    get magazines and books

    pay the cable bill

Third Main Point:

You can actually enjoy a blizzard—if you're with friends.

Supporting Details:

    arrange to be with someone you really like

    make sure your kids are home

    call in sick to your workplace so you're not stranded there

You were given the topic sentence (with proper preparations, you can actually enjoy a blizzard). You created the support. You even found a way to make the paragraph more coherent by grouping specific details under main points: inviting a friend over, making sure your kids are home, and arranging to be stranded at home rather than at work are all examples of how you'd have more fun in a blizzard if you were in good company.

▶ **ACTIVITY 1–3★**

Outlining a Complex Paragraph

Take another look at the outline of a more complex paragraph, and complete a similar outline for your paragraph about how to enjoy a blizzard. Some parts of the outline are already filled in. Turn each point in the rough notes into an entry for this decimal outline.

FIGURE 1-4

Partial Outline of a Complex Paragraph, "How to Enjoy a Blizzard"

Topic Sentence

With the proper preparations, you can enjoy rather than endure that next winter storm.

Support Sentences

1. Sentence making the first main point:

The first step to ensuring delight rather than depression is to stock your home with enough good food to outlast the worst winter can throw at you.

1.1 Additional sentences detailing the support for the first main point:

- Don't forget the most important food group: snack foods.
- Remember tearing out that newspaper recipe for Thai noodles? Now's the perfect time to make that gourmet meal.

2. Sentence making the second main point:

2.1 Additional sentences detailing the support for the second main point:

3. Sentence making the third main point:

3.1. Additional sentences detailing the support for the third main point:

Concluding Sentence (restatement of topic)

▶ ACTIVITY 1–4＊

Writing a Complex Paragraph from an Outline

Referring to figure 15–3, write a paragraph about how to enjoy a blizzard. Compare your paragraph to the suggested answer in figure 15–4.

The same procedure—create a topic sentence and create and organize support—is used to create the paragraphs for longer documents, including research essays—even doctoral dissertations. The study and practice of effective paragraph writing is a powerful way to learn how to improve many of the documents you write in your life outside school. Chapter 4 focuses on writing good paragraphs, the foundation of most of our writing. In the next section of this chapter, you can consider how to move from writing a single paragraph to writing a whole essay.

1.3 IMPROVE YOUR WRITING BY ANALYZING A BRIEF ESSAY

Look at another example of a brief essay, this time a five-paragraph essay, "Pancakes for Sunday Brunch." This is a simple essay about a very concrete topic. It's included because it is simple and concrete and can be analyzed to demonstrate how writers create the content and organization of an essay. Engage in the activities for this little essay until you remember it so well you can use it as a prototype in your own essay writing. In chapters 6 and 7, you can see how the same principles were followed to write more sophisticated brief essays.

FIGURE 1–5

A Simple Brief Essay, "Pancakes for Sunday Brunch"

Introductory
paragraph

Topic sentence

> With time and money scarce in the 1990's, many people satisfy their craving for leisurely gourmet dining by relaxing over inexpensive, homemade meals. Even a busy person can transform a routine Sunday breakfast into an inexpensive, glorious brunch by preparing gourmet pancakes. The secret to wonderful pancakes is to follow three simple steps: select quality ingredients, cook them carefully, and serve the meal with flair.

The successful cook knows that great food begins with great ingredients. Break into a stainless steel bowl two of those brown eggs you got at the market from the farmer who lets her chickens run free. Beat the eggs together with a cup of fresh milk. Add a dash of salt, a teaspoon of baking powder, a splash of vanilla, and a mashed banana that has ripened almost to spoiling. Only a wooden spoon will do to stir in the stone-ground whole-wheat flour. Use just enough to turn the mixture from runny to thick but syrupy. You can tell already that these will be great pancakes.

The chef must now take care to cook the pancakes to perfection. Use butter—not oil—to grease the pan. Heat the skillet until it is hot enough to make a test drop of water sizzle but not so hot that the butter smokes. Ladle as many three-inch puddles of the batter as will fit in your frying pan. Don't flip the pancakes until you see bubbles all over the uncooked top; if you turn them only once, they will be lighter. Take care while cooking, and you'll thank yourself when you eat.

Your delicious pancakes almost guarantee a good brunch, but you can ensure success by presenting the food with flair. Pour hot coffee into a carafe. Fill a small pitcher with maple syrup. Find the butter dish. Select your best matching cups and plates. Fetch the Sunday paper. Put a single rose into a bud vase. Now, get out your favourite tray, and carry the whole meal up to your bedroom and your partner. Present the meal with a flourish.

Conclusion

You selected quality ingredients, cooked them carefully, and presented your food with flair. While away the rest of the morning with your homemade brunch of gourmet pancakes.

By taking apart this five-paragraph essay, you can learn how to write your own essays with a similar structure. The lessons you learn will help you write news releases, research essays, and other kinds of documents. In a single sentence, summarize—in your own words—the main point of the essay. Is your sentence something like this: You can make an inexpensive brunch of pancakes if you select quality ingredients, cook them carefully, and serve the pancakes with flair? You've just expressed the thesis and previewed the main points of the essay about a homemade brunch.

If you look at the essay itself—everything after the title—you'll notice that it has five paragraphs. Three of these paragraphs are quite similar. Which three? In a *boxcar* essay, the support paragraphs in the middle of the essay will share characteristics of paragraphs in general. These garden-variety paragraphs underlie all kinds of documents, including letters to the editor and movie reviews. The first and final paragraphs, however, have special functions: they introduce and conclude essays. Figure 1–6 shows the organization of the introductory, support, and concluding paragraphs for a five-paragraph essay. Just read through the outline for now. You'll refer to it as you analyze the pancakes essay. During the analysis of the essay, you may encounter some unfamiliar terms. Keep in mind that this is an introduction to these terms; you'll have the opportunity to study them in more detail in the next few chapters.

FIGURE 1–6

Outline of a Five-Paragraph Essay

TITLE

PARAGRAPH 1: INTRODUCTORY PARAGRAPH

    Lead-in:

    Thesis sentence, including the preview of the main points:

PARAGRAPHS 2, 3, and 4: SUPPORT PARAGRAPHS

    2.   Topic sentence for the first main point:

       Sentences providing detailed support for the first main point:

Concluding sentence for the first main point:

3.   Topic sentence for the second main point (with transition):

Sentences providing detailed support for the second main point:

Concluding sentence for the second main point:

4.   Topic sentence for the third main point (with transition):

Sentences providing detailed support for the third main point:

Concluding sentence for the third main point:

PARAGRAPH 5: CONCLUDING PARAGRAPH
Summary or restatement of the thesis and main points:

Clincher:

▶ **ACTIVITY 1–5★**

Making a Balloon Outline of a Five-Paragraph Essay

Look at the essay, "Pancakes for Sunday Brunch." Take a close look at the structure or organization of its introductory paragraph. Ideally, it should have two elements: a lead-in and a thesis statement.

The lead-in is the sentence or two the writer creates to try to capture the interest of the reader and to make a favourable impression right at the beginning of the piece of writing. It is discussed in more detail in chapter 5, and in chapter 16 you can see how published authors use lead-ins in their essays. Draw a balloon around the lead-in. Did you balloon "With time and money scarce in the 1990's, many people satisfy their craving for leisurely gourmet dining by relaxing over inexpensive, homemade meals"? Label it *lead-in*.

Take a moment and define the word *thesis*. The thesis statement is the sentence or two in which the writer makes an assertion and, usually, the main points that support the writer's contention. This is further discussed in chapter 2. Circle and label the thesis sentence, including the preview of the main points. Did you balloon "Even a busy person can transform a routine Sunday breakfast into an inexpensive, glorious brunch by preparing gourmet pancakes. The secret to wonderful pancakes is to follow three simple steps: select quality ingredients, cook them carefully, and serve the meal with flair"?

Now look at the body of the essay, the three paragraphs that each develop support for a main point announced in the thesis statement. (Essays don't *have* to have five paragraphs, of course. If you were making only two main points to support your thesis, for example, you might write a four-paragraph essay.) These support paragraphs share common characteristics. Like all paragraphs, they begin with an indentation, and each considers only one main point. The organization of the paragraphs, which is detailed in chapter 4, is

- a topic sentence that states the main idea of the paragraph;

- additional sentences to exemplify, develop, or support the main point; and

- a concluding sentence that reiterates that point. (Sometimes, to make the flow of main ideas smoother, writers may include in a topic sentence a reminder of the previous point. Creating transition clauses or sentences to increase coherence is further discussed in chapter 5.)

Test your understanding of the elements of support paragraphs by ballooning and labelling the topic sentence, support sentences, and concluding sentence for each main point of the essay.

Finally, consider the special characteristics of concluding paragraphs. As described at greater length in chapter 5, a concluding paragraph includes

- a sentence that summarizes or recapitulates (recaps)—in different words—the main points previewed in the thesis statement of the introductory paragraph, and

- a clincher, a sentence or two in which the writer leaves the reader with a memorable final comment.

Balloon and label the concluding paragraph with its recap and clincher. Check your work by referring to the answer in figure 15–5.

As you analyze this simple essay, you can reflect on three other concepts important to writing good paragraphs: unity, coherence, and support.

- Does each paragraph have unity? Does each paragraph really have only one main idea, or does extraneous material distract the reader from seeing the main point?

- Consider how the structure of each paragraph—topic sentence, sentences detailing support for the main idea, and a concluding sentence—draws the thoughts together so that the reader can easily see how they all relate, or are coherent. In a similar way, the organization of the paragraphs—introduction, support, and conclusion—contributes to a coherent document.

Unity and support are discussed in more detail in part 1, and coherence is discussed in part 2.

1.4 CREATE AN ESSAY

Well, you haven't got much ink on your hands, yet, but you have been writing. The first stage in the process is sometimes called pre-writing or planning. When you write, you always spend more time thinking than doing the second-stage drafting—whether handwriting or keyboarding—especially in the early stages of a project. Still, now it's time to do more handwriting.

Having taken an essay apart, you're ready to try to *create* one. After you write an essay collaboratively, you'll find it easier to write one alone.

Many writers find that completing an outline—like the one previously presented—makes it much easier to write a sound essay. Remember "Pancakes for Sunday Brunch"? Take a look at another kind of outline, an outline that the writer of the pancakes essay might have completed before writing that essay. Here's a full-sentence, decimal outline of "Pancakes for Sunday Brunch."

FIGURE 1-7

A Full-Sentence, Decimal Outline of "Pancakes for Sunday Brunch"

Thesis Sentence: Make a glorious brunch of gourmet pancakes by choosing quality ingredients, cooking with care, and serving with flair.

1. Great food begins with great ingredients.
   1.1 Select brown eggs from free-range chickens.
   1.2 Use fresh milk.
   1.3 Add your seasonings.
   1.4 Add your rising agent.
   1.5 Choose whole-wheat flour.

2. Cook your quality ingredients carefully.
   2.1 Fry in butter rather than oil.
   2.2 Be sure the skillet is hot before you ladle in the pancake mix.
   2.3 Flip the pancakes only once.

3. Serve the meal with flair.
   3.1 Serve the coffee from a carafe.
   3.2 Serve the maple syrup from a pitcher, not the bottle.
   3.3 Use a butter dish.
   3.4 Select matching crockery.
   3.5 Fetch the Sunday paper.
   3.6 Put a rose in a bud vase.
   3.7 Serve the meal in bed.

It would be rare to make such a detailed outline before writing a draft, but sketchier outlines are common and useful, perhaps even indispensable. To make an outline, you need main points. Where do the main points come from? How do writers create the main ideas they organize into an outline? You can work through the process. Read on to generate the main points for a five-paragraph essay, take notes, create an outline, and write an essay.

▶ **ACTIVITY 1–6***

Brainstorming for an Essay about the Effects of Photo Radar

Suggest as quickly as possible every effect you can imagine of using photo radar to enforce speed limits on highways, as is done in Alberta and British Columbia and some forty countries around the world. Write notes so that you don't forget important information. Compare your work to the ideas generated by some other students (see figure 15–6).

The list in figure 15–6 is a confusion of conflicting points that looks little like the supporting details listed on the outline for "Pancakes for Sunday Brunch." How can you transform this unwieldy list into something more useful in planning an essay? You need to consider your audience and your purpose. Imagine that you want to convince members of the general public that they will benefit when the government uses photo radar to enforce speed limits. Look over the list again. The list is a mix of positive and negative effects, isn't it? When you designate each effect as positive (P) or negative (N), you end up with a list like the one below:

FIGURE 1–8

List of Positive and Negative Effects of Photo Radar

- more tailgating   N
- ticket doesn't necessarily go to the offender   N
- slower driving speeds   P
- more congested highways   N
- less work for police   P
- police can concentrate on crime instead of radar   P

- province makes more money   P
- insurance costs may be lowered for non-speeders   P
- invasion of privacy   N
- fewer accidents   P
- people will invent devices to fool radar   ?
- engineers will invent better photo radar   ?
- fewer serious accidents   P
- gas savings from driving at lower speeds   P
- less cutting in and out of traffic by speeders   P
- cars will be damaged less in accidents at slower speeds   P
- people will disguise their plates   N

If you want to write an essay, a proposal, or a letter to the editor to support photo radar, you are more interested in the positive effects of using photo radar to enforce speed limits. Still, even with a list of good effects, you do not have a neat, short list of main points. Review the list. Can you suggest a way to organize these disparate points? Can you see some points you could group together under one main idea?

Perhaps the first main point you identify is that driving might be safer. Once you identify that point, you can begin to elaborate on points already recorded and to suggest other related effects. Jot down your ideas about how photo radar might make driving safer, and compare your list to these effects:

First Main Point:
driving might become safer when the police use photo radar to enforce speed limits
Supporting Details:
- slower traffic
- fewer accidents
- less serious accidents
- less cutting in and out of traffic

Can you think of another main point? Perhaps you noted that most people might save money because of photo radar. Note which points might support this idea, and then look at these points of support:

Second Main Point:
when photo radar is used to enforce speed limits, people might save money
Supporting Details:
- slower travel reduces fuel costs
- perhaps insurance premiums will be lowered for owners with fewer citations
- cars that are run at slower speeds will last longer
- the government might use the revenues from fines to reduce taxes
- technicians in photo radar units earn less than police officers, resulting in savings to taxpayers

There's a question mark beside two points that seem neither positive nor negative. One student suggested that some drivers might retire to basement shops to try to invent devices to fool photo radar. Another student said that engineers might try to research more effective photo radar in the hopes of making money by selling this better equipment. You might make the point that implementation of photo radar might lead to more hi-tech research and manufacturing.

Third Main Point:
enforcing speed limits with photo radar might spur high technology
Supporting Details:
- people will invent devices to fool photo radar
- engineers will invent improved photo radar equipment

You have now identified three main positive effects of photo radar. What order would you choose to present these points? That last point is the weakest. If you do include it, you should bury it in the middle of the essay. Start with a strong point, and finish with the strongest point. In between the two stronger points—where it is less prominent than a first or last point—make the weakest point.

You're nearly done creating the content of an essay, and this is a good time to review how well you've met your audience's needs. You were writing for the general public. What can you assume the general public will already know? If you were writing for fifth graders you would certainly want to explain the term *photo radar*, but adults might feel insulted if you assumed they were not familiar with the term. What tone will you set? Will you use a lot of slang? Many potential readers might not think slang is appropriate in an essay about a serious topic like traffic regulations. You haven't completed the content of your essay until you analyze your audience, as discussed in more detail in chapter 3.

Now you're ready to organize an essay that you might title "The Positive Effects of Using Photo Radar to Enforce Speed Limits."

ACTIVITY 1–7 ★

Organizing a Five-Paragraph Essay

Organize this essay by creating an outline like the one shown in figure 1–6, "Outline of a Five-Paragraph Essay." First, brainstorm lead-ins. Suggest one yourself. Now, browse the notes made as students planned the essay; then create a thesis statement, and include a plan of organization for the main points—that is, preview the main points of the essay.

Next, write a topic sentence for each main point that you previewed in your thesis sentence. Look over the lists you made, and under each main point record the point-form notes of specific support. Now, write a concluding sentence for each support paragraph.

Write the sentences for the concluding paragraph. Restate (recap) the main points and create a clincher. Compare your work to the completed outline, "Essay Outline for 'The Positive Effects of Using Photo Radar to Enforce Speed Limits,'" figure 15–7.

▶ ACTIVITY 1–8 ★

Writing a Brief Essay

Working from the outline you created for Activity 1–7, complete the essay by changing the point-form support notes into sentences. Then, conduct a third-stage writing procedure, the final step in the process of writing: revision. Use the "Checklist for Brief Essays" (figure 5–2) to ensure that your essay is complete. Proofread the essay, correcting any deviations from Standard English. Are there any spelling errors? Is everything properly capitalized? Check the appearance of the document. Did you format the essay in the style requested by your instructor? Complete your version and compare it to the group composition shown in figure 15–8 (the essay is formatted in MLA style).

1.5 SOME CONCLUDING THOUGHTS

Writers don't always start with an idea for a topic, develop a thesis, make an outline, and write a whole document. They don't always move so smoothly from the planning of the pre-writing phase, through the draft-writing stage, to the revision stage. Sometimes they plunge into writing *before* they have a plan for the whole project. They may change an outline as they think more clearly about a point. Writers often decide they must gather more information—do more research—as they realize they lack sufficient support for a point they are asserting. They may decide to adjust the essay if they anticipate that some of their intended audience may not completely understand the point asserted.

After a first draft, writers will certainly want to reread, possibly revise. Writers often decide to make major changes to the essay; their revision is far more extensive than simply proofreading for spelling and grammar errors, but they will also want to be sure they have observed all the conventions of Standard English and have met the formatting or appearance requirements of their readers. Knowing the three stages in the process of writing—even though the process is recursive—helps writers to complete sound essays and other kinds of documents.

You may feel awkward and self-conscious writing essays. Any new procedure is apt to feel very strange. (Do you remember the first time you parallel parked?) The skills you must develop to write these formulaic essays, however, are the same skills you bring to essays in the real world, essays that are often considerably longer. And when you write a job application letter, an essay for one of your program courses, an answer on a test, or the minutes to a meeting, you will still need to create good content, organize your message, express yourself in Standard English, and make the document look good. In short, you will still use the COSA formula for all those writing needs. In the next several chapters, you'll have an opportunity to study the details of how to improve your writing.

As you get ready to create your first writing assignment for your teacher, consider two suggestions. First, read Box 1–1: "Make Your Writing Look Great." Follow the suggestions and you're virtually guaranteed to get better marks on assignments you present to any of your teachers. Second, reflect on your teacher's instructions about writing. You form a partnership with your instructor when you take a writing course. Do your part by taking charge of your own development as a writer, because you will spend far less time in class than you will need to spend to become a strong writer. Forge independent study procedures. When your teacher mentions a point about writing, use the index in the text to find out more about that point.

In writing, as in life in general, we are what we make ourselves. Take a proactive approach to your own development as a reader and writer. The more effort you put into your studies, the more you'll benefit.

> **BOX 1–1** Make Your Writing Look Great

When you carefully wrap a gift before presenting it, you show respect for the recipient. As a writer, you must also work to present your written message in an appealing format.

If you follow the guidelines presented in this box, your general school work will look great.

When you write for your instructor, you face a problem that is similar to buying a gift for someone's birthday: you are often unsure about what the recipient would like. Ask your instructor about the guidelines for formatting written work; take notes, and follow closely the advice you're given.

Even when you ask for guidance about the appearance of an assignment, you are going to meet instructors who will not provide the detailed instructions you were hoping for. Some instructors will even say appearance is not important, that they leave those sorts of decisions to each student. You're going to have to rely on your own judgment. This is where you need to apply common sense and an understanding of some widely held ideas about the desirable appearance of commonplace school assignments—because even though some readers (and gift recipients) say it's the thought that counts, they are impressed by an attractive appearance. After all, before the content, organization, or even the Standard English of the paper are noticed, the instructor will notice the appearance of the document.

Follow these guidelines for all the ordinary class work you submit—biographies, short-answer tests, in-class assignments—and your writing will create favourable first impressions.

* *Format your classroom paper in the style recommended by the Modern Language Association (MLA).* The style guidelines of the Modern Language Association are widely observed all over the English-speaking world (Gibaldi). Instructors like to see papers formatted following MLA guidelines because the combined cover/first page makes it very easy for them to tell—at a glance—the assignment, who wrote it, when, and for which course.

  Studying and following the guidelines actually saves you time: you no longer have to take time re-inventing how to set up your assignment; instead, you just quickly and automatically format any general school work in MLA style. Refer to figure 1–9, the "Annotated MLA-Style Version of 'Down-Home Cooking,'" as you read these guidelines, and you will very quickly memorize them.

FIGURE 1–9

Annotated MLA-Style Version of "Down-Home Cooking"

Create a heading—in mixed case—consisting of
- student's name
- teacher's name
- course code
- date work is due (or done for in-class assignments)

Double-space the whole document, including the header and heading

Place the header 1.25 cm from the top edge of paper

Centre the assignment title.

Centre the title of the essay.

Leave right margin unjustified

N.B. The first page is also the cover in MLA style

Create 2.5-centimetre margins on the sides and bottom

Cutler 1

Donovan Cutler

Dr. Douglas B. Rogers

ENGL120 (01)

October 6, 1999

Paragraph One, Draft Two (Classification/Division)

Down-Home Cooking

Where I grew up on Ramea Island, my mother ran a traditional Newfoundland home, including planning evening meals that were different every night of the week, but the same from week to week. On Sundays, we sat down to a big baked chicken dinner with boiled carrots, cabbage, potatoes, and gravy. Such a big meal meant Mondays were leftover days. Tuesday was soup day; usually the soup stock was made from wild game—moose, caribou, or rabbit. If it was a Wednesday, we counted on a boiled dinner, maybe veggies and fish or veggies and salt beef. On Thursdays, meat and mashed potatoes with gravy were the centre of our main meal of the day. The meals on Fridays and Saturdays were even more traditionally Newfoundland. Fridays were fish days; the fish was often battered and fried in oil. For religious reasons, there was never any meat on Fridays. On Saturdays we ate pea soup. There was always salt beef in the soup, and Mom often served pork cakes (ground pork and flour—no rising agent—fried). Although the food changed a little with the seasons—September might mean a partridgeberry pie—there was a reassuring rhythm to these evening meals, which were planned a week in advance, all year long.

* *Create a first page/cover.* Create 2.5 centimetre (one inch) margins at the bottom and sides of your writing. Set a 1.25 centimetre (one half inch) margin at the top. Readers like the appearance of text surrounded by white space. Crowded, dense text tires a reader.

    Write in mixed case. Do not use block capitals. When every letter is capitalized, readers find it harder and slower to read because important information about sentence beginnings, acronyms, and proper nouns is lost.

    Create a header 1.25 centimetres from the top of the page and flush to the right margin. In the header include your last name, a space, and the page number of your work. This header will go onto every page. Should the pages of your assignment become separated, it will be easy for your instructor to put them back in order since each page will have the same unique header and a page number.

    Create a heading for your paper. The heading has most of the information your teacher needs to record a mark for your work. In the next four lines record your name, the teacher's name, the name of the course—and, in parentheses, your course section number—and the date. Align these entries with the left margin.

    Create an informative title so your audience can quickly and easily identify the particular piece of writing. You could label an in-class process essay this way:

Assignment Line: Essay One, Draft One (Process)

Title Line: Pancakes for Sunday Brunch

    Informative titles make life easier for your reader by clearly and quickly identifying the particular piece of work.

* *Observe the MLA guidelines throughout your work.* Start the text on the first line below your title. Double-space all your writing. Your instructor will have more room to write comments, and you'll have less need for re-copying because you'll have space to correct mistakes.

    Observe these general guidelines when submitting school work for which the instructor has not given you explicit directions. Keep in mind, as always, that you should pay close attention to any directions or feedback that suggests your audience prefers you to format your work differently. In part 3 of *Write of Way*, for example, you'll study appearance as you practise writing a research essay, a type of essay in which educated readers expect you to observe detailed formatting conventions so complex it takes two chapters to discuss them. And if you look at the Web pages, you'll learn how to format the different types of documents you need to write to conduct your business and live as a spouse, parent, and citizen.

Try Activity 1–9 to test your ability to follow the MLA conventions for the cover/first page of general classroom work.

▶ ACTIVITY 1–9*

Creating an MLA-Style Essay Cover

Chantal Labelle took Dr. Rogers' course COMM112G, How to Argue. She has just finished a paper she's titled "Why Canada Should Provide Universal Daycare." This is the first sentence in her essay: Daycare: "the care and training of babies and preschool children outside the home during the day" ("Daycare"). She will hand in her research essay on October 14, 2001, the due date. Create an MLA-style cover for her essay. Include an assignment title and the first sentence that begins her text.

PART 1

Creating the Content of Effective Documents

*"Why have I told you all this? To make you change your life!
Rilke was right. Every other reason for writing is insignificant."*
—Jack Ludwig

You write because you've decided it's the most effective way to do a job. You write a letter of complaint so the Good Watch Company will send you a replacement for the wristwatch that expired before the warranty. You write a speech so your peers will elect you to student government. You write an essay to persuade citizens to provide universal daycare so all children have an equal chance to excel at school.

Effective writing begins with an astute analysis of your audience. What information will the Good Watch Company need to decide whether to replace your watch? Did you supply enough details? Will the tone of your speech win or lose you votes? When you ask yourself such questions, you're grappling with what to put into your message, what to leave out; you're creating the content of your document, your message.

You write to get a job done. Reading Part 2 will enhance your audience analysis skills so that your writing *works* for you.

CHAPTER 2

Creating and Supporting Your Thesis

"An essayist is a lucky person who has found a way to discourse without being interrupted."
—Charles Poore

CHAPTER OBJECTIVE

After working your way through the activities, you will use notetaking and outlining to write an essay in which you create and support a thesis.

It's no accident that content is the first element in the COSA formula for good writing. The content—the message—is the most important part of any communication. When you're in a hurry and want to leave a note before you rush out the door, you don't worry about the appearance of the old envelope: you're glad to find anything to write on. When you have a great idea, you don't take time to check every spelling: you just want to scrawl down that idea before it slips away from you. When you're writing a rough draft of a toast to the bride, you don't worry about the paragraphs being in the optimum order: you know you can rewrite later. Nothing in your writing matters more than what is in your heart and head. Good writing begins with a clear expression of those feelings and thoughts.

2.1 DECIDE WHAT TO WRITE ABOUT

Often, you'll have no choice about your topic. If your teacher asks you to discuss the causes of the latest economic downturn, that's what you'll write about. If your boss asks you to compare two photocopiers and recommend a purchase, don't write a love poem. Sometimes, especially in composition courses, you are asked to write to practise a particular method of developing an idea—say, describing a process—and you must choose a process to write about. You've got to write about something, and if you want someone to read it, your topic must be interesting to your audience—often, your teacher. In this first stage of writing, the pre-writing stage in which you create a topic to write about and choose the audience you will write for, you may use one or more of four processes: daydreaming, brainstorming, freewriting, and idea mapping. As you study these techniques for discovering what you want to express to your readers, consider which works best for you. Keep in mind that to create great content, you must be clear about to whom you are writing—and why.

Daydreaming

In the planning stage, before drafting a first version of the document, you spend more time daydreaming than handwriting or keyboarding. To search for a topic, you chat with a classmate. Maybe you read some other essays. Perhaps you muse about jobs you've had or your hobbies. Mulling things over to find a topic is a part of the process of writing.

Daydreaming led Tommy Hall to create "Canada's One-Tier Health Care Is the Better System," the research essay discussed in chapter 7. Trying to think up a topic for a research essay, Hall mused about how he had been irked by commentators who suggested on television and radio talk shows that Canada could no longer afford good health care for everyone. Hall disagreed. Then it hit him: he could write about how Canadians need a health-care system that provides equal care for all citizens. Daydreaming had led him to his essay topic.

▶ **ACTIVITY 2–1**

Daydreaming Essay Topics

Imagine your teacher asks you to write an essay about a Canadian social problem, something that is wrong in our country. Sit quietly for five minutes and jot down any ideas that come to mind. Remember to consider the audience you want to read your message because that will influence the notes you make. Take a moment to evaluate how daydreaming can help you decide what to write about in an essay.

Brainstorming

You may already have used brainstorming to come up with ideas. Many elementary- and secondary-school teachers encourage brainstorming. Those teachers probably told you that the key to effective brainstorming is to accept all ideas. To think up a topic for a process essay, for example, you would be encouraged to jot down—so you won't forget—an idea such as describing the process of putting a stamp on a letter, even though you would not likely write an essay about such an unimportant topic. At this stage, don't try to change or eliminate any idea. When you accept even silly ideas, more creative ideas flow from the subconscious to the conscious mind. Even after you've begun writing, you may brainstorm again to think up more ideas. Brainstorming helps you generate a topic *and* support it. Recall that students used brainstorming to come up with the content for the essay "The Positive Effects of Using Photo Radar to Enforce Speed Limits" (discussed in chapter 1).

▶ **ACTIVITY 2–2**

Brainstorming Writing Topics

As quickly as possible, suggest what it takes to succeed in a job. How can a worker get ahead?

Think about the information you would include if you planned to share these ideas in an article in your school newspaper. Look over your list and reflect on how effectively brainstorming helped you create ideas about this topic.

Freewriting

Some teachers of composition recommend freewriting to get you past an episode of writer's block. When you just can't seem to think of any idea to write about, when you are stymied for a topic, try freewriting. Set a time limit—say, five minutes—and begin to write whatever comes into your head. Don't let your pen stop moving. Write "I can't think of anything" when you can't think of anything more substantive to write. Perhaps freewriting yields a topic because the mind can become very creative when the other choice is tedium.

▶ **ACTIVITY 2–3**

Freewriting to Create the Content for an Essay

Take note of the time, and spend five minutes writing whatever comes to mind as you ponder what you might write to describe the best way to entertain a five-year-old. Imagine that you plan to share the ideas with a first-time babysitter. Examine the ideas you generated. Would this technique be useful to you when you're having trouble thinking up content for your essay?

Idea Mapping

If you find you itch to use the pen in your hand as you consider writing topics, you may like idea mapping. In idea mapping, you use a combination of drawing and note-making to develop a topic. Begin by writing in the centre of a piece of paper a word or two about the topic you are considering. Chantal Clark wanted to write an essay in which she classified information about the way sharing your life with different kinds of pets can improve health by reducing stress. She imagined writing a brief article for a community newspaper. She wrote the word *pets* onto her page and drew an oval around that word, which represented the contention she planned to make in her essay. As she thought of a type of pet to write about—for example, fish—she wrote down that animal name, drew an oval around it, and connected it to the word *pets*. Then she jotted down, circled, and drew lines from the example *fish* to the points she thought up about how keeping an aquarium could reduce stress. She followed the same procedure for *horse* and *dogs*. Look at figure 2–1 to see how Clark developed her idea map.

▶ **ACTIVITY 2–4**

Creating an Idea Map for How Students Can Find the Perfect Place to Live

Working from the idea of the best housing for students, draw an idea map to develop an essay about this topic. Look over your idea map and consider how effective this technique is in helping you create content for your writing.

2.2 WRITE ABOUT AN INTERESTING TOPIC

Quickly now, which of these papers would you rather read: "How to Eat an Avocado" or "How to Drive Your Car for Next to Nothing"? Most of us would rather read about the second topic. It's more important in our lives, and so it's more interesting. Papers about important topics appeal to us—and to our intended audience.

It's no easy job identifying an interesting topic. We've all had passionate interests that seemed very important to us at the time. We itched to tell others what we were thinking. That fascination with the batting averages of the Little Leaguers in your neighbourhood may have diminished as your own children grew up. It probably doesn't seem so important now.

If your essay tells readers information that is obvious, it's uninteresting. How excited can a reader get about an essay entitled "The Wetness of Water"? If you simply state a fact, you haven't created good content for an essay. If you said you were going to write an essay titled "My Lawn Is Made of Grass," you are simply stating a fact; you haven't created an interesting topic. If you announce that Camosun College in Victoria admitted its first students in 1971, you've just stated another fact. So what's a person to do to find an interesting topic?

FIGURE 2–1

Idea Mapping for an Essay about Keeping Pets to Reduce Stress

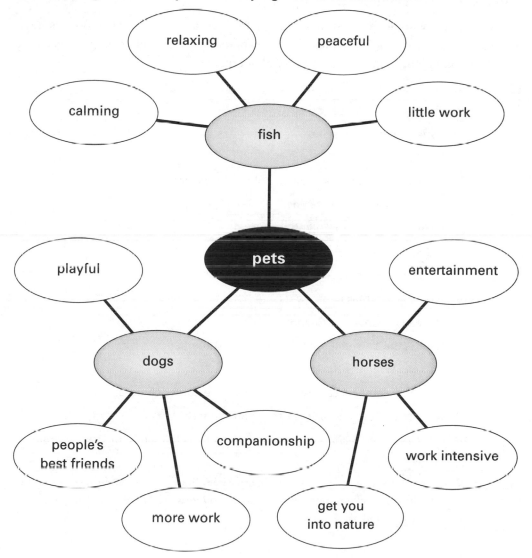

Test the significance of a topic idea by deciding how enthused you would be to write about it. If it's important to you, you can probably write about it with enough insight and passion to interest your reader. You'll still have to analyze your audience, though, to be sure you don't talk over their heads or seem condescending, concerns addressed in chapter 3.

▶ **ACTIVITY 2–5★**

Interesting and Uninteresting Topics

Listed below are essay titles or sentences from essays. Identify each topic as interesting (I) or uninteresting (U). When you indicate that a topic is interesting, suggest the audience that might want to read an essay about that subject.

_____   1. Tuition Fees Are Too High

_____   2. It's Best to Eat Maple Sugar with a Fork

_____   3. Cape Breton Is an Island

_____   4. Nicknames Should Be Banned

_____   5. Canada Should Provide Universal, Free Daycare

_____   6. Economy cars burn less gas.

_____   7. Falling snow can make you feel good.

_____   8. In the spring, the temperature rises.

_____   9. Politics is about government.

_____   10. Exercise can make you sweat.

_____   11. Hockey is popular in Canada.

_____   12. Beer is the downfall of many first-year students.

_____   13. You can ski in the Rockies.

_____   14. Co-op placements can help students make career choices.

_____   15. Medicare should include prescription drugs.

_____   16. _Per Gradus ad Maius_—steps to the greater—is the motto of Grande Prairie Regional College.

_____   17. Dawson College opened in the fall of 1969, the first English-language institution in Quebec's network of CEGEP's _(Colleges de l'enseignment general et professionnel)._

▶ **ACTIVITY 2–6**

Interesting and Uninteresting Topics

Listed below are titles of and sentences from student essays. Identify each topic as interesting (I) or uninteresting (U). Identify the audience that might be interested in the essay.

_____   1. Why People Smoke

_____   2. Why Does Anyone Like Rap Music?

_____   3. The Types of Salad Dressings

_____   4. Corel WordPerfect or Microsoft Word: Which Is Better?

_____   5. Colleges Should Require Students to Own Notebook Computers

_____   6. There are two kinds of municipal voters.

_____   7. There are four seasons in Canada.

_____   8. There are two seasons in Canada.

_____   9. Best-selling books are very popular.

_____   10. The best books are rarely best-sellers.

_____   11. What Makes a Good Salesperson?

_____   12. Picking a Place to Live

_____   13. Snow Is Too Cold

_____   14. How to Survive in the Northern Wilderness

_____   15. Journalism students at Cambrian College publish *The Shield*.

_____   16. Tailgating at a Football Game

_____   17. Students begin attending the CEGEP's after grade eleven.

2.3 WRITE ABOUT ONE TOPIC AT A TIME: CREATE UNITY

Which of these essays would you rather read: "I Like Ice Cream and Skiing" or "Vanilla Ice Cream Is the Perfect Food"? You may find it hard to agree with the second sentiment, but it sounds like a better read. The first essay, with two topics, tries to cover too much. It can be hard to throw out a topic, especially if it is also important to you, but to make a more favourable impression on your reader you should develop only one topic per essay.

▶ ACTIVITY 2–7*

Identifying Essays with Single Topics

A good essay is about a single topic. Write an S beside the essay titles that suggest the essay will be about one topic.

_____   1. How to Clean Cars and Fish

_____   2. The Two Major Causes of Economic Recessions

_____   3. The Causes of Smoking and Drinking

_____   4. The Two Major Types of Computer Printers

_____   5. How to Sing Duets

_____   6. Hoping and Praying for World Peace

_____   7. The Best Café in the World

_____   8. Electricity or Gas: Which Heats Homes Better?

_____   9. Why I Vacation in the Prairies and in the Maritimes

_____   10. Are Twins Really So Similar?

▶ ACTIVITY 2–8

Identifying Essays with Single Topics

A good essay is about a single topic. Write an S beside the essay titles that suggest the essay will be about one topic.

_____   1. The Two Main Reasons People Smoke

_____   2. How to Sing in Harmony

_____   3. Two Types of Dads

_____   4. Why You Should Own a Notebook Computer and a Lunch Bag

_____   5. Decorating for Christmas and Easter

_____   6. Being a Goalie Is Not Easy, Nor Is Being a Younger Sister

_____   7. How to Have Fun in Niagara Falls and Vancouver

_____   8. How to Install Playground Equipment

_____   9. Two Secrets to Earning Great Gratuities

_____   10. The Most Annoying Cyclists on the Road

2.4 MAKE A POINT ABOUT YOUR TOPIC: CREATE A THESIS

You mused, brainstormed, or freewrote and decided on one important topic, perhaps your experiences babysitting. How's this for a first sentence: "I'm going to write about my experiences babysitting"? It's a poor start. Readers can be impatient. They want to know What's your point? What are you going to focus on? Are you going to write about the topic in a vague way, or are you going to narrow your focus to an important aspect of your topic? They want you to get to the point quickly. Write essays that quickly tell readers the focus of your writing—your thesis.

Contrast the first proposal with this one: "Babysitting is an ideal job for a college student." Now you've asserted a proposition; you've stated a thesis. You've done something else critical to an essay: you've created new knowledge. You're not just summarizing someone else's ideas; you're not just reporting on them. You're expressing a new perspective about babysitting. And essays always have this creativity. The thesis of the essay always asserts a perspective. As soon as you can state your thesis, you can begin to create—efficiently—the content of your message. And you can begin to efficiently craft the content of your message to suit your audience.

Essays—brief prose pieces that are usually non-fiction—make a proposition. "Follow my directions," Gram P. Canuck might say about his approach to making pancakes for Sunday brunch, "and you'll enjoy a brunch that is as good as anything you'd eat in a restaurant—and it will cost you way less." Photo radar will produce good effects was the proposition advanced and supported in that cause-and-effect essay you read in the introduction. The persuasive, how-to-do-it (process) paragraph "How to Enjoy a Blizzard" (figure 15–4) asserts that you can enjoy a blizzard if you are prepared for it.

That grade-school assignment "What I Did on My Summer Vacation" was simple storytelling, a narrative, because you probably didn't make a point. And if your elementary-school teacher asked you to write a brief description of a picture, you were writing descriptively, but you probably didn't write a thesis.

In a friendly letter to your sister, you'll narrate the story of your daughter getting lost riding her tricycle farther and farther from her new home as she looked for children to play with. You'll describe in a newspaper advertisement the items for sale at the yard sale you're organizing for your street. But in your working and social life, you will seldom simply narrate or describe. More often, you'll tell the story of your visit to a charming crêperie in Sainte-Adèle as part of an essay about how to attract more tourists to the Laurentians. And you'll describe a computer software program as part of a comparison/contrast analysis in which you recommend the telephony program your company should purchase. You will use your narrative and descriptive skills to help make your point.

You may gain a clearer sense of a thesis by contrasting it with what it is not.

★ **A thesis is not a statement of fact.** "William Unruh won a Killian Prize" does not assert a thesis, it is just a statement of a fact.

★ **A thesis is not an announcement.** "I am going to write about schizophrenia" is an announcement, not a thesis.

★ **A thesis is not a mention of a broad topic.** "Depression" is not a thesis. "David Suzuki should win a Nobel Prize" is a thesis: it expresses a proposition the writer asserts and will try to prove. "Intensifying our efforts to manage schizophrenia would save communities a lot of money" is a thesis statement. "Prozac is the most powerful drug for alleviating depression" is a thesis.

A thesis is a brief statement of the point or proposition of the essay. Essays—in contrast to simple narratives—make and support points. To create a thesis, you will often think first of a broad general topic. Then, as you continue to reflect on the topic, you will need to think of a specific proposition you can make—if you are going to write an essay. Test your understanding of this distinction by completing Activity 2–9.

▶ **ACTIVITY 2–9★**

Identifying Theses

Place a T in front of each essay title that suggests the essay would have a thesis.

_____   1. Schizophrenia

_____   2. Schizophrenia Is Manageable with Drug Treatment

_____   3. Tourist Attractions in Canada

_____   4. Paramount Canada's Wonderland Has the Most Exciting Rides

_____   5. Vancouver Is One of the Great Cities of the World

_____   6. Juvenile Delinquents and Criminals

_____   7. Child Abuse Is the Major Cause of Juvenile Delinquency

_____   8. School Failure Is the Major Cause of Juvenile Delinquency

_____   9. The Web site for the College of the Rockies Is www.cotr.bc.ca

_____   10. The Bug Room Is a Permanent Exhibit at the Provincial Museum of Alberta

► **ACTIVITY 2-10**

Identifying Theses

Place a T in front of each sentence or essay title that suggests the author's essay will have a thesis.

_____   1. Child Abuse

_____   2. We Can Reduce Recidivism among Pedophiles

_____   3. Must-See Attractions for Visitors to Winnipeg

_____   4. The Canadian Museum of Nature Is in Ottawa

_____   5. The Best Museum in Ottawa

_____   6. I am going to write about the trails of Cape Breton.

_____   7. Word-processing Programs

_____   8. WordPerfect Is the Best Word-processing Program

_____   9. This essay is about the Big Nickel Mine.

_____   10. Ten Good Reasons to Visit Sault Ste. Marie

2.5 SUPPORT YOUR THESIS

You create theses for much of the writing you do. What is a job application but a letter that asserts a potential employer should hire you? As soon as you assert a proposition, your audience will expect you to support that contention. You do this by creating main points and supporting each of them with specific details.

Create Your Main Points

You decided what to write about. You narrowed that choice to one topic, found an interesting way to write about it, and created a thesis that presented a proposition, an opinion. Now it's time to create the main points you will assert to support your thesis.

Think of an essay as having three layers of information. Visualize those stone monuments that have stood for more than 5,000 years at Stonehenge in Britain, those slabs and pillars of stone—as shown in figure 2–2—that still make us marvel at how human beings could have constructed them without the use of modern earth-moving machines.

FIGURE 2–2

Stonehenge as a Representation of the Three Levels of Information in an Essay

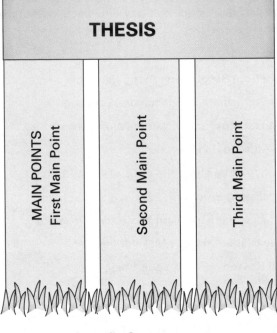

Specific Support

The thesis is the most important level of information in an essay. Visualize the thesis as the huge horizontal slab of rock at the top of one of those constructions.

Remember the paragraph "How to Enjoy a Blizzard" (figure 15–4)? You could easily have expanded it into an essay similar to "Pancakes for Sunday Brunch." Imagine creating an introductory paragraph with a lead-in, a statement of the thesis, and a preview of three points supported in the essay. Your former topic sentence becomes the thesis of this longer document, now transformed into an essay. Take another look at it and state the thesis. Did you express the thesis in words something like these: "You can enjoy a blizzard if you prepare for it"? That simple assertion is the thesis. It is a succinct expression of the controlling idea of the whole new essay you're creating. The thesis is the briefest summation you could make of the proposition of the essay.

Typically, you support this thesis with two or three main points. They're like the strong columns of stone that support the top slab of rock, the thesis. The writer of "How to Enjoy a Blizzard" asserted that there were three main ways to savour a blizzard. Take a minute to reread the paragraph and identify those three main points. Did you identify these points: you can enjoy being snowed in if you arrange to have (1) good food, (2) good entertainment, and (3) good company?

To the extent that you prove—or at least support—these main points, readers will tend to accept the unlikely contention—the thesis—that one can enjoy a blizzard. (The next section of *Write of Way* presents ideas about how to write specific support for your thesis and main points.) The specific details that support the main points and thesis are like the innumerable grains of earth that support the rock constructions at Stonehenge. Without support, the thesis and main points could not stand.

Before we begin to study how to create specific support, try this activity to see if you can detect the relationship between theses and main points.

▶ **ACTIVITY 2–11★**

Matching Theses and Main Points

List the main points that correspond to each thesis.

Thesis One: Each school bus should have a driver and a monitor. (Thanks to Jill Pamenter.)

Thesis Two: Shift work can cause marriages to fail. (Thanks to Marilyn Zacharakes.)

Thesis Three: The high cost of attending college is hurting students.

Main Points:

- It can be depressing to go alone to social events.
- Students work so much their school work suffers.
- Young children will not be picked on.
- Huge debts will create long-term problems.
- The driver will not be distracted as often.
- Going to bed without your partner can make you feel sad.
- Children will be safer boarding and leaving the vehicle.
- Trying to do too much causes health problems.
- Eating alone can make a person feel lonely.

▶ **ACTIVITY 2–12**

Matching Theses and Main Points

List the main points that correspond to each thesis.

Thesis One: To be a winner, a hockey team must have strength in three areas. (Thanks to Sherri-Lin Francis.)

Thesis Two: The Colorado Avalanche is a successful franchise. (Thanks to Tom Cintione.)

Thesis Three: Ice hockey is the best game on earth. (Thanks to Jerry Sokal.)

Main Points:

- Some might argue that baseball is the greatest sport, but hockey is a lot better because it is much faster paced.
- Having a team with a lot of potential also makes for a more successful business.
- No sport comes close to the exciting roughness that characterizes hockey.
- A good offence is absolutely essential to a winning hockey team.
- Even the most powerful offence will sometimes lose the puck; that's why a winning team needs a strong defence.
- Playing in a good market is key to having a successful franchise.
- As Don Cherry endlessly reminds us, fights make a game exciting, and no sport is as receptive to brawling as hockey.
- A franchise with many players who are also team leaders has good potential.
- If you want to put together a winning team, be sure you sign a cager who isn't afraid to put his padded body in front of a frozen disk of rubber travelling a hundred miles an hour.

▶ **ACTIVITY 2–13★**

Creating Main Points

For each thesis, create and record a third main point to support it.

Thesis One: Canada is a great vacation destination because tourists can choose from so many different activities.

1. Tourists can enjoy the shopping and cultural attractions of cosmopolitan cities.

2. Tourists can visit the past by exploring historical sites.

3.

Thesis Two: You can get your family to fire you from your dishwashing chores.

1. Work so slowly that you drive your dish drier up the wall.

2. Be sure to leave food on some of the dishes you wash.

3.

Thesis Three: Babysitting is a great job for college students.

1. After a day with adults, it's refreshing to play with children.

2. The pay is quite good.

3.

Thesis Four: Modern technology is making us lazier.

1. Many products of modern technology, such as videos and CD's, are making us mentally lazier.

2. Modern technology amuses us so well that we are becoming socially lazier.

3.

Thesis Five: Having your wisdom teeth removed is just the beginning of your losses.

1. You will lose your desire to smoke.

2. You will lose your sense of humour.

3.

Thesis Six: You can boost the odds of having a car accident by making the wrong choices.

1. Be inattentive when you drive.

2. Drive an unsafe car.

3.

▶ **ACTIVITY 2-14**

Creating Main Points

Read the first two main points for each of the following theses, and create a logical third main point for each.

Thesis One: I rarely see more than half a movie. (Thanks to Chantal Blanchette.)

1. I barely begin to watch a movie on television before one of my friends drops by unexpectedly.

2. Sometimes I miss the ending of a movie because I answer the telephone.

3.

Thesis Two: Stealing that brand-new red Mustang seemed like a great idea at the time. (Thanks to Kim Marshall.)

1. Joyriding seemed like a harmless thrill until I ended up in jail overnight.

2. Gaining a criminal record that may hurt my career prospects took the fun out of joyriding.

3.

Thesis Three: Even a dedicated dancer faces obstacles to finding enough time to pursue her art. (Thanks to Michelle Finlayson.)

1. Sometimes other important activities, such as school club meetings or family birthdays, conflict with dance lessons or practice times.

2. Some dancers must give up valuable practice time to earn money in part-time jobs.

3.

To write convincingly,

* **Start with a clearly articulated thesis:**

More farmers should grow hemp (not the narcotic variety).

* **Then create main points:**

Growing hemp will keep our farmers working; it makes a fabric tougher, yet softer, than cotton; and it is an environmentally friendly crop.

But a thesis and main points are still not sufficient to create the kind of great content that will lead your reader to accept your point.

* **Finally, write the specific information that supports your viewpoint**. Essentially, you must prove your thesis by supporting each main point with specific, convincing details.

Consider these ideas for how to create this strong specific support.

Create the Specific Support

There's an expression that makes an essential point about the importance of specific support in convincing writing: the devil is in the details. What will make or break your thesis is how convincing you are when the reader examines the details of your support. As you create the details of your support, it is important to visualize the audience for whom you write. Just imagine how differently you would write in a college newspaper about, say, why tuition fees should be frozen, than you would in a letter to your member of provincial parliament. Here are some of the ways you create support for your assertions.

* **Sometimes you choose statistics to create your solid support.** If you're writing a recommendation for the purchase of a particular laser printer, you will doubtless present statistics about projected maintenance costs and the number of copies that can be printed per minute.

* **Sometimes you cite experts to add specific support to your writing**. In recommending a particular printer, for example, you might summarize the evaluations published in computer magazines and consumer's reports.

* **Sometimes you make your specific support more convincing by providing examples or case studies.** You will pique interest in your essay about how our society pressures young women to be thin if you tell us about a friend who suffers from anorexia nervosa.

Whether you choose to write convincingly by citing statistics, experts, or case examples, you should write vividly.

* **Choose words that evoke vivid mental images.** Choose adjectives and adverbs that will help your readers form detailed pictures in their minds.

Contrast these two sentences.

Vague: The park is nice to visit.

Vivid: Cycling gently through Kouchibouguac Park in New Brunswick, your legs won't work as hard as your eyes as they scan the scalloped sand dunes, ocean grasses, forbidding bogs, and sentinel trees.

Doesn't the second sentence help you *see* what the writer wants you to imagine? There is an adjective in the vague sentence (*nice*), but the adjectives in the vivid example provide more convincing detail.

Choose verbs that conjure vivid, multi-sensory images. Contrast these sentences.

Vague: You can find clams and go into caves.

Vivid: Grab a shovel and dig through the bubbling sand for gritty clams. Feel the damp reverberations your voice makes in the moist, cool sea caves.

Notice the way your strong adjectives and evocative verbs work together to let your reader imagine what you are describing:

Vivid: Smell the Old World water splashing your face as you kayak the frothing waves of the highest tides in the world.

Use proper nouns to write more convincingly. Contrast these sentences.

Vague: A relative gave me a gift.

Vivid: When we got back to civilization—Richibucto, New Brunswick—my Aunt Tilly treated me to a lobster dinner at the Habitat Restaurant.

The better sentence uses proper names—*Aunt Tilly* and *Habitat Restaurant*—in place of the vague, general words *relative* and *gift*.

★ **Include convincing details in your support**. Readers like detail. It makes it easier to visualize what the writer is describing.

Consider this conversation:

"Where were you?"

"Out."

"What did you do?"

"Nothing."

Contrast it with this conversation:

"Where were you?"

"Kim, Nyembwe, and I were up at that new restaurant, the Great Canadian Bagel. You have got to try the pesto bagel with spinach and feta and cream cheese. It's so good, I ate three."

Now, consider which conversation might be more likely to ease a parent's worries about a loved member of the family. The detail in the second dialogue reassures dad (probably) that his daughter, although late, has been engaged in healthy, prosocial activity. The first dialogue is not as reassuring.

When you state statistics, cite authorities, present an example, choose vivid words, and include convincing details, you are more likely to convince your audience to your point of view.

▶ **ACTIVITY 2–15★**

Creating the Specific Support

For each of the following theses and main points, jot down some specific support. Thesis One: Each school bus should have a driver and a monitor.

1. Young children will not be picked on.

2. The driver will not be distracted as often.

3. Children will be safer boarding and leaving the vehicle.

Thesis Two: Shift work can cause marriages to fail.

1. It can be depressing to go alone to social events.

2. Going to bed without your partner can make you feel sad.

3. Eating alone can make a person feel lonely.

Thesis Three: The high cost of attending college is hurting students.

1. Students are working so much their school work suffers.

2. Huge debts will create long-term problems.

3. Trying to do too much causes health problems.

▶ **ACTIVITY 2–16**

Creating Specific Support

From the list below, choose a detail that supports each main point.

Thesis One: To be a winner, a hockey team must have strength in three areas.

1. A good offence is absolutely essential to a winning hockey team.

2. Even the most powerful offence will sometimes lose the puck; that's why a winning team needs a strong defence.

3. If you want to put together a winning team, be sure you sign a cager who isn't afraid to put his padded body in front of a frozen disk of rubber travelling a hundred miles an hour.

Thesis Two: The Colorado Avalanche is a successful franchise.

1. Playing in a good market is key to having a successful franchise.

2. A franchise with many players who are also team leaders has good potential.

3. Having a team with a lot of potential also makes for a more successful business.

Thesis Three: Ice hockey is the best game on earth.

1. Some might argue that baseball is the greatest sport, but hockey is a lot better because it is much faster paced.

2. No sport comes close to the exciting roughness that characterizes hockey.

3. As Don Cherry endlessly reminds us, fights make a game exciting, and no sport is as receptive to brawling as hockey.

Choices:

- Fans' blood runs hot from the stunning, violent, sudden moments when the player who, a moment before, was racing along the boards is now struggling to stay upright after a startling check.
- If the fans come out to the arena, faithfully watch their team on television, and buy the team's paraphernalia, the franchise has the income to pay the salaries demanded by the best players.

- Defenders must not only keep the opposing players from crossing the blue line and threatening the goalie, they must resist the urge to score in favour of passing the puck to the offensive players.

- It's the only sport where players can enjoy a good scrap without seeing it on the next episode of *Cops*.

- Good goalies are not only fearless, they are fast and alert.

- Fans are more likely to support a team when they feel it will continue to be successful because many of the players are young enough that they are still developing their talent.

- In a hockey game, you can't take in all the activity going on at once, but in a baseball game, sometimes the most exciting action you see in a minute is the pitcher spitting tobacco.

- The '96 winners of the Stanley Cup, the Colorado Avalanche, had a superb leader in goalie Patrick Roy, who set a good example for the young and improving players.

- A strong centre, one who can reliably win face-offs, is the key to a powerful offence.

> ### BOX 2–1 Learn More about Your Topic
>
> Content is the most important ingredient in the COSA formula for good writing. You write best about what you know best. When you are struggling to write, it is sometimes because you must learn more before you can write more easily—and better. Sometimes, as you imagine your readers, you realize that you need to add detail to your writing or you will not provide enough information to meet your readers' needs.
>
> Occasionally the very act of writing makes me realize that I don't know a topic as well as I thought I did. At other times, I know that I could make my point more effectively if I could write down a particular fact or statistic, but I can't recall that information. I don't really *know* that information. I realize that I need to learn more about my topic.
>
> What do I do when I need to know more before I can continue writing? Sometimes I get lucky: Someone near me does know the information. I just ask a question. "How much was that promised tax cut?" Sometimes I phone the public library. "Could you please help me find a succinct account of how to chair

a meeting?" Once I called Niagara Recycling to find out if I could mix glossy paper with fine paper. (Yes.) I spent months in a university library using electronic card catalogues and other information-retrieval tools to answer one question—are college content-area professors practising writing-across-the-curriculum procedures in Ontario's community colleges—and then I still had to conduct a research study to answer the question. (Not much.)

You get the point: sometimes you must listen, view, read, question, or consult to learn more about the content of the document you are writing. There's more about how to research an academic paper in part 3, and you can visit the *Write of Way* Web pages for suggestions about writing other documents such as news releases or grant applications. The suggestions always include ideas about how to create content that will meet your audience's needs.

As you continue the task of becoming better informed, you will likely run into a problem: how can anyone remember all this information? Consider the suggestions in the next box.

BOX 2–2 Take Notes to Create Great Content

I take a lot of notes. I take notes during faculty meetings and riding association meetings. I take notes during informative television programs. When I read Michael Slade's horrific RCMP novel, *Headhunter*, I took notes so I could try to identify the murderer. (I couldn't.) I write many of these notes into an $8\frac{1}{2}$ by 11-inch weekly planner appointment book. I make notes about Bruce McDonald's films (e.g., Is the Tarantino listed in the credits for *Roadkill* related to director Quentin Tarantino?). (I don't know.) I write on Post-it Notes and attach them to newspaper articles I read, clip, and file.

I could kid you and tell you that I take a lot of notes because I have a poor memory—just an absent-minded professor—but I think my memory's as good as most. But it isn't perfect, and so I write notes.

You will probably find you write different kinds of notes for the various types of work you do. Your notes to prepare a memo will usually be more extensive than your note that a newspaper article has a statistic you might refer to in a letter to the editor. Notes are just external memory—like a computer disk. The notes help you keep track of more information than you can remember unassisted.

In later sections of the book, you can consider notetaking for different writing projects; for example, an important part of notetaking to write an academic paper is carefully recording information you need to give credit to the authors you refer to in the essay and in your bibliography. In the section on writing summaries, you can read more ideas about that particular kind of notetaking.

For now, the important point about notetaking is that even brief notes can make writing better—and easier. Remember how the class brainstormed effects of photo radar? Then you'll recall that the ideas were jotted down. The first notes were just point-form and in no particular order. This is characteristic of rough notes. Yet, as brief and unorganized as those notes were, they were very useful as a step toward the creation of a thesis for the brief essay about the positive effects of photo radar. Imagine how much harder it would have been to create that thesis and the three main points if the writers had trusted only their memories.

2.6 OUTLINE THE SUPPORT FOR YOUR THESIS

As you study the last procedure to create great content for your writing, put together everything you've been considering. Consider the essay "Pancakes for Sunday Brunch." Before I wrote that essay, I was faced with a problem just like you may be faced with in your writing course: I wanted to write a brief boxcar essay, in this case a process essay about how to do something. Here are the steps to follow to create the content.

1. **Decide what to write about.** What four procedures do writers sometimes use to conceive a topic? That's right: daydreaming, brainstorming, freewriting, and idea mapping. I wanted to write a sample essay for my students, an essay that would be simple, concrete, and easy to remember so that students could mentally refer to it to help them write their own essays. Notice that I visualized my readers and their needs as I began to create the content of the sample essay. Daydreaming led me to another thought: we all have concerns about money. And that realization led to the thought that while I love to go out to restaurants, it is an expensive way to eat. A moment later, I thought of the topic of making one's own brunch, one as good as brunch served in a restaurant.

2. **Write about an interesting topic.** Because so many students are struggling to finance their college studies, lots of students would be interested in eating well *and* saving money.

3. **Write about one topic at a time.** Next, I checked the topic idea for unity. Is an essay about how to make an inexpensive homemade brunch about just one topic? Yes.

4. **Make a point about your topic.** Then, I mused: what point would I assert in the essay? The thesis would be that anyone can create an inexpensive gourmet brunch with my famous banana pancakes recipe, the one that turned the Rogers children into the fine physical specimens they are today.

5a. **Support your thesis with main points.** Having created a thesis, I had to create the main points, the columns of support. How would a cook create gourmet pancakes? Brainstorming quickly led to two ideas: you must select great ingredients, but you won't have anything special unless you cook them superbly. I needed one more main point for an example of a standard boxcar essay. I tried freewriting. Over the next few minutes, I wrote ideas that seemed useless for the essay. Then, I wrote, "They'd seem more special if the food was served as in a restaurant." It wasn't an elegant statement, but now I was cooking: serving the food with flair would be the third way to make an inexpensive brunch special.

5b. **Support your thesis and main points.** Still, before I could complete the essay, I had to create specific support; I had to detail the steps of the process of selecting quality ingredients, cooking carefully, and presenting with a certain pizzazz. It was all getting to be too much to remember. Then, I thought about my students collaborating to write "How to Enjoy a Blizzard." To support the topic sentence, we made a list of all our brainstormed ideas. We found our main points among those specific examples of ways to prepare to enjoy a blizzard. But the part of the procedure that jumped to the forefront of my memory was that we looked at an outline for a complex paragraph.

6. **Outline the support for your thesis.** I realized I could sketch an outline to help ensure I created all the content I needed for the essay. I already had the thesis and the main points for the brunch essay. I could start an outline with these main points and then, as I thought them up, write the specific points of support under each main point. My rough outline is shown here:

FIGURE 2–3

Outline of the Main Points of "Pancakes for Sunday Brunch"

Thesis: Make a glorious brunch of gourmet pancakes by choosing quality ingredients, cooking them with care, and serving them with flair.

1. Great food begins with great ingredients.

2. Cook your quality ingredients carefully.

3. Serve the meal with flair.

As I brainstormed the details of my support for each main point, I wrote each detail under the relevant main point. For example, as I thought about the eggs for the pancakes, I thought about Mrs. Epp at the farmers' market just up the street from my home. Mrs. Epp prides herself on giving her chickens the run of her farm, and those huge brown eggs sure taste great.

As I jotted down the details of the specific support, I had finally created the content for my brief essay. Here's what my rough outline looked like:

FIGURE 2–4

Rough Outline of "Pancakes for Sunday Brunch"

Thesis: Make a glorious brunch of gourmet pancakes by choosing quality ingredients, cooking them with care, and serving them with flair.

1. Great food begins with great ingredients.
   - get those good eggs from the market
   - mention banana and vanilla

2. Cook your quality ingredients carefully.
   - melt butter in the pan
   - don't flip the pancakes too early

3. Serve the meal with flair.
   - use a carafe for the coffee
   - use a pitcher for the syrup
   - get the Sunday paper

I could have added more details to the outline, but this was enough to start to write it. You've already seen the result: the more formal, detailed outline is shown in figure 1–7 and the essay itself in figure 1–5.

2.7 SOME CONCLUDING THOUGHTS

The process of writing is not always so linear; it doesn't always go from the creation of the topic, the assertion of a thesis and main points, the detailing of the specific support, and the outlining of the content. Writing is a recursive process: writers may go back to an earlier step or jump ahead to a later stage. Think about the photo radar essay, for example. What did the students think up first, main points or specific details of how photo radar would cause changes in our province? They created the specific support details first. Then, they classified them into main points illustrating that photo radar would benefit citizens. Nor are outlines always so formal as the ones for the pancake brunch essay. Sometimes they never go past some jotted notes—point form, brief, and scattered about the page. But most authors don't feel they really know what is on their minds and in their hearts—the content—until they've at least *mentally* scratched out an outline. To create that content, writers must imagine their readers: will my readers understand my message? Do I need to add more information? Have I set a tone that shows I respect my readers?

Students have learned a lot when they can articulate the logical progression of writing an essay, the progression from topic idea to thesis to main points and support. Use this process to create good content for the essays *you* write.

CHAPTER 3

Analyzing Your Audience

"The pen is the tongue of the hand—a silent utterer of words for the eye."
—*Henry Ward Beecher*

CHAPTER OBJECTIVE

You will increase the effectiveness of your written communications by analyzing your audience to create messages that are appropriate in content and tone.

In chapter 2 you studied how to create a thesis and outline the content of your communication. As you begin to think about a topic, you need to analyze your audience to decide what to include in your writing and what to leave out. You can't create the content of your document until you analyze your audience.

For each type of document you create—a memo or letter to the editor—visualize your reader(s) and plan your message based on your analysis. You will need to meet the information needs of your readers—to make sure that you are understood—and do so in a tone that conveys respect for your audience.

3.1 MEET YOUR AUDIENCE'S INFORMATION NEEDS

Imagine that you walked into your home and found this note: "Please put one foot in front of the other, successively, and walk forward until you arrive at the kitchen cupboard by the sink. Bend down. Open the cupboard door. Reach out your arm and pick up the flour . . . ." Imagine that the note continued—for several pages—to describe in excruciating detail the steps you were to follow to make a pizza for supper. If you know how to make a pizza, then the long note is ineffective because the writer has assumed she needs to write for you information that you already know. The writer has misjudged the information needs of the audience.

Imagine that the note read "Please make a pizza for supper." If you don't know where to look for the yeast or the family pizza recipe, the writer has overestimated your knowledge. Again, the problem is that the writer has failed to meet the information needs of the audience.

It's not easy to give your reader just the right amount of information—no more, no less. As you've explained how to do a job, has a listener impatiently said, "I know, I know. You don't have to tell me all that"? You underestimated the knowledge of your audience.

Whether you write a news article, an essay, or a persuasive speech, you need to assess the background knowledge of your audience to know what to say and what you can assume they already know. In short, audience analysis is an important part of all the writing you do.

Here are some ways to increase your success at analyzing your audience's information needs.

* **Create a comprehensive message.** First, as you look over your notes or outline or draft writing, imagine your audience. Ask yourself whether you've left out any essential background information that your readers are unlikely to know.

* **Edit for brevity.** Once you've drafted your document, consider whether you could express your message more briefly by leaving out information your audience already knows.

* **Test your message on an audience.** When you've done your best at audience analysis, there's still another procedure you can use: test your writing by asking someone else to read and respond to it, preferably someone from your target audience. In your conference, ask questions. Is your reader mystified by any part of your message? Did you assume too much knowledge? Is your reader bored or annoyed? Did you state the obvious?

▶ **ACTIVITY 3-1**

Meeting Your Audience's Information Needs

See for yourself how you customize your communication to meet your audience's need for information. For each of these situations, briefly write a rough draft. To create the content, you're going to have to imagine what your audience needs to know to understand the message you are sending. Make up plausible details. Complete your writing for the first situation, then compare your writing with the example answer in chapter 15.

After that, follow the instructions for the other scenarios. Notice how the content of your messages is strongly influenced by the needs of your audience.

1.* You were getting ready to go to work at Pants 'r' Us, where you are expected to look good. While ironing your shirt, your Sunshine iron began to spew copper-coloured water. Then the iron made a bad smell and went cold. Ordinarily, you'd need only five minutes to iron that shirt; instead, you had to recycle a shirt from your bedroom floor and borrow a neighbour's iron. You were late for work. What will you

   a. say to your boss,

   b. write in an e-mail to a high-school friend attending another college, and

   c. write to the Sunshine company whose iron did not outlast the warranty period?

2. You are supervising young offenders at a bowling alley. The owner is a thoughtful citizen who donates the use of the alley so that the young men can develop pro-social recreational habits. Ralf Dobrovolny, one of the group-home residents, exposes himself to a family bowling in the next lane. Of course you immediately take the young man back to the home. Write a draft of the letter you would send to the owner of the bowling alley to propose that Ralf apologize, promise not to flash again, and miss bowling for two weeks' timeout. Think of your purpose: you want the residents to continue to have bowling privileges. Think of what you will have to say to convince the owner to continue to offer the free bowling. Then write to Ralf's parents. Think of your purpose: you need to inform them of the incident, but you also want to assure them that this kind of behaviour is not that uncommon and that the home is dealing with it effectively.

3. You decide to write an essay for your college newspaper to advise female students how to increase their personal safety, to reduce the chances they will be victims of violence. Jot down the points you will make. Now imagine that you decide to write a similar essay for a newspaper published for grade six students. Jot down the points you would make in *that* essay. How do the lists differ for the two audiences? Why are the lists different?

4. You decide to volunteer to help your candidate win election to the House of Commons because you support a national pharmacare program. The other strong candidate opposes extending the medicare program to cover prescription drug costs. Your first job is to use a telephone script, call citizens on the voter's list, ask their position on pharmacare, and, when you identify supporters or potential supporters, ask if they will take a sign, make a donation, or come and work for the candidate. You're to identify undecided voters because your candidate will phone and speak personally to each of them. You want to be polite to hostile voters, but you don't want to waste any time talking to them. You want to identify supporters so that your election-day

workers can encourage them to vote. You're so good at cold calling that you are soon promoted to coordinator of phone canvassers. You decide to improve the telephone scripts, which start the same but differ once volunteers know if they are speaking to a supporter, a supporter of the opposition, or someone undecided. Sketch out the three new scripts you create for your telephone canvassers.

3.2 CREATE THE RIGHT TONE FOR YOUR AUDIENCE

"Gentle lady, may I implore you to lend your aid to a most vexing difficulty? I would be in your debt if you could take it upon yourself to remove the trash to the curb this morrow." You'd probably be surprised if your mom left you that note instead of this one: "Please put the garbage out this morning." The big difference in these two notes is tone.

The first note is overly formal. It is filled with archaic language (e.g., *gentle lady, implore, this morrow*). You might simply be amused by your mom's tone, but failing to create the tone that suits your audience can sometimes cause trouble. I can remember Miss Booker, my sixth-grade teacher, saying, "I don't like your tone, young man," shortly before I was sent to see Mr. Stevenette, the principal.

Language, both spoken and written, varies in the level of formality. Informal communication includes regionalisms, clichés, slang, and colloquialisms. Formal communication tends to use the more mainstream vocabulary. Sarcasm, irony, and exaggeration are commonplace in informal language. Casual conversation is informal. Formal language is less conversational, more businesslike than casual. Informal language works best in casual situations: we don't want to sound stuffy at a party or in a personal letter. More formal language is appropriate when we are being less casual, more serious. "Hey, baby, how about you and me get hitched?" might not be formal enough for the important event of proposing marriage.

Are you getting the feeling that writers find it hard to set just the right tone? It is challenging. Slang, colloquialisms, regionalisms, clichés, sexist language, wordiness, jargon, and non-idiomatic expression are considered together—in one chapter, under the broad term *tone*—because they all distract the reader from understanding what is in your heart and in your mind just the way a wrong musical note—tone—can ruin your attention to a musical composition.

Imagine your audience as you create the content of your document. Consider the following suggestions, and you will create the tone that will make the best impression on your reader.

⋆ **Use slang sparingly, if at all.** At our most informal moments, we speak and write slang. Slang is highly informal. "How's it hangin'?" may be hot slang today, but it will soon sound as out of date as this possible reply: "Oh, I'm feeling groovy, man."

Is all slang bad? Not at all. Slang in a personal letter or humorous anecdote enlivens the writing. Some slang will even become tomorrow's widely used language. What do you think? Will *snail mail* come into general usage? Put slang in its place, and it will work for you rather than against you.

⋆ **Use colloquial expression to create a conversational tone.** Colloquial speech is also very informal. It creates a casual, conversational tone, but it lacks the newest words or expressions. It is the language of everyday conversation. A lot of good writing has a conversational tone. When travel or food writers use a conversational tone as they describe their experiences, their readers feel like seatmates on that train car or at that café table.

When writing with a colloquial tone, beware becoming too folksy. A memo that begins "I'm going to tell you why we need a new photocopier" sounds amateurish. The writer should be more formal (as well as briefer and more direct).

⋆ **Put regionalisms in their place.** Regionalisms are another kind of informal language that seldom have a place in writing. When I'm sharing a potluck supper with my Maritime cousins, the food is "some good"—and I might tell you so in a personal letter—but that expression would be too informal in my recommendation to purchase a particular brand of scanner. Again, it's not that regionalisms ought to be banned from serious writing: a narrative essay about my vacation at home in Niagara Falls wouldn't be authentic without a mention of going "over the river" (to the United States) for burritos at Casa Cardeñas.

⋆ **Replace clichés with creative expressions.** Clichés, those overused, tired expressions, are more likely to appear in our informal writing. While it may have sounded fresh and new when it was first said, "It's raining cats and dogs" is just a cliché now. "I'd give my right arm to have a dog that is as big as a house and as quiet as a mouse" is boring because we've all heard and read those expressions too many times. When you are draft writing, just scrawl down those clichés that come to mind. When you revise to improve the content of your document, though, express your thoughts and feelings in refreshing, novel ways—if you think it will sound right to your audience—or just state the thought or feeling more directly without using a metaphor. Instead of creating a replacement expression for "It's six of one, a half-dozen of the other," you could write more directly: "Either choice will be fine."

▶ **ACTIVITY 3–2★**

Freshening Up Those Clichés

Write an interesting, new expression in place of these clichés, and then express the ideas more straightforwardly:

1. quiet as a mouse

2. dot every "i" and cross every "t"

3. as white as snow

4. between a rock and a hard place

5. as mad as a hatter

▶ **ACTIVITY 3–3**

Freshening Up Those Clichés

Write a new interesting expression in place of these clichés, or express the ideas more straightforwardly:

1. 110-per-cent effort

2. in a pickle

3. a blanket of snow

4. thick as a brick

5. as happy as a pig in mud

★ **Neuter sexist language.** "Our girls make the best muffins," advertised a Donut Diner near my home. That sign may have driven away more customers than it attracted. The content of the message suggests that only women bake at the doughnut shop. And, the message suggests that management does not respect the dignity of those female workers: *Girls* is a term for female children, not adults. An advertisement that is sexist—like this one—is ineffective because it shows a lack of consideration for some of its audience. Sexist language sets the wrong tone.

It's not hard to rewrite sexist language so that you meet your audience's need to feel you respect them. "Only the best bake for the Donut Diner" or "Our muffins are the best" would have offended none and still asserted that you'd be missing some great food if you drove by this doughnut shop.

Perhaps you think it's unnecessary to train yourself to say *chair, firefighter,* or *server* for the older sexist terms *chairman, fireman,* or *waitress.* Will some children think all their city councillors are men if you always refer to them as *aldermen*? Will some of your potential readers form a negative impression of your writing if you use gender-exclusive language? Create gender-neutral language if you want your writing to be well-received by all readers.

▶ **ACTIVITY 3–4★**

Writing Gender-Inclusive Language

Suggest gender-inclusive language for each of these male-biased, sexist terms.

1. weatherman
2. mankind
3. manhole cover
4. businessman
5. delivery boy

▶ **ACTIVITY 3–5**

Writing Gender-Inclusive Language

Suggest gender-inclusive language for each of these sexist terms.

1. foreman
2. meter maid
3. paperboy
4. rifleman
5. taxman

You might like to read *Words That Count Women Out/In* (2nd ed.) published by the Ontario Women's Directorate in Toronto. It discusses how to write language that shows respect for both men and women.

Writers who try to avoid a male bias in their writing choose non-sexist vocabulary and write sentences that are gender inclusive. Two strategies are commonly used.

★ Avoid sexist language by changing personal pronouns to definite or indefinite pronouns. Contrast these examples:

Sexist: Everyone has his favourite restaurant.

Inclusive: Everyone has a favourite restaurant.

Bias is avoided by changing the masculine pronoun *his* to the definite *(the)* or indefinite *(a)* pronoun.

* Avoid sexist language by changing singular pronouns to plural pronouns.
Contrast these examples:

Sexist: Firefighting is hard on the worker and his family.

Inclusive: Firefighting is hard on workers and their families.

Here the writer avoids biased writing by changing the sentence from singular to plural. The third-person singular personal pronouns (*he* and *she*) and possessive pronouns (*his* and *hers*) indicate gender, but the third-person plural personal pronoun *they* does not, nor does the third-person plural possessive pronoun *their*.

Either of these strategies is preferable to writing the awkward-sounding *her/his* or *he/she*, especially if you do this often. Some speakers and writers choose to alternate the use of *he* and *she* and *his* and *hers*. If you do so, be careful to avoid sexist assumptions. Notice how they are avoided in this example:

Hobbyists pursue their pastimes with passion. He may knit at every meeting. She may golf in every city her work takes her to. He may cook a gourmet meal for friends every Friday night.

▶ **ACTIVITY 3–6***

Creating Messages that Are Gender Neutral

Rewrite these sentences to make them gender neutral:

1. Everyone told his own story.

2. A visitor to Yarmouth should bring his raincoat.

3. A singer-songwriter must be prepared to promote her music by selling her own CD's.

4. A vain person should think less about his appearance.

5. A fool and her money are soon parted.

▶ **ACTIVITY 3–7**

Creating Messages that Are Gender Neutral

Rewrite these sentences to make them gender neutral.

1. Everyone we interviewed said that he enjoyed studying at Algonquin College.

2. When a student living in North Bay wants to attend a local community college, she applies to Canadore College.

3. It's an ill wind that blows no man good.

4. The best laid plans of mice and men often go awry.

5. A dog is man's best friend.

★ **Be succinct.** Some writers, in an attempt to make their writing more formal or scholarly or professional, will become wordy. "Let me draw to your attention the following good points of this cellphone" is wordy. Instead, list the features following a brief, straightforward clause, such as "This cellphone features . . . ."

Worry about writing your message more succinctly *after* you've drafted it. As you reread to see if you've expressed your thoughts and feelings, eliminate words when you find you've repeated a point unnecessarily. Watch for times when you've used a phrase where you could express the information in fewer words. Rewrite when you've expressed an idea indirectly when being direct would be briefer.

Wordy: The most important of the reasons for delaying the fundraiser was the fact that the committee was made up of people who were not working in an energetic way and had not completed the jobs they had agreed to do.

Succinct: The main reason we delayed the fundraiser was that some committee members had not done the work they promised.

▶ **ACTIVITY 3–8★**

Rewrite the following sentences to be as succinct as possible.

1. I would like to tell you about my favourite hobby.

2. There are many varied, different ways or means to extract a tight, unyielding lid or top of a glass container.

3. All personnel should endeavour to comply with the aforementioned rules or guidelines.

4. The reasons, I think, are, in my opinion, that certain malcontents are trying to undo or reverse the decision that was decided upon by a democratic vote at our previous meeting.

5. I would like to ask you if you would consider doing me a favour by telling or informing me about the whereabouts of the washroom.

▶ **ACTIVITY 3–9**

Rewrite the following sentences to be as succinct as possible.

1. In the city of Sudbury, in Northern Ontario, there is a college called Cambrian College.

2. I would like you to please pass the shaker with the salt in it.

3. If you get the opportunity to visit Lloydminster in Saskatchewan, you will have the opportunity to see the Char-Mil Rig, a scale model of an actual oil derrick.

4. It can be very tiring and exhausting giving care to a young infant human being.

5. If you were to read aloud one of Robert Munsch's stories to ten children of preschool age, I think that almost every one of them would like the story.

Why are writers sometimes wordy? Sometimes it's to try to fool the reader into believing the message is better than it really is. Fancy words, though, won't camouflage a poor idea. You do the best job of conveying a sound idea when you write succinctly.

★ **Replace jargon with words more generally known**. Some writers try to achieve a more formal tone by using jargon, the specialized vocabulary of each profession. Here's a sentence that could have been written by a social services worker:

Jargon: **Olaf sometimes engages in aggressive behaviour towards his male sibling because Olaf feels neglected, and he is compensating for the scarce resources of parental attention, even negative attention.**

Here's what the worker saw: Olaf pinched his brother to get attention from his busy parents. The second sentence about Olaf is easier to understand because it is free of jargon.

Is all jargon bad? Not at all. A great deal of what we learn as we become experts is the vocabulary of that activity. We need specialized vocabulary. Try to describe fly fishing without using terms like *rod, cast, line*. The challenge in writing is to create messages—content—that readers can easily understand. If we are using jargon to create an impression of formality, that's probably a bad idea. If we are explaining ideas, and in the process building the knowledge base of the reader—including new vocabulary—then we are using jargon appropriately. When you're thinking of using jargon, always consider it from the perspective of the audience: Will the reader be more likely to understand my message if I use a technical term or should I find another way to express the idea?

★ **Revise until you express yourself in contemporary idiom.** Non-idiomatic expressions can also disturb readers. Look at the following sentence:

X He paid me under a table.

This is really an odd way to pay someone. Probably the writer meant to write "He paid me under *the* table," meaning in a secret or unlawful manner. *Under a table* is non-idiomatic English, yet it differs from the idiomatic expression by only one word. Writing that is even so little awry will take the reader's attention away from what is in your heart and head.

Speakers and writers of English use thousands of idiomatic expressions. These are groups of words whose meaning is not discernible just because one knows the meaning of the individual words such as *under, the,* and *counter.* As you interact with native speakers of English, you learn the meanings of these expressions as naturally as you learn the meanings of tens of thousands of individual words.

Consider this example:

X I'm up a creek; could you give me a hand?

Native users of English don't imagine the speaker in a boat. English-as-a-Second-Language (ESL) users may.

Larger dictionaries often define idiomatic expressions. The new Gage Canadian Dictionary, for example, tells users to search for the meaning of an idiomatic phrase by looking under the entry for the most important word in the expression. Under *ball,* readers will find definitions of *be on the ball, have something on the ball, keep the ball rolling, the whole ball of wax, ball up,* and so forth. Such entries are particularly useful when no one is around to explain an expression, but the best way to learn to speak and write idiomatically is to converse and read extensively. When your teacher points out a non-idiomatic expression, carefully write down how the thought can be expressed idiomatically. Then you can study it, just as you study the spelling of a word you don't know by heart (see the section about spelling, 14.5).

▶ **ACTIVITY 3–10***

Rewriting Non-idiomatic Expressions

Write the idiomatic equivalents of these non-idiomatic expressions.

1. They sold me the pig in a poke.

2. He's not the sharpest pencil in a box.

3. She should pull her own weights.

4. They were helpful: They gave me a finger.

5. At the end of a day, we will have to decide who to vote for.

▶ **ACTIVITY 3–11**

Rewriting Non-idiomatic Expressions

Write the idiomatic equivalents of these non-idiomatic expressions.

1.   We must hang together, or we will all hang in separation.

2.   I wish I could be the fly on the wall.

3.   I am glad I am not a fly in ointment.

4.   She felt like a fish out of the water.

5.   We were hoarse after we gave him three cheer ups.

6.   I am in the jam.

3.3 SOME CONCLUDING THOUGHTS

As you create the content of your document, analyze your audience. Meet their information needs and address them in a respectful tone. Consider practical concerns such as how long the reader expects the document to be. Writers who sensitively analyze their audiences—and give them what they need—will achieve the best results.

Organizing Effective Documents

"What is written without effort is in general read without pleasure."
—*Samuel Johnson*

In part 1, you studied how to create the content of your message. You looked into your heart and head to find what you wanted to express. Because you were writing an essay, you created a thesis—Canada should provide universal daycare—and main points—it would mean children were healthier, smarter, and better adjusted. You imagined your readers and thought about what to say to meet their need for information, delivered with a respectful tone. Then you wrote sentences detailing specific support for your assertion. In part 2, you can study and practise how to organize your message to make the greatest impact on your readers. Keep in mind as you complete the exercises that they are *just* exercises. They draw your attention to specific advice about how to write well, but you can improve your writing only by creating and revising real writing such as essays, progress reports, and business letters. Take the insights you learn from the exercises and apply them to the documents you write. Students who complete the activities, write essays applying the new insights, and read published essays—like the ones in chapter 16—will quickly see that they are learning to write more powerfully. By the time you complete part 2, you will confidently write brief essays, and you'll know how to approach the job of organizing the other documents in your life.

CHAPTER 4

Writing the Paragraphs

"Words and sentences are subjects of revision; paragraphs and whole compositions are subjects of prevision."
—*Barrett Wendell*

CHAPTER OBJECTIVE

You will create the well-organized paragraphs—including topic, support, and concluding sentences—of the quality educated people expect to find in documents written by college graduates.

Each time you write a document, you must organize your writing effectively; for example, in a business letter conveying a message that the reader will not like, you may delay making your main point. In *Write of Way*, effective organization—the *O* in the COSA formula for good writing—is analyzed for every type of document presented on the Web pages. Well-written paragraphs are essential to each of these types of document. Spend some time exploring how to write paragraphs.

4.1 WHAT IS A PARAGRAPH?

Before you read the answer, take a moment to answer the question yourself. A paragraph is a group of sentences about one main point or idea. (Usually, paragraphs begin with an indentation of five spaces or about 1.25 centimetres.)

A paragraph can be as brief as the single sentences reporters write in newspaper articles that quickly move the story along from one piece of information to the next. Most paragraphs, though, have more than one sentence, and as paragraphs become longer, they tend to be organized in a predictable way that makes it easy for readers to understand the main point. This is the typical pattern writers follow when they write a paragraph:

* **Begin with a sentence that states the topic, the main idea or point of the paragraph.** Your topic sentence should tell the reader the main idea you express in the paragraph. Sometimes this will be a fact (e.g., Modern computer hard drives can store a tremendous amount of information). Other times, your topic sentence will state your point of view about an aspect of your topic (e.g., Your grant money will benefit our community in several ways).

* **Add more sentences that support or explain the topic.** These sentences provide the specific details—examples, statistics, reasoned arguments, or anecdotes—that make your writing convincing.

* **Finish the paragraph** with a sentence that briefly summarizes the point made about the topic of the paragraph.

4.2 BEGIN PARAGRAPHS WITH TOPIC SENTENCES

Write good topic sentences—make a point about the single important idea of your paragraph—and readers are more likely to see the world the way you want them to. When you write to express a point of view—including your job application letters as well as your essays—you should create topic sentences to start the commonplace, garden-variety paragraphs that form the body of your documents; for example, look at the second paragraph of the essay "The Positive Effects of Photo Radar" (figure 15–8). What's the first sentence? Notice that it states the topic of that paragraph. In fact, in this case it also *asserts* a main point (that police use of photo radar will make driving safer). By asserting that main point, the writer has reinforced the contention expressed in the thesis, and made it easier for the reader to get the point: photo radar will be good for citizens. That's a demonstration of how effective organization—at just the paragraph level—can help you write well.

Think about the nature of topic sentences. If I asked you to read a paragraph and then asked you what it was about, wouldn't you reword the topic sentence to formulate your answer? Test this idea by reading the following passage and answering the question What was the author's main point?

Children benefit from living with parents who talk a lot with them. Babies who are read to make the sounds of our language at an earlier age. Children develop larger vocabularies when they live with parents who chat while visiting the zoo or the supermarket. When parents and toddlers talk at the supper table about the nature show they watched on television, children learn the sort of information that will make it easier—years later—to understand their textbooks. It's a wise child who chooses talkative parents.

The author's main point? Well, it's stated in the topic sentence, the first sentence, isn't it? And that's the way your comprehension of a reading passage is often assessed: the comprehension-testing questions usually ask you to state the main point of the passage. In fact, if you can state the main point(s)—in your own words—you demonstrate your understanding. When you write a topic sentence in which you clearly articulate the main point of your paragraph, you make it much easier for the reader to comprehend your thoughts and feelings.

Try Activity 4–1 to test your understanding of the concept of topic sentences.

▶ **ACTIVITY 4–1★**

Detecting Topic Sentences

Construct three brief paragraphs from this unorganized mass of sentences. The first step is to identify the three topic sentences. Then find the sentence or two that supports each topic sentence.

- The clear plastic tubing transforms the woods
- The smell of the sap being boiled down makes me forget the mud oozing around my boots.
- Even after you swallow the last crushed bits of grain, the sweet sensation lingers.
- In fact, on variety store and grocery shelves all over North America, you can see the words "Made in Quebec" on bags of granulated maple sugar, on small maple leaves made of maple sugar, and on bottles of maple syrup.
- As you begin to taste the sweetness, it radiates to the furthest corners of your mouth.
- Maple syrup is the best topping for Red River Cereal.
- In the spring, I love to go to a sugar bush.
- Quebec produces the most maple syrup and sugar.

▶ **A C T I V I T Y   4 – 2**

Detecting Topic Sentences

Construct three brief paragraphs from this unorganized mass of sentences. Begin by identifying the three topic sentences.

- The Manitoba Museum of Man and Nature uses "computer-age techniques to give you a quick glimpse into prairie life past and present" (Hall G13), and tourists can also visit the Manitoba Planetarium, the Manitoba Children's Museum, and many more attractions.

- The 930-hectare (2,300-acre) Wascana Centre, a huge greenbelt around Wascana Lake, surrounds the Legislative Building, the Saskatchewan Museum of Natural History, a science centre, a centre for the arts, and so forth.

- Regina is another capital city that looks quite stunning to tourists.

- The city has many attractions including the Edmonton Art Gallery, a space and science centre, and the world's largest mall.

- Winnipeg is underrated as a tourist destination.

- The picturesque river valley location is just the start of a visitor's delight with Edmonton.

▶ **A C T I V I T Y   4 – 3 ⋆**

Practise Creating Topic Sentences

Read the following brief essay. For each set of blank lines, create a topic sentence, such as those Renée DeLong, a student in a culinary skills program, wrote in the original version of her essay.

How to Prevent Accidents in the Kitchen

Avoid accidents in the kitchen by always observing basic safety procedures. Be thoughtful about knives, stoves—even the floor you walk on.

_____

_____ When you have to walk across the kitchen, don't carry your knife with the sharp tip pointing out. Always walk with your arm hanging down at your side, with the knife blade facing your back. When washing dishes, never leave a knife in the water in case someone else puts a hand in the water. It's safer to wash and put a knife away as soon as you've finished using it.

_____ Never leave pot handles protruding past the edge of the stove. Point them inward so that no one walking by can accidentally bump a hot pot off a burner. Form the habit of always putting on an oven mitt before you handle a pot. Don't forget that an electric element that is no longer red can still burn you.

_____ Never leave water, spilled food, or anything else on the floor. If you spill grease, and cannot clean all of it off the floor, pour salt on it to prevent falls.

When you're in the kitchen, follow safety procedures so that you don't hurt yourself with your knives, stove—or floor. Remember: even a small accident can kill the joy of cooking.

▶ **ACTIVITY 4–4**

More Practice Creating Topic Sentences

Read the following brief essay. For each set of blank lines, write a topic sentence, as engineering technology student John Szekeres did in the original of his essay.

Pirating Software

Computer programs can really help us produce work, including exciting reports, newsletters, or Web pages. Unscrupulous people who pirate software (use computer programs that they have not paid for) hurt us all by driving up prices and discouraging the development of new, even more powerful programs.

_____ The manufacturer of the software must recover the costs of developing the software. When people illegally copy the program for free, the company receives no money. The software manufacturer will have to make more money from each copy that honest customers purchase. Legitimate users will pay more for programs that many people have pirated.

_____ Sluggish sales mean that there is less money to pay software engineers to write new programs. This may mean, for example, that a word processing program is not revised, so that to create more sophisticated documents the legitimate customer will have to learn a whole new program rather than an updated version of the same program. Eventually, honest customers end up with fewer programs to choose from because software piracy discourages developers.

Illegally copying computer software increases the cost for everyone and slows the development of better programs. We should all discourage software piracy.

4.3 LIMIT EACH PARAGRAPH TO ONE MAIN IDEA

As you organize your paragraphs, remember that each one makes one main point. Just as you limit a document to a single topic—to achieve unity—express one main idea in each paragraph. If there's more than one key idea, move one to its own paragraph. Apply this advice in Activity 4–5.

▶ **ACTIVITY 4–5★**

Limiting a Paragraph to One Main Idea

The following topic sentences are flawed. They suggest the paragraphs will develop *two* main ideas. Underline the second point or idea, the part you should move into a separate paragraph so that each paragraph is about one main idea.

1. Follow these easy steps to make yogurt and beer at home.

2. We should make our school buses safer for children and reduce the chance of food poisoning by using bleach on our kitchen dishrags.

3. Gardening and gourmet cooking are engrossing hobbies.

4. Autistic children seldom learn to communicate verbally, nor do they learn how to become independent workers.

5. Many new jobs and regulations are being created in call centres.

▶ **ACTIVITY 4–6**

Limiting a Paragraph to One Main Idea

The following topic sentences are flawed. They suggest the paragraphs will develop *two* main ideas. Underline the second point or idea, the part you should move into a separate paragraph so that each paragraph is about one main idea.

1. We should teach our children to read better and to become more physically fit.

2. We should stop mowing our lawns and treat lifeguards with more respect.

3. Schizophrenia and Alzheimer's disease have many causes.

4. You can improve your fishing techniques and learn to build a deck.

5. There are many benefits to caring for a pet, and it is good for your health to meditate, too.

4.4 ORGANIZE SUPPORT WITHIN YOUR PARAGRAPHS

In chapters 1 and 2, you

- considered how to create the content of an effective essay, the thesis, main points and support, and
- outlined the support for a brief essay about a pancake brunch.

The supporting detail for an essay is organized into paragraphs. The more effectively you organize the support within a paragraph, the better you convey your thoughts and feelings. Whether you write out an outline (such as shown in figure 2–4, an outline of the essay about gourmet pancakes) or only mentally outline your support, you should consider the order of each supporting sentence in each paragraph. You can effectively organize chronologically, emphatically, and logically; sometimes you decide the order of the points is not important, that no particular order is best: you may order such points randomly.

Organizing Support Chronologically

Process essays use chronological order to show readers the steps they must follow in sequence to perform some activity, such as cooking a pizza. Note the way Nicole McCoy uses chronological order to tell readers—step after step—how to make the perfect pizza.

Although you need a sound foundation of light, stretchy dough, you really begin to create the ideal pizza when you spoon on the sauce. Don't use a bland commercial pizza sauce; create your own with a mixture of tomato paste, chunky salsa, oregano, basil, salt, sugar, and lots of well-cooked ground beef. Top the sauce with a sprinkle of fresh fontina cheese, but don't use too much: you don't want to obscure the flavour of the sauce. Bake that pizza in a 450-degree oven until it's a golden brown. Cut it into large slices. Then, drizzle on a simmering mixture of garlic butter and Parmesan cheese. At last it's time to bite into this perfect pizza.

When you conceive a writing topic and decide that your reader will be sure to understand if you describe each step in order, you still need to identify your contention and—probably—jot down some point-form notes, details that will support your point. Don't slow down the pre-writing by taking the time to decide the optimal order, but as you begin to draft a first version of your message, organize the details in the way that will best convey your point. I often do this by adding numbers to my sketchy outline, numbers that show the order I'll follow to write the support sentences of my paragraph. I wish you could see how many numbers I scrawled onto copies of the drafts as I wrote parts of this book: you'd be convinced notetaking is essential to most writing.

Organizing Support Emphatically

Sometimes you can make your point more convincingly by arranging your supporting details in emphatic order. In emphatic order, you present your strongest piece of support *last*. When you use emphatic order, you start supporting your point with the second-strongest piece of evidence. Place support points of moderate value between the first and last points because people tend to more clearly remember first and last impressions. Weak points are less noticeable in the middle of an essay. Note the way Debra Oreskovich uses emphatic order in her paragraph about camping.

> How much I enjoy a camping trip depends on how well I prepare for it. It's very important to look through brochures, Web pages, and guides to pick a great place to camp. These help me find the rustic, family-oriented campgrounds I prefer. I also know that it's important to check the weather in the area I want to visit: heavy thunderstorms—or worse—can not only damage gear, they can hurt campers. Referring to a list helps me take care of a critical concern: packing the necessary gear—tent, sleeping bags, Hibachi, charcoal, cookware, cutlery, crockery, toilet items, books, matches, and insect repellent—and food—non-perishable items for all the meals. But with camping so popular, the most important part of my preparing is to phone ahead to reserve a campsite.

Organizing Support Logically

Sometimes you will make your point most effectively by organizing your support logically. Take a look at the following paragraph:

> It is alarmingly easy to become dependent on sedative drugs. Those dreadful feelings of despondency and listlessness that descend on us when we lose someone we love can tempt us to gain at least a little release by

taking a sedative. The sedative can cause the side effect of disturbing our sleep. The sleep disturbances can make us feel lethargic, and this feeling can cause us to feel more depressed so that we look to the drug to help alleviate the melancholy.

Each point leads logically to the next, building a conclusion that almost compels the reader to accept it.

As you look over your rough notes for an essay you're writing, consider whether arranging your points in a logical order might be an effective way of communicating your message.

Organizing Support Randomly

Consider this paragraph:

Amateur historians will have lots to do while visiting Calgary. In Heritage Park Historical Village, live interpretations and exhibits—including a steam locomotive and a paddlewheeler—show what life was like before 1915. A Blackfoot teepee and a settler's cabin at the Glenbow Museum are just two of the artifacts illustrating the heritage of the Canadian West. The Fort Calgary Historic Park includes the fort built by the North West Mounted Police when they arrived in 1875. You can step into yesterday while visiting Calgary today.

In this paragraph, history buffs learn of three examples of historical exhibits in Calgary. If you re-arranged the order of those examples, would your paragraph be more effective? Not really. For some points, it does not matter in what order you organize your supporting details.

Try the following exercise to test how well you understand the ways you can organize your support to make your point.

▶ ACTIVITY 4–7*

Ordering Support within Paragraphs

First, indicate the type of organization you would prefer, and then write numerals to show the optimal order for the specific details of the support.

1. If you want to apply for one of the thousands of places in more than 100 full-time programs at New Brunswick's community colleges, make sure to:

    • Enclose official transcripts of marks from high school and other educational institutions you have attended.

    • Enclose your non-refundable application fee.

- Enclose your completed application form.
- Enclose your information about related education and training experience.
- Send all your materials early enough to be received in Campbellton, NB, by March 1.

2. The New Brunswick College Admissions Service (CAS) examines three criteria to ensure that each spot in the community college system goes to the most suitable applicant.

- Applicants' abilities and skills are examined to determine suitability for the proposed program.
- Candidates' academic performance in English and mathematics is considered.
- College applicants are evaluated for work or training relevant to the desired training program.

3. Although the use of pesticides in agriculture has resulted in impressive crop gains, we are all paying a cost for this bounty.

- Pesticides can cause cancer, miscarriages, birth defects.
- Agricultural aircraft pilots have higher mortality rates.
- Pests are becoming resistant to our pesticides.
- Pesticides reduce bird and fish populations.

4. There is a vicious cycle that can promote alcoholism.

- You feel restless and uneasy because of sleep deprivation.
- You drink alcohol to reduce stress.
- Sleep troubles cause stress.
- You sleep poorly because of alcohol.

5. Mitch Shepherd outlined several steps to snowboarding.

- To help control your speed, carve back and forth across the hill; the wider the turn, the slower you will go.
- Slowly shuffle towards the hill until you start your descent.
- Once you learn the carve technique, you must learn to stop by turning your body and board ninety degrees while keeping your balance and digging the back edge of your board into the snow as hard as you can.
- At the top of the hill, strap your feet into the board, ninety degrees to the hill.

▶ **ACTIVITY 4–8**

Practise Writing Paragraphs that Include Topic Sentences and Well-Organized Support

Practise writing topic sentences and effectively ordering support for them by writing complete paragraphs for each item in Activity 4–7*. Create new topic sentences and express the support in your own words.

▶ **ACTIVITY 4–9**

Organize Support within Your Paragraphs

Practise organizing support within paragraphs by indicating the type of organization you would prefer and then writing numerals to show the optimal order for the support.

1. If you want to have a good time at the football game, you need to plan a good tailgate party. (Thanks to Richard DeLong.)

   - After you set up, you can join the other party-goers in playing a little parking-lot football.

   - When you arrive at the stadium parking lot, search for a prime spot. It's great if you can park right next to a Johnny-on-the-Spot.

   - As game time nears, it's time to move the party into the stadium; after all, you've got to see if your team will win.

   - As soon as you and your friends jump out of the car, open the trunk, find the cooler, and grab a cool one. That first drink tastes so good.

   - Before you head out for the day, be sure you've packed everything you need: steaks and salads, beverages, the barbecue, a football to toss around.

   - When you start to notice the pleasant aroma of steak, hot Italian sausage, and roast chicken, it's time to fire up the barbecue.

2. You're standing at the bar when you notice him and he notices you. You flash him a seductive smile. He smiles back and begins to glide toward you, manoeuvring through the crowd. All of a sudden, you see he is holding a white cylinder; the tip is glowing. No, it can't be. Your dreamboat is a smoker. You turn your back on him. There's nothing less attractive than a guy who smokes. (Thanks to Kerri A. Bray.)

   - The worst part of a romantic relationship with a smoker is that kissing him is about as pleasant as kissing an ashtray.

- One of the worst parts of dating a smoker is that he always wants to smoke right after dinner, and if you're not finished dinner you will certainly not want to continue eating once he lights up.

- Even if you're upstairs, you'll know the moment he walks into your house because you can smell his distinctive cologne: Eau du Maurier Light.

3. Owning a pet can help you lower your blood pressure. (Thanks to Chantal Clark.)

- Listening to the serene sound of bubbling water as you watch your tropical fish swim can deeply relax you after a hard day's work.

- Petting a dog can be so soothing that volunteers in some hospitals now take dogs to visit patients who are experiencing the stress of illness.

- Many people lower their blood pressure by grooming a horse and enjoying nature while horseback riding.

4. It's always a depressing start to a day to discover as you get ready to go to work that you have a flat tire, but you can hurry on your way if you change your tire efficiently. (Thanks to Bill Terreberry.)

- Finally, put your flat tire and jack into the trunk and get on your way to work.

- Then proceed to jack up the car.

- Begin by using your tire iron to loosen and remove the lug nuts on the flat.

- Lower the jack and tighten the nuts even more.

- Next, slide your spare onto the exposed bolts and tighten them as well as you can.

- That will permit you to remove the flat tire.

4.5 ENSURE COHERENCE WITHIN PARAGRAPHS

Well-organized writing is easier to read. When you begin a paragraph with a topic sentence, you make it easier for readers to see the point you are making. There are two main ways to increase the connections among ideas within paragraphs: use synonyms and repetition to help readers see the connections among points and include words that directly indicate how information is interconnected.

★ **Create coherence by using synonyms and repetition.** You can help your reader see the connections among all the details of your support for your thesis by repeating a keyword; the repetition reminds your readers of your thesis. Or, you can choose synonyms or synonymous terms. In both cases, you succeed in reminding your audience of your point.

Complete this activity to test how well you can detect Craig Farrish and Rob Deslauriers's use of repetition to create coherence.

▶ **ACTIVITY 4–10★**

Creating Coherence by Repeating Key Words

Read "Outlaw Spanking: Repeal Section 43 of the Criminal Code" (see section 7.5). Count how many times the authors used the word *repeal* to emphasize their contention that Canadians should outlaw spanking.

▶ **ACTIVITY 4–11**

Increasing Coherence by Using Synonyms

In "How to Be Fired from Your Dishwashing Job" (see section 7.1), Heidi Lambert wanted to remind readers that this was a process essay about how to escape the family chore of dishwashing. She emphasized that point by using, throughout the essay, synonymous terms for being fired. Read her essay, and record all the terms that mean the same as *being fired*.

★ **Choose words to emphasize connections within the paragraph.** Within a paragraph, good writers often choose words and phrases to show readers the connections among the points. In other words, writers use certain words to make the message more coherent.

Some words draw readers' attention to the *relationships* among ideas. Words like *another* and *also* show connections between ideas. *For example* and *such as* show readers that you are using examples to illustrate the points you make in the essay. *On the other hand* and *conversely* suggest readers look closely at contrasts within the information. *First* and *finally* draw readers' attention to the development of ideas in the information.

Complete the next activity to reinforce your awareness of words that writers can use to create more coherent messages.

▶ **ACTIVITY 4–12★**

Detecting Cohesion Signals

Read the following paragraph and underline the words that Amy Lonergan used to organize her sentences into a coherent, chronological account of how to fib successfully.

If you've decided to tell a white lie to get you out of some awkward situation, such as why you can't go out on Friday night, you had better try my procedure. The first step is to think up a plausible excuse. Anything too far-fetched will clearly show the victim that you have put no time or effort into this project at all. Next, be careful to memorize your fib. Stumbling over your words while telling a white lie may result in your having to tell the truth! Finally, you must master the skill of uttering the fib while looking directly into his eyes. This last step may take some time to perfect, but if you look away shiftily, he'll know you're not telling the truth. Following these few rules will let you fib with the best—or worst—of them.

▶ **ACTIVITY 4–13**

Detecting Cohesion Signals

Underline the words the author used to hold together—to create cohesion among—the sentences in these paragraphs.

1. Nova Scotia Community College was established in 1988 from pre-existing vocational and technical institutions such as the Institute of Technology and the Nautical Institute. On fourteen campuses across Nova Scotia, 7,000 students study full-time. In addition, more than 10,000 study part-time. The College offers more than 135 programs including dental assisting, carpentry, and funeral services. Not all programs are offered at every campus; for example, students must attend Truro Campus to study ecotourism. Within the NSCC system, there are also many ever-changing customized educational opportunities, including on-the-job training.

2. If you were born in another country, to become a Canadian citizen you must first pass an interview by a citizenship judge. The judge will ask questions to determine if you speak enough French or English to participate in the community. You must show a general understanding of Canada's form of government. You must also know citizens' rights and responsibilities. In addition, if you want to become a new Canadian, you need to know how to vote. Finally, you will be quizzed about Canadian history and geography. It isn't hard to pass the citizenship test, but you might want to study materials you can get from the office of your local member of parliament.

You'll employ these techniques to increase the coherence of complete essays, as discussed in chapter 5.

4.6 FINISH PARAGRAPHS WITH CONCLUDING SENTENCES

When you effectively organize a paragraph, you may write a concluding sentence to remind your audience of the point you made in that paragraph. Concluding sentences can ensure that readers will not get partway through another paragraph trying to understand a puzzling jump from one idea to another. A good concluding sentence will concisely sum up your point. It increases the likelihood that your reader will quietly agree with you and get ready for your next idea.

Writers often conclude sentences by recapitulating or restating the main idea of the paragraph, but they try to express the idea in a new, refreshing way so that the paragraph doesn't seem repetitious or boring. When you recap the main idea, you make it easier for readers to understand your point. Since too many concluding sentences in the support paragraphs can make the writing sound stilted, use these summarizing sentences sparingly. Analyze your audience: will adding a concluding sentence to this paragraph ensure that you are understood, or will your reader think you're re-explaining the obvious?

Do Activity 4–14 to test your understanding of how to write concluding sentences for paragraphs.

▶ ACTIVITY 4–14*

Writing Concluding Sentences

1. Replace the blank lines with appropriate concluding sentences.

    The federal government provides services that affect all Canadians. This is the level that determines citizenship. The national government also sets foreign policy and creates a national economic policy. The federal government is responsible for printing money, and it provides a postal service.

    _____

    _____.

2. Add a concluding sentence to James Marshall's description of one of the types of fighters that train at the Shamrock Club.

    The third type of fighters are boneheads. They don't train rigorously and don't listen to the coaches' advice. They often quit working when the coaches are not watching. They also look for easy spars. They build themselves up to seem more skilled than they are and then brag about nothing.

    _____

    _____.

3. Add a concluding sentence to this paragraph Damian Rogers wrote in a grant application to the Trillium Foundation.

A number of other groups contribute financial support because they believe the youth caucus of the Ontario Environmental Network (OEN) is doing valuable work. The OEN itself provides administrative support, including office space, telephone answering, photocopying, word processing, bookkeeping, and coordination. Other supporters include national environmental organizations (e.g., Canadian Environmental Law Association), community-based groups (e.g., Clean North), and—of course—student/youth organizations (e.g., Ontario Public Interest Research Group, Toronto). _____

_____

_____.

▶ **ACTIVITY 4–15**

Writing Concluding Sentences

Replace the blank lines with appropriate concluding sentences for this essay Alan Abercrombie wrote.

Casinos

I have no enthusiasm for the new gambling casino about to open in Niagara Falls. Although a lot of people see the casino as a cure-all for all of Niagara's problems, I believe it will hurt local charities, further impoverish those who can least afford to gamble, and create more gambling addicts.

Casino Niagara will hurt the fundraising efforts of local church and community groups. The relatively small prizes offered at service club and other charity bingos will no longer interest anyone. The less glamorous settings of the charity casinos will mean the gamblers will no longer show up. Yes, the provincial government will take a lot of money from the new casino, but _____

_____

_____.

The new casino will make many of the poor in Niagara even poorer. I have always felt that it was the people who could least afford it who did most of the gambling, people down on their luck and the unemployed hoping for a quick fix to their financial problems. Even though most of the money taken into the casino will stay there, it is hard for some people not to feel that they're the exception to the rule, that they will be big winners. The casino is just another _____

_____

_____ .

Having a casino in a community is bound to create new gambling addicts. A small segment of the population will not be able to resist the temptation of a chance to make lots of money without much work. They will show up at the casino on a daily basis, become addicted to the excitement of gambling, leave their families destitute, and be tempted to steal so they can gamble some more. Some people find it so hard to resist one more attempt to win that they wet their pants rather than take the time to go to a washroom!

_____

_____ .

When I contemplate the negative impact the casino will have on our community, I cannot look forward to it, to less money for our local charities, less money for our poor families. Our only gain will be more gambling addicts among us.

Complete Activity 4–16* to test how well you can identify and arrange the components of a paragraph.

▶ ACTIVITY 4–16*

Organizing Paragraphs

To practise organizing paragraphs, construct three from these sentences. Find the topic sentence, support sentences, and concluding sentence for each paragraph. Copy them onto three separate sheets, one for each paragraph.

- When an epic film like *Braveheart* is panned and scanned for a home-viewing video, viewers miss key visual information, such as the lush scenery and the massive number of revolutionaries, because only the central action survives the reformatting to make a version that fills a television screen. A letterbox version of John Carpenter's *Christine* captures the director's intent to show you how terribly outnumbered the protagonist is in that high-school hallway, but in the pan-and-scan version, viewers cannot experience the dread because they can't see the whole threat.

- Most people think it's too hard to write music, but if you follow my procedure, you may surprise yourself with a good song.

- The right approach can make waiting on tables pleasant—and profitable.

- Make a good first impression by smiling, making eye contact, introducing yourself, and handing out menus. Your second step is to take beverage orders and enthusiastically describe the specials of the day. When you believe the customers have decided what to order—the menus will probably be resting closed on the table—return with the drinks, and ask if the patrons would like to order. Punch the food order into the restaurant's computer, and check the progress of the cooking so that you can serve the food as soon as it is ready.

- Video distribution companies should stop releasing films in pan-and-scan formats.

- Send the distribution companies a message: Whenever possible, rent your videos in letterbox versions.

- First, pick a style—folk, alternative, blues, or metal—for your song. Then pick up your guitar and strum chords in that style until you start to sense a melody within your chord progressions.

- Service that is efficient—but not intrusive—almost always leads to a good tip.

- During the meal, ask if everything is okay. When you see that the diners have finished eating, clear the table of everything that is no longer needed and find out if anyone would like a dessert, coffee, or tea. Bring the bill with the beverages.

- Keep playing your chords and humming your melody until you create some lyrics. After a while, you'll feel an urge to ask your friends to listen to a brand-new song.

▶ ACTIVITY 4–17

Organizing Paragraphs

To practise organizing paragraphs, construct three paragraphs from these sentences. Find the topic sentence, support sentences, and concluding sentence for each essay and copy them out on separate sheets, one for each paragraph. (Thanks to Richard DeLong, Rosanne Celina Michaud, and David Bennett.)

- In the final stage of healing, you feel more energetic and it seems worthwhile to seek out your friends. You realize that you've passed through a healing process and life is good again.

- Economy cars, with their cheap prices and great gas mileage, seem like the right choice for starving students. However, with their smaller engines and bodies, they don't hold up over time. Few students consider full-sized cars because their price tags are almost as large as their motors, and they consume twice as much gas as economy cars. Mid-sized cars seem to have the best of both worlds: they're quite economical and durable.

- The moment your heart breaks, you have already begun the healing process.

- After rejecting economy and full-sized cars, students often resolve their car-buying dilemma by purchasing mid-sized cars.

- Finally, turn the machine on, and very soon you'll be able to smell the sweet aromatic scent of that very necessary coffee.

- Students, because of their limited budgets, find it challenging to decide what kind of used car to buy.

- If you're like me—and most of North American society—getting your morning coffee is the most important part of the day.

- First, you feel such intense pain that you cry and cry. You feel so desolate, so deeply sad; nothing seems worth doing, not even eating. Gradually, as the weeks go by, the pain eases a bit and the depression starts to lift. You may be startled when you laugh while watching a sitcom, even if you're in tears again a few minutes later.

- As you groggily make your way into the kitchen, your sleep-filled eyes and cloudy brain guide you straight to the coffee machine. Proceed to grasp the carafe carefully because if you break it now you're in deep trouble. Bring it to the sink, and fill it to the maximum level. Return it to the machine and pour it in. Now you need to get a filter (or a paper towel if—tragically—you've run out of filters). Now add the proper amount of coffee: lots.

▶ **ACTIVITY 4–18**

Practise Organizing Paragraphs

Using one of the essays outlined in Activity 4–9, write a paragraph that includes a strong topic sentence, support sentences arranged for maximal effectiveness, and a concluding sentence that leaves readers—other college students—feeling that the writing was well organized. Reread your paragraph and rewrite it if you feel you could make it more coherent by adding transition words.

4.7 SOME CONCLUDING THOUGHTS

You've studied how to write effective paragraphs, the building blocks of most written communication. In chapter 5, you will have the opportunity to transform paragraphs into one particular kind of document, brief essays. The activities in chapter 5 will also prepare you to write better research essays (as discussed in part 3) and how to improve your writing of all the different kinds of documents presented on the *Write of Way* Web pages.

Organizing Brief Essays

"If you would be a reader, read; if a writer, write."
—*Epictetus*

CHAPTER OBJECTIVE

After completing the activities in this chapter, you will have a clear understanding of how to organize brief essays.

5.1 MOVING FROM SINGLE PARAGRAPHS TO ESSAYS

Paragraphs form the body of many different kinds of writing, from essays to job applications. Some demands for writing require only a single stand-alone paragraph. An answer to a test question is often only a paragraph in length. To apply for a college program, you may have to write a statement of why you should be admitted to that particular program; the application may leave room to write only a single paragraph. Before studying how to write effective essays, take another moment to consider single, individual paragraphs.

Garden-variety, single paragraphs fill the spaces between introductions and conclusions in all kinds of writing, including essays. Each paragraph begins with a topic sentence that identifies the main idea developed in the paragraph (e.g., The biggest crop in the Niagara peninsula is cut flowers). Next come the sentences that support the main idea (e.g., statistics showing the value of the major Niagara crops). Commonplace paragraphs often end with a concluding sentence that restates the point, if this will help the reader understand the main idea (e.g., When people think of Niagara, they think of grapevines and peach orchards, but flowers are the main source of farm incomes).

Not only is an essay longer than a single paragraph, an essay differs in another fundamental way: an essay always includes a thesis statement; an essay makes a contention. By contrast, a garden-variety paragraph begins with a topic sentence that indicates only the main idea of the paragraph, which could be a contention or simply a statement of fact. "Nicknames should be abolished" makes an assertion, and could be the topic sentence of a paragraph or the thesis of an essay. "Our biggest crop in the Niagara peninsula is cut flowers" is a topic sentence that could begin a paragraph that simply states a fact.

Non-fiction writing varies from being quite objective—an incident report that tries to objectively describe a fight in a group home or an information summary of a larger document, a summary that simply aims to find a briefer way of expressing the essential information of the original—to very subjective—an essay recommending that Canadian parents not spank their children.

You've looked at an outline of Donovan Cutler's paragraph "Down-Home Cooking" (figure 1–1). It is organized just as readers expect:

- topic sentence,

- support sentences, and

- concluding sentence.

In chapter 2, you studied how to create theses and support sentences. You studied how to write concluding sentences in section 4.6. It's time to practise organizing all this information into well-formed essays.

You may recall from chapter 1 that a paragraph can be more complex, such as the paragraph "How to Enjoy a Blizzard" (figure 15–4). As you reread that paragraph, search for the three main points that support the topic sentence (you can enjoy a blizzard) and note the way each main point is supported by additional detail. Take another look at figure 15–3, the outline for the paragraph about enjoying a blizzard. Imagine that you were going to write a humorous article for a college newspaper. Brainstorm additional points you could make for your plan to enjoy a blizzard. At a point, you may decide that the amount of support you've created is just too much to fit into a single paragraph. The increasing number of main points or the greater amount of supporting detail means that you can create a paragraph for each main point. Perhaps you'll write a longer introduction and a lengthier conclusion. It's time to organize a longer document, a multi-paragraph essay. Figure 1–6 shows an outline for such an essay, a five-paragraph essay. Does your longer essay have to be five paragraphs? No, your essay need only be long enough to effectively make your point, and that could make it ten, twelve, or four paragraphs long.

The fundamental structure of a multi-paragraph essay is very similar to the organization of a complex paragraph:

- the thesis is stated (it replaces the topic sentence of the complex paragraph);

- each main point is successively made and supported; and finally,

- the conclusion reminds readers of the main idea.

Test your understanding of the components of a multi-paragraph essay by completing Activity 5–1.★

▶ ACTIVITY 5–1*

Identifying the Components of Brief Essays

After reviewing the balloon version of "Pancakes for Sunday Brunch" (figure 15–5), use the labels from figure 1–6, "Outline of a Five-Paragraph Essay" (introductory paragraph, first support paragraph, second support paragraph, third support paragraph, and concluding paragraph) to make a balloon version of "Make That a Veggie Burger."

Make That a Veggie Burger

The rapid expansion of vegetarian items on menus across Canada is a sign that more people are choosing to become vegetarians. People still eating other animals always ask, "Why did you become a vegetarian?" Many vegetarians hope that as they explain why they chose vegetarianism, the questioner will choose vegetarianism, too, for three reasons: Become a vegetarian because it is good for your health, environment, and conscience.

For some, choosing a healthy diet means becoming a vegetarian. Eating less fat—particularly animal fat—reduces the likelihood of developing cancer and heart disease. Dean Ornish, a physician and professor of medicine, recommends a low-fat diet that eliminates meat and dairy products. His studies suggest that this diet can even reverse some symptoms of heart disease. Choose vegetarianism for a lifestyle that leads to better health.

The destruction of the rain forests to clear grazing land for beef cattle has led some people to vegetarianism: they want to tread more lightly on the earth, to treat the environment more gently. Others are disturbed to read about how cattle manure runs off the ground and pollutes streams and groundwater. Far more land is needed to feed people meat than to produce enough grains, vegetables, and fruits to sustain human life. If you care about the environment, choose to be a vegetarian: it is an important way to care for our planet.

Some people become vegetarians because they can't in good conscience kill other animals. If animals have enough consciousness to know their interests—such as preferring to stay alive—their wishes must be considered. Look at the way we resolve conflicts of interest with other animals with consciousness, human animals. You want to drink alcohol and drive your car. I'm worried you'll hurt me by driving drunk. We consider both interests and decide a limit to the alcohol permitted in the bloodstream: you can still have a beer after work, but I don't have to worry that you'll be driving while impaired. If you have decided not to ignore the interests of non-human animals, choose to become a vegetarian.

More and more people are becoming vegetarians. If you care about your health, your environment, and your conscience, choose vegetarianism.

▶ **ACTIVITY 5-2**

Identifying the Components of Brief Essays

After referring to figure 1–6, create a similar outline for Sean Davidson's "Bar People."

Bar People

Ask the servers in a busy nightclub, and they will tell you they've seen it all. Bar patrons are a very diverse group, ranging from minors, to couples, to hard-core drinkers.

It is impossible, unfortunately, to eliminate minors from the bar scene. Whether through fake ID's or incompetent doorkeepers, minors manage to sneak in. From a server's point of view, these are the worst customers: they tip poorly, if at all. Because they cannot handle their alcohol, minors often instigate arguments and fights. Until someone comes up with a foolproof way to determine age, minors will continue to make life interesting for servers.

Couples are generally the most pleasant people to serve. They are too wrapped up in each other to create problems in the bar. In order to impress their dates, people on dates tip well and drink less. Couples are almost perfect customers unless they do become intoxicated and overly amorous for a public place.

It's hard to rate heavy drinkers as customers. They can go from being your best customers of the night to your worst. They generally tip well early in the evening, but as the money runs low, the next beer is more important than leaving a tip. Hard-core drinkers can be selfish and inconsiderate about leaving the bar: they don't care that the server of alcohol can be held responsible for any accidents caused by a drunk patron. Although a server stands to make a lot of money from these customers, they pose a great risk and can be very unpleasant when refused service.

Minors, couples, and hard-core drinkers all make life interesting for a server in a bar. They're why I'd rather sell drinks than shoes or stereos.

Once you've memorized the main elements of brief essays, and the order of those components, turn your attention to studying the introductory, support, and concluding paragraphs.

5.2 THE UNIQUE STRUCTURE OF INTRODUCTORY PARAGRAPHS

Take a closer look at introductory paragraphs. Look again at figure 1–6, the outline of a five-paragraph essay; look particularly at Paragraph 1: Introductory Paragraph. Examine the elements readers expect in the introduction to an essay and the order they expect to encounter these elements: lead-in, thesis, and—usually—a preview of the main points. Read this section to learn more about how to organize powerful introductions to the essays you write.

Lead-ins

Your readers begin to *judge you* as soon as their eyes focus on your writing. You've created a document with an attractive appearance because you want your readers to form a favourable first impression. Your efforts to make a good impression should include creating a strong lead-in. Other writers call this a *grabber* (Green and Norton), a *motivator* (Bailey and Powell), or a *hook* (Wingersky, Boerner, Holguin-Balogh, Gossin, and Stancer), but all these terms express a similar underlying belief: you have only a few moments to capture the attention of your reader and to arouse a desire to read your document.

Most of the time, you will not worry about writing an effective lead-in until you've generated a thesis, main points, and support and have outlined your essay. Then, you'll want to pay particular attention to the beginning.

Look to the content of your document to create the lead-in, the first words your audience will read. As you re-familiarize yourself with your content, be on the lookout for some information that would capture your reader's interest. Here are some ways writers often lead readers into documents.

★ **Telling a story makes a good lead-in.** Contrast these two ways of introducing the same essay.

OK: Using cosmetic surgery to disguise the appearance of children with Down syndrome does not increase their IQ, achievement test scores, or school grades.

Better: All through my pregnancy, I dreamed of my baby. When—after seventeen hours of labour—I gazed into her face, my dreams for her were shattered as I realized she had Down syndrome. I wondered if the cosmetic surgery they were using in Germany to disguise this condition would help my beautiful baby be more successful at school. Right then I planned to research the topic. I found out that such cosmetic surgery did not increase IQ, achievement test scores, or school grades.

Sometimes an anecdote or a case study can make a powerful lead-in to an essay.

★ **Making a startling statement can be a good lead-in.** "Working shifts can ruin your marriage." That really catches the reader's attention. Your reader isn't expecting such a claim, and he or she is therefore motivated to read the rest of the essay.

You can also startle readers into attention by asserting an unexpected point of view. Here's an example: "Most people think that attending daycare strains the emotional bond between children and their parents, but such child care actually promotes better parent–child bonding." An opinion startlingly different from popular belief will spark interest.

★ **An apt quotation is a good lead-in.** A Goderich, Ontario, judge—in dismissing charges against a mother who had punished her 11-year-old daughter for mess-ing her room and blaming her sister—said, "Parents are entitled to use a belt . . . . There were welts, but I guess you expect to find welts when you use a belt" (Jourard D2).

That quotation is a strong lead-in to an essay opposing spanking. It is powerful because it has the immediacy of speech, and it hints at a story. Quotations can do that.

"The state has no place in the bedrooms of the nation," said former Prime Minister Pierre Elliott Trudeau in an interview in December 1967. His statement has served as a lead-in for many essays.

Your dictionary is another effective source of material to quote. Quoting a definition can sometimes grab the attention of readers. "Blood money: Money gained at the cost of another person's life, freedom, welfare" was the lead-in to Toronto health policy consultant Michael Rachlis' essay decrying a tax cut financed by reducing welfare payments. That quotation really does grab your attention, even if you disagree with Rachlis' opinion.

* **A question can make an interesting lead-in.** Consider this essay lead-in: "Would you like to babysit seventy children for forty-five minutes? Would you like to do that with your back to the children? How would you like to do it while driving a forty-foot school bus?"

Jill Pamenter hooks her audience by asking those questions. Her questions make her readers concerned about children's safety. The questions helped Jill persuade readers to support her quest to ensure that school buses are staffed with two adults: a driver and a monitor.

Questioning is a powerful way to pull a response from your readers. It can really grab their attention and motivate their desire to find out what you have to say.

▶ **ACTIVITY 5–3**

Creating Lead-ins for Essays

Create a lead-in for each of the incomplete introductory paragraphs. Read through the statement of the thesis and the preview of the main points. Write a lead-in with a tone appropriate to the topic.

1.* _____

_____

_____ I decided to quit my job at a local sawmill, and come back to college, because management frequently assigned unscheduled overtime, always paid low wages, and often ignored safety regulations. (Thanks to Chris Barr.)

2. _____

_____

_____ Even in cars equipped with air bags, you should still wear your seat belt because you can avoid the neck and spinal column injuries possible even at low speeds and the fatal injuries possible in high-speed crashes. (Thanks to Greg Henderson.)

3. _____

_____

_____ To be a successful film actor, you need to know exactly what to do when you hear the words "Rolling," "Speed," and "Action." (Thanks to Michael D. White.)

4. _____

_____

_____ If you want to avoid the drunks you sometimes run into at parties, pay close attention to the way someone approaching you walks and talks. (Thanks to Aaron Smallbone.)

5. _____

_____

_____ Air bags in cars reduce neither accidents nor insurance costs. (Thanks to Andrew MacLeod.)

Thesis and Preview of Main Points

Once you've created a lead-in for the introduction to your essay, it's time to state your thesis, and this almost always means simultaneously previewing your main points.

Usually you include the thesis and the preview of the main points in the same sentence. Express the main points in a parallel form. Look at these examples:

Poor: You'll have a wonderful time at Point Pelee Provincial Park swimming, birding, and to go for hikes.

Good: University College of the Cariboo is a good place to study biology, chemistry, or mathematics.

The second sentence is better because the words in the series are expressed in a parallel structure that reads more smoothly. Read more about parallel structure in section 12.12.

5.3 ORGANIZE THE SUPPORT PARAGRAPHS

Within each paragraph, you organized your points of support chronologically, emphatically, logically, or randomly. Remember the discussion in which the class determined the order for discussing the main effects of using photo radar to enforce speed limits? Follow the same procedure as you plan your organization of the main points of your essay. Remember, too, that after you arrange your main points in the optimal order, use the same order when you preview those main points in your introductory paragraph. Your readers will expect you to use the same order in both parts of the essay. Indeed, readers will often glance back to the preview section of your introduction to see which point you will make next in the essay. You make your essay more coherent when you ensure the same order for the main points in the preview and in the body of the essay; all the information is more tightly tied together.

► BOX 5–1 Ensure Coherence between Paragraphs

When you tightly connect all the paragraphs of your essay, you make it easier for your readers to understand you. You achieve that coherence partly by organizing well-formed essays with introductions, support, and conclusions. You create outlines—outlines of the content, as shown in figures 1–7 and 2–4, and outlines of content and organization, as shown in figure 15–7—to write essays with strong cohesion.

You can employ another technique to create cohesion: use transition words.

*Create coherence by using transition words. In figure 1-6, "Outline of a Five-Paragraph Essay," you can see the words *with transition* in parentheses at the beginning of paragraphs 3 and 4. These are logical points in five-paragraph essays where you can ensure your readers see the relationship of a previously mentioned point with the point you make next. You can begin your topic sentence by briefly repeating the point you just made in the previous paragraph.

Look at these two versions of a middle section of a five-paragraph essay. Notice how the second version has transition in the topic sentence.

No Transition:

One act of cheating can have devastating effects on a student's reputation and finances.

Plagiarism also hurts the community.

Transition:

One act of cheating can have devastating effects on a student's reputation and finances.

Not only does plagiarism hurt the individual, it also harms the community.

Test your understanding of how to create transition by completing Activity 5–4.

▶ ACTIVITY 5–4*

Creating Transitions between Paragraphs

Read this portion of "Shamrock Club Boxers," and rewrite it to create more cohesion between the paragraphs by adding a reminder of the previous point to the topic sentences for the paragraphs about casual participants and boneheads.

They work hard and have a strong desire to win their bouts. These top competitors live totally healthy lifestyles.

Some of the fighters at the Shamrock Club participate more casually. These boxers don't have the same dedication as the first type. Boxing is only a secondary activity in their lives. They do the work at a slower pace and don't get the same attention from the coaches. Casual participants don't usually choose as healthy a lifestyle.

The third type of fighters are boneheads.

▶ ACTIVITY 5–5

Creating Transitions between Paragraphs

Read Theresa Duff's essay "Sign Language in School," and create more cohesion between the paragraphs by adding a reminder of the previous point to the topic sentence about the next point.

Sign Language in School

Imagine never being able to hear anything around you. Worse, imagine that you couldn't talk with the people in your life. High schools should offer courses in American Sign Language—just as they offer courses in other languages—because many students are interested in learning Sign to benefit themselves and deaf people.

Many high school students are more interested in learning sign language than French, Spanish, German, or Latin. One of the goals of second language learning is to develop the intelligence of the language learner, and students know that learning Sign would be just as stimulating as learning a spoken language. Some students would also like to learn Sign because it would enable them to become more rounded people by making it easier to communicate with a greater diversity of humankind, just as learning any other second language. Many students, who must now wait until college, are interested in learning to sign while at high school.

_____

_____ it could also financially benefit the learners. Potential employers might be impressed by job applicants who know Sign. Deaf people shop, too, and a company or store with employees who can communicate with deaf customers could attract more business. And, of course, there are jobs for interpreters and other kinds of workers in schools, service agencies, and group homes.

_____

_____ it would be a great benefit to our deaf citizens. It is very hard for people born deaf to learn to communicate by speech and to lip-read. It is considerably easier for people who can hear to learn sign language. If more students could learn Sign while at high school, it would enrich them and improve the lives of deaf people in our community.

High schools should offer courses in sign language because many students want to learn to sign; they know that it would be interesting and would be valuable to themselves and to deaf people.

5.4 THE UNIQUE STRUCTURE OF CONCLUDING PARAGRAPHS

After you have created the content for an essay and outlined your plan of development, turn your attention to your ending. Partings leave impressions that are nearly as important as introductions, so you want to write a strong concluding paragraph.

Look again at figure 1-6, the outline of a five-paragraph essay. Read about the elements of the final paragraph. What are the two parts of a concluding paragraph? You're right: a restatement or recap of the thesis—usually the main points, too—and a clincher.

Restatement of the Thesis

The restatement of the thesis gives the writer one last opportunity to remind the reader of the contention in the writing. It's your last chance to ensure your reader *gets* the point. You don't want to sound repetitious, so create new ways to express the main ideas. Sometimes those synonyms you used to create greater coherence can be used here, too. Other times, you can summarize or reinforce your point more forcefully by repeating the words you used in the introductory paragraph.

Look again at "The Positive Effects of Using Photo Radar to Enforce Speed Limits" (figure 15–8). In this instance, the writer simply repeated the thesis and main points.

The Clincher

Writers often choose to finish an essay with some final comment created to linger in the mind of the reader, to leave the reader with a good final impression. Here are two suggestions for creating good clinchers.

> *** If your topic is not too serious, you can finish with a humorous comment.** Some essays finish with a humorous point, like the clincher for "The Positive Effects of Using Photo Radar to Enforce Speed Limits" (figure 15–8). It reminds us that we might end up in a photo radar photograph any time we are in a car, so we might want to stay home on a bad-hair day. The essay closes with the words "Oh, well, you can always wear a hat."

> *** If your essay has a serious tone, write a clincher that will make a final sober comment.** The essay about plagiarism is quite sombre in tone (see section 7.3). This sort of sober-minded advice seems a good parting comment:

Imitation may be the sincerest form of flattery, but when you want to borrow other people's ideas, give them credit by naming the authors and indicating where their work was published.

▶ **ACTIVITY 5–6***

Writing Concluding Paragraphs

Imagine the essays that might be written from the following decimal outlines. For each, write a concluding paragraph that includes a recap of the thesis (and main points) and a clincher.

1. Thesis: There are several benefits to learning to play a musical instrument.

    1. People who learn to play a guitar, piano, or band instrument will find that their skill always makes it easier to meet new friends.

2. Learning to play an instrument to accompany oneself while singing provides the musician with an enjoyable hobby.

3. Putting your brain through the work of learning to play music can actually make you smarter.

2. Thesis: Taking our children along on routine trips to do chores may be a little more work than going alone, but it benefits our kids.

    1. The conversations we have at the supermarket or garage—and the people we meet who also talk with our children—help our children develop better language skills.

    2. While bakeries and hardware stores are old hat to us, our children learn more about their world whenever they visit these places with us.

    3. The give-and-take of getting along with other people when we share outings helps our children develop more social skills.

3. Thesis: Lenny Gallant is a fine singer-songwriter.

    1. Gallant's distinctive voice draws you into his songs.

    2. When you listen to Lenny Gallant's story-songs, you sometimes feel as though you know the people he sings about.

    3. Gallant, a PEI native, has a talent for telling Canadians stories about themselves.

4. Thesis: It's a good practice to write routine classroom assignments in MLA style.

    1. Most teachers will form a positive impression of a paper formatted in MLA style.

    2. When you routinize a way of formatting your assignments, you save yourself time.

    3. Writing in MLA style is a kind of courtesy that is very helpful for the reader; for example, teachers can quickly find the information they need to record a mark for the writer.

5. Thesis: There are many reasons why we should make it financially easier for students to attend college.

    1. To succeed in the global economy, Canada will need highly educated citizens, and more capable people would attend college if we removed economic barriers to attendance.

    2. A democracy works better when citizens are more informed, and a college education helps students become more knowledgeable about the world.

    3. Students would learn more effectively if they were not preoccupied with money concerns.

▶ **ACTIVITY 5–7**

Writing Concluding Paragraphs

Imagine the essays that might be written from the following decimal outlines. For each, write a concluding paragraph that includes a recap of the thesis (and main points) and a clincher.

1. Thesis: Several factors make it difficult to quit smoking.

    1. It's tough to quit smoking when you are constantly reminded of cigarettes when you see other people puffing away in the doorways of every building you enter.

    2. Peers who are still smoking can make it hard to quit because they often urge you to join them for a smoke.

    3. Memories of how much you enjoyed smoking can tempt you to light up again.

2. Thesis: If you visit Niagara Falls, there are three attractions you must see.

    1. Journey Behind the Falls—tunnels you can look out of right into the falling water—is one of the best attractions in Niagara Falls.

    2. Another must-see is the Imax film *Niagara: Miracles, Myth, and Magic*.

    3. The best thrill in Niagara Falls—short of going over in a barrel—is riding the Maid of the Mist ferryboat right up to the face of the falls.

3. Thesis: The Lung Association deserves your support.

    1. Your donations will help the Lung Association fund medical research into lung disease.

    2. The Lung Association offers educational programs to help asthmatic children and adults suffering from chronic lung disease such as emphysema.

    3. You should give a donation to the Lung Association to support its stop-smoking programs.

4. Thesis: There are three ways we can help children learn to read words on sight.

    1. To help children learn to read independently, we should encourage young children to read easy text and guess at the words they cannot yet read on sight.

    2. If we teach children how to do phonic analysis, they will have a procedure to try when they don't recognize words on sight.

    3. When we quietly tell a child a word she doesn't recognize while reading aloud, we help the child learn to recognize it on sight.

5. Thesis: Students need to consider three factors to find a great place to live while attending college.

    1. Students need to investigate several places to find a home that meets their first requirement: low cost.

    2. Most students also need to consider location in looking for a place to live while at school because they can save a lot of money if they can walk to school.

    3. A place with good atmosphere is also important to students because they spend a lot of hours at home.

5.5 PUTTING IT ALL TOGETHER TO WRITE BRIEF ESSAYS

You can take certain actions at the beginning of your composition course that will help you maximize how much you improve your writing. Look closely at your course outline. Determine if you will be able to choose your own topics for the essays you will write. Then, plan the essays you're going to write. Perhaps you would like to write about topics related to your program. Perhaps there are social issues that concern you. To prepare to write meaningfully about these topics, you may want to do some research. You might research casually by reading particular sections of a textbook, or you may go to a library and use information-retrieval tools to research a topic. As you imagine your audience, you'll know whether you need to learn more to write your essay.

This approach is obviously more work than just writing off the top of your head. Everyone finds it easier to write about what they know well, and harder to write about topics with more sophisticated content. Analyzing your college's policy for appealing a course grade is harder than a composing a humorous essay about how you can get your family to fire you from dishwashing chores. Yet, the kind of writing you will do in the workplace is more like that essay about appealing a grade. Some of the sample essays in chapter 7 were written by students after they did some research.

Chapters 6 and 7 present essays with various numbers of paragraphs to help you develop a sound understanding of essay writing. To do so, you've got to be able to adjust your essays to the length you need, which could be four, six, or sixty paragraphs. That's also why you'll be asked to make outlines or balloon versions of essays. When you can create an appropriate outline to help you construct an essay, you've developed a very useful writing skill.

As you get ready to hand in a writing assignment, take a moment to consider why your teacher is going to mark it. The first reason is obvious: to earn her paycheque, the teacher must submit grades for each student. Teachers of writing, however, usually have much nobler reasons for marking your papers: they sincerely want to help you write better. They believe that students are empowered when they become capable writers. Scratch an English teacher, and you'll almost always find someone who passionately wants to help all students be the best they can be. So, your teacher will write feedback on your assignment to help you improve as a writer.

This feedback really can help you transform yourself into a more capable writer. You can begin to make the most of this feedback even before you hand in your assignment. Apply everything you know about writing so that your document is as good as you can make it. That way, the feedback will accurately indicate precisely what you *still* need to learn to improve your writing. You can get down to the business of self-improvement as a writer.

You may find it helpful when planning an essay to create a scratch outline. Figure 2–4 shows a scratch outline of just the content of that essay about making a pancake brunch, while figure 1–6, "Outline of a Five-Paragraph Essay," shows an outline of both the content and organization of a brief essay. Remember: you create an outline to help you write a better essay, so your outline need only be sufficiently detailed to help you write faster and better. Figure 5–1 shows an even simpler scratch outline of the content of an essay. When planning your essay, you might save time by jotting your ideas into a copy of the outline below. (If your essay makes more than four main points, you will have to add to this scratch outline.)

FIGURE 5–1

Scratch Outline of an Essay

Thesis:

_____

_____

_____

First Main Point:

_____

_____

_____

Point-form notes of specific support for the first main point

- _____
- _____
- _____
- _____

Second Main Point:

_____

_____

Point-form notes for the second main point

- _____
- _____
- _____
- _____

Third Main Point:

_____

_____

Point-form notes for the third main point

- _____
- _____
- _____
- _____

Subsequent Main Points:

_____

_____

Point-form notes for the n-main point

- _____
- _____
- _____
- _____

Create your outline as you plan your essay. You may find that to write an effective essay you need to create a scratch outline of the content but need only refer to the outline of the content and organization.

After you've completed a draft of your essay, use the checklist to be sure your essay is sound. Test your essay to see if you can give a yes to every question (figure 5–2).

FIGURE 5–2

Checklist for Brief Essays

Introductory Paragraph

_____ Did I begin with a strong lead-in?

_____ Did I state my thesis?

_____ Did I preview my main points?

Support Paragraphs

Paragraph developing the first main point

_____ Did I begin my first support paragraph with a topic sentence about the first point I previewed in the thesis sentence?

_____ Did I detail convincing support for the first main point?

_____ Did I effectively conclude the paragraph?

Paragraph developing the second main point

_____ Did I begin my second support paragraph with a topic sentence about the second point I previewed in the thesis sentence?

_____ Did I detail convincing support for the second main point?

_____ Did I effectively conclude the paragraph?

Paragraph developing the third main point

_____ Did I begin my third support paragraph with a topic sentence about the third point I previewed in the thesis sentence?

_____ Did I detail convincing support for the third main point?

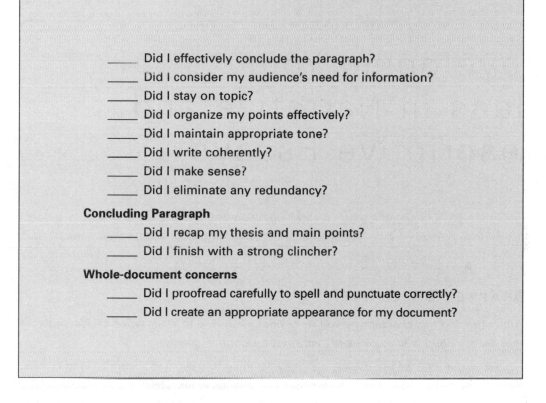

_____ Did I effectively conclude the paragraph?

_____ Did I consider my audience's need for information?

_____ Did I stay on topic?

_____ Did I organize my points effectively?

_____ Did I maintain appropriate tone?

_____ Did I write coherently?

_____ Did I make sense?

_____ Did I eliminate any redundancy?

Concluding Paragraph

_____ Did I recap my thesis and main points?

_____ Did I finish with a strong clincher?

Whole-document concerns

_____ Did I proofread carefully to spell and punctuate correctly?

_____ Did I create an appropriate appearance for my document?

5.6 SOME CONCLUDING THOUGHTS

If you follow the advice and the activities in this chapter, you will improve your writing. You can also make progress by reading the sample essays and working your way through the analysis questions about them (see chapters 6 and 7). In part 5, you can study how published writers developed their ideas. Still, there's only so much progress that comes from studying and completing exercises. The more often you write _entire_ essays, the faster you will learn to write better.

CHAPTER 6

Developing Your Ideas in Narrative and Descriptive Essays

"The life of a writer is tragic: the more we advance, the farther there is to go and the more there is to say, the less time there is to say it."
—*Gabrielle Roy*

CHAPTER OBJECTIVE

After studying this chapter, you will write brief essays—and other types of documents—that are enriched with stories and evocative, descriptive details.

From the time we are babies, we enjoy listening to narratives, hearing good stories. Picture books, cartoons, comic books, our first chapter books, television sitcoms, or the latest best-selling thrillers or romance novels—we enjoy stories throughout our lives. "You know it was a fluke that Anne Michaels' first novel, *Fugitive Pieces*, won the Orange Prize," says a friend. Now you want the whole story of how Michaels' publisher hadn't even submitted the book for consideration, that only two days before the judges short-listed the books, judge Alison Pearson learned of the book from a friend, "an editor for a rival publishing house" ("Book Contest" A4). Pearson showed it to the chair of the panel, who also loved it, and Anne Michaels won the $70,000 prize.

Rich, specific, detailed description also makes those stories more interesting. The effective storyteller helps us visualize the people and places of the story. In the next two sections of *Write of Way*, you'll have a chance to learn how to enliven your writing with stories and descriptive details—and how to use storytelling and description in effective essays. In each section, you can read examples of brief essays and answer discussion questions about them; then you can consider suggestions for topics you might write about.

College students wrote most of the example essays. The viewpoints expressed by the writers are bound to annoy or even anger some readers. Good writers often challenge our personal beliefs or values. You'll learn to write better by discussing the papers. When you really disagree, why not write a rebuttal?

6.1 NARRATING

You often have a reason to write a narrative, to tell a story; for example, in the chapter 6 essay "It Takes a Whole Village to Raise a Child," the author told four anecdotes to illustrate child neglect and tried to arouse readers to take better care of Canada's children.

You often tell stories at social events. To roast a good citizen at a fundraising dinner, you might tell a story to reveal the character of the person being roasted. I'm already planning to narrate two stories at my parents' fiftieth wedding anniversary: One is about how my dad cancelled—after it had already started—a meeting, choosing instead to drive me to hear Prime Minister Lester Pearson; I'd wanted so much to go to an election rally that I'd told Dad I was going to hitchhike. Another is about how my mum reacted when she caught me reading a mildly pornographic novel I'd found on my paper route. She just quietly—more with sorrow than with anger—suggested that with so many fine books to read, it was a shame to see me wasting time. That comment influenced me more than harsh words or a spanking could have. I hope retelling those stories in an anniversary toast will help me go a little ways towards thanking my parents for a lifetime of caring.

Much of news-article writing is narrating the sequence of events; storytelling, really.

Sometimes you want to tell a story just because it's a great anecdote to share. It's easy to imagine André Bryan (his essay follows) telling his story as a stand-up comedy act. You may see Kari Longboat's story in her autobiography. The stories in "It Takes a Whole Village to Raise a Child" could be told in a daycare fundraising letter, a speech, or a letter to the editor.

Consider the following guidelines when you want to tell a story.

* **Decide the best order for telling the events of the story.** Almost always you'll choose to tell the story in chronological order, just the way the story unfolded; however, sometimes you can get a good effect from changing the order, perhaps telling the ending and then flashing back to explain, for example, just how you ended up sleeping on the couch.

* **Use your knowledge of the process of writing.** Brainstorm, daydream, and jot notes in the pre-writing stage. Once you've outlined your narration—perhaps a story you're going to tell in an anniversary-party toast—do your draft writing as quickly as you can, not slowing down to worry about spelling or punctuation. Later you can revise your writing to make certain it conveys what is in your head and your heart—and does so in Standard English and with a pleasing appearance. (Remember the COSA formula.)

* **Consider using dialogue.** You can best tell some stories by writing dialogue. When you read André Bryan's tongue-in-cheek account of a visit to a grocery

store, you'll agree that the story comes alive because you hear the actual words of the shoppers.

★ **Consider using the first person.** Kari Longboat's reminiscence is told in the first person: "I recall a place I used to visit, and it now reminds me of summer, hot dogs, and family." The first-person perspective creates a sense of immediacy; you feel almost as though you are there with the storyteller. Longboat's personal tale, told in her own voice, puts readers in touch with their own memories of childhood. Perhaps you can best tell *your* story in the first person.

6.1.1 Examples of Narrative Essays

It Takes a Whole Village to Raise a Child

I was looking for the parenting books in one of those new box stores that cram together under one giant roof a couple acres of CD's, magazines, computer programs, and children's books. (I was hoping I wouldn't discover that someone else had already created the next book I was planning to write, a book about teaching children to read and write.) Then I saw it: a row of the niftiest gear to share with kids—a water balloon tug-of-war toy, a new Nerf-type miniature football with fins to make it easier to guide through the air, and a Velcro-like mitt that would let even very young children catch a soft, fuzzy ball. First the memories hit me: How much fun it had been to play with new toys when my children were little. Then, the depression sandbagged me: How sad that some children rarely have such experiences. Over the next few hours, four memories surfaced, and I felt again so strongly that we really must take better care of all our children.

I remembered Michael and remembered that we need to ensure that all our children have the opportunity to be a part of our culture. Karen, Michael's mom—neglected and abused during her own childhood—attended a fitness, life skills, and parenting program. Karen had sat through the children's storytime as the preschool teacher read nursery rhymes. Later, she stopped the teacher and said, "How did that poem go—the one about the egg and stuff: 'All the king's horses and all . . .'? I ain't never heard it before, but it sure did make Michael laugh."

I remembered Roy Ito, principal of Lloyd George Public School, a school so under the shadow of the giant Dofasco steel plant in north-end Hamilton that there were mornings when you could trace your name in the dust on the desks, and I remembered that we even need just to feed some of our children better. Roy—uncharacteristically—looked sombre. He was feeling down, he said, because he was taking the boys to play basketball: you could look across the court and pick out his students, not by their uniforms, but just because most of them were a head shorter than their wealthier opponents. As a cocky young consultant, I'd belatedly noticed the same phenomenon when I asked a preschool teacher in a nearby daycare centre if this was her group of three-year-olds; she told me these children would soon go to kindergarten!

I remembered a college student introducing me to Heather, a woman who couldn't read as well as her daughter who was struggling in grade one, and I remembered that we need to take better care of our children's educational needs. I struggled to ask—to understand without embarrassing Heather—when she had begun to realize that for her, learning to read was hard. "I knew right in grade one that I wasn't getting it, that the other kids could read and I couldn't," she said. Failed grades, special education classes, early school leaving—Heather never got enough individual attention to overcome that slow start. Now she wanted—more than anything—to be able to help her daughter avoid that frustration and failure.

Some people who make it take a lot of credit for their success. They say, "I worked hard; I deserve the rewards of success." Many of them don't realize that in the race for success, not everyone gets a fair start. When some children live with parents who grew up in the culture of poverty, when too many children—and even one is too many—don't even have a healthy diet, and when some children don't get the help they need in school, they're being asked to begin the race from several metres behind the starting line. That leisurely Sunday afternoon cappuccino and browse—and those goofy toys I've always been fascinated by—reminded me that on Monday morning I'd better renew my commitment to join the efforts to take better care of all our children.

Talk about a Funny Fetish by André S. Bryan

On a trip to the grocery store the other day, I discovered my companion had an odd fetish. As we strolled along the rows of sweet-smelling produce, she demonstrated an uncontrollable urge to fondle fruits and vegetables.

As we walked, she rubbed her hand along the fuzzy outer skin of a kiwi fruit. As the soft mist from the store's sprinkler showered the broccoli, leaving tiny beads clinging to the buds, she said, "Isn't that fascinating?"

"Wet vegetables? Not really," I replied.

As we continued to stroll along the rows with their multi-coloured displays of fruits, each stand drew a comment from my friend. She picked up a McIntosh apple, rubbed it over her cashmere sweater until the fruit glistened brilliant red, and then she exclaimed, "Isn't that beautiful?"

As I tripped on the thick yellow garden hose and came to rest in a display bin of "Product of the USA" sweet corn, I attempted to cover my clumsiness with the comment, "Not as beautiful as you, dear."

She helped me back to my feet and urged me to finish an apple that she had already begun to eat. Then she massaged a bunch of grapes and a cantaloupe, simultaneously. As she popped a few of the grapes into her mouth and mine, she sighed, "Feel how they explode. Isn't that titillating?"

"No," I explained. "In this country, it's shoplifting." And I hurried out past the checkout girls in their red and white uniforms, vowing never to return to that Fortino's. At least not with my friend with the fetish.

A Place I Used to Go by Kari Longboat

Did you ever have a favourite place you went to when you were a child growing up? Maybe at the time you never realized the memories you were creating. I recall a place I used to visit, and it now reminds me of summer, hot dogs, and family.

I remember sweltering summer days where I came close to crying tears of boredom because it was too hot to even move. Then, my dad would come home to our hot house in Ohsweken and say, "Let's go to Port Dover and get a foot-long," meaning a hot dog. Mom was always glad to make the sweaty car ride just to get away from wilting from the heat of the stove. So we would all pack into the car and go to Port Dover, a real tourist town, boarded up all winter, but a charming, busy, lakeside town to visit during hot summer days.

It may seem strange that a hot dog is a treasured childhood memory, but I can't think of Port Dover without thinking of hot dogs. These hot dogs were supper—and a treat. I remember that what I liked best was picking from a smorgasbord of unique toppings to put on the foot-long. There was a fantastic choice: crispy, cool shreds of lettuce; transparent chopped onions; thick chunks of juicy tomatoes; skinny strands of cheddar cheese; colourful coleslaw; ravishing red pickled beets; and—of course—mustard and ketchup. I remember eyeing the dog with hungry, almost starving, eyes. Then came the first savoury bite. I recall how lucky I felt when most of my hot dog stayed intact, not sliding onto the ground or all over my shirt.

Other times when I recall Port Dover, I think of the timeless beach, and that reminds me of my family and our togetherness. We'd all go for a walk. We are a big family, so I don't remember going much of anywhere with everyone. But when I think of Port Dover, I think of squishing six kids—four of them monster teenage boys—into that puke-green grocery-getter to travel to our tiny getaway. And we'd walk by the noisy arcades, the tiny souvenir shops, and onto the short sandy beach with the long stone dock, and I'd be overwhelmed by a sense of joy that I was with my family.

Summer, hot dogs, and a place I used to go are all parts of a special dream of not so long ago.

▶ **ACTIVITY 6–1**

Analyzing Narrative Essays

Thinking about the Content

1. Quote the sentence that asserts the contention—the thesis—of "It Takes a Whole Village to Raise a Child."

2.* Most of the stories in "It Takes a Whole Village to Raise a Child" provide the support for the thesis. How many different stories are narrated in that essay? Briefly identify them.

3. Which story most effectively uses dialogue to move the story along?

4.* Why did each writer choose to write in the first person?

5. Which word in André Bryan's essay ought to be changed to eliminate sexism?

Thinking about the Organization

6. Which pieces of writing most closely conform to the organization of five-paragraph essays?

7.* Each of the writers organizes the support in a similar way. What is the method used to organize the details of the stories?

8. The introductory paragraph of "It Takes a Whole Village to Raise a Child" does not have a preview of the main points. Why doesn't it? Rewrite the thesis sentence so that it does preview the main points. Which version is better? Why?

6.1.2 Ideas for Your Narrative Essay

To write an essay that includes narration, think up a topic and choose a method for developing your idea (describing a process, explaining a cause, and so forth). Be sure to create a thesis.

You might, for example, decide to write a persuasive essay in favour of honesty being the best policy. This could be your thesis: Three recent events have reminded me that it's best to be honest. In the support paragraphs of the essay, you would tell the three stories to illustrate that point.

You might think of a topic after reading the title of these narrative essays other students have written.

- Stay in School
- The Best Helping Hand Is at the End of Your Arm
- Happiness Is Contagious
- Technology Is a Lifesaver

6.2 DESCRIBING

The success of some of our writing depends upon effective description. When a restaurant menu makes your mouth water in anticipation, you have been reading powerful descriptive writing. Effective advertisements of all kinds lead consumers to form irresistible images.

Evocative description, though, has more uses than just advertising. A persuasive essay recommending a way to reduce school violence will be more convincing if your writing makes readers *visualize* the school as it is now, and what it could become. An explanation of how to brew beer at home will be more useful to home brewers if it helps them form mental images of the process.

Consider these ideas as you get ready to write effective description:

★ **Give your reader details.** You always need detailed specific support for the propositions you make in your essays, but detail is especially necessary in descriptive writing. Contrast these two sentences:

Vague: There are many small animals in the woods around the lodge.

Detailed: You can't walk far into the woods before you see the chipmunks tunnelling into the leaves in front of your feet.

Write the generalities that come into your head when you're racing through your draft writing—but when you revise, change those general words into evocative, specific detail.

★ **Consider all pertinent senses when writing description.** Descriptive writing doesn't just help readers see the scene or person, it makes them aware of texture, sounds, odours, pressure, temperature, humidity. Descriptive writing evokes a multisensory, I-was-there experience. Don't overdo it, but as you revise your writing, consider adding detail that will evoke more than one sense.

★ **If it's a descriptive *essay*, create a thesis.** It's true that you use descriptive writing in many different kinds of documents, but to write an *essay* that is descriptive, you need to make a proposition; you need a thesis. For example, you might describe a bedroom by including this thesis statement: As soon as you opened the bedroom door, you could tell that Jarod loved heavy metal music.

6.2.1 Examples of Descriptive Essays

Vacation Paradise by Chris Barr

Northern Ontario boasts some of the most breathtaking scenery in our country, and nowhere is it more pronounced than in the area around Georgian Bay. There is no better way to appreciate the grandeur of this land than to spend some time at many of the local lodges that dot the edges of the bay. Because of its unspoiled beauty, abundant wildlife, and cozy accommodations, I would recommend Hidden Bay Resort as the lodge of choice.

As you drive down the sandy lane off the main road, there is little to indicate the great beauty beyond. A heady, perfumed scent comes from the red pines and from a lush carpet of delicate, multi-coloured wildflowers that rise from the needle-thatched forest floor. You emerge from the forest atop a grey-and-pink crest of smooth granite to see a small, impossibly blue bay fringed by narrow, mysterious, reedy channels, with a backdrop of birch and aspen trees and a hard-packed, white sandy beach.

There are animals and birds everywhere. Saucy, striped chipmunks come up to the campsites to beg for food. Bandit raccoons prowl at night. You sometimes see a black bear stop at the outskirts of the camp and peer in, curious. Across the bay, you see moose grazing the yellow and white water lilies. Loons trill their sad, chilling songs from dawn until dusk. Majestic ospreys soar above the water and then plummet into the bay, only to rise again with a large bass or pike. Yellow warblers the colour of sunflowers sing in the pines.

The accommodations are basic but cozy. When you walk through the cabin door, the sweet smell of cedar hits you before you hear the bang of the screen door. The windows are covered with colourful, hand-sewn, cotton curtains. The large kitchen has a fridge, stove, and sink, but what you're drawn to is the old, blackened wood stove beside a conical pile of firewood that will warm you through the night. At the end of the kitchen is a table for six. To the left of the table is a long, narrow sitting room with a worn but comfortable couch that is the perfect place to sit to lose yourself gazing at the bay outside. The beds in the single bedroom guarantee a good night's sleep: They have the sun-sweet smell and the comforting texture of flannelette sheets.

Everyone should take time off from routine life and enjoy a slower, less stressful way of living. For sheer beauty, fascinating nature, and old-fashioned, cozy accommodations, Lake Shebeshabong is the place to go.

Spices for Indian Cuisine by Beth Ashton

Ever wonder how they season those savoury, colourful meals at East Indian restaurants? The spices for East Indian cuisine can be divided into three general categories: spices for flavour, colour, and heat.

The main flavouring spices are cumin, coriander, cloves, pepper, cardamom, asafetida, cinnamon, mustard, and ginger. Some flavouring spices have very specific uses: Asafetida is used primarily as a flavouring for <u>papadams</u>, which are wafer-like appetizers. Many of these spices are widely used in almost any Indian dish: Cumin, coriander, cardamom, pepper, cloves, and cinnamon are present in almost every curry. Cardamom, cinnamon, and cloves are often used to add flavour to many desserts, including <u>beebeek</u>, a kind of coconut cake.

The second category of spices—those for colouring—are used to change the appearance of plain foods or to enhance the look of a curry. The two main colouring spices are saffron, which is a lovely red-gold colour, used, for example, to transform plain white rice into a sun-coloured dish, and turmeric, a bright Tonka-truck-yellow spice that enhances the appearance of dishes such as <u>murg kari</u>, an elegant chicken curry.

The last group of spices, those used for heat, is made up of different kinds of pepper, such as black, white, cayenne, and many kinds of fresh hot peppers. Cayenne pepper is used not only for its spiciness but also for its bright red colour.

Although the lines between the categories of spice are somewhat unclear—because spices are often valued for more than one of their properties—Indian cuisine brings together these three general spice categories in almost every dish to create a harmony of flavour, colour, and heat.

▶ **ACTIVITY 6–2**

Analyzing Descriptive Essays

Thinking about the Content

1.* Pick three places in "Vacation Paradise" where Chris Barr could have written more specific detail that would have helped readers form an even clearer picture of his favourite resort. Rewrite to enhance the description.

2. Which support paragraph in "Spices for Indian Cuisine" could benefit from more convincing detail that would help Beth Ashton make her point? What kind of information would you add?

3.* Why is the following rewrite of the first two sentences of Chris Barr's last point not nearly as good as his original writing?

   There's good accommodation at Hidden Bay Resort. You'll be very comfortable and you'll like the old, comforting articles.

4. What senses are aroused by Beth Ashton's essay "Spices for Indian Cuisine"?

Thinking about the Organization

5. Write a topic sentence for Chris Barr's second main point, that the animals are a prime attraction of Hidden Bay Resort.

6.* Create a decimal outline of Chris Barr's contention that a principal attraction of Hidden Bay Resort is abundant wildlife. (You may wish to look at the decimal outline of the pancakes essay, figure 1–7.)

7. Add a clincher to "Spices for Indian Cuisine."

6.2.2 Ideas for Your Descriptive Essay

Here are some ideas to consider as you prepare to write your own descriptive essay. As you read the list, you might note that if you add rich descriptive details, you can often improve essays that explain causes or describe processes.

You might write a descriptive essay about some phenomenon you've learned about in your content courses (e.g., how to write a powerful script for a telemarketing promotion, or the causes of metal fatigue when machinery operates at high temperatures).

Write an essay that reviews an art show, a film, a book, or a concert.

Look over this list of essay titles; it may help you think up a topic for your essay.
- A Day at the Beach
- My Friend
- Twisted Metal
- My Room
- Skydome
- Ryan's House

6.3 SOME CONCLUDING THOUGHTS

We've been telling stories and describing what we've experienced ever since our species invented language. Perhaps that's why we take so naturally to writing narrative and descriptive essays. In chapter 7, you'll have the chance to write essays to describe processes, to explain causes and effects, and to argue persuasively. While you develop your ability to learn to write expository and descriptive essays, you'll also develop the skills you need to write job applications, grant proposals, and the other kinds of documents you must be able to write to prosper in this information age.

Developing Your Ideas in Expository and Persuasive Essays

"The most original thing a writer can do is write like himself.
It is also his most difficult task."
—*Robertson Davies*

CHAPTER OBJECTIVE

After analyzing the sample essays in this chapter, you will be able to write brief, attractive, well-organized expository and persuasive essays in Standard English.

As you create the content of your essay—the *C* in the COSA formula for effective writing—you develop your ideas in different ways. Sometimes you may write to classify some aspect of the world; for example, you might categorize the boxers you've trained with, as James Marshall did in "Shamrock Club Boxers," an essay presented later in this chapter. You might explain the causes of a phenomenon, as Marilyn Zacharakes did in "Shift Working Your Way to Divorce." You might compare and contrast the way the police and courts treat youthful and adult offenders. You might describe a process, as in "How to Kill *The English Patient:* Adapt it to Film." You might try to persuade your readers to your way of thinking, as Craig Farrish and Rob Deslauriers did in "Outlaw Spanking."

You use all these methods to develop your ideas. Thinking about the ideas presented in this chapter will help you become more proficient at systematically explaining ideas that you propose. Each rhetorical mode (or method of developing ideas) is explained briefly, and then you are invited to read and analyze sample essays to learn to write similar material more powerfully.

7.1 EXPLAINING PROCESSES

Explaining how to carry out a procedure—say, how to use a word-processing program—is probably the toughest kind of writing you do.

To explain a process, you must consider the your audience's needs. You want neither to bore them by explaining the obvious, nor mystify—and frustrate—them by leaving out some information necessary to understanding the process. Imagine being the reader trying to understand the steps you describe. Does your text include all the information the reader needs to understand the process?

Jot notes—point form will do fine—as you visualize each step in the process. Organize the points of a process essay chronologically. Create an outline of the major steps in the process (your main points) and the more specific details of how to carry out that process (see figure 5–1). It's hard to do effective process writing without this kind of pre-writing.

How long does an effective process essay need to be? The answer can't be a number of words: your essay is long enough when your reader can understand the process you've described.

Analyzing the sample essays in this section will help you describe processes effectively. Read some of the published essays that have good process writing (see the list at the end of the table of contents). Remember to listen carefully to your teacher's instructions so that you write an essay that's the correct length and uses the assigned rhetorical mode (method of developing ideas). If you must choose your own topic for a process essay, you may want to brainstorm ideas and pick the one that can most easily be expressed in the length your teacher requests.

7.1.1 Examples of Process Essays

How to Appeal a Grade

If you're attending Olds College in Alberta, you can appeal a grade by following the directions in the "Student Rights and Responsibilities" section of the calendar. If you have a hard-to-resolve disagreement, you may need to go through three steps: discussion with the instructor who assigned the grade, an appeal to the ombud, and an appeal to the Academic Council.

The calendar says that if you feel an assigned grade is too low, you should first speak directly to the instructor. Before booking a meeting, you should assemble all relevant assignments. Look at other students' assignments and the grades they received. Jot an outline of the points you want to make. If you've prepared effectively, and if you listen to your instructor's point of view, you may come to an agreement about the grade.

You may appeal to the ombud if you are unable to come to an agreement about a final grade, but you must do so in writing within thirty calendar days of becoming aware of the prob lem. The ombud will facilitate a meeting between you and the instructor. If it is thought to be helpful, the ombud will also invite the appropriate academic dean. The ombud will help you and your teacher discuss the grade. If you and your instructor still disagree about the grade, the ombud will, within fifteen days, convene the Academic Council Appeals Committee.

The final decision in a grades appeal is made by the Appeals Committee. At Olds College, the committee comprises a student representative, a faculty representative, and a Board appointee. As the appellant, you may bring to the appeal one person for support or advocacy. The members of the committee will listen to both points of view. All three committee members must vote, and the decision must be reported within three days.

Years go by, and students in class after class agree with their instructors' grades. Still, it's reassuring to know that in case of disagreements, Olds College has created a clear appeals process from the instructor to the ombud to the Academic Appeals Committee.

How to Be Fired from Your Dishwashing Job by Heidi Lambert

People often dread washing dishes. I know I'd rather clean a whole house and leave the dishes. As far as I can remember, I have done dishes only about six times in my life. This is because of the way I used to do them. If you want your family to fire you from your job as a dishwasher, follow my plan: take your time, miss some food, and break some dishes.

One way to get canned as a family dishwasher is to wash so slowly that you drive your drier crazy. You can count on your drier to complain so bitterly—and loudly—that your mother will take over. Persist in being the world's slowest dishwasher, and eventually you will be replaced: Time seems so valuable to everyone.

All good dishwashers know you have to really scrub to remove all that stuck-on food, so be sure to leave food residues on the dishes you wash. Finding dirty dishes is pretty gross. Don't scrub, and your family will just decide you have no future as a dishwasher.

If working slowly and missing food on plates and cutlery haven't got you dismissed from dishwashing, you're going to have to resort to breaking dishes as you work. Now, of course, it is perfectly possible to drop a dinner plate when it's covered with slippery detergent, but you've got to do it with the skill of a Genie Award winner: you've got to convince your audience your mishap was a mistake. After a few instances of slippage, your family will outsource your dishwashing responsibilities.

Working slowly, sloppily, and clumsily will ensure your family terminates your dishwashing job. Just be careful they don't downsize you right out of the family.

How to Kill *The English Patient*: Adapt it to Film

About the time I was reading page 102 of *The English Patient*, my students began to wonder about my mental health. Within just a few minutes, tears welled up in my eyes as Hana, the nurse from Toronto, tried to help Kip defuse a bomb, and then—as their danger passed—an unsuccessfully suppressed chortle of relief and joy burst out of me. Other people were startled by the sighs, laughs, and sharp intakes of breath interrupting my silent reading as I journeyed through Michael Ondaatje's novel, like a first-time rider on a roller coaster—in the fog. Book reviewer Pico Iyer has identified part of the novel's allure: "One by one, he introduces his characters . . . leading us through their lives as through the darkened corridors of a huge and secret house. Loves flicker, footsteps echo, lines of poetry recur. All four feel their way through darkness, by hand and memory, and with all the phantom sensuousness that darkness brings. The effect is a little like Borges on a love-potion" (1). Screenwriter/director Anthony Minghella ruined *The English Patient* by radically simplifying the language, the plot, and the characterization.

Minghella simplified the language to transform a ravishingly rich book into a pedestrian movie. "Ondaatje alchemizes . . . with a poet's fluent radiance. Scene after scene shimmers with the jeweled brilliance of Arab poetry" (Iyer 1). Minghella, though, exults in the medium of film—"the most potent art form we have. It can show you the close-up of a woman's neck and give you a whole world, a desert landscape, in the next cut. That expanding and contracting eye, the iris, is so visceral" (qtd. in Johnson, "Erotic" 3). But it is the language of the novel that more effectively evokes our imaginations. Iyer writes that Kip, the East Indian Sikh sapper, "walks through cities where corpses are strung from trees and sleeps beside angels in deserted churches. . . . Woven through such flights are colorful threads of historical arcana: richly researched evocation of the 'desert Englishmen' of the '30s, lilting allusions to Herodotus and Kipling, catalogues of the winds that blow across the sands. The result is a realism that could not be more magical" (1–2).

The film adaptation is also disappointing because it simplifies the book's plot. In an article in *Maclean's*, Brian D. Johnson expressed it this way: "Minghella had to lose entire sections of the story" ("Erotic" 1). Film viewers never walked the English countryside as Kip learned the dangerous trade of bomb disposal with the unflappable Miss Morden and her boss, Lord Suffolk, the amateur *Lorna Doone* researcher, all the while adjusting to the nearly-as-dangerous minefields of class-ridden British society. Even the book's climax is removed for the film adaptation: viewers never understand how the atom bombs dropped on Hiroshima and Nagasaki drive Kip back to India into a life where—years later—his love of Hana still haunts him.

Character simplification, though, is probably the worst procedure Minghella uses to adapt *The English Patient* to film. Not only are whole characters completely absent—most significantly Kip's Empire-despising brother—the film makes Katharine Clifton, wife of Geoffrey Clifton—the airplane-flying, amateur desert explorer—a principal character, in place of Hana. And what a simplification of the character of Katharine! In the film, she explains away the torturous, adulterous relationship by saying, "I always loved you," but the book better captures the difficulty of understanding human behaviour by offering no such easy explanation for their affair. Kip is also subjected to character simplification; in the film he is a clichéd caricature devoid of convincing background detail. And the meagre glimpse viewers are offered into the past of David Caravaggio—the thief who has lost his thumbs—reduces that character's depth and believability. Entirely gone is Ondaatje's invisible narrator, who knows each character's thoughts. As Brian Johnson notes, "That dry, discerning narrative tone . . . found at the heart of Canadian fiction [is] perhaps what makes our literature so compelling . . . and our films so difficult" ("The Canadian" 45). Without it, none of the characters in the film are as interesting.

Saul Zaentz spent $60,000,000 producing a film that replaces a complex, slowly aged cheddar with plastic, neon-orange processed cheese. Even without lingering over the evocative text—and you will—it takes about seven hours to read *The English Patient*. To adapt it to film—even one 160 minutes long—requires simplifying the language, the plot, and the characters. Every time I compare the satisfaction of reading a great novel with the pleasure of watching a film adaptation, I resolve to spend more time reading.

Works Cited

Iyer, Pico. "Magic Carpet Ride." Rev. of *The English Patient*, by Michael Ondaatje. *Time* 2 Nov. 1992: 71+. CMAS FullTEXT Elite. CD-ROM. Ebsco. Feb. 1997.

Johnson, Brian D. "The Canadian Patient." *Maclean's* 24 Mar. 1997: 42–46.

—. "Erotic Geography." *Maclean's* 18 Nov. 1996: 64+. *CMAS FullTEXT Elite.* CD-ROM. Ebsco. Feb. 1997.

Ondaatje, Michael. *The English Patient*. 1992. New York: Vintage–Random House, 1993.

▶ **ACTIVITY 7–1**

Analyzing Process Essays

Thinking about the Content

1.* Read this version of paragraph two of "How to Be Fired from Your Dishwashing Job."

One way to get canned as a family dishwasher is to wash so slowly that you drive your drier crazy. You can count on your drier to complain so bitterly—and loudly—that your mother will take over. My sister always runs to Mom, just to bug me. Persist in being the world's slowest dishwasher, and eventually you will be replaced: Time seems so valuable to everyone.

Which is better, the original or the revision? Why?

2. Quote the sentence that asserts the thesis of "How to Appeal a Grade."

3.* What is the second main point that Lambert asserts in "How to Be Fired from Your Dishwashing Job"?

4.* Quote the thesis sentence of "How to Kill *The English Patient:* Adapt it to Film."

Thinking about the Organization

5.   Here's another version of the second supporting paragraph of Lambert's essay "How to Be Fired from Your Dishwashing Job":

     Finding dirty dishes is pretty gross. All good dishwashers know you have to really scrub to remove all that stuck-on food, so be sure to leave food residues . . . .

     Which version is better? Why?

6.* Study figure 15–5, the balloon version of "Pancakes for Sunday Brunch." Then create a balloon version of "How to Appeal a Grade."

7.   What is the clincher for "How to Be Fired from Your Dishwashing Job"? Why isn't the clincher's tone more sombre?

7.1.2 Ideas for Your Process Essay

Just reading a list of suggested topics for papers sometimes helps you think of a topic you can get enthusiastic about, and enthusiasm helps you write better.

- how to become an entrepreneur
- how to pursue a hobby (write about just one hobby)
- a procedure from one of your content-area courses
- how to alleviate a social problem (pollution, poverty, unemployment, racism)
- a procedure from a familiar workplace

Here are some titles of process essays other students have written. Perhaps a title will give you an idea for your own process essay.

- How I Watch Television
- How to Fight the Cable Company
- How to Survive the Move to College
- Preparing for an Interview
- Creating a Healthy Marriage
- How to Know You Have a True Friend

7.2 CLASSIFYING

Quickly now, what are the two most common types of post-secondary institutions in Canada? You probably answered, "Colleges and universities." You know how to classify these institutions.

You know a lot about how phenomena are divided or classified in the world. And often, when you experience difficulty categorizing something, you realize that you need to learn more; for example, is cobalt a magnetic substance? Does copper belong in the category of magnetic substances?

Experts know how to classify in their area of expertise. A botanist can tell you the meaningful categories or classifications of plants. An ambulance attendant can categorize types of accident injuries. A security specialist can classify offences as indictable and non-indictable. A graduate of a culinary skills program can describe the types of disinfectants used to clean a kitchen. In your field of study, part of what will make you an expert is an increased ability to categorize your content area.

You will often need to write about how something is classified; for example, if you are asked to recommend a new scanner for an office computer, you will have to find out about types of scanners before you can make a recommendation.

Read and analyze the sample essays to sharpen your ability to write about how the world is classified.

7.2.1 Examples of Classification Essays

College Communication

In a college serving more than 5,000 full-time and 25,000 part-time students in a region of more than a quarter of a million people, an enormous amount of communication targets three groups of people: students, staff, and community.

Niagara College reaches out to students in many ways, sometimes before they've chosen to attend the school. The Marketing and Communications department sends promotional material to high school guidance counsellors. College representatives speak at secondary schools. The calendar, called the Career Guide, is sent out to anyone who requests it. The College maintains Web pages. College programs are advertised in local papers, including the Tribune, the Standard, and the Review. Students are given more specific information once they enrol. They are also given a Student Handbook of important information (e.g., dates of sports activities and college policies). Once they've begun their studies, students receive course information sheets, course handouts, midterm progress reports, final grades, and transcripts. The Niagara News, although primarily a training vehicle for journalism students, also provides a way for employees of the college to communicate with students. The attempts to communicate continue after graduation, because the College disseminates information about finding jobs and publishes materials aimed at alumni.

The administration also directs a lot of communication at the staff at the College. In Touch, a newsletter published by Marketing and Communications, tells of staff changes, new programs, guest speakers, successes and challenges facing the school. When staff log on to the mainframe computer, they may see announcements. Throughout the year, many memos communicate new parking regulations, news about the budget, or committees that are looking for members. Minutes of meetings are sent by internal mail. The telephone voice-mail system spurs the exchange of a lot of information. CRNC is mostly a practical lab for the Broadcasting: Radio, Television and Film program, but it is also a source of news at the College. Departmental, divisional, and college-wide meetings facilitate communication. Throughout each academic year, there is a tremendous amount of information directed at staff.

The College also directs a lot of information at the general public. Media advisories and news releases announce major news—like the naming of the Maid of the Mist Centre—to radio stations and newspapers. Job openings and guest speakers are advertised in newspapers. N-Compass, an occasional newspaper about College events and news, is distributed through newspapers and some direct mail. If you call the College and end up on hold, you will hear announcements of College events. The president and many other members of the College share information at the service clubs, political organizations, and public and private functions they attend. Much communication is directed at community members who serve on the Board of Governors or the advisory commit-tees, in which people working in the field help ensure that programs teach what is necessary for success. The College takes a multifaceted approach to communicating with the community.

From e-mail to snail mail, from the telephone lines to the radio waves, the College initiates a great deal of communication with its students, staff, and community.

Shamrock Club Boxers by James Marshall

Look around the Shamrock Club, and you'll notice that the boxers in training look pretty much alike: sweaty and focused. Underneath the similarities, though, there are three types of fight-ers: competitors, participants, and boneheads.

Canadian greats, such as Billy Irwin, Mike Strange, and Don Gignac, are dedicated competitors. They come to the gym regularly, keep their mouths shut, and listen to the coaches. They work hard and have a strong desire to win their bouts. These top competitors live totally healthy lifestyles.

Some of the fighters at the Shamrock Club participate more casually. These boxers don't have the same dedication as the first type. Boxing is only a secondary activity in their lives. They do the work at a slower pace and don't get the same attention from the coaches. Casual partic-ipants don't usually choose as healthy a lifestyle.

The third type of fighters are boneheads. They don't train rigorously and don't listen to the coaches' advice. They often quit working when the coaches are not watching. They also look for easy spars. They build themselves up to seem more skilled than they are and then brag about nothing. Every gym has its boneheads.

When you're new to a gym, you won't be able to tell which fighters belong to which category. But it won't be long before you know the competitors, the participants, and the boneheads.

Why Do They Tell Us Not to Spank Our Children?

Perhaps it's understandable that parents are confused about whether or not to spank chil-dren to make them behave. The Vancouver Province gave front-section coverage to this story about spanking: Al Riopel, a thirty-year-old Esquimalt sailor, "was fined $300 and put on probation for six months" (Bermingham 1) for strapping his nine-year-old daughter. He had used his belt to hit her twice on the bottom.

Eight months earlier, however, a newspaper story told us that another spanker—American tourist David Peterson—had been acquitted in a London, Ontario, courtroom. Angry at his five-year-old daughter for pushing his two-year-old son out of the car and closing the door on his fingers—he was not hurt—Peterson had "laid her on the trunk of the car, pulled down her pants and . . . spanked her" (Chidley 1). Two spankings, two court cases—opposite trial outcomes.

Although spanking remains popular with the public—a Toronto Star poll showed "70 percent of Canadian parents believe it is sometimes necessary to use physical discipline" (Bleich 1)—Peterson's lawyer, Michael Menear,

> canvassed more than twenty experts, hoping to find one who would climb onto the witness stand and say that what David Peterson had done was not harmful to his daughter. None of them would, because professionals who study child abuse and corporal punishment are unanimously anti-spanking. 'There just isn't a study to be found that shows that spanking is a method of choice,' concludes one researcher after a literature review of the field. (Hercz 2)

If parents read newspaper and popular magazine accounts of adults charged with assault for spanking their children, what would they learn about why child-guidance experts advise parents not to spank? Parents would read that spanking is ineffective and bad for children—and parents.

Writing in Saturday Night, Robert Hercz (2) comments: "Some studies conclude that corporal punishment, in the long run, is no more effective than other means of discipline."

In an article originally published in the St. John's Telegram, Jean Edwards Stacey (1) captures a point of view common among child-mental-health experts: "Spanking your child might not land you in jail but the practice should be strongly discouraged, says psychologist Christine Clancy . . . . When it comes to spanking the debate shouldn't be about whether or not it's legal—the issue is whether . . . it does any good . . . . Spanking doesn't teach children how to change their behavior." If it did, surveys like the one conducted by Family Relations would not reveal that the average preschooler receives 150 spankings a year ("Discipline" 1).

Parents read about alternatives to spanking—articles mentioned distraction; child-proofing; using rewards, logical consequences, and time-outs; and lots of talking and explanations—because among spankers, "85 per cent believe that it is ineffective" (Stainsby 2).

In newspapers and magazines, parents also read that child experts say spanking is not only ineffective, it's bad for children. "The more spankings a child is subjected to, the more likely he or she is to be physically aggressive with siblings and in school, and as an adult with spouses and children, according to psychologist Dr. Terry Luce," notes Marnie Larsen-Ko (1), director of the Association Against Physical Punishment of Children. Larsen-Ko also notes that spanked children do more poorly in school.

Dr. Emmett Francoeur, a pediatrician and member of the Canadian Pediatric Society, says "many adults suffer low self-esteem because they were spanked as children" (qtd. in Bueckert 1). They are also more likely to become thieves (Stainsby 2).

Spanking can even kill kids: "An average of 44 Canadian children are killed by family members each year, 35 of them by parents" (Stacey 2). "There are studies from all over the world that show that the majority of child-abuse incidents began as corporal punishment, says Joan Durrant, whose area of expertise at the University of Manitoba is corporal punishment" (qtd. in Hercz 3). As psychologist Luce notes, "the No. 1 [sic] cause of accidental death of infants is parents who beat them under the guise of discipline" (qtd. in Larsen-Ko 1).

Many parents will find themselves nodding in agreement with the finding of a new survey by Joan Durrant: "The single most likely outcome of a spanking . . . is parental guilt" (qtd. in Hercz 4). Immediately after Don Wierenga of Lacombe strapped his eleven-year-old daughter for defying his order to be ready to go to church, he was so filled with remorse that he "immediately notified Social Services, signed up voluntarily for anger-management counselling and pleaded guilty to the subsequent assault charge" (Woodard 1).

Sherri Lutz, in Family Violence: A Handbook for First Nations Workers, also recognizes this link between hurting children and feeling guilt: "Abusers and survivors may also experience fear and shame about family violence" (13).

As Hercz notes, "The community at large may be travelling that same road. The percentage of parents, especially young parents, who spank is dropping, and they are feeling notably ambivalent about it" (4).

Parents have an excellent opportunity to consider the comments of child-care experts about spanking because the popular press routinely presents such expert opinion in stories about spanking. Most of the authorities advise parents not to spank because it doesn't make children behave better, it has bad effects on children—making it likelier that they'll get in trouble for aggression and theft, for example—and it makes parents feel guilty. As more citizens become familiar with the issue, perhaps spanking will fall into even greater disfavour. As Hertz notes, "Most parents spank because they were spanked, not because they've considered the issue. If they did, they might begin to talk themselves out of the practice" (4). Hercz quotes Michael Menear—the lawyer for American tourist David Peterson—as saying, "I went through my own personal journey as I was representing Mr. Peterson." Although Menear has not totally eschewed spanking, he added, "I see it as a good thing to find other ways of disciplining kids."

Works Cited

Bermingham, John. "Father Hit for Spanking: Court Fines Him $300 for Assault: Testing the Limits of a Parent's Right to Punish." Province [Vancouver] 29 Jan. 1996: A6. Canadian NewsDisc. CD-ROM. CEDROM-SNi. 1995–1996.

Bleich, Doreen M. "Spanking Kids." Briarpatch Apr. 1996: 10. Canadian Periodical Index Quarterly (CPI.Q). CD-ROM. Gale. Feb. 1997.

Bueckert, Dennis. "Don't Spank Your Kids, Pediatricians Say; Spanking Ideas." Edmonton Journal 8 Oct. 1996, Final ed.: A1/Front. Canadian NewsDisc. CD-ROM. CEDROM-SNi. 1995–1996.

Chidley, Joe. "Spanking on Trial: Should Parents Ever Strike Their Children." Maclean's 8 May 1995: 24. Canadian Periodical Index Quarterly (CPI.Q). CD-ROM. Gale. Feb. 1997.

"Discipline." Psychology Today May/June 1996: 18. CMAS FullTEXT Elite. CD-ROM. Ebsco. 1984–Oct. 1996.

Hercz, Robert. "Bum Rap." Saturday Night Nov. 1995: 20+. CMAS FullTEXT Elite. CD-ROM. Ebsco. 1984–Oct. 1996.

Larsen-Ko, Marnie. "No Excuse for Hitting Children: Every Act of Violence Against a Child Leaves a Permanent Emotional Scar." Calgary Herald 10 June 1996: A6. Canadian NewsDisc. CD-ROM. CEDROM-SNi. 1995–1996.

Lutz, Sherri. Family Violence: A Handbook for First Nations Workers. Brentwood Bay, BC: First Nations Education Association, 1994.

Stacey, Jean Edwards. "Words Better Than Blows—Psychologist; Spare the Rod." Edmonton Journal 17 Mar. 1996: G2. Canadian NewsDisc. CD-ROM. CEDROM-SNi. 1995–1996.

Stainsby, Mia. "Time to Stop the Spanking: Corporal Punishment of Children Can Lead to Dysfunction in Their Adult Lives As Well As Inducing Feelings of Shame and Inadequacy in the Caregivers Who Carry Out the Process: Banning Spanking in Sweden Cut Child Abuse." Vancouver Sun 22 July 1996, Final ed.: B6. Canadian NewsDisc. CD-ROM. CEDROM-SNi. 1995–1996.

Woodard, Joseph K. "Anything But Spanking: The Never-Hit Campaign Gears Up With Federal Support." Alberta Report 15 July 1996: 34–35. Canadian Periodical Index Quarterly (CPI.Q). CD-ROM. Gale. Feb. 1997.

▶ **ACTIVITY 7–2**

Analyzing Classification Essays

Thinking about the Content

1.* What is the thesis of "Why Do They Tell Us Not to Spank Our Children?"

2. What is the thesis of "Shamrock Club Boxers"?

3.* Quote the topic sentence for the third main point that James Marshall used to support his contention that there are three categories of fighters at the Shamrock Club.

4. Is an example of communication inadequately described in the second paragraph of "College Communication"? Does the author assume too much knowl-

edge on the part of the reader? In "Shamrock Club Boxers," phrases such as "work hard" and "live totally healthy lifestyles" do not evoke concrete images. Create some specific details to support James Marshall's claims.

5.* In your own words, write the thesis and main points for "College Communication."

6. Study figure 5–1 and write an outline of paragraph two of "Shamrock Club Boxers."

7. Given that the writer asserts that the essay reveals what parents would learn about the inadequacies of spanking if their only sources of information were stories in newspapers and popular magazines, indicate a source of information that does not belong in this essay.

Thinking about the Organization

8. Which of the essays lacks a clincher? Write one.

9.* Which support paragraph in "Shamrock Club Boxers" has the weakest concluding sentence? Write a better one.

10. What is the clincher for "Why Do They Tell Us Not to Spank Our Children?"

7.2.2 Ideas for Your Classification Essay

Here are some ideas to consider as you create a topic for a classification essay:
- stereotypes
- characteristics of a job (e.g., sales professional)
- classifications that are a part of the jargon of the vocation you are studying

Here are some titles of classification essays other students have written. Perhaps a title will give you an idea for your essay.

- Canada's Most Popular Sports
- Fishing Techniques
- True Friends
- My Moods
- Communication with the Deaf
- The Joy of Camping
- Discipline Techniques for Raising Responsible Children

Remember, too, to look at some of the published essays in which authors classified information. The list is on pages vii–viii.

7.3 EXPLAINING CAUSES AND EFFECTS

From the time you were a tiny baby, you were always trying to figure out the causes of what you experienced. You heard a novel sound, for example, and you crawled over to find out what made it. As you grew up, you tortured your parents with questions: "Why is the sky blue?" "What makes the thunder sound?" It doesn't end in childhood. If your bicycle starts to make an unusual sound, you try to figure out the cause. Scientists look for the causes of human illness.

We are all amateur scientists trying to predict the effects of certain changes in our lives. "If I change college programs, what will happen to me?" is just another way of asking, "What will the effects be if I switch programs." If I smoke cigarettes, will I harm my health? What will happen if Quebec becomes an independent country? What will happen if we reinstate the death penalty?

A great deal of accumulated human knowledge is the understanding of causes and effects. When you know that salmonella from raw poultry can cause food poisoning, you can avoid it by cooking chicken and eggs thoroughly and using disinfectants on kitchen surfaces. We can act differently because we know that when women drink alcohol during pregnancy, their babies may suffer from fetal alcohol syndrome.

On the job, you may explain the causes of some phenomenon or its effects. You might, for example, write a memo about the effects of purchasing a new photocopier. You might describe the reasons for (the causes of) the overuse of convenience copies when less expensive copies can be run by the print centre in your business.

If you decide to write an effects essay, you will find it necessary—in planning your contention—to carefully create the wording of your thesis. Here's a wording that clearly shows you are writing about effects: Because welfare rates have been reduced, more people are having their utilities cut off, visiting food banks, and being evicted.

Here's another thesis statement that clearly shows the writer is discussing effects: Reducing the number of children in each primary school classroom will improve students' scores on standardized achievement tests, reduce the incidence of failed grades, and reduce the need for special education. The wording makes it clear that the writer is discussing the effects of educating children in smaller groups.

An essay entitled "Why Teens Drop Out of School" clearly shows that the writer is explaining causes.

Before you write an essay exploring causes or effects, read the sample essays in this section. Marilyn Zacharakes suggests that the strain of living with a shift worker can break up a marriage. Helena Dykstra draws upon her experiences working as an aide in an elementary school. Each of the example essays deals exclusively with causes or effects. Your essay will be clearer if you make a choice to write about either—but not both—causes or effects.

7.3.1 Examples of Essays Explaining Causes or Effects

Plagiarism's Harvest

The <u>Canadian Oxford Dictionary</u>—the best Canadian dictionary I've ever seen—defines the action of plagiarizing as to "take and use (the thoughts, writings, inventions . . . of another person) as one's own" ("Plagiarize"). At colleges, students who commit plagiarism sometimes do it accidentally; when students use the ideas and language they find in their review of the research on their topic, they may not know the conventions for citing the authors of the information, to give them credit for writing that information. Sometimes students deliberately write their own names on papers written by someone else or excerpt sections of published writers and fail to document who really wrote those words. Plagiarism has terrible effects for both the student plagiarists and the community.

Capilano College in North Vancouver imposes strong penalties for plagiarism, as do all educational institutions. "Students are responsible for ensuring that they understand and follow the principles and practices of proper documentation and scholarship" (<u>Capilano College Calendar</u> 32). Students caught pretending to have written a paper that was authored by someone else receive a zero for that essay. The College may consult with the instructor involved and penalize the students more; the College may even expel plagiarists. One act of cheating can have devastating effects on a student's reputation and finances.

Plagiarism also hurts the community. If people pass off other people's writing as their own, the winners of essay and poetry contests are suspect. These contests help to encourage beginning writers to undertake the hard work of learning to write well. If plagiarism became commonplace, it would undermine the ability of songwriters, novelists, and other writers to earn money. Such loss of income potential might mean a great novel is never written, to the loss of all of us. If scholars lie about what they write, the public might doubt they can be trusted in other ways. The public might not believe the medical research published in journals. The consequences of plagiarism are so dreadful that it must be strongly discouraged.

Plagiarism harms both students and their communities. Imitation may be the sincerest form of flattery, but when you want to borrow other people's ideas, give them credit by naming the authors and indicating where their work was published.

Shift Working Your Way to Divorce by Marilyn Zacharakes

Divorces are quite common among shift workers. People who continually work shifts are more and more often finding that they are losing their marriage partners because they don't like to sleep alone, to attend social functions alone, or to eat dinner alone.

When you get married, you do so thinking you will have someone to sleep with. Then your partner comes home and says, "I have a job, but it's shift work. It won't be for long." So you try to hang in there, but in the end, the shift work wins. You get tired of sleeping alone, and you start to wander away.

When you live with a shift worker and a special occasion like a wedding comes up, it's really hard to go by yourself. You're always hoping that the event will fall on his day off, but it never does. You go to these weddings, birthday parties, and christenings, and you go alone. Sooner or later you get tired of sitting alone and telling people that you are married, and you begin to wander away.

When you live with a shift worker, you are always eating alone. Sometimes you grow so tired of feeling lonely that you decide to go out for dinner. When you start going out for dinner, you end up meeting someone, and he buys you dinner, and you realize that the shift work won.

Shift work is not meant for married people. People need people. You can't go through life sleeping, socializing, and eating without your partner. It never fails: sooner or later you get so tired of being alone that you end up going astray, and your marriage ends in divorce.

Education for Exceptional Learners by Helena Dykstra

"In 1982, the Canadian Charter of Rights and Freedoms formally banned discrimination on the basis of disability" (Jones 122). Despite the passage of the Charter, parents have sometimes been forced to take school boards to court to fight to have their exceptional learners—children "who deviate from the norm in terms of physical, mental, behavioral, emotional, developmental, or learning characteristics" (Lerner, Mardell-Czudnowski, and Goldenberg 3)—placed in regular classrooms. For example, the Brant County Board of Education decided that eleven-year-old Emily Eaton, who has cerebral palsy, would benefit more from being placed in a segregated class than in a regular-education class. In February 1995, the Ontario Court of Appeal ruled that she had the "right to attend school with able children, despite the school board's insistence that she be segregated" (Jones 122). Still, the Brant board decided to appeal the ruling to Canada's Supreme Court. Such opposition is difficult to understand because the Charter says people with disabilities should not be discriminated against, and authoritative educational opinion clearly suggests that exceptional students progress best when they are identified early, begin school early, and are integrated in regular classes.

The years from birth to six are crucial to the development of children, both those with special needs and those without. Identification of those at risk is the first step in providing appropriate service. "When handicapped and at-risk children are identified early, their chances for academic success increase and the long-range effects of their handicap decrease" (Lerner, Mardell-Czudnowski, and Goldenberg 15). Whatever the risk factor for the child, early identification can lead to implementation of appropriate programs for growth and development, while the child can benefit the most.

Whether this early education is home-based, centre-based, or a combination (Beirne-Smith, Patton and Ittenbach), these early experiences affect growth and development. The stimulation provided by early education programs improves IQ's and prevents children from falling too far behind their peers. The benefits of early stimulation are summarized by Lerner et al.: "There is a growing conviction that all children benefit from a generalized early education program. A basic assumption of early childhood education is that a stimulating environment and appropriate instruction can greatly influence a child's ability and improve the likelihood of school success" (9).

Mainstreaming—placing all children in regular classes—provides several benefits for exceptional learners as well as the other children in the class. Chisholm offers this favourable review of mainstreaming exceptional students:

> When integration works well, there is almost no arguing with its benefits. 'There is growing evidence that integrated children learn better academically in a mixed class,' says Gary Bunch, a professor of education and psychology at Toronto's York University. 'They also have better self-esteem and a wider circle of friends; most of them have never had anyone call them before.' As adults, Bunch believes that such individuals will have a better chance of thriving, with less likelihood of depending upon institutional care. (53)

On October 9, 1996, the Supreme Court struck down the decision of the Ontario Court of Appeal (Barnes A2). The court indicated that "it is not discrimination to place a handicapped child in a special education class against the parents' wishes" (Bueckert A5). The ruling indicates the need for provincial governments to ensure the optimal progress of exceptional children by mandating early identification, early education, and mainstreaming. "For Emily, the battle has, in a sense, already been won. She attends grade six at a nearby Catholic school that has provided her with an educational assistant in a regular classroom. She's happy, she's made new friends and doesn't want to switch schools again" (Bindman A12).

Works Cited

Barnes, Alan. "Court Okays Special Classes." *Toronto Star* 10 Oct. 1996: A2.

Beirne-Smith, Mary, James R. Patton, and Richard Ittenbach. *Mental Retardation.* 4th ed. New York: Merrill, 1994.

Bindman, Stephen. "Disabled Girl Takes Battle to Top Court." *Toronto Star* 9 Oct. 1996: A12.

Bueckert, Dennis. "Not Discrimination to Put Child in Special Needs Class, Court Says." *Toronto Star* 7 Feb. 1997: A5.

Chisholm, Patricia. "Schooling the Disabled." *Maclean's* 27 Mar. 1995: 52–54.

Jones, Deborah. "Swimming In the Mainstream: Disabled Kids in Regular Schools." *Chatelaine* Oct. 1995: 59+.

Lerner, Janet, Carol Mardell-Czudnowski, and Dorothea Goldenberg. *Special Education for the Early Childhood Years.* 2nd ed. Englewood Cliffs, NJ: Prentice-Hall, 1987.

▶ **A C T I V I T Y   7–3**

Analyzing Essays Explaining Causes or Effects

Thinking about the Content

1.* Quote the sentence in "Plagiarism's Harvest" that states the essay's thesis and the preview of the main points the writer develops to support his contention.

2. Paraphrase the thesis and main points of "Shift Working Your Way to Divorce."

3.* How many main points are made in "Plagiarism's Harvest"? Paraphrase them. Is this a five-paragraph essay?

4. Quote Helena Dykstra's thesis.

5. Which sentence in "Plagiarism's Harvest" spoils the unity of the first paragraph?

Thinking about the Organization

6.* Quote the clincher for "Plagiarism's Harvest."

7.* In "Shift Working Your Way to Divorce," which method of organizing the support does Zacharakes use: chronological, emphatic, logical, or random?

8. What type of lead-in is used in "Plagiarism's Harvest"?

7.3.2 Ideas for Essays about Causes or Effects

Here are some ideas for an essay about causes or effects.
- the causes of social problems (runaways, shoplifting, child abuse, spouse abuse, drug abuse)
- the effects of raising highway speed limits, age for drinking, tuition fees, minimum wage
- causes of some phenomenon you're studying in one of your program courses

If you're trying to think of a topic for your own essay, look over these titles.

- How TV Affects Our Children
- Babies Having Babies
- Drinking and Driving
- What Wrecks My Mood
- The Joys of Commuting
- Why I Can't Stop Smoking

7.4 COMPARING AND CONTRASTING

We so readily develop ideas by comparing similarities or contrasting differences that we do it constantly. Your friend introduces a new girlfriend, and you're struck by the similarities to her previous girlfriend. You go to see a movie because it stars a favourite actor, and you can hardly believe how different he seems in this film. In fact, if you are discussing the film, one way to make your comments more interesting is to compare the new film to other films.

The process of comparison helps you understand what is important. You compare and contrast items—say, televisions—you are considering purchasing. The remote controls differ. Which would you enjoy using? The warranties differ. How important is that to you? You make these comparisons, too, about far more important concerns, such as who you will vote to represent you at city hall, the legislature, or parliament.

Imagine that you want to contrast two teachers you know. You could group together all the information about one teacher. Then you could group together the contrasting information about the other teacher. Your thesis might be "Professors Burhanuddin Rabbani and Abdullah Hakim have very different teaching styles." This kind of organization is called a block comparison. You'll have an opportunity to organize a block comparison later.

You could choose to compare those teachers in a different way. You could, for example, identify characteristics that distinguish good teachers. Perhaps you decide politeness is important, as is an ability to explain things. Fairness in marking assignments is also important to you. You identify as unimportant how well they dress or the political party they support. Now that you've determined the significant characteristics, you're ready to contrast those two teachers. You might create a thesis such as "When you consider politeness, clarity, and fairness, it's easy to see who is the better teacher." Then you contrast each teacher on the basis of these characteristics. You are writing a point-by-point comparison.

Read and discuss the questions for the following essays. (Special thanks to Ralph Malcolm, a court officer in Ontario, for technical information about youth and adult offenders.)

7.4.1 Examples of Essays that Compare and Contrast

Adult and Youth Offenders

A common comment about crime is that youth who commit crimes get off with a slap on the wrist. How accurate is this perception that youthful criminals are coddled? How different are the experiences of arrest, investigation, and court for a person fifteen years old and one thirty-five?

Thanks to a 911 call from a concerned citizen, two police officers were waiting at the curb to arrest Jake and Jake, Jr. as they carried out the television they had stolen during their break-in of the Chans' home. Officer Young said to Junior, "You're under arrest." Jake got the same message from Officer Ma Ture, and both suspects were read their rights. Officers Young and Ma Ture had to read from cards to caution the thieves because the caution was about twenty lines long and even included an 800 number to call for legal aid. So far, the two suspects had been treated almost identically.

Their experiences of detention began very similarly, too. Both were handcuffed. Jake and Junior were each searched for evidence and to ensure the safety of the officers. They were both taken to the police station for an investigation interview. They were both allowed to seek legal counsel. Since the evidence was rather incriminating—the Chans had wisely engraved Mrs. Chan's social insurance number onto a metal piece on the back of their television set—Junior was charged under authority of the Young Offender's Act of the Criminal Code and Jake under the regular Criminal Code. It was night and the police were unable to summon a Justice of the Peace to the station, so the suspects were both held overnight pending a bail hearing the next day. Because he was a youth, Junior was placed in a segregated cell. If it hadn't been so late, Junior would have been held at the David S. Horne Home, a youth holding facility. Jake was kept overnight, too, in a cell area holding other adults. Since neither Jake nor Junior had a criminal record, the JP released them both the next morning on an undertaking to show up for a court date. Both found the whole experience of investigation quite unpleasant—and they were glad Junior hadn't been exposed to hardened criminals—but when they compared notes, they were struck by how similarly they had been treated.

The next phase for both miscreants was to go to court. Jake's case was tried in the Criminal Division of the Ontario Court of Justice. Junior's case went to the Family Division. A Community and Social Services probation officer made a predisposition report on Junior. A probation officer for the Solicitor-General prepared a pre-sentence report for Jake. If Junior had been sentenced to a juvenile correctional facility, he would have had to serve his entire sentence. If Jake had been sentenced to a correctional centre, he would have been eligible for early release before he served all his time. Because the pre-sentence reports were favourable, they were placed on probation and sentenced to six months of community service because they were first offenders. Jake had to keep the sidewalks of seniors clear of ice, and Junior had to help at the food bank. Jake and Junior commiserated later over a bottle of Lysol that things could have been worse.

From arrest to investigation to court, Jake and Junior were treated similarly. While the public may feel that judges should sentence lawbreakers to harsher penalties, when it comes to the indictable offence of break and enter, it seems that youth offenders are not treated much differently than adults.

Sisters by Chris Barr

I often wonder how siblings can be so different when they had the same parents and grew up in the same household. My mother and my aunt are a case in point. Their lifestyles, personalities, and physical characteristics are as different as night and day.

My mother and my aunt have contrasting lifestyles. My mother lives a modest but full life. During my childhood, she was a devoted homemaker. When I was a teenager, she went to work with my father in the family business. She lives in an older, three-bedroom bungalow in a quiet village and drives a 1987 Firefly. Now that she is retired, my mother has more time to enjoy her family and friends, and she makes yearly trips to England and the Caribbean. My aunt, on the other hand, lives a jet-set life. She was a fashion model and married a wealthy man from a prominent British-Jamaican family. While my cousin was growing up, a nanny looked after her. My aunt divides her time between grand homes in London and Port Antonio, Jamaica. She drives a Mercedes. She's had no need to work, and she travels extensively.

These sisters have very different personalities. My mother is stable, calm, giving, and loving to both family and friends. She is a good listener, easy to talk to. However, her sister can be very moody, stubborn, bossy, self-absorbed, and aloof. They really are very different in personality.

Physically these sisters are polar opposites. My mother is five feet, seven inches. Her wavy, jet-black hair frames a round face. She has soulful dark brown eyes, a button nose, and full lips. She has an average frame. She is neither too heavy nor too thin. My aunt stands nearly five feet, ten inches tall. She has straight, ash-blond hair. Her face is strikingly angular. She has a perfectly proportioned nose and thin lips. Her eyes are beautiful, huge and hazelnut coloured with flecks of emerald green. She has the lean, svelte body of a jungle cat. If you saw them together, it would not occur to you that they were sisters.

My mother and her sister are very different in lifestyle, personality, and appearance. Perhaps it is their differences that allow them to be best friends.

▶ ACTIVITY 7–4

Analyzing Essays that Compare and Contrast

Thinking about the Content

1.* "As different as night and day" is the way Chris Barr contrasts his mother and aunt. Suggest a refreshing, novel simile that would be more interesting to read.

2. In one sentence—in your own words—state Chris Barr's thesis, and preview his main points.

Thinking about the Organization

3.* Which paragraph in "Adult and Youth Offenders" has no topic sentence? Write one.

4. Create a thesis statement, including a preview of main points, and decimal outline for "Adult and Youth Offenders," but organize it in block style. There will be two main points. (You might want to look at figure 1–7, "A Full-Sentence, Decimal Outline of 'Pancakes for Sunday Brunch.'")

5.★ Which word in "Sisters" serves to make the third paragraph more coherent by making it easy for readers to see the contrast between the sisters' personalities? In the paragraph on physical differences, add a word or phrase that makes the contrast even sharper.

6. Which paragraph in "Sisters" lacks a concluding sentence? Does it need one? What would you suggest?

7.★ Indicate for each essay whether the block or point-by-point method of comparison was used.

7.4.2   Ideas for Essays that Make Comparisons

Here are some ideas for essays that present comparisons:
- comparing life experiences (e.g., living in the country or city, growing up in two different cultures, being single or married)
- comparing processes you're studying in your program courses (e.g., two types of disabilities)
- comparing two entertainment or work experiences (a novel and a film, two jobs, or going to the movies versus chatting over coffee)

If you're having trouble deciding on a topic for your comparison/contrast essay, you may find it helpful to browse these essay titles:

- College and High School
- Vacations with Family, Vacations with Friends
- Boyfriends and Husbands
- Country Life Versus City Life
- Rock Music and New Country Music
- WordPerfect or Word?

7.5 ARGUING AND PERSUADING

We argue all the time. You could call it by another name. You could say that a day doesn't go by that you don't try to persuade someone to your point of view. Think about it. Have you ever asked your boss to alter a work schedule? Have you tried to talk someone into loaning you a car? If you answered yes to either of these questions, you've argued. You've tried to persuade someone to your point of view.

When you write a brief persuasive essay, you assert a point of view and support your argument. There are several ways to do this:

- You may organize your support into a logical argument
- You may marshal statistical data to support your point of view.
- You may conduct some research or rely on your memory to create support for your argument by citing experts on your topic.
- You may tell a story that illustrates your point.

Basically, your job is to advance a viewpoint and try to present convincing evidence that you are correct.

In the workplace, you may have many opportunities to argue. You may write a memo to advance a plan. You may write a business letter to convince an unhappy customer that she should pay her bill.

As citizens, too, we often encounter arguments. When you read an editorial urging you to vote a certain way, you are considering someone else's opinion. When you write a letter to the editor, you are making your own attempt to persuade readers to your way of thinking.

Do you think that prostitution should be legalized? Are you against raising tuition for students? Do you favour raising the minimum wage? You've got viewpoints that you may wish to propose to other citizens.

There are whole courses on argument. There's a lot to learn to argue persuasively. You can't learn it all in one writing course, but here are some procedures to follow to write effective direct-approach persuasive essays.

You may write your argument using one of the methods you've studied to develop ideas in essays. You might argue that the best way to improve the performance of post-secondary students is to test them all, and then use the results of the standardized tests to admit only the highest scoring students. You are considering processes. You might compare two ways of dealing with criminals—imprisonment or requiring restitution—and argue that one way is better. As you muse about your topic, you'll think of the method that will best express your thoughts and feelings.

To write an effective essay, remember the steps you usually take: create a thesis, main points, and support. Jot notes. Plan an outline. There's one additional concern with an argument: remember that the person seen as the nicest usually wins the argument. Be sure to write with a tone that shows respect for your readers. You may anticipate that they will disagree with you, but don't belittle their perspective. Finally, study the example essays. For the first essay, Rob Deslauriers looked back into his own childhood and, with Craig Farrish, wrote convincingly that spanking should be abolished. Their research provided lots of support for their viewpoint. Your persuasive essay will be better if you write about a topic you care about passionately. That's what Barb Tarr did when she thought about her childhood and constructed a powerful argument against nicknames.

7.5.1   Examples of Persuasive Essays

Outlaw Spanking: Repeal Section 43 of the Criminal Code by Robert A. D. Deslauriers and Craig R. Farrish

An eight-year-old boy in Winnipeg disobeyed his parents and opened a bag of sunflower seeds (Jourard D2). His father "turned on him slapping him across the back and shoulder and repeatedly kicked him." Justice Joseph O'Sullivan said, "The force applied was well within what has been accepted by parents in this province." The judge was correct: Legal precedents show other discharges for offences, including a Goderich, Ontario, mother who struck her "11-year-old daughter on the behind, leaving welts" (Jourard D2). Section 43 of the Criminal Code of Canada is what legitimizes this violence: "Every schoolteacher, parent or person standing in the place of a parent is justified in using force by way of correction toward a pupil or child, as the case may be, who is under his care, if the force does not exceed what is reasonable under the circumstances" (Milligan 30). Canada should repeal Section 43 because it contradicts other sections of our criminal code and violates our Charter of Rights and Freedoms and the United Nations Convention on the Rights of the Child.

Section 43 should be repealed because it permits parents and other adults to hurt children in ways that would be criminal offences if the victims were adults. If someone pulled down my pants and spanked me—as happened to a five-year-old in a London, Ontario, parking lot (Hess A1)—he would be breaking Section 265(1) of the criminal code: "a person commits assault when, without the consent of another person, he applies force intentionally to that person, directly or indirectly" (Milligan 207). If someone hit me with a belt and left welts, he would be guilty of breaking Section 267 of the Criminal Code of Canada: "Every one who, in committing an assault, carries, uses or threatens to use a weapon . . . or causes bodily harm is guilty of an indictable offence" (Milligan 210). We should repeal Section 43 because it permits assaults on our children in the guise of discipline.

We should repeal Section 43 to make it clear to all adults that disciplining children by hitting them violates children's fundamental Canadian rights. Consider Section 7 of the Charter of Rights and Freedoms: "Everyone has the right to life, liberty and security of person" (Milligan MS6). Surely the boys at St. John's School in Alberta don't feel secure when they can be hit by a "foot or two of heavy belt or a leather barber's strap" (Taylor 31). The courts have interpreted Section 43 to define as reasonable force punishments that cause bruising, swelling, nosebleeds, and even chipped teeth, but surely this can be considered the kind of "cruel and unusual treatment or punishment" forbidden in Section 12 of the Charter (Milligan MS6). We should make it clear to all adults that it is wrong to discipline children by hitting them.

Finally, we should repeal Section 43 and forbid spanking because it violates the United Nations Convention on the Rights of the Child. The agreement, which was signed by Prime Minister Brian Mulroney in 1990 (Fuller 22), "requires all signatories to take all appropriate legislative measures to protect the child from all forms of physical or mental violence" (McGovem 32). To live up to the letter and spirit of the Convention, we must outlaw spanking.

We must repeal Section 43 because it violates other Canadian laws, our own Charter of Rights and Freedoms, and an agreement with the UN. Section 446 of the Criminal Code states: "Every one commits an offence who willfully causes or, being the owner, willfully permits to be caused, unnecessary pain, suffering or injury to an animal or bird" (Milligan 288). This is absolutely nauseating: We live in a country that says it is a criminal offence to injure an animal, yet degenerate parents can kick, slap, push or beat their children with belts—and get away with it under the protective shelter of Section 43.

Works Cited

Fuller, Patty. "Another Assault on the Family." *Alberta Report* 13 Dec. 1995: 22–23.

Hess, Henry. "Father's Spanking of a Child Not a Crime, London Judge Rules." *Globe and Mail* 27 Apr. 1995: A12.

Jourard, Ron. "Holding the Rod, Sparing the Child." *Globe and Mail* 10 Apr. 1993: D2.

McGovem, Celeste. "It Smacks of Social Engineering." *Alberta Report* 27 June 1994: 32–33.

Milligan, David. *Milligan's Correlated Criminal Code and Selected Federal Statutes*. 1994. St. Catharines: Beacon Hill Law Book, 1995.

Taylor, Peter. "Strapless All the Rage." *Alberta Report* 7 May 1990: 30–31.

What's in a Name? by Barb Tarr

"What is in a name?" asked Shakespeare. Many people today would answer, "Nothing." This is evidenced by the increasing use of nicknames in today's society. The sad part is that many of the recipients of these nicknames have no say about their newfound identities. I, for example, have had the grave misfortune of being baptized many times over the years: Chuck, Harley, and—more recently—the Barbinator, to name a few. I believe I speak on behalf of many when I say that nicknames should be abolished because they conceal the logic behind our parents' choosing our birth name, they are annoying, and they are hard to discard.

Parents-to-be spend hours discussing the name they will give their new baby. Their discussions are so passionate that they can become arguments as husband and wife recall names of relatives past and present, friends, and idols. As the couple consult books about the history and origin of names, they learn that Damian means constant one and Linda means beautiful. Names are suggested and discarded until, finally, they find the perfect name. All the work researching, debating, and choosing the name will be obscured when their child's peers bestow a nickname. Parents probably wish they could abolish nicknames.

The originators of nicknames think that they are funny, but the names are annoying to everyone else. The nicknamed person has to hear the name—say, Clutzy—and the ensuing laughter, every day. The rebaptized has no choice but to speculate about the origins of the moniker, and the story is not likely flattering. Even worse are the awkward silences that follow attempts by the baptizers to explain the name. That accident in the gym that seemed so screamingly funny at the time—at least to some—undoubtedly loses something in the retelling. The nickname and the endless recounting of the story of its origins become so annoying that almost everyone wishes to banish the nickname.

Another good reason for banning nicknames is that it is so hard to get rid of them. An example from my hometown immediately springs to mind: Steven MacDougall, 25, was forced to announce his engagement under his nickname, <u>Goose</u>, or no one would have realized who was getting married. There's no end to the troubles caused by persistent nicknames: imagine trying to explain to your new fiancée, as she meets your college friends, why they all call you <u>Loverboy</u>. The next time you are on the verge of giving someone a nickname, think about the forty-year-old at his high school reunion yelling across the floor, "Hey, Bob! Remember? It's me, <u>Stinky</u>!"

I hate nicknames because they conceal our meaningful birth names, annoy almost everyone, and are hard to get rid of. The remedy to this problem is to abolish their use. To all of you who still disagree, I ask you to consider that even though "a rose by any other name would smell as sweet," no one would rush to smell a <u>stinkweed</u>.

▶ **ACTIVITY 7–5**

Analyzing Persuasive Essays

Thinking about the Content

1.* Quote the thesis for "Outlaw Spanking: Repeal Section 43 of the Criminal Code."

2. Read this version of Barb Tarr's second paragraph.

Parents-to-be spend hours rapping about the name they will lay on their new baby. Their discussions are so awesome that they can become nuclear as the old lady and her old man yak about their kith and kin. As they hit the books about the history of names, they dis each other and pick a rad name. It's all for nothing when the other kids lob a nickname. Parents probably wish they could nuke nicknames.

Which is better, the original or the revision? Why?

3. Keep the topic sentence, but rewrite the rest of the third paragraph of "What's in a Name?" to increase the power of the support. Make up an example—and another nickname—to develop the point more convincingly.

4.* Review figure 2–4, "Rough Outline of 'Pancakes for Sunday Brunch.'" Create a similar outline of the content of the fourth paragraph of the essay "What's in a Name?"

Thinking about the Organization

5. How many times does Barb Tarr use the word *abolish* or variants of that word? What synonyms of *abolish* does she use? Why does she use these words so often?

6.* What is the principal technique Deslauriers and Farrish use to lead in to "Outlaw Spanking: Repeal Section 43 of the Criminal Code"?

7. In which paragraph of "What's in a Name?" could the topic sentence be improved to remind us of the thesis? Write a better one.

7.5.2   Ideas for Persuasive Essays

Here are some topics you could write about.

- You could write to suggest a change in social policy that would improve our lives (e.g., universal daycare, reinstatement of the death penalty, legalization of marijuana, denticare)
- Compare two procedures from your content-area studies and recommend one as superior

You might generate a topic for your persuasive essay by reading through the titles of papers other students have written.

- Quit Smoking
- Get a Pedicure
- TV: A Bad Babysitter
- No Makeup
- Pay Your Child Support
- Move to the Country

7.6 SOME CONCLUDING THOUGHTS

By working through chapters 6 and 7, you've developed your ability to create brief essays to express your ideas and your feelings. Working your way through part 3 will let you apply your new skills to writing research essays. You'll also find that you can apply what you've learned to write strong job application letters and résumés, types of writing explored on the *Write of Way* Web pages.

From Brief Essays to Research Essays —and Beyond!

"Publication is a self-invasion of privacy."
—*Marshall McLuhan*

Write of Way aims to help first-year college students improve their writing. In the first part of the book, you've studied and written brief essays. Part 3 shows you how to write research essays.

If your introductory writing course doesn't include topics such as writing grant proposals or wedding toasts, use the related Web pages—see the last section of the table of contents at the front of the book—as a reference when you face these writing tasks. Want to join a service club? Would you like to serve on the student activity council? Are you a little nervous because you don't know the rules for participating in that Zonta, Optimists, or minor hockey association meeting? Read the Web section on agendas and minutes. There's no faster way to become a key person in an organization than to volunteer to keep minutes or be the recording secretary. Need to write a letter to complain about shoddy service, perhaps the low quality of the food services at your campus? Review the suggestions, emulate the sample, and you'll create good content, you'll organize it well, and you'll create an appearance that will make a good impression on your audience. When you follow the COSA formula, you're more likely to get your way! Although *Write of Way* can be only an introduction to this real-world writing, there's enough information to start you writing for your life.

Writing Research Essays

"I quote others in order to better express my own self."
—*Montaigne*

CHAPTER OBJECTIVE

You will use modern information-retrieval tools to review relevant literature and write a research essay.

Research is the "careful hunting of the facts or truth" ("Research"). When you write a research essay, your goal is to tell your readers what you believe is the truth about a topic. In chapter 8, you can read about how Tommy Hall researched health insurance in Canada and the United States, and how he came to assert—in a research essay—that Canada's public health-insurance system is better.

In the best of all possible worlds, you would apprentice with an experienced partner to learn to write a research essay. Since you may not have a partner to help you write your best paper yet, you can learn by reading about researching a topic. Along the way, you can do several assignments and read through simulations of the steps of researching and writing. If you complete the assignments as best you can, you can really improve your researching, notetaking, outlining, and essay-writing skills. You can more quickly learn to write a research paper if you *act* as well as *read*.

When students learn that they will be writing a research paper, most gasp. It just sounds like way too much work—an impossible task. Yet, almost everyone soon writes a solid research paper.

They write a good essay because they already know a great deal. So do you. There's only a little new learning. Think about it. You know how to create a brief essay by brainstorming a topic—say, not liking nicknames—and narrowing your focus and creating a thesis: Nicknames should be abolished. You make notes. You outline main points: Nicknames disguise our parents' reasons for naming us, they are annoying, and they are hard to get rid of. You know how to create specific support for each main point. (Remember how Barb Tarr related the anecdote of a friend's having to publish his wedding announcement under the nickname *Goose* because that's the only way his friends would know he was getting married?) You know how to introduce and conclude brief essays. The only new learning is

- how to research your topic and

- how to document, to indicate to your readers who wrote the information and where it was published.

Before you begin a detailed look at how to write a research essay, though, take a general overview.

8.1 STUDY THE CONTENT OF A SAMPLE RESEARCH ESSAY

If you study an example of the type of essay you must write, you'll find it easier to write your own paper. Do Activity 8–1 to increase your general understanding of research essays.

▶ **ACTIVITY 8–1**

Studying a Sample Research Essay

The aim of this activity is to give you an opportunity to continue building a mental model of a research paper. If you have a clear conception of a research essay, you will write a better paper. As you read the sample essay, think about how you could succinctly summarize it. Try to state the thesis and the main points Hall made in his research essay. If you will be writing a paper in MLA style, read "Canada's One-Tier Health Care Is the Better System" in chapter 9. If you will be writing a paper in APA style, read "Canada's One-Tier Health Care Is the Better System" in chapter 10. Then, continue reading this chapter.

You've finished reading the paper already? Good. Let me ask you: can you summarize that essay in one sentence? Is your summary anything like this: Canada's one-tier, tax-supported health-care system is more economical, efficient, and fair than a two-tier system? If so, you've understood Hall's contention, his thesis, and his main points.

Your own essay should make an assertion in a similar fashion. Even if your instructor assigns an essay topic, you will have to express a viewpoint. Whether you are assigned a topic or create your own, start to think not just about your essay topic in general, but about your contention.

Take a closer look at the content of a research essay. Refer again to the essay "Canada's One-Tier Health Care Is the Better System," and write your answers to Activity 8–2. When you're finished, compare your answers to those given in chapter 15.

▶ ACTIVITY 8–2*

Analyzing the Content of a Research Essay

1. Quote the sentence in which Hall states his thesis and previews his main points.

2. In your own words, state each of the essay's main points.

3. Study the full-sentence, decimal outline of "Pancakes for Sunday Brunch" (figure 1–7). Write a similar outline for the first main point of Hall's essay "Canada's One-Tier Health Care Is the Better System." For each point of specific support, write in parentheses the author of the information and the page number on which the information is printed. Complete your outline, and compare it to the outline provided in chapter 15. (If you want to practise APA-style documentation, record within the parentheses the author, year, and page number, as shown in chapter 10.)

As you looked closely at the details of Hall's essay, you may have wondered: how did he learn all this information about Canada's health-insurance system? How did he decide what to write about? How will *I* create the content of *my* research essay? You know that informative content is the most important component of a successful essay, and you're wondering how to create that content.

In chapter 2, you studied how to use daydreaming, brainstorming, idea mapping, and freewriting to create the material for a brief essay. Hall daydreamed his way into a topic: he was irked by television commentators saying health care was becoming too expensive for taxpayers, that Canada should privatize health care, as the United States has. Hall wondered if Canada's health-care system wasn't better than the two-tier approach in the United States. He decided to read about this topic. Judging by the number of publications listed in the bibliography of his paper, he certainly found a lot of information about health care, didn't he?

As you read through his bibliography—the list of works cited in an MLA-style paper, the references list in an APA-style paper—you notice the titles of books and articles about health insurance. Finding material about *any* topic has never been easier thanks to modern information-retrieval tools such as electronic card catalogues, CD-ROM databases, and Internet search engines.

Hall first looked for a book about health care. He looked up the term *health* in the catalogue of the permanent collection of the library, but there were so many titles about topics such as fitness, nutrition, and prevention of disease that he decided to try a narrower term: *health insurance*. The catalogue did not use that term; the catalogue said, "See *insurance, health*." Under the heading *insurance, health—Canada*, Hall found the McGilly book, *Canada's Public Social Services*. Under *insurance, health—Ontario*, Hall saw a book with the words *national health insurance*. He looked for call numbers of books under this heading, and struck pay dirt with a book he found in his search: *Looking North: What We Can Learn from Canada's Health Insurance System*. The title itself supported his hunch that Canada's system was better. Then, right in the preface, Arnold Bennett said that "health care costs Canadians far less than Americans" (xvii). Hall was beginning to think that his thesis might be that Canada's system was better and that a main point supporting this assertion was that it was less expensive. He wanted to be sure to remember this information—he was almost certain he would need it in his essay—so he decided to jot a note. He wrote the quote on a small file card, labelling it "cheaper." He knew he would need to reference that information, so he noted the name of the author and the page number. Look at figure 8–1 for an example of the notes Hall made as he read more information about how the Canadian health-insurance system is more "economical." Note that Hall saved time by writing in point form.

FIGURE 8–1

File Card of Note Taken

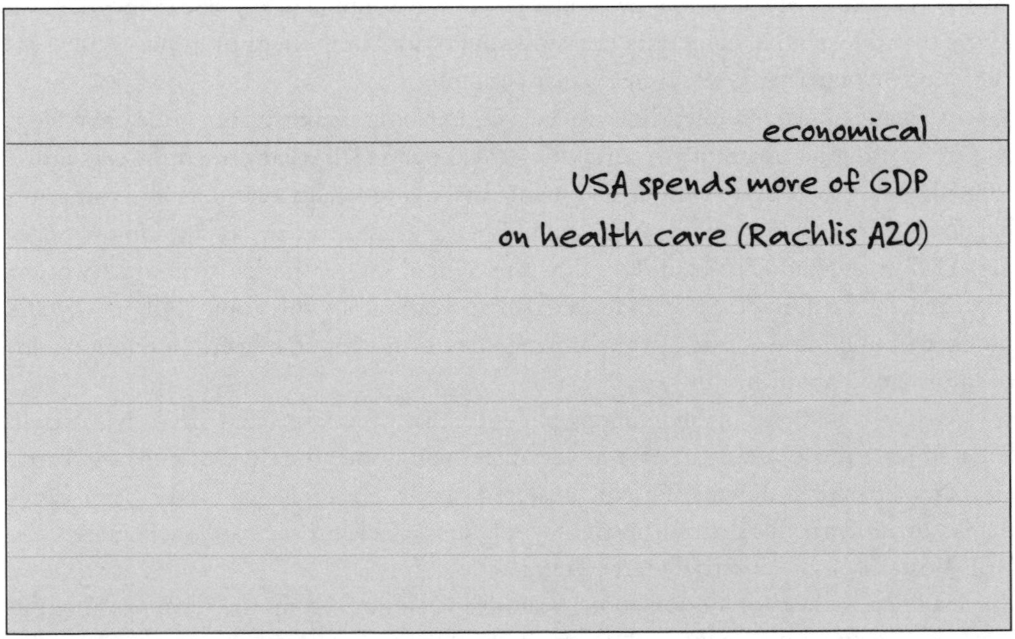

economical

USA spends more of GDP
on health care (Rachlis A20)

Figure 8–2 shows that he also took the time to create a file card for all the information he would need to include in his bibliography. This allowed him to quickly find his way back to the source document in case he decided to include a direct quotation or needed to re-study a point.

In the first article in *Looking North for Health: What We Can Learn from Canada's Health Care System*, Hall found another main point to support his thesis: Beatty noted that although we spend less per person, we have lower infant mortality rates (34). The public health plan is more efficient at giving greater health to greater numbers.

Once Hall had created a thesis and a couple main points, he could read more pointedly. He could more quickly decide what was relevant to his essay, and which text he could skip over and ignore. As he created each main point, he labelled a file folder and began to put his notes into it.

Hall's teacher had suggested that students must read several sources to be sure they were learning the important information about a topic. Reading only a few documents might mean that students were reading an eccentric viewpoint, not information held in general high regard by people well-informed about the topic. Hall decided to supplement his reading of books with articles from journals, magazines, and newspapers.

FIGURE 8–2

File Card of Note Taken

Rachlis, Michael.

"Shopping for Care Nonsensical."

Toronto Star.

January 19, 1996. p. A20.

He asked a college librarian to suggest how he might search for articles about health insurance. The librarian suggested that he look in an electronic database and recommended the Canadian Business and Current Affairs (CBCA) database, which was on CD-ROM and could be accessed through computer terminals in the reference area of the library. The librarian explained that the CBCA database consists of the titles and other information about articles published in about 500 mainly Canadian business and general journals and magazines. It also indicates information about where to find articles published in ten Canadian newspapers and news services. The full text of many of these documents is stored right on the CD's so students can read it on the monitors, or print those documents, or save them to computer disk to be viewed in a word-processing program on another computer. The most wonderful thing about the database, added the librarian, is that it is as easy to find articles on a topic as it is to find a book in a library card catalogue.

The librarian said that there were two ways to look for articles about health insurance. She recommended that Hall conduct a subject search. Hall watched as the librarian used a Microsoft Windows 95 software program to load the CBCA database and, guided by instructions on the monitor screen, type *health care* into a window. Another window indicated that there were 107 articles filed under this heading in the database. She also said that he could search the database using keywords, such as *health insurance* (which identified 708 articles that had that term somewhere in the text) or *one-tier* (which yielded 31 hits). Sometimes he was able to read the whole article right on the monitor (or save it on a computer disk to read later on his home computer); other times, he noted the publication title, date, and pages and had to find hard copies of the articles in the library's collection of back issues or on microfilm. Hall was quickly able to learn about health insurance by reading the material he found in his search of the literature. For example, when he read this comment by Dr. Joel Lexchin, "In the 1960s, the Canadian society made the decision that no one should be denied medical care on the grounds that they couldn't afford it," Hall knew he had another main point: a universal health insurance system is better because it treats rich and poor people fairly.

Although Hall did not search the Internet for information, he could have. The college librarian said that he could use one of the computers connected to the Internet, and that she would show him how to use a search engine, such as Open Text or Yahoo! Canada. She said that he could enter keywords, much as he did to use the CBCA database. Hall remembered that his teacher had said that some information on the Internet was of questionable value, that researchers had to be careful to consider the reliability of the information. Since Hall had already found more information than he could read, he decided not to search for more via the Internet. He continued to make his notes and put them into file folders (including a new one for information about Canada's one-tier health-insurance system being fairer).

> BOX 8–1 Researching on the Internet

Tommy Hall missed some valuable information by not looking on the Internet. If he had entered "National Forum on Health" into the Yahoo search engine, he would have found, on the first of 426 Web pages, a link to a government of Canada Web site on which the entire report was published.

As with any source of information, you must judge critically what you read on the Net. Material published in textbooks, specialized encyclopedias and dictionaries, peer-edited journals, and reputable newspapers and magazines— these materials are more reliable than musings on personal Web pages. Original sources, such as the Forum's report, though, are high-quality, primary information sources. You will find that more and more organizations publish their reports on the Internet, because it is less expensive than mailing hard copies.

Writing Effective Summaries

Good notetaking skills are essential in creating effective documents, including essays. In a world where information is being created faster and faster, summarizing has also become a survival skill. Inundated by information—much of it printed—we hardly have the time to read pertinent documents one time, let alone more than once. Fortunately, reviewing a well-prepared set of informative summaries takes less time than rereading whole documents. When you learn to summarize well, you've learned an important study-reading skill.

If you write research papers, you will quickly learn the value of summarizing. Once you survey the literature to become informed about your topic, you must tell your audience the information you learned. In paragraph after paragraph, you will find yourself paraphrasing—in fewer words—the essence of the other writers' findings.

Sometimes you have other reasons for writing an informative summary. The *Publication Manual* of the APA requires each paper to have a summary; they call it an abstract: "a brief comprehensive summary of the contents of an article" (American 8). The abstract is one of the most important parts of your document. If your paper is published, the abstract will be included in databases where other researchers will find it as they review the literature pertinent to their research interest. Those researchers will decide—as they read your abstract—whether to read or ignore the whole document.

Busy bosses in social service agencies and big-box retail stores often assign employees to write longer summaries, called executive summaries, of convention presentations; meetings; and articles, books, reports, and other documents.

Creating the Content of an Effective Information Summary

* **Decide the length of your summary.** Summaries are often about ten per cent of the length of the original. If you're writing for someone else, ask your reader how long the summary should be.

* **Read through the whole document.** Read to understand the article. Don't worry yet about which information you will include in your summary.

* **Be sure you understand the main point.** Whether you are summarizing your own article or someone else's, your most important job is to understand the main point of the article. Audience analysis is crucial. Why does your reader want a summary? What is her purpose in reading it? The answers will help you decide what material in the original document you must include in your summary.

As you read through the original, look for the most important information the author develops in the document. Be sure to include this information in your summary. The author of the original may have signalled the key information by using words indicating causation (e.g., *because*, *consequently*) and important basic information (e.g., *fundamental*, *significant*, *crucial*).

Create a topic sentence that expresses the main idea in a brief, clear way. The main point Suzanne Ziegler makes in a newspaper article entitled "Failing Young Children Jeopardizes Their Future at School" (see 16.4) is that it is better to socially promote low-achieving students than to fail them.

* **As you begin to reread, make point-form notes of the most important information.**

* **Select the most important details.** Once you've identified the most important point of the article, you're well on your way to an effective summary. Now you must imagine your audience's need to read enough significant detail to clearly understand your summary. The topic sentence above tells the most significant point Ziegler made, but it is not sufficient for a summary because it is difficult to understand her contention without more information. The summary doesn't give us some of the specific details essential to supporting Ziegler's assertion. Notice how much more convincing the summary becomes if we add specific support: Compared to other weak students who are socially promoted, failed students don't learn as much and more frequently drop out of school.

⋆ **Paraphrase rather than quote information.** You can almost always express someone else's ideas more succinctly by using your own words, rather than quoting the words of the source document.

⋆ **Try to express your summary in the same tone used by the author of the original document.** Be neutral about the content of the summary. Remember that you are summarizing someone else's document; express your point of view in documents *you* author.

Organizing an Effective Informative Summary

⋆ **Begin the summary by naming the author and document title in the first sentence.**

⋆ **Start by stating the main point of the document.** Create an effective summary by beginning with the main point. Then, add a sentence with the next most important information. Always organize the summary so that even if readers quit before the end, they will know the most important information.

Unlike essays, summaries do not require clinchers. Summaries end with a whimper, not with a bang.

Making Your Summary Look Good

⋆ **Create a single block of text and centre it on the page.** Omit the usual paragraph indent for a summary.

You'll have many opportunities to practise summarization. When you are listening to your instructor in class or to a speaker in a meeting of a business or service club, listen closely for the main points and write them down. Add a brief example or illustration, and those notes will help you remember the occasion more clearly. Don't take so many notes that you do not listen efficiently to the speaker, but take enough that you keep yourself alert by the effort you must make to summarize effectively.

If you pause to summarize news articles or textbook sections—mentally or in writing—you will understand and remember better.

▶ ACTIVITY 8–3⋆

Summarizing Information

You can practise summarizing information by completing this activity. Imagine that you are a prisoner advocate working with inmates released to attend school. You have collected and placed in a library many articles that you believe can help prisoners succeed in school. You have decided to catalogue these materials. Rather than just writing descriptive summaries telling what's in each document, you've decided it would be more helpful to your clients to write informative summaries that would clearly state the most important information in the articles. That way, even if your clients decide not to read an entire document, they will learn the most important information. Remember that to create a good summary you should find the main point of the passage, add any detail needed to support the most important information, and express it in your own words. Read "You Can Learn to Read Better" (16.1), one of the articles the prisoners might want to read. This essay is about 1,500 words long, so write a summary of about 150 words.

8.2 STUDY THE ORGANIZATION OF A SAMPLE RESEARCH ESSAY

You've analyzed the content of a sample research essay. You've learned how one student created the content of such an essay. Now examine the way writers organize research essays. Complete the following activity.

▶ ACTIVITY 8–4*

Analyzing the Organization of a Sample Research Essay

1. Review figure 1–6 ("Outline of a Five-Paragraph Essay") and figure 15–7 ("Essay Outline for 'The Positive Effects of Using Photo Radar to Enforce Speed Limits'"). Notice that there are three main sections in the general outline of an essay and in the specific essay about photo radar: an introduction, support paragraphs, and a conclusion. Research essays are organized into the same sections. Show that you can identify these sections in Hall's research essay by quoting the first few words that begin each part and the last few words that end each part of "Canada's One-Tier Health Care Is the Better System."

INTRODUCTION TO THE ESSAY

SUPPORT PARAGRAPHS

CONCLUSION TO THE ESSAY

2. Indicate the lead-in, the part of the essay where the author attempts to arouse your interest so that you'll read the paper.

3. Quote the sentence in which the author states how he organizes the exploration of the topic, the text in which he previews the main points.

4. Indicate in the concluding section of the text where the author recapitulates the thesis and main points of the essay.

5. Quote the clincher, the text the author writes to leave the reader with a memorable last thought.

How did Tommy Hall organize his paper so well? Once he created his thesis and main points, he could also think more efficiently about the organization of the whole essay: the introduction, the support paragraphs, and the conclusion.

Since Hall had already created the thesis and main points of the introduction, he noted, on cards labelled *Introduction*, information that might capture the reader's interest. He was also thinking about his audience, and so he was on the lookout for background information that would make it easier for readers to follow his argument.

He quickly knew that he had so much information about each of his main points that he would have to write several paragraphs to develop each point. He had already decided to begin by discussing the economics of a one-tier system, to move to arguing for its efficiency, and to finish his support by asserting the fairness of a one-tier system of public health insurance. He had created a solid plan for the organization of his paper.

As Hall read, he was also watching for material that could conclude the paper, particularly a good clincher. When he came to the last sentence in Robert Evans' paper, he was sure he'd found his clincher. He carefully recorded this quotation onto a file card. He also made a card for the bibliography. He wrote on that card all the information needed for his bibliography so he would not have to return to the library to retrieve the book again.

At a point, Hall looked over his notes and knew he had enough material to write his essay. He knew he had sound organization. He had gradually constructed a detailed outline. His thoughts turned to checking the appearance requirements (MLA or APA) for his essay.

Why should you study this essay so closely? To help you remember a basic model of a typical research essay. If you can visualize a complete research essay, you'll be more effective in studying the details of how to create such an essay. You may also conclude that the organization of a research essay is highly similar to the organization of a brief essay. You can more easily complete a research paper if you conceptualize the task as creating an introduction, in which you assert your thesis and main points; creating the body of the essay, in which you support your main points; and creating a conclusion, in which you remind your readers of your thesis.

8.3 STUDY THE APPEARANCE OF A SAMPLE RESEARCH ESSAY

Previewing Hall's paper introduced you to the appearance of an MLA- or APA-style paper. You'll use one of these styles to format your research essay. Do the next activity to increase your understanding of how to format modern research papers. Try Activity 9–1 now if you're writing a research paper in MLA style, or Activity 10–1 if you're writing in APA style. Continue reading this chapter after you complete one of those activities.

Before Hall began typing into his word-processing program, he reviewed the style requirements. Even though he knew he might revise his essay, he decided to observe the style guidelines in his first draft; he knew he would save some time if he did not have to extensively revise before preparing his final version of his research essay.

He started to learn how to format his paper by reviewing the textbook and the sample paper. Then he continued by creating the cover for his project. He created the page layout and header with his word processing software, remembering to double-space all the text. He began to refer to his outline and his notes to write the introduction.

He created the bibliography as he wrote. Every time he was uncertain about how to set up a reference, he went back to the sample paper and the textbook. Because he was word-processing the document, it was easy to insert each reference alphabetically onto a list at the end of his electronic document. Gradually, he was able to refer to earlier parts of his own paper to consistently observe the conventions of the style he was emulating. Over several sessions at the computer, Hall worked straight through to the end of his paper. Tommy Hall had his first draft.

After completing the first draft, Hall set aside the paper for a couple of days. Then he retrieved the file into his word-processing program and reread his essay, trying to imagine how it would seem to his instructor. Hall pretended that he was reading the paper for the first time. He tried to determine if it made sense, if it was effectively organized, if it adhered to the style he had emulated. He decided to change the order of some of the points of support for his second main point. When he had done that, he felt he had written a good paper.

Hall decided that he was nearly ready to submit the paper. He moved his cursor to the beginning of the document and used the spell checker feature of his word-processing program. He decided to read the essay one last time. He remembered the suggestion that proofreaders detect more errors if they read a paper beginning with the last sentence and then read each sentence back to the beginning of the paper. (Such a reading makes no sense, but it does make it easier to detect grammar and punctuation errors.) After proofreading, he printed two copies of his essay. He filed one copy—in case his instructor's car was burgled. Hall was finally ready to submit the other copy to his teacher.

8.4 SUMMARY OF THE STEPS FOR WRITING A RESEARCH ESSAY

You've previewed a research essay to examine its content, organization, and appearance. Here's a summary of the steps you must take to write such an essay.

1. **Select a Topic and Research It.** Even if you're assigned a topic for your research essay, you still need to choose how to approach that topic. Create your content by using the techniques you studied to write short essays: daydreaming, brainstorming, idea mapping, and freewriting. Always keep in mind who you are writing for: meet the needs of your reader.

   When you are asked to create your own topic, look at your course materials. If you must write a research essay, be on the lookout for an essay topic as you read your textbook. When you find yourself wishing the textbook author had told you more about a topic, take charge of your own learning by researching that topic.

   When the textbook stimulates you to research a topic, you have a head start on finding other relevant information. Almost certainly the author has cited material from the research literature. When you go into the library, look up and read those specific references. Look up the text's references in a database of research and see which keywords or descriptors refer to them. You'll find more related research using the same keywords in your information-retrieval attempts. You'll still need to review the literature more extensively, but you've made a start. Remember that the three main sources of information will be the catalogue of the library's permanent collection, CD-ROM's with databases of materials published in periodicals, and the Internet. Ask your teacher and a research librarian to tell you the major information tools used by researchers of the subject you are researching. They can help you find guides to writing in specific disciplines; for example, Prentice Hall publishes a student writer's manual series (e.g., *The Political Science Student Writer's Manual* by

Gregory M. Scott and Stephen M. Garrison). The series includes guides for writing about history, philosophy, and sociology. Addison Wesley Longman publishes the Short Guide Series (e.g., *A Short Guide to Writing about Art* by Sylvan Barnet); other guides focus on biology, chemistry, film, literature, history, science, and social science).

If you find too much material with the keywords or terms you use, narrow your search by using more specific words; for example if, in searching for articles about money laundering, the word *crime* returns too much information, try looking for the exact phrase *money laundering*. If you now find too little information, try *fraud* or the term *white-collar crime*. Ask a library worker how to do this for the information retrieval tools you're using, and read the help screens or instruction manuals provided for the software.

When you read the materials you find in your search of the literature, use the notetaking skills you studied in part 2. To save yourself time, summarize information.

2. **Create a Thesis, Main Points, and Support.** As you read more about your topic, you will need to create a thesis. What are you going to assert? Remember that Hall decided to write about why Canadians needed a health-care system for everyone. He had a topic, but he still didn't have a thesis. As he conducted his literature search, Hall began to believe that his essay should assert that Canada's one-tier health-care system was better than the United States' two-tier alternative. After more reading, Hall had his thesis and his main points: Canada's system is economical, efficient, and fair. However, he still needed more content. He needed specific support—statistics and quotations from experts—details that showed the economy, efficiency, and fairness of a one-tier system. He plunged back into reading the newspaper articles and books to search for more evidence to support his point of view. You've got to do the same.

3. **Organize the Essay.** As you finish researching your topic, think about what you will say in your introduction and conclusion. Watch for a stunning statistic or startling quotation that will make a good lead-in. Be sure to make a note about any quotation that you think would make a memorable last thought, your clincher. Consider creating file folders of material you might use in the introduction and conclusion. As you take a moment to review one of these files, you may suddenly know what you want to say in these important sections. You may find, too, that it is easier to organize your essay if you review your answer to Activity 8–4, "Analyzing the Organization of a Sample Research Essay."

4. **Meet the Appearance Requirements for Your Essay.** Be sure you understand how your professor wants you to format your research essay. Pay close attention to

comments made during classes, and read carefully any handouts. If you can, examine a sample paper in the required style. Some students like to try to emulate these style requirements as they create the first draft. Others like to wait until they are keying the final draft.

5. **Revise the Draft.** It's a good idea to set your first draft aside for a day or two. Then try to read it from your teacher's perspective. Think of the COSA formula. During your audience analysis, rewrite any sections that you feel assume too much background information; delete writing that belabours the obvious. Be sure the tone of the research essay is fairly formal, but not stuffy. Is the paper well organized? Did you write using Standard English? Did you meet the appearance requirements?

6. **Proofread the Essay.** Once you have finished your revision, proofread the paper. Start at the end of the paper and, sentence by sentence, check that you have spelled and punctuated correctly. Many students use the spelling and grammar checking software in their word-processing programs. Be wary of your software's advice; these electronic proofreaders are not completely reliable.

8.5 SOME CONCLUDING THOUGHTS

Well, you've done it. You've written an essay—your new personal best, I hope. It probably feels good to have reached the end of the project; however, in many ways, you've just begun.

You can start to increase your essay-writing ability the moment your instructor returns your paper. Act on the feedback your instructor provided. At the least, thoughtfully consider the comments. Imagine how your paper would be different if you had known about and acted on this advice *before* you submitted the final draft. Save your paper, and as you get ready to write another read through it and reflect on the comments. Plan to write an even better essay next time.

If you have a strong desire to improve your essay-writing ability, don't just read your instructor's feedback, act on it: revise this paper before you start another essay assignment. Make it better in every way you can. Your instructor may not provide an opportunity to do this for additional marks—most instructors are so busy they have difficulty getting through first and only markings—but if you write it again, you can make the kind of improvement that comes only from rewriting. You'll have an even better model paper to use as an aid to writing your next essay.

CHAPTER 9

Writing Research Essays in MLA Style

"The general practices the MLA Handbook *describes are followed by writers of studies and reports that serve the needs of many different readers, in government, business, industry, the professions, the academy, and the media."*
—*Phyllis Franklin, Executive Director, Modern Language Association*

CHAPTER OBJECTIVE

After completing the activities in this chapter, you will be able to write a research essay in MLA style.

The Modern Language Association (MLA) was founded in 1833. The precursor of the *MLA Handbook for Writers of Research Papers* (Gibaldi)—aimed at high school and undergraduate students—and the *MLA Style Manual and Guide to Scholarly Publishing* (Gibaldi)—for graduate students, scholars, and professional writers—was published as the "Style Sheet" in 1951. MLA members and scholarly publishers almost immediately adopted the conventions. Today, students, scholars, editors and publishers around the world refer to the handbooks to prepare reports, journal articles, and books, particularly in the humanities (e.g., English and other languages, history, and classics). In addition, much writing in business, technology, and science is based on slight variations of the MLA conventions. When you learn MLA style, you learn to present writing in a way that's well-regarded all over the world.

The newest edition of the *MLA Style Manual and Guide to Scholarly Publishing*—the second—includes how to cite electronic publications such as e-mail and CD-ROM's. When the Modern Language Society updates its documentation conventions, it posts them to its Web site (www.mla.org). The examples in this chapter reflect the 1998 style manual and the 1998 Web site postings of the latest MLA conventions. Visit the *Write of Way* Web pages to see, in the copy of the research essay posted there, any further changes in documentation conventions.

If you're reading this section of *Write of Way*, it's probably because an instructor has asked you to write a research essay in MLA style. If that's the case, and you already know how to write a college-level research essay, read this chapter to learn how to format your essay in MLA style. If you feel that it would be helpful to further study how to write a research essay, you may want to stop reading here, and go to chapter 8, "Writing Research Essays."

9.1 EXAMPLE OF AN MLA-STYLE ESSAY: "CANADA'S ONE-TIER HEALTH CARE IS THE BETTER SYSTEM"

▶ **ACTIVITY 9–1**

Studying a Research Essay in MLA Style

The easiest way to learn to write a paper in MLA style is to begin by examining one. Look at Tommy Hall's research essay "Canada's One-Tier Health Care Is the Better System," and take a moment to answer each question as you read through the discussion of this MLA-style paper.

FIGURE 9–1

MLA-Style Paper

> Hall 1
>
> Tommy Hall
>
> Dr. Douglas B. Rogers
>
> ENGL323G
>
> January 24, 1999
>
> Canada's One-Tier Health Care Is the Better System
>
> Rich or poor, if you live in Canada, you can go to the doctor and be referred to a hospital when you're sick. Canada's publicly funded, one-tier health-care insurance system makes this possible. Similar social welfare systems

are commonplace in Europe, but the United States provides a startling alternative: a two-tier combination of social-welfare Medicare and free-enterprise private health insurance. One result is that forty million people have no health insurance at all, and "another 40 million have such inadequate coverage that a major illness could lead to personal bankruptcy" (Rachlis A20). In the United States, families have become destitute because their private insurance did not cover the costs of care for leukemia or neonatal care.

Some say our public health insurance system ought to cover dental, optical, drug, and other health-related costs—more as Justice Emmett Hall proposed to the Parliament of Canada in 1964 (Bergman 24). Waiting periods for services do vary somewhat in the provinces, and a few people do travel to the United States for treatment, but most would agree the Canadian system is close to one-tier. It does come near realizing the principle of equal access. Despite inequities that remain in our health-care system, Canada's one-tier, publicly supported, health-insurance system is better than two-tier alternatives because it is more economical, efficient, and fair.

Our one-tier health-care system is less expensive than the two-tier system in the United States. Of all the industrialized countries, the United States, with its two-tier system of health insurance, spends the most on health care (Terrana 14). The many private health-insurance plans in the United States push up the costs of providing health care: "Current U.S. estimates put the extra administrative costs generated by private coverage—pure paper-pushing—at about $100 billion annually," estimates Robert Evans, a professor of economics at the University of British Columbia's Centre for Health Services and Policy Research ("Canada Should" B6).

In a comparison of the U.S. and Canadian health-insurance systems, Perrin Beatty notes, "As recently as 1971, the United States and Canada spent about the same percentage of gross national product (GNP) on health care, 7.6 percent and 7.4 percent, respectively. By the end of the 1980s, our total health care spending was much lower, at 8.6 percent, than that of the United States, at 11.4 percent" (33).

Beatty estimates that more than three times as much money is lost to administration costs in the United States than in Canada (34).

Arnold Bennett, an American advocate of health-care reform in the United States, compares the health-insurance systems of the two countries and concluded that in reality "health care costs Canadians far less than Americans are paying" (xvii).

Michael Rachlis noted that the 1,500 private insurance companies mean that the United States will spend 15 per cent of its GDP on health care—5 per cent more than any other country (A20).

Not only is our one-tier health insurance system economical, it is efficient: It ensures the greatest health for the greatest number of citizens.

The first publicly funded hospital-insurance plan was created by Tommy Douglas' CCF Government in Saskatchewan in 1946. It came about partly because of concerns about the poor health of Canadians (e.g., high infant mortality and tuberculosis). These concerns surfaced in reports like the National Sickness Survey of the early 1950's:

> The health of the population was conceded by all qualified observers to be far below the standard attainable with existing knowledge, skill, and national wealth . . . . almost all commentators agreed that the high cost of a trip to the hospital, and to a lesser extent, the cost of treatment by a doctor, deterred people from seeking care when they should have done so and hereby contributed significantly to the low level of health in Canada, even among people not thought of as 'poor.' (McGilly 233)

When contemporary neoconservatives urge a health-care system in which each individual pays her own way, they don't mention that Canada had such a system—and the general health of the nation was low. Look at what happened as tax-based public hospital and medical health-care insurance came into effect in 1968.

Perrin Beatty (34), in an address in the United States, documented the changes:

> Has it improved the health of the population? We think it has. At the
> time we introduced the first element of our plan in the early 1950s,
> our infant mortality rate was running 40 percent higher than
> Australia's, 30 percent higher than the United Kingdom's, and 5
> percent higher than the United States' . . . . Today our infant mortal-
> ity rates are 30 percent lower than yours and among the lowest in
> the world, at 7 per 1000 live births.

Any kind of cost—fee-for-service or user fee—discourages the poor from using medical services. Beatty notes that pregnant women began coming earlier to physicians when they did not have to pay out of pocket.

Another example comes from Lexchin, a member of the Medical Reform Group, who notes that prescription user fees mean that "the poor may stop using important drugs such as insulin and heart medications, admissions to nursing homes rise, and there is a deterioration in the care that people with mental illness receive" (A23).

Gordon Guyatt notes that restrictions on prescriptions in New Hampshire caused more admissions to nursing homes and emergency rooms and "the increased medical costs for mental health patients was 17 times the savings in drug costs" (qtd. in Toughill A17).

Preventative medical actions are less expensive and are part of the reason why a system where everyone can seek necessary medical treatment without worry about cost means more health for all members of that society. Our medicare system might be even more efficient at ensuring health for all if it included free prescription drugs.

A one-tier health-care system treats all Canadians fairly: Rich and poor can get essential medical help. "In the 1960s, the Canadian society made the decision that no one should be denied medical care on the grounds that they couldn't afford it" (Lexchin A23).

The Canada Health Act itself specifically requires equity: It "requires provincial medicare plans to cover all medically necessary services" (Hamilton A1/Front).

Benjamin Freedman, professor at the McGill Centre for Medicine, Ethics and Law, and clinical ethicist at the Sir Mortimer B. Davis Jewish General Hospital, captures this valuing of equality: "Canada has a health-care system in which, roughly speaking, everyone is in the same boat. If the wealthy and powerful want better care—new drugs, shorter waiting lists, technological improvements—they have to change the system itself, making it available to everyone else at the same time" (B2).

Most Canadians who want a fair system would agree with Robert Evans: "Two-tier medicine would benefit some Canadians; that's why they want it.

They always have. An 'upper tier,' where the wealthy pay privately for preferred access to publicly insured services, would definitely be good for bank presidents and their doctors. Overall, our system would be less equitable, more costly, and less efficient. Most of us would lose" ("Canada Should" B6).

Freedman (B2) notes that allowing some people to pay more to get better medicine would lead some health-care professionals to leave the public system, reducing overall quality. And, as Evans notes, the wealthy are not clamouring for a truly pay-as-you-go system—it would be prohibitively expensive—they still want to have the public system pay; then, they'd add some money ("Canada Should" B6).

Many others agree that a two-tier system means that most people get poorer health care. Gwyn says, "The second, public, tier becomes a third-rate system" (D3). And Lewis notes, "The well-to-do desert the public system for private insurance schemes, and their support for the tax-based public system dwindles" (A19).

Most Canadians continue to agree with Linda McQuaig: "The notion that we must cut back on our *public* expenditures is based on the questionable assumption that our *private* expenditures are something more important—that Nintendo is more important than library services (164). Canadians have shown that they are willing to pay the taxes to keep a one-tier health insurance system because it is fairer."

Prime Minister Chrétien's remarks capture the Canadian fondness for our medicare system:

> There is a wide consensus in our country about preserving our distinctive state-funded health-care system called medicare. Under our system, you can go to the doctor of your choice. You are admitted to a hospital if you need to be. Period. Not if you have enough money. Or the right private plan. The fact is that no one in Canada needs to worry about medical bills. It is one of our proudest achievements. Canadians want to keep medicare. And we will. (qtd. in Marleau B2)

Columnist Richard Gwyn goes even further in describing medicare as the system that knits Canadians into a national community, the "symbolic railway of the 21st century" (D3).

You might think that we can count on our public health-care system being with us for a long time, given that so many Canadians are so fond of it. Perhaps not. Dr. Clement Richer, president of the Quebec Federation of General Practitioners, believes that rich people should be able to obtain CAT scans and other procedures more quickly than other citizens: "Some of our patients feel discriminated against, not to be able to pay to get exams more quickly . . . . If those who can afford it get service more quickly, I don't see any problem" (qtd. in Hamilton A1/Front).

There are some people who do not want all Canadians to have equal
access to health care, but most Canadians prefer to keep their publicly
funded health-insurance system because it is economical, efficient, and fair.
As Robert Evans notes ("Health Care" 27), "The system we have seems to
be a remarkably good compromise of quality, affordability, equity, and humanity. Not bad, eh?"

Hall 10

Works Cited

Beatty, Perrin. "A Comparison of Our Two Systems." Bennett and Adams

28–39.

Bennett, Arnold. Preface. Bennett and Adams xv–xxiv.

Bennett, Arnold, and Orvill Adams, eds. *Looking North for Health: What We Can

Learn From Canada's Health Care System*. San Francisco: Jossey-Bass, 1993.

Bergman, Brian. "Conscience of Canada: Emmett Hall Helped to Shape

Social Programs." *Maclean's* 27 Nov. 1995: 24.

——. "Canada Should Shun a Two-Tier System: The Wealthy Might Gain,

But at the Expense of Others." *Gazette* [Montreal] 20 May 1995, Final

Weekly Review: B6.

Evans, Robert. "Health Care in the Canadian Community." Bennett and

Adams 1–27.

Freedman, Benjamin. "Klein's Alberta, Two-Tier Medicine Would Pillage

Public Health Care." *Gazette* [Montreal] 12 Mar. 1995, final ed.: B2.

Gwyn, Richard. "Two-Tier Health Care Would Point to Two-Tier Society."

Toronto Star 1 Oct. 1995: D3.

Hall 11

Hamilton, Graeme. "Let Wealthy Pay for Fast Care: MDs; Head of Physician's

Group Calls for Two-Tier Medicare System." *Gazette* [Montreal] 2 May

1995, final ed.: A1/Front.

Lewis, Steven. "Canada's Health-Care Debate: First, Strip Away the Myths."

Globe and Mail 9 May 1995, Metro ed.: A19.

Lexchin, Joel. "Eves' Prescription for Inequality." *Toronto Star* 1 Jan. 1996: A23.

Marleau, Diane. Letter. *Gazette* [Montreal] 1 June 1995, final ed.: B2.

McGilly, Frank. *Canada's Public Social Services: Understanding Income and Health

Programs.* Toronto: McClelland and Stewart, 1990.

McQuaig, Linda. *The Wealthy Banker's Wife: The Assault on Equality in Canada.*

Toronto: Penguin, 1993.

Rachlis, Michael. "Shopping for Care Nonsensical." *Toronto Star* 19 Jan. 1996:

A20.

Terrana, Anna. "The National Forum on Health: High-Quality, Affordable

Health Care for all Canadians." *Chinatown News* 18 Feb. 1995: 14.

Toughill, Kelly. "Higher Medical Costs Coming for All." *Toronto Star* 24 Jan.

1996: A17.

Let's look at the first page, which is also the cover. It has an interesting appearance, doesn't it? What do you see nearest the top? Flush right, 1.25 centimetres from the top is the header: it's the last name of the writer and the page number. All the other margins are 2.5 centimetres. (Perhaps you're familiar with the appearance of this essay because you've been observing the advice in Box 1–1, "Make Your Writing Look Great." The advice in the box is largely based on the guidelines of the Modern Language Association.)

Glancing down the page, what do you see next? On this first page, the heading includes a line each for the writer's name, teacher's name, course name, and the date the work is submitted.

Notice that the title of the paper is centred and typed in mixed case: the important words are capitalized.

The next line of print is indented. Finally, you've reached the essay proper, and you're ready to read the introduction. Just before you do, glance through the rest of the essay. Remember: you just want to get an idea of what an MLA-style essay looks like. Notice that the header is on every page. All the lines of text are double-spaced. There are a lot of quotation marks and colons, and there are many more parentheses, aren't there? Inside the parentheses, the surnames indicate who wrote the information and the numerals indicate the page numbers on which the information is printed.

The last heading you see is "Works Cited," the list of materials referred to in the essay. Look on page 2 of "Canada's One-Tier Health Care Is the Better System." What is the third name you see? It's Bergman. Look for that name on the works-cited page. The entries are alphabetized by the writers' surnames. Ahh, there's Bergman. In the body of the essay, Hall told—in a brief code—where he found the information just presented in the essay. Hall cited the author of the information (Bergman) and the very page number (24) where Bergman presented that information. All the information you need to find and read that material is recorded in the list of works cited: Brian Bergman's article was titled "Conscience of Canada: Emmett Hall Helped to Shape Social Programs." It appeared on page 24 of *Maclean's* magazine in the issue published on November 27, 1995. In an MLA-style paper, there is always this congruity: the source of information that you cite in the text of the essay—where you usually indicate only the author and the page number—is always cited—with full publication information—on the works-cited page. A parenthetical documentation style is quite handy, isn't it?

Your preview of this paper has familiarized you with the appearance of an MLA-style paper. You'll use MLA style to format your research essay. As always, the content is most important in a research essay. Still, appearance matters, too, and so further details of how to format a paper in MLA style are presented here. Read on if you're ready to format your paper in MLA style. If you want to learn more about how to create an essay, leave this section, for now, and read chapter 8, "Writing Research Essays."

9.2 DOCUMENT SOURCES IN THE TEXT

When you write in MLA style, you must indicate in your text who wrote the specific information that you found in your search of the literature and precisely where in the published work that information appears. Later, you completely document the source in your works-cited list.

Look at the example of how Hall documented a source in the text of "Canada's One-Tier Health Care Is the Better System":

Columnist Richard Gwyn goes even further in describing medicare as the system that knits Canadians into a national community, the "symbolic railway of the 21st century" (D3).

As is usually the case, citing the author and the page number is sufficient to tell the reader who wrote—and where—the specific idea that the current medicare system unifies Canadians, just as the railway did in the nineteenth century. Many pages in documents posted on the World Wide Web are unnumbered. When you refer to an unpaginated Web document, simply note the author. If paragraphs or sections *are* numbered, include such numbers; for example, you might write (Smith, pars. 20–21). The numbers after *pars.*, an abbreviation of *paragraphs*, tell the reader where in the Web document you found the information you discuss or quote.

Here are some additional requirements of MLA style.

✳ When citing authors and page numbers, parenthesize as little as possible. A lengthy parenthetical comment interrupts your reader's thoughts. Look at the problem created by this documentation decision:

X You can conserve water (City of Niagara Falls) if you think conservation is important.

Parenthetically citing such a lengthy corporate author in the middle of the sentence creates too large an interruption. Make it a little easier for your reader to follow your thinking by parenthesizing as little of a reference as possible. Instead do as Hall did in the second example below where the author's surname, Beatty, is incorporated into the essay text and only the page number is parenthesized.

The City of Niagara Falls suggests several ways to conserve water.

✳ For short quotations, incorporate the quotation and documentation into your text. Most of the time you will probably reword the information you learn in your literature search, just as in this example:

Beatty estimated that more than three times as much money is lost to administration costs in the United States than in Canada (34).

But sometimes you will feel that the source expresses the information so well that you want to quote the writer's exact words. If the quotation comprises four or fewer lines of your paper, simply incorporate those words with your own, as in this example:

Gwyn says, "The second, public, tier becomes a third-rate system" (D3).

Note that the parenthetical element, the page number, precedes the punctuation that ends the sentence containing the quoted material. Notice that Hall has placed even this brief parenthetical element at the end of the point he is making so he interrupts the reader's thoughts as little as possible.

★ **Embed documentation around indented quotations.** When you include a direct quotation longer than four lines (three lines of verse), remember to omit the quotation marks and indent the whole quotation 2.5 centimetres (10 characters) from the left margin. Continue double-spacing and observe the usual 2.5-centimetre (one-inch) right margin.

Try to give the reader the information about your longer quotations—who wrote the information and on which pages it was printed—in the text rather than in parentheses, just as you did for quotations that are incorporated into your text. Look at this excerpt from Hall's paper to see how it is done.

Prime Minister Chrétien's remarks capture the Canadian fondness for our medicare system:

> There is a wide consensus in our country about preserving our distinctive state-funded health-care system called medicare. Under our system, you can go to the doctor of your choice. You are admitted to a hospital if you need to be. Period. Not if you have enough money. Or the right private plan. The fact is that no one in Canada needs to worry about medical bills. It is one of our proudest achievements. Canadians want to keep medicare. And we will. (qtd. in Marleau B2)

Only the print source and page number have been parenthesized. And that interruption occurs at the end of a natural break in the writing, a place where the reader would normally pause to consider what has been said so far. Note that the quotation concludes with the ending punctuation of the quoted material. The parenthetical reference to the page number has simply been included at the end of the block quotation.

Do not begin a block quotation with a paragraph indentation, even if there is one in the original text. But if you quote more than one paragraph, indent each subsequent paragraph three additional character spaces.

★ **When citing two authors with the same surname, precede each surname with the author's first initial:**

C. Davies asserts this view (22), and so does D. Davies (126).

★ **Cite co-authors in text and parenthetically.**

Miezitis and Rogers wrote about reflective and impulsive children in grade one classrooms: Generally, teachers prefer to distance themselves from impulsive children (Miezitis and Rogers 11).

When you cite a publication with more than three authors, print the surname of the first author and then use *et al.* in place of the other names. Finish with the page number unless you are referring to the work as a whole.

X: Miller, Bogale, Sonnes, and Chan recommended a new name for the attraction (37).

OK: Miller et al. recommended a new name for the attraction (37).

⋆ **When citing multiple works by the same author, add a shortened version of the title of each work.** Notice the way Hall did this in the essay "Canada's One-Tier Health Care Is the Better System."

And, as Evans notes, the wealthy are not clamouring for a truly pay-as-you-go system—it would be prohibitively expensive—they still want to have the public system pay; then, they'd add some money ("Canada Should" B6).

As Robert Evans notes ("Health Care" 27), "The system we have seems to be a remarkably good compromise of quality, affordability, equity, and humanity. Not bad, eh?"

⋆ **Cite organization authors.**

The Canadian Red Cross Society (n.p.) recommends that you dive carefully.

Cite a corporate or organization author when the publication, in this case a brochure, does not indicate the name of an author. Give the page number, as usual, even after a corporate author. In this example, no page number is indicated because the pamphlet is unpaginated. This work could be referred to in a parenthetical citation, but the corporate author's name is so long it would tend to interrupt the reader's thoughts. Since the organization name is not the name of a document, don't enclose it with quotation marks or italicize it.

⋆ **Cite the volume number as well as the page number when referring to multivolume works.** This entry (**Britton 2: 312**) means that Britton wrote the information referred to on page 312 of the second volume of the work indicated in the list of works cited.

⋆ **Don't cite page numbers when referring to whole works.** Don't indicate a page number in the following sentence because the reference refers to the work as a whole, not some specific part.

You'll find many examples of fine writing in *Canadian Classics: An Anthology of Short Stories* (Metcalf and Struthers).

* Don't cite page numbers for documents arranged alphabetically (e.g., dictionaries and encyclopedias). Document a reference to a dictionary or encyclopedia entry in this fashion:

The game of crokinole derives from the French word *croquignole*, a flick ("Crokinole").

Essentially, the word is treated as an article title. You can see on the works-cited page that it has been included in the *c*'s, its appropriate place in an alphabetized list. The additional bibliographic information is given there, too. There is no need for a page number in the text or works-cited entry because a reader will easily find the entry since a dictionary's entries are arranged alphabetically.

* Use semicolons between multiple citations in a single parenthetical reference. To show widespread agreement among authorities, you may want to briefly refer to several experts by citing them in a parenthetical reference in your text. In this excerpt, the author has indicated that several people writing about the information superhighway have described how to bank by modem. Notice that each citation is separated by a semicolon.

Already some people are banking from home (Antonoff et al. 98; Israelson D4; Vizard 30).

* Cross-reference two or more references to the same document. The next group of references shows how your works-cited page might look in an earlier stage of your essay before you realize that one work has been referred to three times. (Note that *Ed.* is capitalized when it stands for *edited by*, but *ed.* when it means *editors*.)

Beatty, Perrin. "A Comparison of Our Two Systems." *Looking North for Health: What We Can Learn From Canada's Health Care System*. Ed. Arnold Bennett and Orvill Adams. San Francisco: Jossey-Bass, 1993. 28–39.

Bennett, Arnold. Preface. *Looking North for Health: What We Can Learn From Canada's Health Care System*. Ed. Arnold Bennett and Orvill Adams. San Francisco: Jossey-Bass, 1993. xv–xxiv.

Evans, Robert. "Health Care in the Canadian Community." *Looking North for Health: What We Can Learn From Canada's Health Care System*. Ed. Arnold Bennett and Orvill Adams. San Francisco: Jossey-Bass, 1993. 1–27.

Is it really necessary to repeat so much information? The MLA guidelines advise that you cross-reference instead. Look at these revised entries to see how to do this.

Beatty, Perrin. "A Comparison of Our Two Systems." Bennett and Adams 28–39.

Bennett, Arnold. Preface. Bennett and Adams xv–xxiv.

Bennett, Arnold, and Orvill Adams, eds. *Looking North for Health: What We Can Learn From Canada's Health Care System.* San Francisco: Jossey-Bass, 1993.

Evans, Robert. "Health Care in the Canadian Community." Bennett and Adams 1 27.

Now the author has completed only one reference for the whole work and made three briefer references to parts of the document.

* **Cite an indirect source of information by using *qtd. in* (quoted in).** In the following quotation, Hall indicates that he knows what Dr. Clement Richer said, not because Hall heard him, but because Hall read a quotation of Dr. Richer's remarks in reporter Graeme Hamilton's article "Let Wealthy Pay for Fast Care: MDs; Head of Physician's Group Calls for Two-Tier Medicare System." If you examine Hall's works-cited entry, you can see that this was published in the Montreal *Gazette* on May 2, 1995, on page A1 of the front section.

Dr. Clement Richer, president of the Quebec Federation of General Practitioners, believes that rich people should be able to obtain CAT scans and other procedures more quickly than other citizens: "Some of our patients feel discriminated against, not to be able to pay to get exams more quickly . . . . If those who can afford it get service more quickly, I don't see any problem" (qtd. in Hamilton A1/Front).

* **For classic prose works, cite more than just the page number**. Classic prose works have been published in several editions. When you indicate the page numbers of *your* edition of the classic, your reader will be frustrated in following your discussion if she is using a different edition, unless you provide additional information such as references to chapter numbers. In your parenthetical reference, cite the page number from your edition, then cite the book or chapter number (**112; ch. 6** or **214; bk. 2, ch. 3**).

* **For classic plays and poems, omit page numbers and cite part and line.** If you quote lines 6 and 7 in the second scene of act 1 of William Shakespeare's *Taming of the Shrew*, cite this information parenthetically, in this way:

(1.2.6–7.)

Some teachers prefer students to use Roman numerals for play parts (e.g., **I.i.6–7**), but the MLA handbook recommends using Arabic numerals.

Robert Hayman wrote the first poetry in English in what would become Canada. These lines show where his heart stayed: "Although in cloaths, company, buildings faire, / With England, New-found-land cannot compare:" (lines 1–2).

Once you have indicated that you are citing lines, you can omit the word *lines*, and just include the numbers of the lines.

* Indent dialogue quoted from plays. When you quote dialogue between characters in a play, indent the quoted material 2.5 centimetres or ten characters from the left margin. At the new left margin, type in block capitals the character's name, then a period. Now quote the first line. If the character speaks for more than a line, indent the remaining lines an extra three spaces after the one-inch left margin. When a new character speaks, begin by typing that name at the one-inch, indented left margin and follow the same procedure as for the first character. Complete the indented dialogue quotation by parenthesizing the line numbers quoted from the play. In the following example, Robertson Davies did not provide line numbers.

> MRS STEWARD. How fortunate. I have excellent grape jelly.

> MRS MOODIE. I dote upon grape jelly. (598; act 1)

* Favour the present tense. Use the present tense when discussing the research literature ("Evans notes") and your analysis ("Canadians like their health-insurance system").

9.3 DOCUMENT SOURCES IN THE LIST OF WORKS CITED

The citing of the author and page number in the text is the first step you take to help your reader distinguish your ideas from the intellectual contributions of others. Each entry in the body of your writing is matched by an entry in the works-cited section. In *Works Cited*, you provide all the information your reader needs to obtain that cited material for personal study. That spirit—make it easy for your reader to find the documents you refer to—is the reason for the detailed information in this section.

As you look over the detailed instructions for completing a works-cited list, you may be fatigued by the prospect of how much work it takes to carry out these instructions. This is a good time to remind you of two important points. Perhaps hearing them again, in this new context, will refresh your spirits.

You go to the effort of preparing a works-cited list as a courtesy for your reader. Do this well, and you make a good impression on your reader because you make it easy for him or her to find the writings that you discuss in your research. Since you spend more time reading than writing, most of the time you benefit from someone else's work. That writer made it easy for you to find the source documents.

There is another advantage to learning to use this system of documentation: Once you become efficient at using these guidelines—I don't think anyone ever memorizes them—you will find that you can complete bibliographies more quickly. Knowing the standard ways to record the information means you won't waste time re-inventing logical ways to create a bibliographical entry.

★ **Place your list of works cited at the end of your paper.** After the last page of the text of your essay, start a new page to list works cited. Continue the page numbering in the header. If you concluded your essay on page 12, your works-cited page has the same header as the rest of your essay, but the page number is 13. Continue to double-space. Centre the title *Works Cited*. If the works cited span more than one page, do not repeat the title, just continue with the alphabetized list of entries.

★ **Alphabetize all the entries in the works-cited list.** As they read through an essay, readers often flip to the works-cited list to read the details about the work referred to in the body of the paper. You alphabetize the entries to make it easy for your readers to find each entry of interest.

★ **Use common abbreviations in the works-cited list.**

Ed. for edited, ed. for editor

trans. for translator

★ **If a works-cited entry exceeds one line in length, indent the next line (or lines) one tab or five spaces (1.25 centimetres) from the left margin.** Entries are easier to read if each begins with a hanging indent, as indicated in the following example.

Bennett, Arnold, and Orvill Adams, eds. *Looking North for Health: What We Can Learn From Canada's Health Care System.* San Francisco: Jossey-Bass, 1993.

★ **Leave one character space after each piece of punctuation in citations.** When using word-processing software (with proportional spacing), leave a single space after commas, periods, question marks, and colons in works-cited entries. For example, leave a single space after a colon that separates a title of a work from its subtitle.

★ **Study these examples to create a correct entry for the different types of documents you refer to.** As you prepare your works-cited list, look through the list below for an example of the same type of document you refer to in your paper. Then follow the guidelines for that type of publication to create a correct works-cited entry for your reference material. You'll do it with increasing speed and ease as you become more familiar with the conventions. This section is organized into Citing Whole Documents (Books and Pamphlets), Citing Articles in Books and Periodicals, Citing CD-ROM's and Other Electronic Sources, and a miscellaneous section, Citing Other Publications. Within each category, the key words are alphabetized to make it easier to find an example of the type of work you must reference. Still, you will probably feel that creating a list of works cited is a tedious job. It is. It requires painstaking, fastidious attention to detail. Yet it also requires creativity and intelligence, so you can't just go on automatic to do the job. You'll often have to consult more than one example to reference a document you refer to in your essay; for example, if you read an article from a magazine—but you never held that magazine in your hands because you found the article while browsing the Net—you'll need to refer to entry 29 ("article in magazine") and example 40 ("public online posting").

Citing Whole Documents (Books and Pamphlets)

1. book by anonymous or unknown author
2. book by corporate author
3. book by editor, translator, or compiler
4. book by one author
5. book by two or three authors
6. book by multiple authors
7. book in language other than English
8. book in multiple volumes
9. book in republished edition
10. book in second and subsequent editions
11. book in series
12. book in translation
13. book with multiple publishers
14. book with publisher's imprint
15. book/brochure without publication information or pagination
16. books by same author, editor, translator
17. books by same authors
18. conference proceedings
19. dissertation (published)
20. dissertation (unpublished)
21. government publication
22. pamphlet
23. report

Citing Articles in Books and Periodicals

24. abstract from abstracts journal

25. afterword

26. article in anthology

27. article in journal (each volume is paginated)

28. article in journal (each issue is paginated)

29. article in magazine

30. article in microfilm collection

31. article in newspaper

32. article in reference book

33. article that is serialized

34. editorial

35. foreword

36. introduction

37. letter to the editor

38. preface

39. review

Citing CD-ROM's and Other Electronic Sources

40. public online posting

41. publication from online database

42. publication from CD-ROM, diskette

43. publication from periodically updated CD-ROM database

Citing Other Publications

44. advertisement

45. audio recording

46. cartoon/comic strip

47. e-mail

48. film

49. interview

50. legal source

51. letter

52. lecture

53. map

54. manuscript

55. memo

56. musical composition

57. performance

58. radio or television program

59. speech

60. video recording

61. work of art

Citing Whole Documents (Books and Pamphlets)

Before studying the specific conventions for various whole works, take a close look at a sample entry to increase your familiarity with the most common elements of a works-cited entry.

Saul, John Ralston. *The Unconscious Civilization.* **Concord: Anansi Press, 1995.**

Begin with the name of the author. Then present the title; if you're listing the title of a whole work, use italics if you are word processing or underline if you are handwriting. Next, state the city in which the book was published. Follow that with a colon, and indicate the name of the publisher. You may omit words such as *Co.*, *Inc.*, and *Publisher.* Place a comma after the publisher and complete the entry with the date of the publication. Note the use of the comma to separate the author's surname and given name(s). Use the period to separate elements of the entry and to conclude it. You will accurately prepare an MLA-style works-cited list if you attend to similar details in the sample entries.

1. book by anonymous or unknown author

When there is no author listed on the title page, substitute the title for the author's name. Alphabetize that entry by the first important word of the title (not the articles *a, an, the*). This entry would be entered with the *s*'s, not the *t*'s.

The Sponges of Lake Winnipeg. Brandon: Wishful Books, 1996.

2. book by corporate author

When an association or committee publishes a book, they do not always list an author on the title page. Cite as the author the name of the group, even if they have also published the work.

Delrina (Canada). *Getting Started Guide.* Toronto: Delrina, 1995.

3. book by editor, translator, or compiler

Record an editor, translator, or compiler in the same way as an author, but after the surname(s), write the abbreviation *ed.* or *eds.*; *trans.*; *comp.* or *comps.* (in lowercase), followed by a period.

Arnold Bennett and Orvill Adams, eds. *Looking North for Health: What We Can Learn From Canada's Health Care System.* San Francisco: Jossey-Bass, 1993.

4. book by one author

McQuaig, Linda. *The Wealthy Banker's Wife: The Assault on Equality in Canada.* Toronto: Penguin, 1993.

5. book by two or three authors

Reverse the surname and first name for only the first author. Separate the given and surnames with a comma and add *and* before the author's last name.

Norton, Sarah, and Brian Green. *Essay Essentials.* Toronto: Holt, Rinehart and Winston, 1991.

Silverman, Rita, William M. Welty, and Sally Lyon. *Case Studies for Teacher Problem Solving.* 2nd ed. New York: McGraw-Hill, 1996.

6. book by multiple authors

For books written by more than three authors, you may simply indicate the first author, and—after a comma—add *et al.* (Latin for *and others*), or you may record all the authors, in the same way you did for works by three authors.

McCown, R.R., et al. *Educational Psychology: A Learning-Centered Approach to Classroom Practice.* Canadian Edition. Scarborough: Allyn & Bacon, 1996.

7. book in language other than English

Proceed as for an English–language book.

Fiot, Jacques. *Le Français Par Les Mots Croises.* Paris: Librairie Hachette, 1969.

8. book in multiple volumes

Brown, Russell, and Donna Bennett, eds. *An Anthology of Canadian Literature in English.* 2 vols. Toronto: Oxford University Press, 1982.

9. book in republished edition

When you are using a reprint of a book, note the year the book was originally published. Put that date right after the title. This example also indicates that Collins Crime is an imprint used by Collins Publishers.

Wright, Eric. *Smoke Detector.* 1984. Don Mills: Collins Crime–Collins, 1985.

10. book in second and subsequent editions

Kerrigan, Donna, Ray Matthews, and Gary Webb. *Who's Going to Read This Anyway?* 4th ed. Toronto: Holt, Rinehart and Winston, 1991.

11. book in series

If the title or half-title page indicates that a book is part of a series, place the series name, any number, and a period just before the publication information.

Gerson, Carole, and Gwendolyn Davies, eds. *Canadian Poetry: From the Beginnings Through the First World War.* New Canadian Library. Toronto: McClelland & Stewart, 1994.

12. book in translation

Proceed much as for an edited book.

Atwood, Margaret. *Marquee au Corps.* Trans. Helene Filion. Montreal: Les Quinze-Filiale de Sogides, 1983.

13. book with multiple publishers

Note that the order of the publishing companies is the same in the entry as it is in the book.

Paikeday, Thomas M., ed. *Penguin Canadian Dictionary.* Markham: Penguin Books Canada; Mississauga: Copp Clark Pitman, 1990.

14. book with publisher's imprint

Collins published this book under the imprint *Collins Crime.* Indicate this in the works-cited list by starting with the imprint and then putting a hyphen before the name of the parent publisher. In the example, the *1983* indicates that the book was first published in 1983. Omit this information if you're using a first edition.

Wright, Eric *The Night the Gods Smiled.* 1983. Toronto: Collins Crime Collins, 1984.

15. book/brochure without publication information or pagination

Sometimes books do not have some of the information you are expected to record for a works-cited entry. Use these MLA conventions to tell your readers the information that was not available from the publication. Capitalize and punctuate just as though you had the usual information.

n.d.   (no date of publication)
n.p.   (no place of publication)
n.p.   (no publisher)
n.pag.   (no pagination)

Canadian Red Cross Society. *Safe Diving.* N.p.: Canadian Red Cross Society, 1989. N.pag.

Commemorative Services of Ontario. *The Facts about Cremation.* Toronto: Commemorative Services of Ontario, n.d.

16. books by same author, editor, translator

When you want to cite another book by the same writer, do not repeat the author entry. Instead, type three hyphens, a period, and the next title. Alphabetize the list of the author's works by book title. If the writer served as editor or translator, write the three hyphens, a comma, and the corresponding abbreviation (e.g., *ed.*).

McQuaig, Linda. *Shooting the Hippo: Death by Deficit and Other Canadian Myths.* Toronto: Viking-Penguin, 1995.

———. *The Wealthy Banker's Wife: The Assault on Equality in Canada.* Toronto: Penguin, 1993.

17. books by same authors

Proceed as you did for books by same author. Do this only if the multiple-author teams are identical; otherwise, make a new entry for each unique writing team.

18. conference proceedings

Liu, Mingho. "On-Line Identification of Coherent Generators Using Multilayer Feedforward Neural Networks." *Proceedings of the IEEE International Conference on Industrial Technology.* Guangzhou, China. 5–9 Dec. 1994: 803–807.

19. dissertation (published)

Model the following entry for a dissertation published by University Microfilms International. Note that the title is italicized.

Rogers, Douglas B. *Are College Content-Area Professors Practicing Writing Across the Curriculum?* Diss. State U. of New York at Buffalo, 1993. Ann Arbor: UMI, 1994. 9335162.

20. dissertation (unpublished)

Rogers, Douglas B. "Are College Content-Area Professors Practicing Writing Across the Curriculum?" Diss. State U. of New York at Buffalo, 1993.

21. government publication

Begin the entry with the name of the government. Then note its particular department or agency. Canadian federal government documents are published in Ottawa by the Queen's Printer.

Canada. Ministry of Industry. Statistics Canada. *Household Facilities by Income and Other Characteristics.* Ottawa: Queen's Printer, 1993.

22. pamphlet

Follow the same conventions as for a book.

Canadian Red Cross Society. *Safe Diving.* N.p.: Canadian Red Cross Society, 1989. N.pag.

23. report

If a report is published as a whole, rather than as part of a collection, italicize the title. If there is no author noted, and it's published by the organization, start with the name of the corporation or organization. If you found the report on the Internet, add the additional information, as indicated in the section on electronic sources.

Ferris, Jackie, and Tania Stirpe. *Gambling in Ontario: A Report From a General Population Survey on Gambling-Related Problems and Opinions.* N.p.: Addiction Research Foundation, 10 Aug. 1995.

Information Technology Association of Canada. *The Canadian Information Infrastructure: An Agenda for Action.* June 1994. 24 July 1996 <http://www.itac.ca/ITAC/agendaen.html/>.

Citing Articles in Books and Periodicals

24. abstract from abstracts journal

To create an entry for an abstract you obtained from a journal of abstracts, begin by citing the publication data for the full-length document. Then, if it is not evident from the title, add the word *Abstract*. Finish with the publication information for the source of the abstract. Note that you do not need to indicate the page number of the abstract if it is presented in the journal in a way that makes it as easy for the reader to find as numbered pages would.

Gilbert, Sharon L. "Perspectives of Rural Prospective Teachers Toward Teaching in Urban Schools." *Urban Education* 30 (1995): 290–305. *Child Development Abstracts and Bibliography* 70.1 (1996): item 125.

25. afterword

Treat an afterword the same way as you would a foreward (see item 35 in this list), but substitute the word *Afterword*.

26. article in anthology

When an essay, poem, or other work is published in a collection, follow the conventions for citing a book, with these additional considerations. Cite the author of the piece and the title. The title will usually be within quotation marks because it is a part of a document, not a whole work. Now, name the whole work. Separate these elements with periods. Next, use an abbreviation to indicate the editor or translator of the whole work (the abbreviation *Ed.* is read aloud as "edited by"), and write out the name in the first name, surname order. Finish the entry with the city, publisher, date, and page numbers of the piece cited, as in this entry:

Evans, Robert. "Health Care in the Canadian Community." *Looking North for Health: What We Can Learn From Canada's Health Care System.* Ed. Arnold Bennett and Orvill Adams. San Francisco: Jossey-Bass, 1993. 1–27.

27. article in journal (each volume is paginated)

Most academic journals are paginated by volume. That means that several issues together constitute one volume of the journal. Sometimes the journal's volume will correspond to the calendar year, but more often a particular volume is made up of all the issues published in an academic year, typically September to June. If the volume is continuously paginated, each new issue of the journal starts numbering one page number higher than the last page of the previous issue. It is easy to find particular pages because the whole volume is paginated. Thus, you need to indicate only the volume number of the journal. Leave out the issue number. After the year, do indicate the pages on which the article is printed. Notice that the names of periodicals, including newspapers and magazines, are italicized; they are followed by *no* punctuation.

Rogers, Douglas B. "Assessing Study Skills." *Journal of Reading* 27 (1984): 346–354.

28. article in journal (each issue is paginated)

When a journal begins each new issue by numbering from page one, a reader will find it easier to find a particular issue if you cite the number of the issue in your works-cited list. In the following example, the *16* indicates the volume number and the *2* the issue number.

Miezitis, Solveiga and Douglas Rogers. "Teacher Interpersonal Distancing and Pupil Behaviour." *Ontario Psychologist* 16.2 (1984): 9–12.

29. article in magazine

Examine the following entries to see the conventions for citing a magazine article. Here are a few more considerations. When the article is not printed on consecutive pages, cite the page number for the first page and a plus sign. For a magazine, even when it indicates volume and number, cite just the day (if indicated), month (as abbreviations, except for May, June, and July), and the year, as shown below.

Frost, Mimi. "Up in Smoke: Why Teen Girls Don't Quit." *Chatelaine* July 1996: 29+.

Bergman, Brian. "Conscience of Canada: Emmett Hall Helped to Shape Social Programs." *Maclean's* 27 Nov. 1995: 24.

30. article in microfilm collection

Provide the information for the print version (if there is any). Follow with the information about the microform.

Kurfis, J. *Do Students Really Learn from Writing?* (1985). ERIC Document Reproduction Service No. ED 293 123.

31. article in newspaper

Here are a few extra requirements you must meet to correctly cite a newspaper article.

• Omit introductory articles from newspaper names: write **Calgary Herald**, not **The Calgary Herald**.

- Add the name of the city to an entry for a local newspaper: write *Free Press* **[London]** or *Free Press* **[Winnipeg]**.

- If the newspaper publishes more than one edition, indicate the edition you referred to. After the date, add a comma and an abbreviation for the edition.

Ramsay, Cynthia. "Don't Recycle the Same Old Myths About Health Care." *Globe and Mail* 15 May 1995, Metro ed.: A13.

- Use a plus sign (+) to indicate nonconsecutive pages of an article. Write the number of the first page of the article and, immediately, a plus sign if the article is not printed on consecutive pages.

Airhart, Sharon. "On-Line Recipe Exchange Lets Users Cook Up a Storm." *Toronto Star* 17 May 1995: E1+.

32. article in reference book

Follow the guidelines for a piece in an anthology: start with the author's name (if available) and then the title of the part. For a well-known reference work, record only the edition and year of publication. You do not even need to indicate page numbers if the entries of the work are arranged alphabetically. Cite an editor when the piece is from a little-known reference work and provide all the usual publication information.

"Crokinole." *The Canadian Oxford Dictionary.* Toronto: Oxford University Press, 1998.

33. article that is serialized

If an article is published under one name by one author but in two or more issues of a periodical, create one works-cited entry for the series. If each part of the series has a different title, list them all. After the usual bibliographic information, add a note that indicates the article is part of a series. You will have to think creatively to ensure that your reader gets all the information needed to find the material you cited.

Israelson, David. "Canada in Castro's Cuba." *Toronto Star* 13 July 1996: F1+; 14 July 1996: D1+; 15 July 1996: E1+.

Sarah, Robyn. "The Dumbing-Down of Literacy." *Globe and Mail* 30 May 1996: A24. Third of a series begun 28 May 1996.

34. editorial

Most editorials are unsigned, so begin the entry with the title of the editorial. Follow the title with the descriptive term *Editorial.*

"Traffic Plans Beg for Answers." Editorial. *Niagara Advance* 14 Mar. 1995: 4.

35. foreword

Begin the entry with the name of the writer of the book part. Then type the name of the book part (*Foreword*) and a period. Follow this with the name of the whole work. If the writer of the part is the same as the editor or writer of the whole work, indicate the last name again, but precede it with *By*. If the writer or editor of the part is different from the writer of the whole, precede the name with *By*, and then cite the complete name of the writer of the whole document. Write this name beginning with the given name and following with the surname. Complete the entry in the usual way, and add the page numbers that comprise the part.

Monty, Jean C. Foreword. *Canadian Internet Handbook.* By Jim Carroll and Rick Broadhead. Scarborough, ON: Prentice Hall Canada, 1994. xiii–xvi.

36. introduction

Follow the instructions for citing a foreword, but substitute the word *Introduction*.

37. letter to the editor

Cite a letter to the editor as you would any other newspaper article except that instead of an article title, you will type *Letter*. The titles that newspapers sometimes give to letters are not part of the letters, so don't include those titles in your citations.

Rogers, Douglas B. Letter. *Standard* [St. Catharines] 10 Apr. 1996: B5.

Rogers, Linda. Reply to letter of Dick Harrington. *Standard* [St. Catharines] 19 July 1996: B5.

38. preface

Proceed as for a foreword, substituting the word *Preface*.

Bennett, Arnold. Preface. *Looking North for Health: What We Can Learn From Canada's Health Care System.* Ed. Arnold Bennett and Orvill Adams. San Francisco: Jossey-Bass, 1993. xv–xxiv.

39. review

Cite the reviewer's name and the title of the review. Write *Rev. of* and indicate the title of the work reviewed. Place a comma and name the author, choreographer, or other type of artist. Add relevant information when citing a review of a performance. If the review is of more than one work, list titles and artists in the order indicated by the reviewer, and separate entries with commas. If the reviewer is not indicated, begin the entry with the title of the review; if the review is untitled, begin the works-cited entry with *Rev. of*, and alphabetize the entry by the title of the work reviewed.

Galway, Conchita. Rev. of *The Art of Mary Pratt: The Substance of Light.* Vancouver Art Gallery. 20 Dec. 1995–3 Mar. 1996. *Planet of the Arts* [Emily Carr Institute of Art and Design, Vancouver] Feb./Mar. 1996: 22.

Doughty, Howard A. Rev. of *False God: How the Globalization Myth Has Impoverished Canada*, by James Laxer, and *The Wealthy Banker's Wife: The Assault on Equality in Canada*, by Linda McQuaig. *The College Quarterly* 1.1 (1993): 20.

Citing CD-ROM's and Other Electronic Sources

It is really just the relative newness of these media that gives writers pause for thought about how to refer to them in a works-cited entry. For the most part, you can treat them as you would books, magazines, and so forth, but include the additional information that a reader needs to find them. If you are citing a document that *does* exist in printed form, record that information first. Continue by presenting the information that tells the address or path the reader must follow to find the electronic version that *you* read. When citing any document that could be altered after you read it, record the date on which you accessed it. In this section, the references to authors Gates, Madige, and McBane are from "Internet Ethics."

40. public online posting

The Internet provides several different ways to publish information. Study the examples to see how to document these materials. Generally, you begin your entry with the name of the writer, the title of the electronic posting, the date it was posted, the name of the forum, and the source; include the date you accessed the information; and conclude with the universal resource locator (URL) between angle brackets. If formatting requirements lead you to break up an URL, separate after a slash, and do *not* add a hyphen.

The first example shows how to document one of the most common electronic sources, a paper published to a Web site.

Canada. Industry Canada. "Chemicals and Bio-Industries." *Strategis: Industry Canada Online.* 17 July 1996 <http://www.strategis.ic.gc.ca>.

If Industry Canada had dated this document, you would note that date just after the title of the material.

The following example shows how to document material that can be downloaded via the file transfer protocol (FTP). The second date shows when the writer downloaded the file. If the document is a whole work, rather than a part of a larger document, italicize the title. If Gates' book was part of a project, the name of the project—just in mixed case, with no quotation marks or italics—would be noted before the publication date.

Gates, Gary. *Shakespeare and His Muse*. 1 Mar. 1996. 17 April 1997 <ftp.guten.net.gproject/texts/english/bard/research/muse.txt>.

The next example shows how to document a posting on a listserv.

Kaufman-Lacusta, Maxine. "MidEast Peace Now." Online posting. 1 Oct. 1998. Quaker Peace and Social Action Listserv. 1 Oct. 1998 <http://www.quaker-p@earlham.edu>.

To document information taken from a Usenet news group, study this example:

Madige, Ellen. *How to Build a Better Mousetrap*. Online posting. 16 Jan. 1996. 21 Jan. 1996 <news: sci.tech.inventions.mousetrap>.

Refer to material from an online chat by first naming the online speaker. If McBane had titled her posting, that title—within quotation marks—would follow her surname.

McBane, Lisa. Online posting. 8 Mar. 1996. 9 Mar. 1996 <telnet://telnetworld.sensemedia.net:6677,#egypt>.

The next example, from the *MLA Style Manual and Guide to Scholarly Publishing* by Joseph Gibaldi (217) shows how to document an article that was first published in hard copy and is also available via a gopher. The publication date is noted first, then the access date.

McDonald, Henry. "The Narrative Act: Wittgenstein and Narratology." *Surfaces* 4.4 (1994): 21 pp. Jan. 1997 <gopher://surfaces.umontreal.ca:70/00/Articles/Ascii/Vol4/A-McDonald.txt>.

The following example shows how to document material that came from someone's World Wide Web home page.

Rogers, Linda. Home page. 18 July 1998 <http://www3.sympatico.ca/douglas.rogers>.

When a page is untitled, use a brief description, such as *Home page*.

41. publication from online database

Study this example from the MLA Web site:

Victoria Women Writers Project. Ed. Perry Willett. Apr. 1997. Indiana U. 26 Apr. 1997 <http://www.indiana.edu/~letrs/vwwp/>.

The first date indicates when the document was last revised. The second date tells readers when *you* read the document.

42. publication from CD-ROM, diskette

To cite a document/program published on a diskette, follow the conventions for a book, but just before indicating the city of publication, add the work *Diskette* and a period.

Feldstein, Sandy. *Practical Theory*. Diskette. Van Nuys, CA: Alfred, 1983.

43. publication from periodically updated CD-ROM database

When you find a document by searching a CD-ROM database—perhaps the *Canadian NewsDisc*—begin your citation by noting the hard-copy source of the document. Then, italicize the title of the database, name the publication medium, note the name of the publisher of the database, and conclude with the date of publication of that version of the electronic database.

Larsen-Ko, Marnie. "No Excuse for Hitting Children: Every Act of Violence Against a Child Leaves a Permanent Emotional Scar." *Calgary Herald* 10 June 1996: A6. *Canadian NewsDisc*. CD-ROM. CEDROM-SNi. 1995–1996.

Citing Other Publications

44. advertisement

Start your works-cited entry with the subject of the advertisement, neither italicized nor in quotation marks. After a period, write the word *Advertisement*, and follow that with another period. Finally, include the usual information about the publication in which the advertisement appears.

National Film Board of Canada. Advertisement. *This Magazine*. Mar./Apr. 1996: 12.

The Great Canadian Bagel. Advertisement. *Newsworld*. 10 July 1996.

45. audio recording

Decide which artist you want to emphasize, and begin the entry with that surname. Next, use periods to separate title of recording, other important contributing artists, and the city of publication. Place a comma between the city and the year of publication, as in this example where the additional information reveals that Aglukark self-published the CD in 1992 and that EMI Music Canada is a publisher's imprint of Thorn EMI.

Aglukark, Susan. *Arctic Rose*. 1992. Mississauga: EMI Music Canada–Thorn EMI, 1994.

In the next example, note the addition of the word *Audiocassette*. Since the CD has become the standard form for recorded music and spoken-word, you do not need to indicate when a recording is a CD. Indicate when you cite less common formats such as audiotape, LP, or videodisc.

Connors, Stompin' Tom. *More of the Stompin' Tom Phenomenon*. Audiocassette. N.p.: Crown Vetch Music Ltd., 1991.

46. cartoon/comic strip

Begin the entry with the surname of the cartoonist. Add the title of the cartoon (if it has one), the word *Cartoon*, and finish with the information about the publication, as usual.

Bell-Lundy, Susan. *Between Friends*. Cartoon. *Toronto Star* 11 July 1996: F8.

47. e-mail

Begin your works-cited entry with the surname of the writer of the e-mail. Next, tell the name of the e-mail—if your correspondent titled it—and put quotation marks around it; otherwise, describe it (*E-mail to the author* or *E-mail to President Patterson*). Conclude with the date of the communication.

Rogers, Damian. "I'm a Little Short this Month." E-Mail to Douglas B. Rogers. 5 May 1999.

48. film

Cite a film as you would cite a video recording, except that you do not need to note that it is a film because this is considered the usual format.

49. interview

Begin the entry with the surname of the person interviewed. Add any pertinent information including the following: title, label *Interview* (if that is not apparent in the title), and the usual publication information.

Polley, Sarah. "The Adventures of Sarah Polley." Interview. *This Magazine* Mar./Apr. 1996: 13.

Rogers, Damian. Personal interview. 19 May 1999.

50. legal source

Refer to bills, laws, acts, and other legal documents by name:

British North America Act

Bill 167

Canada Student Financial Assistance Act

Constitution Act, 1982

Canadian Charter of Rights and Freedoms, Sec. 15(2)

Canada Business Corporations Act, R.S.C. 1985 (The abbreviation stands for *Revised Statutes of Canada*.)

Refer to legal decisions in this way:

Regina v. Arnold. Canadian Criminal Cases. 88 C.C.C. (3rd) 92–95. Nova Scotia Court of Appeal. 1994.

> The abbreviation *R.* can be used for *Regina.* The name of the case has been followed by the published source of the judgment and the specific information that tells the reader in which edition and on which pages the decision is printed. The entry concludes with the name of the court that made the decision and the date.

51. letter

Proceed much as you did for e-mail. Name the sender, name the document, and indicate the date of the correspondence.

Household Financial Centre. Letter to Douglas B. Rogers. 22 May 1999.

52. lecture

Follow the guidelines for a speech, substituting the label *Lecture* for *Speech*.

53. map

The question mark indicates uncertainty about the year of publication; the date was not clearly stated on the map.

Atlantic Provinces and Quebec. Map. N.p.: Canadian Automobile Association, 1995?

54. manuscript

Begin a citation for an unpublished manuscript with the surname of the author. Indicate the title. Provide a brief description of the document, and note the date.

Rogers, Douglas B. "Review of *Reading Assessment in Practice*." A paper submitted to *Teaching Education*, January 1996.

55. memo

Cite memos as you cite e-mail, but use a label that includes the word *Memo*.

Niagara College Payroll Department. Memo about delayed paycheques. 25 May 1999.

56. musical composition

Begin the citation with the surname of the composer. Then italicize the title of the work, unless it is identified technically only by form, key or number.

Mendelssohn, Felix. Symphony no. 3 in A minor, op. 56.

Tchaikovsky, Peter Ilyich. *Variations on a Rococo Theme for Cello and Orchestra*, op. 33.

57. performance

Cite a performance much as you would a video recording.

Wilcox, David, perf. Sean O'Sullivan Centre for the Arts, St. Catharines. 10 July 1996.

58. radio or television program

Include in your works-cited entry as many of these elements as possible, in this order: title of episode (if applicable); title of program, italicized; title of series (if appropriate); name of any network involved; call letters for local station; city; and date of broadcast.

Bennett, Willie P. Interview with Shelaugh Rogers. *Morningside*. CBC, CBL, Toronto. 8 July 1996.

59. speech

Include all the information essential to telling the reader precisely where you heard the speech: name of speaker, title of oral presentation, the occasion, the location, and the date.

Rogers, Douglas B. "Are College Content-Area Professors Helping Students Learn to Write?" Learned Societies Congress/Canadian Society for the Study of Higher Education. Brock University, St. Catharines. 25 May 1996.

60. video recording

Begin the entry with the name of the film or video, unless you want to emphasize the role of some other person important in the recording. In such a case, begin the entry with that person's name. Add information about actors and producers if you think it is important to the discussion in your paper. Just before citing the production company, indicate that this is in videocassette or laser disc or any format other than film.

Father and Son. Dir. Colin Browne. Videocassette. National Film Board of Canada. 1992.

61. work of art

Begin the entry with the surname of the artist. Italicize the name of the work next. Name the gallery or private individual that houses the piece, and name the city. You may include the date the work was created; put it right after the title. If you refer to a photograph of a work, include in your entry the source of the reproduction.

Pratt, Mary. *Balancing Oranges. Toronto Star* 16 June 1996: B1.

MacDonald, James Edward Hervey. *Thomson's Rapids, Magnetewan River*. 1910. McMichael
  Canadian Art Collection. Kleinburg, Ontario.

▶ ACTIVITY 9–2*

Creating a Works–Cited Page

Try Activity 9–2 to test your understanding of how to create an MLA-style works-cited
page.

Naomi Epstein wrote a five-page essay using the following materials. Create the
works-cited page for her paper. Check your own work.

Andrew Nikiforuk's Globe and Mail article Andrew Nikiforuk Views a Video That
Focuses on the Classroom appeared on page 22 on March 12, 1993.

Public Education: Can We Keep It? by Arnold Fege was published in the magazine
Educational Leadership, November, 1992, on pages 86–89.

The subtitle of Class Warfare is the Assault on Canada's Schools. The writers are
Maude Barlow and Heather-jane Robertson. The Toronto company Key Porter Books
published the book in 1994.

9.4 SOME CONCLUDING THOUGHTS

It's tiring work, isn't it, trying to observe all the MLA conventions in your writing?
It may help to remember that the work is for a good cause: when writers make reading easy, we all benefit—because we all read far more than we write.

CHAPTER 10

Writing Research Essays in APA Style

"The Publication Manual of the American Psychological Association *is the style manual most used by writers and students in psychology, the other behavioral and social sciences, nursing, criminology, and personnel areas."*
—*The Publication Manual of the American Psychological Association*

CHAPTER OBJECTIVE

After completing the activities in this chapter, you will be able to write a research essay in APA style.

Most professionals and students in social sciences (including psychology, sociology, anthropology), nursing, criminology, and personnel refer to the *Publication Manual of the American Psychological Association* (American Psychological Association) for guidance about the style or appearance of their documents. They've done so for a long time: the precursor of the *Publication Manual*—as it is usually called—was published as a seven-page insert in the *Psychological Bulletin*—in 1929!

The advice to authors was first referred to as the *Publication Manual* in 1952. The American Psychological Association continued to make periodic revisions, and in 1994 they published the 368-page fourth edition. The *Publication Manual* has become a standard around the globe.

If you're reading this section of *Write of Way*, it's probably because an instructor has assigned a research essay and asked you to write it in "APA format." This is a trickier requirement than you might realize because the *Publication Manual* makes an interesting distinction between *copy* and *final* manuscripts: "The author of a thesis, dissertation, or student paper produces a 'final' manuscript; the author of a journal article produces a 'copy' manuscript (which will become a typeset article)" (331).

As the manual itself notes, "The APA *Publication Manual* is intended primarily as a guide to preparing manuscripts for journal publication" (331). Because that is its goal, some of its recommendations lead to documents that look peculiar to most readers; for example, adherence to the recommendations for a *copy* manuscript means a cover that looks awkward and sparse and references that lack hanging indents. Indeed, the manual goes on to recommend that "schools should provide students (and typists) with written guidelines" for documents that are final copies and that "instructions to students to 'use the *Publication Manual*' should be accompanied by specific guidelines for its use" (332).

Underneath the surface differences of copy and final manuscripts are the document conventions that most people agree are the core of APA style. These conventions ensure that readers can discern who wrote the ideas and information presented in the essay.

Write of Way presents the core rules for documenting research in the body of the text and in the bibliography. This chapter also models and explains the conventions for preparing final copies of documents in APA style. It recommends hanging indents for references and italic typeface in word-processed documents, instead of underlining. If you wish to submit an article for publication in a journal requiring APA style, you can refer to the *Publication Manual* for the additional requirements. You will already know most of the conventions presented there.

To study how to create a research essay, read chapter 8 before returning here and finishing this chapter. If you're ready to learn the specific APA conventions, read the rest of this chapter now.

10.1 EXAMPLE OF AN APA-STYLE ESSAY: "CANADA'S ONE-TIER HEALTH CARE IS THE BETTER SYSTEM"

▶ ACTIVITY 10–1

Studying an Essay in APA Style

The easiest way to learn to write an essay in APA style is to begin by examining one. Look at figure 10–1, Tommy Hall's research essay "Canada's One-Tier Health Care Is the Better System." Then answer the questions as you read about the format of the paper.

FIGURE 10–1

APA-Style Paper

Canada's One-Tier 1

Canada's One-Tier Health Care Is the Better System

Tommy Hall

Nunavut Arctic College

Canada's One-Tier   2

Abstract

Canada's one-tier health-insurance system is more economical, efficient, and

fair than a two-tier system, such as that in the United States. A survey of

recently published books and newspaper and newsmagazine articles revealed

that Canada's one-tier system consumes a smaller percentage of gross domestic

product, yet—in contrast to a system that has tens of millions of under- and

uninsured people in the United States—pays for basic care by physicians and

hospitals for all its citizens. The publicly funded health-insurance system

ensures that citizens have an equal opportunity to enjoy good health.

Canada's One-Tier Health Care Is the Better System

Rich or poor, if you live in Canada, you can go to the doctor and be referred to a hospital when you're sick. Canada's publicly funded, one-tier health-care insurance system makes this possible. Similar social welfare systems are commonplace in Europe, but the United States provides a startling alternative: a two-tier combination of social-welfare Medicare and free-enterprise private health insurance. One result is that forty million people have no health insurance at all, and "another 40 million have such inadequate coverage that a major illness could lead to personal bankruptcy" (Rachlis, 1996, p. A20). In the United States, families have become destitute because their private insurance did not cover the costs of care for leukemia or neonatal care.

Some say our public health insurance system ought to cover dental, optical, drug, and other health-related costs—more as Justice Emmett Hall proposed to the Parliament of Canada in 1964 (Bergman, 1995, p. 24). Waiting periods for services do vary somewhat in the provinces, and a few people do travel to the United States for treatment, but most would agree the Canadian system is close to one-tier. It does come near realizing the principle of equal access. Despite inequities that remain in our health-care system, Canada's one-tier, publicly supported, health-insurance system is better than two-tier alternatives because it is economical, efficient, and fair.

One-Tier Health Insurance Is More Economical

Our one-tier health-care system is less expensive that the two-tier system in the United States. Of all the industrialized countries, the United States, with its two-tier system of health insurance, spends the most on health care (Terrana, 1995, p. 14). The many private health-insurance plans in the United States push up the costs of providing health care: "Current U.S. estimates put the extra administrative costs generated by private coverage—pure paper-pushing—at about $100 billion annually," estimated Robert Evans (1995, p. B6), a professor of economics at the University of British Columbia's Centre for Health Services and Policy Research.

In a comparison of the U.S. and Canadian health-insurance systems, Perrin Beatty (1993) notes:

> As recently as 1971, the United States and Canada spent about the same percentage of gross national product (GNP) on health care, 7.6 percent and 7.4 percent, respectively. By the end of the 1980s, our total health care spending was much lower, at 8.6 percent, than that of the United States, at 11.4 percent. (p. 33)

Beatty (1993, p. 34) estimated that more than three times as much money is lost to administration costs in the United States than in Canada.

Arnold Bennett (1993), an American advocate of health-care reform in the United States, compared the health-insurance systems of the two countries and concluded that in reality "health care costs Canadians far less than Americans are paying" (p. xvii).

Michael Rachlis (1996, p. A20) noted that the 1,500 private insurance companies mean that the United States will spend 15 per cent of its GDP on health care—5 per cent more than any other country.

One-Tier Health Insurance Is More Efficient

Not only is our one-tier health-insurance system economical, it is efficient: It ensures the greatest health for the greatest number of citizens.

The first publicly funded hospital-insurance plan was created by Tommy Douglas' CCF Government in Saskatchewan in 1946. It came about partly because of concerns about the poor health of Canadians (e.g., high infant mortality and tuberculosis). These concerns surfaced in reports like the National Sickness Survey of the early 1950's:

> The health of the population was conceded by all qualified observers to be far below the standard attainable with existing knowledge, skill, and national wealth . . . . almost all commentators agreed that the high cost of a trip to the hospital, and to a lesser extent, the cost of treatment by a doctor, deterred people from seeking care when they should have done so and hereby contributed significantly to the low level of health in Canada, even among people not thought of as 'poor.' (McGilly, 1990, p. 233)

When contemporary neoconservatives urge a health-care system in which each individual pays her own way, they don't mention that Canada had such a system—and the general health of the nation was low. Look at what

happened as tax-based public hospital and medical health-care insurance came

into effect in 1968.

Perrin Beatty (1993, p. 34), in an address in the United States, documented

the changes:

Has it improved the health of the population? We think it has. At the

time we introduced the first element of our plan in the early 1950s,

our infant mortality rate was running 40 percent higher than Australia's,

30 percent higher than the United Kingdom's, and 5 percent higher

than the United States' . . . . Today our infant mortality rates are

30 percent lower than yours and among the lowest in the world, at

7 per 1,000 live births.

Beatty noted that pregnant women began coming earlier to physicians

when they did not have to pay out of pocket. Any kind of cost—fee-for-

service or user fee—discourages the poor from using medical services.

Another example comes from Lexchin (1996), a member of the Medical

Reform Group, who noted that prescription user fees mean that "the poor

may stop using important drugs such as insulin and heart medications, admis-

sions to nursing homes rise, and there is a deterioration in the care that

people with mental illness receive" (p. A23).

Gordon Guyatt noted that restrictions on prescriptions in New Hampshire caused more admissions to nursing homes and emergency rooms and "the increased medical costs for mental health patients was 17 times the savings in drug costs" (cited by Toughill, 1996, p. A17).

Preventative medical actions are less expensive and are part of the reason why a system where everyone can seek necessary medical treatment without worry about cost means more health for all members of that society. Our medicare system might be even more efficient at ensuring health for all if it included free prescription drugs.

One-Tier Health Insurance Is Fairer

A one-tier health-care system treats all Canadians fairly: Rich and poor can get essential medical help. "In the 1960s, the Canadian society made the decision that no one should be denied medical care on the grounds that they couldn't afford it" (Lexchin, 1996, p. A23).

The Canada Health Act itself specifically requires equity: It "requires provincial medicare plans to cover all medically necessary services" (Hamilton, 1995, p. A1/Front).

Benjamin Freedman (1995), professor at the McGill Centre for Medicine, Ethics and Law, and clinical ethicist at the Sir Mortimer B. Davis Jewish General Hospital, captured this valuing of equality:

Canada has a health-care system in which, roughly speaking, everyone is in the same boat. If the wealthy and powerful want better care—new drugs, shorter waiting lists, technological improvements—they have to change the system itself, making it available to everyone else at the same time. (p. B2)

Most Canadians who want a fair system would agree with Robert Evans: Two-tier medicine would benefit some Canadians; that's why they want it. They always have. An 'upper tier,' where the wealthy pay privately for preferred access to publicly insured services, would definitely be good for bank presidents and their doctors. Overall, our system would be less equitable, more costly and less efficient. Most of us would lose. (p. B6)

Freedman (1995) noted that allowing some people to pay more to get better medicine would lead some health-care professionals to leave the public system, reducing overall quality. And, as Evans (1995) noted, the wealthy are not clamouring for a truly pay-as-you-go system—it would be prohibitively expensive—they still want to have the public system pay; then, they'd add some money.

Many others agree that a two-tier system means that most people get poorer health care. Gwyn (1995) said, "The second, public, tier becomes a third-rate system" (p. D3). And Lewis (1995) noted, "The well-to-do desert the public system for private insurance schemes, and their support for the tax-based public system dwindles" (p. A19).

Most Canadians continue to agree with Linda McQuaig (1993): "The notion that we must cut back on our *public* expenditures is based on the questionable assumption that our *private* expenditures are something more important—that Nintendo is more important than library services (p. 164). Canadians have shown that they are willing to pay the taxes to keep a one-tier health-insurance system because it is fairer.

Conclusion

Prime Minister Chrétien's remarks captured the Canadian fondness for our medicare system:

> There is a wide consensus in our country about preserving our distinctive state-funded health-care system called medicare. Under our system, you can go to the doctor of your choice. You are admitted to a hospital if you need to be. Period. Not if you have enough money. Or the right private plan. The fact is that no one in Canada needs to worry about medical bills. It is one of our proudest achievements. Canadians want to keep medicare. And we will. (as cited in Marleau, 1995, p. B2)

Columnist Richard Gwyn (1995) went even further in describing medicare as the system that knits Canadians into a national community, the "symbolic railway of the 21st century" (p. D3).

You might think that we can count on our public health-care system

being with us for a long time, given that so many Canadians are so fond of it.

Perhaps not. Dr. Clement Richer, president of the Quebec Federation of

General Practitioners, believes that rich people should be able to obtain CAT

scans and other procedures more quickly than other citizens: "Some of our

patients feel discriminated against, not to be able to pay to get exams more

quickly . . . . If those who can afford it get service more quickly, I don't see

any problem" (as cited in Hamilton, 1995, p. A1/Front).

There are some people who do not want all Canadians to have equal

access to health care, but most Canadians prefer to keep their publicly funded

health-insurance system because it is economical, efficient, and fair. As Robert

Evans (1993, p. 27) concluded, "The system we have seems to be a remarkably

good compromise of quality, affordability, equity, and humanity. Not bad, eh?"

References

Beatty, P. (1993). A comparison of our two systems. In A. Bennett & O. Adams

(Eds.), *Looking north for health: What we can learn from Canada's health care*

system (pp. 28–39). San Francisco: Jossey-Bass.

Bennett, A. (1993). Preface. In A. Bennett & O. Adams (Eds.), *Looking north*

for health: What we can learn from Canada's health care system (pp. xv–xxiv).

San Francisco: Jossey-Bass.

Bergman, B. (1995, November 27). Conscience of Canada: Emmett Hall

helped to shape social programs. *Maclean's, 108,* 24.

Evans, R. (1993). Health care in the Canadian community. In A. Bennett &

O. Adams (Eds.), *Looking north for health: What we can learn from Canada's*

health care system (pp. 1–27). San Francisco: Jossey-Bass.

Evans, R. (1995, May 20). Canada should shun a two-tier system: The wealthy

might gain, but at the expense of others. *Gazette* [Montreal], p. B6.

Freedman, B. (1995, March 12). Klein's Alberta, two-tier medicine would

pillage public health care. *Gazette* [Montreal] (final ed.), p. B2.

Gwyn, R. (1995, October 1). Two-tier health care would point to two-tier

society. *Toronto Star,* p. D3.

Hamilton, G. (1995, May 2). Let wealthy pay for fast care: MDs; Head of physician's group calls for two-tier medicare system. *Gazette* [Montreal] (final ed.), p. A1/Front.

Lewis, S. (1995, May 9). Canada's health-care debate: First, strip away the myths. *Globe and Mail* (Metro ed.), p. A19.

Lexchin, J. (1996, January 1). Eves' prescription for inequality. *Toronto Star*, p. A23.

Marleau, D. (1995, June 1). [Letter to the Editor]. *Gazette* [Montreal] (final ed.), p. B2.

McGilly, F. (1990). *Canada's public social services: Understanding income and health programs.* Toronto: McClelland and Stewart.

McQuaig, L. (1993). *The wealthy banker's wife: The assault on equality in Canada.* Toronto: Penguin.

Rachlis, M. (1996, January 19). Shopping for care nonsensical. *Toronto Star*, p. A20.

Terrana, A. (1995, February 18). The national forum on health: High-quality, affordable health care for all Canadians. *Chinatown News*, p. 14.

Toughill, K. (1996, January 24). Higher medical costs coming for all. *Toronto Star*, p. A17.

Look at the first page, the cover. It has an interesting appearance, doesn't it? At the top of the page, you see the header, which consists of an abbreviated title of the essay, a five-space gap, and the number of the page. Every page begins with the header, which can be created easily in word-processing programs.

The header makes it easy for the reader to reassemble the paper should it come apart. When journal editors send a submitted article for review, they do not want the reviewers to know who wrote the paper. The editors remove the first page before sending the manuscript to the reviewers. When the reviews are returned, the editor can easily reassemble them by matching the manuscript page headers.

The header is placed flush-right to the margin, about 2.5 centimetres (one inch) from the top margin. APA style recommends margins of this size top and bottom, left and right. These are the default values for most word processors. Although it will not be apparent until page 2, the right margin is always unjustified.

The title of the paper appears next. Notice that it is presented in a plain form: The font is common, such as Courier or Times New Roman, and it is not embellished by italics or underlining. There are no quotation marks or ending punctuation. The title is in mixed case, though, with all the important words capitalized. It's centred on the page—top and bottom, left and right.

The author's name is printed below the title. The *Publication Manual* recommends that you choose one form for your name and use it consistently in all your written work. Otherwise, people will be unsure if Tommy H. Hall is the same writer as T. Hall, Tommy Hall, and so forth.

The essay writer indicates on the last line on the page the name of the school where the work has been done.

APA style requires double-spacing of all text. Since single-spacing is the usual default for word processors, adjust the line spacing.

Look at page 2. Again, you'll notice the header, but now it indicates the second page of the paper. Then the word *Abstract* is centred. Beneath it is a brief but comprehensive information summary of the paper. Most student papers should have abstracts of between 75 and 100 words, but some teachers may ask for greater length. Note that for an abstract, the writer omits the usual five-space paragraph indent and that page 2 presents *only* the abstract.

The first line of print on page 3 is the header. Then, the title of the paper is presented once again. (A reviewer would be seeing the title for the first time.) Then the text of the paper begins. Note that APA style requires each paragraph to begin with a 1.25-centimetre (one-half-inch) indent. Use the tab key.

Glance through the paper at the headings in the text. Find the first one. Is it "One-Tier Health Insurance Is More Economical"? Notice that it is centred and in mixed case. If an additional level of headings were needed, each would be flush-left, in mixed case, and underlined.

Note the remaining headings: "One-Tier Health Insurance Is More Efficient," "One-Tier Health Insurance Is Fairer," "Conclusion," and "References." The headings make the paper easier to read.

Turn back to page 3, and glance over the next few pages considering this question: Which piece of punctuation is more common in this essay than in the novels and newspaper articles you read? There are more colons and quotation marks, and many more parentheses. Inside those parentheses you type surnames, dates, and page numbers. The surnames tell who wrote the information discussed in that part of the essay. The date tells the year the material cited was published, and the page number tells the precise page on which that material is printed.

Turn to the second-last page of the essay. Look down the page until you read an entry that begins with the name *Bergman*. What does this entry tell you? The bibliographic entry tells the writer's name, the date of the publication, the title of the work, and where it was published.

Look at page 3 and find Bergman's name. Note that here in the body of the essay, Hall told—in a brief code—where he found the information just presented in the paper. Hall cited the author of the information (Bergman), the year of publication (1995), and the very page number (24) where Bergman's information was published. All the information you need to find and read that material is recorded in References: B. Bergman's article was titled "Conscience of Canada: Emmett Hall Helped to Shape Social Programs." It appeared on page 24 of *Maclean's* magazine in the issue published on November 27, 1995. In an APA-style paper, there is always this kind of congruity: the source of the information you cite in the text of the essay—where you indicate just the author, year of publication, and (often) the page number—is always cited with complete publication information on the references page. This parenthetical, author-date-page documentation style is quite handy, isn't it?

Your preview of the paper has familiarized you with the appearance of an APA-style paper. That's the style you will use to format your research essay. As always, the content is most important, but appearance matters, too. Further details of how to format a paper in APA style are presented here. Read on if you're ready to format your paper in APA style. If you wish to learn more about how to create an essay, leave this section, for now, and read chapter 8, "Writing Research Essays."

10.2 DOCUMENT SOURCES IN THE TEXT

When you format an essay in APA style, you must document the information you find in your search of the literature. Indicate the author of any material you refer to and the date the material was published. When you directly quote the material, you must also report in your text the page number where the quoted text is printed. Indicate the page number even when you are paraphrasing if doing so will help your reader locate specific information, especially in longer or more complex text.

★ Incorporate into the text documentation and brief quotations (fewer than forty words). Look at this example of how Hall used the APA parenthetical documentation style because his quotation was fewer than forty words:

Columnist Richard Gwyn (1995) went even further in describing medicare as the system that knits Canadians into a national community, the "symbolic railway of the 21st century" (p. D3).

The *Gywn* citation is one of the more common ways to document a source. Hall embedded Richard Gwyn's name in the running text of the sentence; Hall needed to parenthesize only two elements. The year is noted close to the author so that readers who choose to look immediately for this entry in the references will find the matching citation easily and quickly. The page number has been parenthesized immediately after the quotation. Note that the ending punctuation is placed *after* the parenthetical element.

The entire reference could have been parenthesized. Imagine that Hall had written

Medicare has even been called Canada's "symbolic railway of the 21st century" (Gywn, 1995, p. D3).

★ Block quotations longer than forty words. When you quote material longer than forty words, create a free-standing block of text. Start a new line, and use the indent feature of your word processor to create a temporary margin five spaces (about 1.25 cm) to the right of the usual margin. Maintain your double-spacing, and let your text extend to the usual right margin. Omit the quotation marks. If your quotation extends to additional paragraphs, indent those an extra tab space (1.25 cm). These conventions are illustrated in the following example.

In a comparison of the U.S. and Canadian health insurance systems, Perrin Beatty (1993) noted:

> As recently as 1971, the United States and Canada spent about the same percentage of gross national product (GNP) on health care, 7.6 percent and 7.4 percent, respectively. By the end of the 1980s, our total health care spending was much lower, at 8.6 percent, than that of the United States, at 11.4 percent. (p. 33)

Note that the reference to the page number is placed outside the final punctuation of block quotations.

* Cite both authors in your text in all references.

Miezitis and Rogers (1984) found that teachers preferred to distance themselves from impulsive students.

* Cite all three, four, or five co-authors the first time you refer to them.

Applebee, Lehr, and Auten (1981) noted in the National Study of Secondary School Writing in 1979 that students do very little connected writing.

Then, on subsequent references to this material, simply write:

Applebee et al. (1981).

* Use *Author et al.* when a work has six or more authors. Just record the surname of the first author, even the first time you refer to a work with six or more authors.

* Cite works by title when no authors are indicated. Cite the first few words of the reference list entry, usually the title, when you do not have the name of the author of the work. Note the comma after the title part of the entry. (If an organization has authored a document, though, see "Cite organization authors.")

People can order groceries from a home computer ("How Peapod," 1995).

* Cite works by title when the author is listed as anonymous. Cite in the text just the first few words of the title of the work when the author is unknown or has remained anonymous. See the previous example.

* When citing authors with the same surname, precede each surname with the author's first initial(s):

C.P. Davies (1998) and D.D. Davies (1997) have criticized this practice.

* List multiple citations of one author's works in a single parenthetical reference in chronological order. If you refer to several works by the same author, list them from oldest to newest:

Rogers has long been interested in teaching reading and writing (1981, 1984, 1988, 1996).

* When multiple publications by the same author have the same date, use suffixes to distinguish them. If several publications have the same publication date, use suffixes. The suffixes will be assigned in the references section by the alphabetical order of the titles of the works.

That year he published several studies about emergent writing (Graves, 1997a, 1997b, 1997c).

* When you cite two authors in the same parenthetical reference, alphabetize by surname. Note how the semicolons separate the citations.

A few studies showed a different trend (Gill, 1996; Ghiz, 1995; Hill and Mohammed, 1998).

* Cite organization authors. When an organization publishes a document, write out the whole name of the organization the first time it appears in your text. If the abbreviation of the group's name is well-known, the abbreviation can be used in subsequent references to that document. Otherwise, write out the name of the organization each time you refer to the document it published. That name is not a document title, so don't enclose it with quotation marks or italicize it.

To research a speech about visual impairment, you might contact the Canadian Institute for the Blind (CNIB). The CNIB has published many pamphlets about vision.

Diving after drinking is dangerous (Canadian Red Cross Society, 1989).

* For classic works, cite parts instead of page numbers. You do not need to list major classical works in the references. In the text of your paper, refer to them by part; the parts will be consistent in different editions of the work.

If you quote lines 6 and 7 in the second scene of act 1 of William Shakespeare's *Taming of the Shrew*, cite this parenthetically in this way:

(1.2.6–7)

Notice that no page has been indicated because this is a classic work.

* Cite the date of your version when citing old works.

William Shakespeare's *Taming of the Shrew* (1623/1992)

* Cite personal communications only in your text. Because your reader cannot refer to this material, do not include it in your references section. In the text, make such citations this way:

A. A. Rogers (personal communication, May 28, 1999).

* Don't cite page numbers when referring to whole works. Simply record the author and date. If you want to draw your reader's attention to a particular part, such as a chapter, do it in this fashion:

There is an excellent discussion of this in Gordon (1999, chap. 4).

* Refer to bills, laws, acts, and other legal documents by name.

British North America Act

Bill 167

Canada Student Financial Assistance Act

Constitution Act, 1982

Canadian Charter of Rights and Freedoms, Sec. 15(2)

Canada Business Corporations Act

See "Legal Sources" in the next section for instructions about how to fully reference this type of citation. The complete reference is provided for the Canada Business Corporations Act.

★ **Abbreviate citations to legal cases in your text.** In the text, follow this form when you refer to a case:

Regina v. Arnold, (1994) or (*R. v. Arnold*, 1994).

See "Legal Source" in the next section for how to document legal sources in the references.

★ **Cite an indirect source of information by using** *as cited in.* In the following quotation, Hall indicates that he knows what Dr. Clement Richer said not because Hall heard him, but because Hall read a quotation of Dr. Richer's remarks in reporter Graeme Hamilton's article "Let Wealthy Pay for Fast Care: MDs; Head of Physician's Group Calls for Two-Tier Medicare System." If you examine Hall's reference entry, you can see that this was published in the Montreal *Gazette* on May 2, 1995, on page A1 of the front section.

Dr. Clement Richer, president of the Quebec Federation of General Practitioners, believes that rich people should be able to obtain CAT scans and other procedures more quickly than other citizens: "Some of our patients feel discriminated against, not to be able to pay to get exams more quickly . . . . If those who can afford it get service more quickly, I don't see any problem" (as cited in Hamilton A1/Front).

★ **Shift tenses logically.** When discussing material published previously, use the past tense (e.g., "Lexchin noted") or the present perfect tense (e.g., "Several authorities have reported"). Use the present tense to express conditions and ideas at the time you are writing the paper (e.g., "Canadians prefer").

10.3 DOCUMENT SOURCES IN THE REFERENCES SECTION

The citing of the author-date information in the text is the first step you take to help your reader distinguish your ideas from the intellectual contributions of others. Each reference in the text must match an entry in the references list. Each entry in the references list will include all the information necessary for a reader to retrieve and consult the work. The entry in the text will acknowledge the contribution of another writer and guide the reader to the corresponding entry in the references list.

As you look over the detailed instructions for completing a references list, you may be fatigued by the prospect of how much work it will take to carry out these instructions. This is a good time to remind you of two important points. Perhaps hearing them again, in this new context, will refresh your spirits.

You go to the effort of preparing a list of references as a courtesy for your reader. Do this well, and you make a good impression on your reader because you make it easy for the reader to examine personally the writings that you found in your research. And, since you spend more time reading than writing, most of the time *you* will benefit from someone else's work. *That* writer will have made it easy for you to find the source documents.

There are two other advantages to learning to use this system of documentation: Once you become efficient at using these guidelines—I don't think anyone ever memorizes them—you will find that you can complete bibliographies more quickly. Knowing the standard ways to record the information means you don't have to waste time reinventing logical ways to create a bibliographic entry. And, when you know the information you need for your references section, you can ensure that you take down all the information necessary so you do not need to revisit the library to search out those materials a second time.

* **Place your list of references at the end of your paper.** After the last page of your essay, start a new page to list references. Continue the numbering in the header. If you concluded your essay on page 12, your reference page will have the same header as the rest of your essay, but the page number will be 13. Continue to double-space. Centre the title *References*. If the references span more than one page do not repeat the title, just continue with the alphabetized list of entries.

* **Alphabetize all the entries in the list of references.** As they read through an essay, readers often flip to the references list to read the details about the work referred to in the body of the paper. You alphabetize the entries to make it easy for your readers to find each entry of interest.

* **Arrange multiple one-author entries by year of publication.**

Toughill, K. (1995, December 24). Prescription fees harmful to health, pharmacists say. *Toronto Star*, p. A11.

Toughill, K. (1996, January 24). Higher medical costs coming for all. *Toronto Star*, p. A17.

* **If a reference entry exceeds one line in length, indent the subsequent line (or lines) one tab or five spaces (1.25 cm) from the left margin.** An entry is easier to read if it begins with a hanging indent, as indicated in the following example.

Terrana, A. (1995, February 18). The national forum on health: High-quality, affordable health care for all Canadians. *Chinatown News*, p. 14.

* **Use common abbreviations in your references list (e.g., chap., ed., n.d. [no date], p. or pp. [page, pages], trans., vol.).** When providing the city in which a publisher is located, indicate the province or state, unless the city is well-known for publishing. Use the Canada Post abbreviations for the names of provinces and states (e.g., BC for British Columbia).

* **Study these examples to create a correct entry for the different types of documents you refer to.** As you prepare your references list, look through the list below for an example of the same type of document from which you derived information for your paper. Then follow the guidelines for that type of publication to create a correct entry for your reference material. You'll do it with increasing speed and ease as you become more familiar with the conventions. This section is organized into Referencing Whole Documents (Books and Pamphlets); Referencing Articles in Books and Periodicals; Referencing CD-ROM's and Other Electronic Sources; and a miscellaneous section, Referencing Other Publications. Within each category, the key word is alphabetized to make it easier for you to find an example of the type of work you must reference.

Even when you read the instructions and examine the examples, you will find it demanding to create a references list. You will often have to think creatively and use information from more than one example to properly reference some of the works you find in your search of the literature. And on top of staying alert and thinking cleverly, you must be painstakingly fastidious in attending to detail.

Referencing Whole Documents (Books and Pamphlets)

1. book by anonymous or unknown author

2. book by corporate author

3. book by editor, translator, or compiler

4. book by one author

5. book by two or more authors

6. book in language other than English

7. book in multiple volumes

8. book in republished edition

9. book in second and subsequent editions

10. book in translation

11. book with multiple publishers

12. book/brochure without publication information or pagination

13. brochure

14. conference proceedings

15. dissertation (published)

16. dissertation (unpublished)

17. government publication

18. pamphlet

19. report

Referencing Articles in Books and Periodicals

20. abstract from abstracts journal

21. afterword

22. article in anthology

23. article in journal (each volume is paginated)

24. article in journal (each issue is paginated)

25. article in magazine

26. article in microfilm collection

27. article in newspaper

28. article in reference book or collection

29. editorial

30. foreword

31. introduction

32. letter to the editor

33. preface

34. review

Referencing CD-ROM's and Other Electronic Sources

35. public online posting

36. publication from CD-ROM, diskette

37. publication from periodically updated CD-ROM database

38. publication from online database

Referencing Other Publications

39. advertisement

40. audio recording

41. cartoon/comic strip

42. e-mail

43. film

44. legal source

45. letter

46. lecture

47. manuscript

48. speech/paper presented

49. video recording

50. work of art

Referencing Whole Documents (Books and Pamphlets)

Before studying the specific conventions for various whole works, take a close look at a sample entry. This examination will increase your familiarity with the most common elements of a reference entry.

Saul, J. R. (1995). *The Unconscious Civilization*. Concord: Anansi Press.

Begin with the name of the author. To reduce the probability that the worth of a publication is judged by the gender of the writer, APA reference style requires that you indicate only the initials of given names. Next, indicate the year of publication, in parentheses, followed by a period. Then, note the title of the whole work, in italics if you are word processing or underlined if you are handwriting. Capitalize only the first word of the title and subtitle, if there is one (and any proper nouns). Next, state the city in which the book was published. Follow that with a colon, and indicate the name of the publisher. You may omit words such as *Co.*, *Inc.*, and *Publisher*. Note the use of the period to separate elements of the entry and to conclude it. You will accurately prepare an APA-style references list if you attend to these details.

1. book by anonymous or unknown author

When there is no author listed on the title page, substitute the title for the author's name. Alphabetize that entry by the first important word of the title (not the articles *a, an, the*). This entry would be entered with the *s*'s, not the *t*'s.

The sponges of Lake Winnipeg. (1996). Brandon: Wishful Books.

2. book by corporate author

When an association or committee publishes a book, it does not always list an author on the title page. Cite as the author the name of the group, even if they have also published the work, but if this is the case, near the end of the entry, use the word *Author* instead of repeating the corporation name.

Delrina (Canada). (1995). *Getting started guide* [Software Manual]. Toronto: Author.

3. book by editor, translator, or compiler

Record an editor, translator, or compiler in the same way as an author, but after the surname(s), write the abbreviation *Ed.* or *Eds.*; *Trans.*; *Comp.* or *Comps.* (in parentheses), followed by a period.

Bennett, A., & Adams, O. (Eds.). (1993). *Looking north for health: What we can learn from Canada's health care system.* San Francisco: Jossey-Bass.

4. book by one author

McQuaig, L. (1993). *The wealthy banker's wife: The assault on equality in Canada.* Toronto: Penguin.

5. book by two or more authors

Reverse the surname and first name for all the authors. Separate the entries with commas and add an ampersand (the *&* symbol) before the last name.

Norton, S., & Green, B. (1991). *Essay essentials.* Toronto: Holt, Rinehart and Winston.

McCown, R.R., Driscoll, M., Roop, P., Saklofske, D. H., Kelly, I. W., Schwean, V. L., & Gajadharsingh, J. (1996). *Educational psychology: A learning-centered approach to classroom practice* (Canadian Edition). Scarborough: Allyn & Bacon.

6. book in language other than English

Proceed as for an English-language book.

Fiot, J. (1969). *Le Français par les mots croises.* Paris: Librairie Hachette.

7. book in multiple volumes

Brown, R., & Bennett, D. (Eds.). (1982). *An anthology of Canadian literature in English.* (Vols. 1–2). Toronto: Oxford University Press.

8. book in republished edition

When you are using a reprint of a book, record the year the book was originally published and complete the bibliographic information. Conclude the entry with, parenthesized, the clause *(Original work published 19xx).* There is no ending punctuation after the parenthesized material.

Wright, E. (1985). *Smoke detector.* Don Mills: Collins. (Original work published 1984)

9. book in second and subsequent editions

Kerrigan, D., Matthews, R., & Webb, G. (1991). *Who's going to read this anyway?* (4th ed.). Toronto: Holt, Rinehart and Winston.

10. book in translation

Proceed much as for an edited book.

Atwood, M. (1983). *Marquee au corps* [Bodily harm]. (Helene Filion, Trans.). Montreal: Les Quinze Filiale de Sogides.

11. book with multiple publishers

Note that the order of the publishing companies is the same in the entry as it is in the book.

Paikeday, T. M. (Ed.). (1990). *Penguin Canadian dictionary.* Markham: Penguin Books Canada; Mississauga: Copp Clark Pitman.

12. book/brochure without publication information or pagination

Sometimes books do not have all the information you must record for a reference. Use these conventions to tell your readers the information that was not available from the publication. Capitalize and punctuate just as though you had the usual information.

n.d.   (no date of publication)
n.p.   (no place of publication)
n.p.   (no publisher)
n.pag.   (no pagination)

Commemorative Services of Ontario. (n.d.). *The facts about cremation.* Toronto: Commemorative Services of Ontario.

13. brochure

Reference a brochure as you would a book.

Canadian Red Cross Society. (1989). *Safe diving*. N.p.: Canadian Red Cross Society.

14. conference proceedings

Liu, M. (1994). On-line identification of coherent generators using multilayer feedforward neural networks. *Proceedings of the IEEE International Conference on Industrial Technology* (pp. 803–807). Piscataway, NJ: IEEE Service Centre.

15. dissertation (published)

For a dissertation published by University Microfilms International, follow these conventions.

Rogers, D. B. (1994). Are college content-area professors practicing writing across the curriculum? *Dissertation Abstracts International, 54*(01), 2966A. (University Microfilms No. DA 9335162)

16. dissertation (unpublished)

Rogers, D. B. (1993). *Are college content-area professors practicing writing across the curriculum?* Unpublished doctoral dissertation, State University of New York at Buffalo.

17. government publication

Proceed as for a book. Begin the entry with the name of the author or group. Canadian federal government documents are published in Ottawa by the Queen's Printer.

Ministry of Industry. Statistics Canada. (1993). *Household facilities by income and other characteristics*. Ottawa: Queen's Printer.

18. pamphlet

Follow the same conventions as for a brochure.

19. report

If a report is published as a whole, rather than as part of a collection, italicize the title. If there is no author noted, and the report is published by an organization, start with the name of the corporation or organization. If you found the report on the Internet, add the additional information as described in the section on electronic sources.

Ferris, J., & Stirpe, T. (1995). *Gambling in Ontario: A report from a general population survey on gambling-related problems and opinions*. N.p.: Addiction Foundation.

Information Technology Association of Canada. (1994/1996, July 24). *The Canadian information infrastructure: An agenda for action* [Online]. Available Internet: http://
   www.itac.ca./ITAC/agendaen.html.

Referencing Articles in Books and Periodicals

20. abstract from abstracts journal

Add *[Abstract]* between the abstract title and the period if the journal title does not
include the word *abstract*. Note that you do not need to indicate the page number of
the abstract if it is presented in the journal in a way that makes it as easy for the reader
to find as numbered pages (e.g., the abstracts are alphabetized).

Note that the volume number—but not the issue number—is treated as part of the
journal title; underline or italicize it, too.

Gilbert, S. L. (1996). Perspectives of rural prospective teachers toward teaching in urban
   schools. *Child Development Abstracts and Bibliography, 70*(1), 125.

21. afterword

Reference an afterword the same as you do a foreword (see item 30 in this list).

22. article in anthology

When an essay, poem, or other work is published in a collection, such as an anthology, follow the conventions for citing a book, with these additional considerations. Cite
the author of the piece and the title. Now, write *In* and list the author(s), initials first
followed by surname(s). Then, in parentheses, use an abbreviation to indicate the editor
or translator of the whole work. Follow with a comma, and then name the whole work.
Indicate the page(s) inside parentheses (p. or pp.), and finish the entry with the city and
publisher, as in this entry.

Evans, R. (1993). Health care in the Canadian community. In A. Bennett & O. Adams (Eds.),
   Looking north for health: What we can learn from Canada's health care system
   (pp. 1–27). San Francisco: Jossey-Bass.

23. article in journal (each volume is paginated)

Most academic journals are paginated by volume. That means that several issues
together constitute one volume of the journal. Libraries will usually bind together all
the issues of a volume. Sometimes the journal's volume will correspond with the calendar year, but more often a particular volume is made up of all the issues published in an

academic year, typically September to June. If the volume is continuously paginated, each new issue of the journal starts numbering one page number higher than the last page of the previous issue. It is easy to find particular pages because the whole volume is paginated. Thus, you need indicate only the volume number of the journal. (Leave out the issue number.) After the volume number, do not use *p.* or *pp.*, just record the page number(s).

Note that in references to pages of articles in journals, APA style does not use the abbreviation *p. (pp.)*.

Rogers, D. B. (1984). Assessing study skills. *Journal of Reading 27,* 346–354.

24. article in journal (each issue is paginated)

When a journal begins each new issue by numbering from page one, a reader will more easily find a particular issue if you record the number of the issue in your references list, as in the following example in which the *16* indicates the volume number and the *2* the issue number, which—unlike the volume number—is not italicized.

Miezitis, S., & Rogers, D. (1984). Teacher interpersonal distancing and pupil behaviour. *Ontario Psychologist, 16*(2), 9–12.

25. article in magazine

Examine the following entries to see the conventions for citing a magazine article. When the article is not printed on consecutive pages, cite all the page numbers; separate them with commas. Do not precede the page numbers with *p.* or *pp.* For a magazine, cite the day (if indicated) and month. Record the volume number, too.

Frost, M. (1996, July). Up in smoke: Why teen girls don't quit. *Chatelaine, 69,* 29, 31, 33, 78, 80, 82, 84.

Bergman, B. (1995, November 27). Conscience of Canada: Emmett Hall helped to shape social programs. *Maclean's, 108,* 24.

26. article in microfilm collection

Kurfis, J. (1985). *Do students really learn from writing?* (ERIC Document Reproduction Service No. ED 293 123).

27. article in newspaper

Here are a few extra requirements you must meet to correctly cite a newspaper article.

★ **Add the name of the city to an entry for a local newspaper.** Write *Free Press* **[London]** or *Free Press* **[Winnipeg]**.

*   **If the newspaper publishes more than one edition, indicate the edition you referred to.**

Psachas, M. (1995, May 15). [Letter to the Editor]. *Gazette* [Montreal] (final ed.), p. A1/Front.

*   **Use** *p. (pp.)* **to indicate page numbers.**

Ramsay, C. (1995, May 15). Don't recycle the same old myths about health care. *Globe and Mail*, p. A13.

*   **Indicate all nonconsecutive pages of an article.** Write the page numbers of every page of the article, and use commas between them.

Airhart, S. (1995, May 17). On-line recipe exchange lets users cook up a storm. *Toronto Star*, pp. E1–E2.

Freedman, B. (1995, March 12). Klein's Alberta, two-tier medicine would pillage public health care. *Gazette* [Montreal] (final ed.), p. B2.

28. article in reference book or collection

Follow the guidelines for a piece in an anthology. Start with the author's name (if available) and then the title of the part. For a well-known reference work, just give the edition and year of publication. You do not even need to record page numbers if the entries of the work are arranged alphabetically. Cite an editor when the piece is from a little-known reference work, and do provide all the usual publication information.

Crokinole. (1998). *Canadian Oxford dictionary.* Toronto: Oxford University Press.

29. editorial

Most editorials are unsigned, so begin the entry with the title of the editorial.

Traffic plans beg for answers. (1995, March 14). [Editorial]. *Niagara Advance* [Niagara-on-the-Lake], p. 4.

30. foreword

Treat a foreword the same as you would any other article in a collection.

Monty, J. C. (1994). Foreword. In J. Carroll & R. Broadhead, *Canadian Internet handbook* (pp. xiii–xvi). Scarborough, ON: Prentice Hall Canada.

31. introduction

Follow the instructions for citing a foreword, but substitute the word *Introduction*.

32. letter to the editor

Cite a letter to the editor as you would any other newspaper article except that instead of recording an article title, type, in square brackets, *Letter*.

Rogers, D. B. (1996, April 10). [Letter to the editor]. *Standard* [St. Catharines], p. B5.

Rogers, L. (1996, July 19). [Reply to letter of Dick Harrington]. *Standard* [St. Catharines], p. B5.

33. preface

Begin the entry with the name of the writer of the book part. Then type the name of the book part (*Preface*) and a period. Follow this with *In* and the name(s) of the author or editor of the whole work. Add the name of the work, and add the page numbers that comprise the part. Finish with the city and publisher.

Bennett, A. (1993). Preface. In A. Bennett & O. Adams (Eds.), *Looking north for health: What we can learn from Canada's health care system* (pp. xv–xxiv). San Francisco: Jossey-Bass.

34. review

Cite the reviewer's name and the title of the review. Write, within square brackets, *Review of . . .*, filling in the word *book, film,* and so forth, and the title of the work reviewed. If the review is not titled, use the information within the brackets as the title. If the reviewer is not indicated, begin the reference entry with *[Review of . . .]*

Galway, C. (1996, February–March). [Review of *The art of Mary Pratt: The substance of light.* Vancouver Art Gallery. December 20, 1995–March 3, 1996]. *Planet of the Arts* [Emily Carr Institute of Art and Design, Vancouver], p. 22.

Doughty, H. A. (1993). [Review of the books *False god: How the globalization myth has impoverished Canada* and *The wealthy banker's wife: The assault on equality in Canada]. The College Quarterly* 1(1), 20.

Referencing CD-ROM's and Other Electronic Sources

It is really just the relative newness of these media that gives writers pause for thought about how to refer to them in a reference entry. Treat them as you would books or other publications, but include the additional information a reader needs to find items published electronically.

35. public online posting

Begin your entry with the name of the writer, indicate the title of the electronic posting and the publication date, and describe the posting and the source. If you cannot supply the publication date, indicate the date you accessed the material. Indicate *Available*, if the document can be retrieved, and provide the information necessary to get it. The sample references for Gates, Madige, and McBane are from "Internet Ethics."

Industry Canada. (1996). Chemicals and bio-industries. *Strategis: Industry Canada Online* [Online]. Available Internet: http://www.strategis.ic.gc.ca

Gates, G. (1996, March 1). *Shakespeare and his muse* [Online]. Internet. Available FTP: ftp.guten.net.gproject/texts/english/bard/research/muse.txt

Madige, E. (1996, January 16). *How to build a better mousetrap* [Online]. Internet. Available Usenet: sci.tech.inventions.mousetrap

McBane, L. (1996, March 8). [Online]. Available IRC: telnetworld.sensemedia.net:6677,#egypt

36. publication from CD-ROM, diskette

To cite a document/program published on a diskette or CD-ROM, follow the conventions for a book, but just before indicating the city of publication add the word *Diskette* or *CD-ROM* (inside square brackets). Use a period to end this element, and treat the bracketed word as part of the title. Do not underline or italicize the names of computer software.

Feldstein, S. (1983). Practical theory [Diskette]. Van Nuys, CA: Alfred.

37. publication from periodically updated CD-ROM database

When you find a document by searching a CD-ROM database—perhaps the Canadian NewsDisc—begin your citation with the author, date, and title. Add, in brackets, *CD-ROM*. Then tell the name of the CD-ROM database, the producer of the CD-ROM publication, and the date of the version you accessed.

Larsen-Ko, Marnie. (1996, June 10). No excuse for hitting children: Every act of violence against a child leaves a permanent emotional scar. *Calgary Herald,* p. A6. [CD-ROM]. Canadian NewsDisc. CEDROM-SNi. 1995–1996.

38. publication from online database

Treat the document the same as a public online posting, but note the name of the database (Internet, CompuServe).

Referencing Other Publications

39. advertisement

Start your entry with the subject of the advertisement. After a period, write the word *Advertisement*, bracket it, and follow with another period. Finally, include the usual information about the publication in which the advertisement appears.

National Film Board of Canada. (1996, March–April). [Advertisement]. *This Magazine,* 12.

The Great Canadian Bagel. (1996, July 10). [Advertisement]. *Newsworld.*

40. audio recording

Decide which artist you want to emphasize, and begin the entry with that surname. Note the date of copyright. In this example, the additional information reveals that Aglukark recorded the CD in 1992 and that EMI Music Canada is a publisher's imprint of Thorn EMI. Place the period that ends the title part of the entry *after* the indication of the medium.

Aglukark, S. (1994). *Arctic rose* [CD]. Mississauga: EMI Music Canada–Thorn EMI. (1992).

Connors, S. T. (1991). *More of the Stompin' Tom phenomenon* [Audiocassette]. N.p.: Crown Vetch Music Ltd.

41. cartoon/comic strip

Begin the entry with the surname of the cartoonist and the date of publication. Add the title of the cartoon (if it has one), the word *Cartoon* (in brackets), and finish with the information about the publication, as usual.

Bell-Lundy, S. (1996, July 11). *Between friends* [Cartoon]. *Toronto Star,* p. F8.

42. e-mail

This is a personal communication that your reader cannot retrieve. In the text of your writing, indicate it by a parenthetical reference such as this: "**(A.K. Wigg, personal communication, August 2, 1997**)." Do not make an entry for your references list.

43. film

Reference a film the same way as a video recording, but note that it is a film.

44. legal source

Refer to bills, laws, acts, and other legal documents by name. Note the source. In parentheses, give the date the law was enacted.

Canada Business Corporations Act, R.S.C. (1985). (The abbreviation stands for Revised Statutes of Canada.)

Reference legal decisions in this way:

Regina v. Arnold. 88 C.C.C. (3rd) 92–95. (Nova Scotia Court of Appeal. 1994).

The abbreviation *R.* can be used for *Regina.* The name of the case has been followed by the published source of the judgment—the volume, source (Canadian Criminal Cases), and page(s). The entry concludes with the name of the court that made the decision and the date, parenthesized.

45. letter

Treat a letter the same as e-mail. Do not include a letter in your references entries.

46. lecture

Since a lecture or speech cannot be retrieved by your readers, reference it in the text as you would a personal communication and do not enter it into your references list.

47. manuscript

Begin a citation for an unpublished manuscript with the surname of the author. Parenthesize the date. Indicate the title. Provide a brief description of the document.

Rogers, D. B. (1996). Review of *Reading assessment in practice.* Manuscript submitted for publication.

48. speech/paper presented

Include information that will enable the reader to know precisely where you obtained the information: name of speaker, title of oral presentation, the occasion, and the location.

Rogers, D. B. (1996). *Are college-content area professors helping students learn to write?* Paper presented at the Learned Societies Congress/Canadian Society for the Study of Higher Education, Brock University, St. Catharines, ON.

49. video recording

Begin the entry with the name of some person important in the recording (e.g., the director). Indicate the date. After the name of the recording, write *[Video]* and a period. Then indicate where it is available. Don't punctuate after the parentheses.

Browne, C. (Director). (1992). *Father and son* [Video]. (Available from National Film Board of Canada)

50. work of art

Begin the entry with the surname of the artist. Italicize the name of the work next. You may include the date the work was created; put it right after the title. Name the gallery or private individual who houses the piece, and name the city. If you refer to a photograph of a work, include in your entry the source of the reproduction.

Pratt, M. (1996, June 16). *Balancing oranges* [Painting]. *Toronto Star,* p. B1.

MacDonald, J. E. H. (1910). *Thomson's Rapids, Magnetewan River* [Painting]. McMichael Canadian Art Collection, Kleinburg, Ontario.

Try Activity 10–2★ to test your understanding of how to create an APA–style references section.

▶ **ACTIVITY 10–2★**

Creating a References Page

Imagine that Mohamed Fayed has written a six-page essay called "Making the Grade" using the following materials. Create the references page for the paper. Check your own work by examining figure 15–11.

Andrew Nikiforuk's Globe and Mail article Andrew Nikiforuk Views a Video That Focuses on the Classroom appeared on page 22 on March 12, 1993.

Public Education: Can We Keep It? by Arnold Fege was published in volume 50 of the magazine Educational Leadership, November, 1992, on pages 86–89.

The subtitle of Class Warfare is the Assault on Canada's Schools. The writers were Maude Barlow and Heather-jane Robertson. The Toronto company Key Porter Books published the book in 1994.

10.4 SOME FURTHER THOUGHTS ABOUT ESSAY COVERS

Adding an MLA-Style Assignment Cover Sheet

The cover/first page of an APA-style essay is very sparse. It does not give instructors enough information to easily recognize the project or even know which class the writer attends. It better serves the needs of a journal editor than a college instructor. You may want to create a cover in MLA style for your APA-style essay. (See figure 1–9, "Annotated MLA-Style Version of 'Down-Home Cooking.'") You may be using this style for your in-class assignments.

The MLA cover does indicate the information that instructors want to see—quickly—when they begin to mark a stack of papers. The heading and the assignment title (e.g., "Research Essay Assignment") of MLA-style papers are more informative than the cover of a paper formatted in APA style. If you decide to create such an assignment/cover page, simply attach it to the front of your APA-style paper and begin the numbering of the APA-style paper on the next page. In that way, you'll show that you've learned to write in APA format, and you'll present the work with an appearance that makes it easier for your instructor to record your mark. Try Activity 10–3 to see if you can design an MLA-style cover for a research essay assignment.

▶ ACTIVITY 10–3*

Creating an MLA-Style Cover Sheet for an APA Essay

Kim Honsberger took the course ENGL097, Teach Kids to Read and Write, with Dr. Douglas B. Rogers. She wanted to create an MLA-style cover sheet for a research essay assignment she had to write in APA style. She intended to hand the paper in on the due date, April 1, 2003. Create a cover page for her.

Another Choice of Assignment Cover Sheet

The limitations of the APA-style cover have led many institutions to create instructions for covers suitable for their students. Figure 10–2 shows an example of a common variation on such covers. Again, check with your instructor before you put such a cover on your essay.

FIGURE 10–2

Variation on MLA- and APA-Style Covers

Canada's One-Tier Health Care Is
the Better System

Tommy Hall

Early Childhood Education Program

Submitted in partial fulfillment
of the requirements for the course
Psychology of Early Childhood
George Brown College
Toronto, Ontario

March, 2006

10.5 SOME CONCLUDING THOUGHTS

Working through chapters 8 and 10, you've taken a close look at how to write and format a research essay in APA style. What you have to say—your content—is always more important than its appearance, but go to the effort to follow the APA guidelines, and you will ensure that your readers form a favourable first impression of your essay. Good luck on that paper.

PART 4

Writing Standard English

"We like that a sentence should read as if its author, had he held a plough instead of a pen, could have drawn a furrow deep and straight to the end."
—*Henry David Thoreau*

When you write a thoughtful, organized message—with an inviting appearance—you're well on your way to effectively expressing yourself. You've successfully shown strength in three components of the COSA formula for good writing: good content, effective organization, and attractive appearance. Your efforts to communicate your thoughts and feelings, though, can be thwarted by failure on the third criterion by which writing is judged: is the message written in Standard English?

Perhaps you aren't convinced that Standard English is easier to read than non-standard English. You may reason that as long as the reader can tell what you mean, isn't it just nitpicking to insist on "all that grammar stuff"? Read this passage from *Riddley Walker:*

On my naming day when I come 12 I gone front spear and kilt a wyld boar he parbly ben the las wyld pig on the Bundel Downs any how there hadnt ben none for a long time befor him nor I aint looking to see none agen. He dint make the groun shake nor nothing like that when he come on to my spear her wernt all that big plus he lookit poorly. (Hoban 1)

Russell Hoban's haunting novel of the near future shows us what can happen to the language If we can't standardize our usage. And consider what would happen if everyone innovated when writing. Bernard Shaw parodied English spelling by suggesting *ghoti* as a possible way to spell *fish* (/gh/ like *rough*, /o/ like *women*, /ti/ as in *station*). If we didn't bother to consult a dictionary, we would soon be unable to read one another's spellings. If we all creatively punctuated sentences, we would soon find it hard to understand what we wrote to one another.

When writers choose to write in Standard English, they are saying that they will go to some extra effort to make it easier for others to read. Users of Standard English aren't being finicky or stuffy—not most of them, anyway. They are simply trying to make reading easier. It's a kind of courtesy or good manners to go to the extra effort to create a more comfortable reading experience for your audience. Considerate writers work hard to make a good impression.

Part 4 describes and explains how to construct sentences that conform to the conventions or rules of Standard English. From discussing how to write complete sentences to how to capitalize proper nouns to highlight important information, the aim is to help you tell your audience your thoughts and feelings.

A teacher of writing is invaluable to your efforts to develop more skill as a writer. You are probably unaware of your deviations from written Standard English; you intuitively feel that you are writing correctly. A composition instructor can name the types of errors you make. Then, you can play your indispensable role in self-development: you can look up and read in part 4 how to avoid or correct that error.

You don't need to read every word of part 4. You probably know most of it. You need read only those sections that discuss the errors identified by your teacher.

Can you learn to write Standard English without a teacher? I wrote part 4 to try to make that possible, but it's much harder than improving with the help of a teacher. Chapter 11 discusses the fundamentals of creating complete sentences with correct agreement. Learn the content of chapter 11, and you will avoid the most common errors college students make. You may already know most of the content of chapter 12. Many students arrive at college with these skills; I've included the material so that if your teacher *does* draw your attention to such errors, you can quickly bring yourself up to speed on these conventions. Chapters 13 and 14 will help you learn to control the fundamentals of punctuation and other mechanical conventions of writing in Standard English and ensure that you have the advanced literacy skills employers expect of college graduates. Diligent study and practise of the accompanying exercises permits you—through independent effort—to make much progress, but you'll learn faster with a teacher.

If you find yourself puzzled by any explanations, it is probably because some of the vocabulary is unfamiliar to you. Try reading right through an explanation because, although you will meet terms from formal grammar, the information is usually reiterated in less formal language. You should find that you learn the vocabulary of grammar through this immersion approach. If you remain puzzled about a term, use the index to find it in the appendix; it presents the fundamentals of English grammar. You may find that it is helpful to refer occasionally to this background material.

CHAPTER 11

The Fundamentals: Creating Complete Sentences with Correct Agreement

"Words, sentences, books: so much more than simple pleasure,
so much the very heart of life itself."
—*Neil Bissoondath*

CHAPTER OBJECTIVE

After reading this chapter, you will be able to create complete Standard English sentences with correct agreement.

11.1 AVOID FRAGMENTS

Look at this construction: While living in Port Colborne. What do you think? Is it a grammatical sentence? Go with your intuition. Do you feel that something is missing, that it is not a complete sentence, that it doesn't express a complete thought? You're correct: it's only a part—a fragment—of a sentence. Use your strengths as a listener and speaker of English to help you write better. If your teacher is pointing out that you sometimes write fragments, though, you will find it helpful to study the text in this section to add specific, explicit comprehension to your intuitive feel for a complete sentence.

Sentences are complete when they have at least a subject—an agent, someone or something that does something—and a verb—a word that indicates the action occurring in the sentence—and when they express a complete thought. When a sentence is lacking an essential part, it is really only a fragment.

A sentence fragment looks like a sentence: it begins with a capital; it ends with a period or a question or exclamation mark. If it lacks a subject or verb, though, it is only a fragment. If it expresses less than a complete thought, it's only a fragment.

Consider some fragments and how they can be rewritten as complete sentences. There are two strategies for transforming fragments to sentences: rewrite the fragment as a complete sentence, or attach the fragment to an existing sentence or main clause.

* **Rewrite the fragment—phrase, clause, or list—as a complete sentence.**
  Here are some examples of fragments created when a phrase, clause, or list is written as though it made a complete sentence.

X (fragment): The writer of the comic strip *Between Friends*.

You can feel that something is missing. This fragment is missing an action word—a verb—so it cannot be a sentence. Here it is rewritten as a complete sentence.

Sandra Bell Lundy, who lives in Port Colborne, Ontario, writes the comic strip *Between Friends*.

X (fragment): When she created the comic strip *For Better or For Worse*.

That last construction is only a fragment, in this case a clause. (Clauses like this are called *subordinate* or *dependent* because they cannot stand as sentences, no matter how they are punctuated.) Although it has a subject and a verb, it is not a complete sentence because it does not express a complete thought. Here the fragment has been rewritten as a sentence.

Lynn Johnston became well-known in Canada when she created the comic strip *For Better or For Worse*.

This is also a fragment:

X (fragment): For example, Linwood Barclay, Arthur Black, Joey Slinger, and William Thomas.

We can rewrite by embedding this list in a complete sentence with a subject (*humourists*) and verb (*write*) and expressing a complete thought.

Four fine humourists write newspaper columns: Linwood Barclay, Arthur Black, Joey Slinger, and William Thomas.

* **Attach a fragment to a complete sentence.** The following example contains a fragment.

X (fragment): Lundy doesn't write *Between Friends* to be funny. To take an inside look at women.

The fragment, an infinitive phrase, can't be a sentence because it does not express a complete thought, but it could be attached to an existing sentence (or independent clause).

Lundy doesn't write *Between Friends* to be funny but to take an inside look at women.

A whole subordinate clause can be punctuated as if it were a sentence, yet it is really a fragment, as in the second construction in this example.

X (fragment): Lynn Johnston became a very successful cartoonist. When the strip began daily publication.

The second construction is a fragment, a subordinate clause, but it can be transformed into part of a complete, complex sentence by attaching it to the preceding sentence, which is an independent clause that does express a complete thought:

Lynn Johnston became a very successful cartoonist when the strip began daily publication.

A different rewriting produced the next sentence; note that the fragment has become an introductory element for the sentence.

When the strip began daily publication, Lynn Johnston became a very successful cartoonist.

To test your knowledge of how to avoid writing fragments by writing complete sentences, complete Activity 11–1.

▶ **ACTIVITY 11–1***

Avoiding Fragments

Follow the instructions in each item.

1. Is the following a fragment or a sentence? Kerry Powell (B4) writing about Alberta's at-risk wildlife.

2. Is the following a fragment or a sentence? The biggest hawk in North America, the ferruginous hawk.

3. Begin with the fragment and write one complete sentence. Ferruginous hawks soared the skies in most of Alberta. In the early 1900's.

4. Rewrite to make one complete sentence by ending with the fragment. They like to live in open areas. Including grasslands and fallow pastures.

5. Rewrite to make one complete sentence by starting the sentence with the fragment. When they are feeding their young. The parents eat about 480 gophers.

6. Rewrite to make one complete sentence by beginning the sentence with the fragment. Ferruginous hawks can live for twenty years. In the wild.

7. Finishing with the fragment, rewrite to make one complete sentence. The hawks are endangered. Because cultivation of the land reduces their habitat.

8. Finishing with the fragment, rewrite to make one complete sentence. Farmers know the hawks control rodent pests. Especially gophers.

11.2 DIVIDE FUSED SENTENCES BY FULLY SEPARATING THEM

To write a complete sentence, you not only need to avoid writing fragments, you need to construct and punctuate the sentence to clearly identify the main idea. The main idea in a sentence is expressed in the independent clause. There are several ways to construct and punctuate sentences to ensure that your writing makes independent clauses primary.

There's a problem in the next example: there are two main ideas in one sentence. In fact, there are two sentences fused together.

X (fused): Dr. Tom Connors wrote *Stompin' Tom: Before the Fame* he wanted to tell about his life.

There are two main ideas, and the simplest way to give primacy to each is to divide this fused construction into two grammatically correct sentences. Find the end of the first independent clause (the complete thought), and finish it with a period. Start the second complete thought (independent clause) with a capital, as in the next example.

Dr. Tom Connors wrote *Stompin' Tom: Before the Fame*. He wanted to tell about his life.

Now, there is a separate sentence for each complete thought. Each independent clause is primary.

There are other ways to fix fused sentences, but before examining them, see if you can do a perfect job on Activity 11–2.

▶ **ACTIVITY 11–2★**

Dividing Fused Sentences

Use just periods and capitals to write complete, grammatical sentences in place of these fused constructions.

1. Stompin' Tom's famous songs include "Bud the Spud" and "Tillsonburg" "Bud the Spud" is about a renegade potato hauler, and "Tillsonburg" tells about harvesting tobacco.

2. "Sudbury Saturday Night" celebrates the lives of working people "Lady k.d. lang" praises another singer-songwriter.

3. Tom Connors was born in the Depression in Saint John he and his single mom were forced on the road when he was three years old.

4. He was abused in St. Patrick's Orphanage he lived with a foster family, too.

5. By age 13, he had run away he learned to play guitar and sing for his supper.

6. He travelled Canada sometimes the police would jail him for vagrancy.

7. For years, he's worn a black cowboy hat and his stompin' boots legend has it that he's used the boots to pound a beat right through a sheet of plywood.

11.3 MEND COMMA SPLICES

In fused sentences, independent clauses—expressing complete thoughts—aren't separated at all. Comma splice errors occur when only a comma separates complete thoughts, as in this example.

X (comma splice): Mr. Dressup stopped taping his kids' TV show in 1996, he felt it was time to retire.

A comma is insufficient to separate two complete thoughts. The easiest way to fix a comma splice is to put a period at the end of the first complete thought (independent clause). Then, begin the second clause with a capital and create a second complete sentence.

Mr. Dressup stopped taping his kids TV show in 1996. He felt it was time to retire.

You'll have to proofread carefully to notice if you've run together two complete thoughts and joined them with only a comma. Test yourself by correcting these constructions that contain comma splices.

▶ ACTIVITY 11–3★

Mending Comma Splices

Using only periods and capitals, correct any constructions that contain comma splice errors.

1. Negro Creek Road in Holland Township near Owen Sound, Ontario, has an interesting history, it was named after blacks who settled the area before 1850 (Avery, "Blacks" A10).

2. These early settlers had escaped slavery in the United States, some other black pioneers had come from England.

3. The 1851 census showed about fifty black families living near Negro Creek and Negro Lake, they arrived before European settlers.

4. The Holland Township council renamed the road Moggie Road, George Moggie was an early white settler.

5. Howard Sheffield, who can trace his roots back nine generations to the first settlers, wanted the name reinstated, a delegation presented Council with a petition signed by more than 100 black and white citizens.

6. Eventually, five thousand people signed a petition to restore the old name, late in 1997, the Holland Township council put Negro Creek Road back on the map (Avery, "Negro Creek" A16).

11.4 SEPARATE SOME INDEPENDENT CLAUSES WITH A COMMA AND A CONJUNCTION

When you place absolutely no punctuation between two independent clauses—complete thoughts—you've created a fused sentence, as in this next example.

X (fused): Walter Ostanek won a Grammy Award for the Best Polka Album three years in a row he runs Walter Ostanek's Music Centre in St. Catharines, Ontario (Murphy A1).

If you put a comma between the two independent clauses, as in the next example, you would make a comma splice error.

X (comma splice): *Happiness is Polkas* was his forty-eighth recording, he has performed for more than four decades.

You've seen that the simplest way to separate the complete thoughts is to put a period at the end of the first and begin a new sentence by capitalizing the first word of the second independent clause. There is another way to separate two independent clauses grammatically yet keep them in the same compound sentence: use a comma and a coordinating conjunction, as in the next sentence.

The second most popular newspaper in Canada is the *Globe and Mail*, and it is available from sea to shining sea.

Any of the joining words (which are called coordinating conjunctions)—*and, but, for, nor, or, so,* and *yet*—can join independent clauses. When two clauses are joined by coordinating conjunctions, each independent clause remains a main clause; the writer is indicating that the ideas are equally important. Don't forget that these conjunctions are not always preceded by a comma—Jacques and Jill went up the hill—but they must be if they join independent clauses. Each independent clause will always express a complete thought and have both a subject and verb, as in this next sentence.

Polka King Walter Ostanek didn't win four Grammies in a row, but he did enjoy partying at the awards in Los Angeles.

▶ ACTIVITY 11–4★

Separating Independent Clauses with a Comma and a Coordinating Conjunction

Where appropriate, insert commas in the following sentences so that you correctly join independent clauses with a comma and a coordinating conjunction.

1. Do you like to clean your home and have people over for coffee?

2. Oh, you're not really that fond of the cleaning but you like chatting over a great cup of coffee.

3. You may have found the main reason for the growing popularity of cafés and it is not just good coffee.

4. Espresso and cappuccino are the old favourites at cafés but patrons are more often ordering chococcino and other exotic drinks.

5. Chococcino is prepared like a cappuccino but you steam chocolate milk into strong espresso coffee.

6. In Niagara Falls, one of my favourite cafés is the Italian Ice Cream Parlour and Café and I particularly like their cappuccino.

7. When I'm near the University of Toronto, I drop by the Future Bakery Café so that I can drink a bowl of coffee and watch the world pass by.

8. Gathering in a café with a few co-workers lets me dump the stress of work before I go home yet it doesn't leave me sleepy the way a beer does.

9. I like to combine browsing a bookstore and sipping a coffee yet I rarely find café bookstores such as the Bookshelf Café in Guelph.

10. The next time I'm in Winnipeg, I'm going to the Roasting House so I can try their espresso. I hear it's excellent.

11.5 SEPARATE SOME INDEPENDENT CLAUSES WITH A SEMICOLON

When two independent clauses express ideas that are closely related, the semicolon separates them more effectively than a period. The semicolon joins the complete thoughts in a way similar to the combination of a comma and a coordinating conjunction: both clauses express equally important main ideas. The combination of a comma and a conjunction makes the relationship of the two clauses very clear and should be used when you want to ensure the reader sees the relationship. The semicolon forces the reader to a longer pause—almost as long as for a period—so the semicolon is the right choice when you want your readers to take notice of the relationship of your first idea to the second, yet you do not feel the ideas need to be tied together as explicitly as a comma and a conjunction would bind them.

I want to go to the Calgary Stampede; I am planning a business trip to Calgary in July.

The sentence above and the one below convey similar thoughts. The sentence above uses a semicolon to draw the reader's attention to the close relationship of the main ideas. In the second example, the author leaves nothing to chance and uses a comma and a coordinating conjunction to show the cause–effect relationship clearly.

I want to go to the Calgary Stampede, so I am planning a business trip to Calgary in July.

A contrast is a close relationship commonly signalled by a semicolon:

Young adults play all day and play all night; middle-aged adults work all day and sleep all night.

▶ **ACTIVITY 11–5***

Separating Independent Clauses with a Semicolon

Using only a semicolon, fix each fused construction.

1. Nellie McClung showed her concern for women's rights early in 1890, at age sixteen, she signed a petition for women's suffrage.

2. She became a popular speaker for the Women's Christian Temperance Union she became a popular writer with the publication of *Sowing Seeds for Danny*.

3. In 1914, suffragette Nellie McClung led Manitoba women in seeking the right to vote Premier Sir Rodmond Roblin led the opposition.

4. Premier Roblin said, "I don't want a hyena in petticoats talking politics to me" McClung said, "Never retract, never explain, never apologize—get things done and let them howl."

5. Premier Roblin presided over Manitoba's parliament Nellie McClung held a mock parliament.

6. Premier Sir Rodmond Roblin said, "Nice women don't want the vote" suffragette Nellie McClung said, "Politics unsettles men."

11.6 SEPARATE SOME INDEPENDENT CLAUSES WITH SEMICOLONS AND CONJUNCTIVE ADVERBS (OR TRANSITION PHRASES)

The next sentence shows another way that two independent clauses can be combined in a compound sentence that gives equal weight to two main ideas and suggests to readers the close relationship of the ideas.

During the 1995 Quebec referendum, SaskTel provided a free, five-minute telephone call to Quebec; consequently, many people in Saskatchewan reached out and touched someone in Quebec.

The adverb *consequently* modifies the verbs *reached out* and *touched*, and serves as a way of joining the first independent clause with the second. Analyze the punctuation. If you imagined taking the word *consequently* out of the sentence, you would still need a semicolon to join the remaining—and related—independent clauses. Now imagine re-inserting the conjunctive adverb "consequently." *Consequently* becomes a non-essential word that introduces the second main clause. (As explained in "Separate an Introductory Element from the Independent Clause," you are observing a convention of Standard English when you put a comma between the introductory element and the main part of the sentence, the independent clause in which the author expresses a complete thought.) The following words can perform the dual role of adverb and conjunction:

accordingly, also, anyway, besides, consequently, finally, furthermore, however, incidentally, indeed, instead, likewise, meanwhile, moreover, nevertheless, next, otherwise, still, subsequently, then, therefore, thus

You follow similar procedures to punctuate sentences with transition phrases or conjunctive adverbs. Look at this sentence:

In St. Albert, Alberta, on her eighth birthday, Tanya Cowan gave birth to daughter Katelyn; by the way, Katelyn—also born on February 29—may become a young mom.

You can choose from many transition phrases to convey subtle relationships between some of your independent clauses. Here is a list of some common transition phrases you might use:

after all, as a result, at any rate, for example, in addition, in fact, in my opinion, in other words, on the contrary, on the other hand, to tell the truth

▶ ACTIVITY 11–6★

Separating Independent Clauses with Semicolons and Conjunctive Adverbs (and Transition Phrases)

Use the semicolon (and any additional punctuation needed) to edit these sentences.

1. Singer-songwriter Gordon Lightfoot immortalized a Great Lakes shipping disaster "The Wreck of the Edmund Fitzgerald" told how the ore freighter sank in Lake Superior in 1975.

2. For years, no one knew exactly what had happened to the ship however a Michigan entrepreneur videotaped the wreck in 1994.

3. All twenty-nine crew members died during a fierce storm a gigantic wave probably swamped the *Edmund Fitzgerald*.

4. At a dedication ceremony at the Great Lakes Shipwreck Museum in Whitefish Point, Michigan, the ship's brass bell tolled twenty-nine times that is relatives rang the bell once for each lost crew member.

5. The bell then sounded once more that day appropriately Gordon Lightfoot stepped forward to ring it in memory of all the sailors lost to the Great Lakes (Sepkowski A28).

11.7 USE A COMMA TO SEPARATE AN INTRODUCTORY ELEMENT FROM A MAIN CLAUSE

You punctuate to make it easier for readers to understand your writing. To make it easy for readers to spot your main clause, in which you express your main idea, use a comma to separate any introductory words from the independent clause. Consider this example:

To honour the first Canadian-born prime minister, a CEGEP is named John Abbott.

The main idea is in the independent clause, *a CEGEP is named John Abbott*. The sentence, though, starts with some introductory words. The comma at the end of this introduction alerts the reader to the more important information that follows—in the main clause. There are many different kinds of introductory elements, and you will make your writing easier to read if you follow each with a comma, and then write the independent clause. When you are reading a novel or newspaper, you will occasionally see a short introductory element *not* followed by a comma, but you can be more confident that readers will understand if you do use the comma.

  ★ **Use a comma after *yes* or *no* preceding a main clause**

Yes, Assiniboine Community College has a campus in Brandon, Manitoba.

  ★ **Use a comma after a phrase that precedes a main clause**

At numerous off-campus locations, thousands of students study part-time.

If the phrase is very short, you do not need to follow it with a comma:

At age four I started to watch *Mr. Dressup*.

  ★ **Use a comma after a clause that precedes a main clause**

When Manitoba transformed its three technical vocational schools into community colleges, the Manitoba Vocational Training Centre was renamed Assiniboine Community College.

* **When someone is addressed in a sentence, use a comma after the name**

Uma, I'm glad you're my friend.

* **Use a comma after a mild interjection that precedes a main clause**

Oh, look who just came in.

* **Use a comma after a conjunctive adverb or transitional phrase**

Incidentally, L.R. Wright is one of my favourite mystery writers. In my opinion, her Staff Sergeant Alberg—she introduced him in *The Suspect*—is a fascinating character.

ACTIVITY 11–7*

Separate Introductory Elements from Main Clauses

Edit these constructions to make them grammatically correct sentences. One sentence is correctly punctuated. Write a C beside it, and don't change it. Underline the number of the sentence for which you could add a comma, but don't have to.

1. When you try to name Canadian landscape painters the members of the Group of Seven probably come to mind.

2. Arguably the most famous of the Group of Seven artists Tom Thomson (1877–1917) changed the way Canadians looked at common objects such as trees.

3. Peeking out of the woods near Kleinburg, Ontario the McMichael Canadian Art Collection exhibits many paintings by Tom Thomson, A.J. Casson, and other members of the Group of Seven.

4. Not only can you view their paintings, you can also look at works by contemporary Native Canadian artists.

5. In addition to viewing all this art you can explore more than 100 acres of the kind of landscape that inspired the artists.

6. Even if you don't go outside you can still view the scenery through the gallery's floor-to-ceiling windows.

7. If you are interested in purchasing prints or art books visit the Gallery Shop.

8. If you stay past lunch don't worry; you can eat at the McMichael Restaurant.

9. In the summertime you can even eat your meal on the outdoor terrace.

10. If you are near Toronto it's worth the forty-minute drive to visit the McMichael Canadian Art Collection.

11.8 SEPARATE NON-ESSENTIAL LANGUAGE FROM THE INDEPENDENT CLAUSE

The main idea of a sentence is always expressed in the main clause. By using commas to set off non-essential information, you make it easier for your reader to attend to the basic information.

* Identify parenthetical expressions with commas

Holland College, as some of you may know, is in Charlottetown.

You should vote for Thomson, in my opinion.

* Identify non-restrictive clauses and phrases with commas

You can study nursing at Mohawk College, which is in Hamilton.

The dependent clause *which is in Hamilton* provides additional information about the college, but it is not essential to the fundamental meaning of the sentence. Contrast that sentence with this one:

St. Clair is the community college that is in Windsor.

Now the dependent clause *that is in Windsor* contains information essential to the basic meaning of the sentence; without that information, you cannot identify which particular college is being discussed. Note that you use the relative pronoun *that*, rather than *which*, in this restrictive clause. The contrast between restrictive and non-restrictive clauses can be seen in the following two sentences, which, although alike in appearance, have quite different meanings:

Car sellers who lie are a hazard to the public.

Car sellers, who lie, are a hazard to the public.

The first construction restricts the discussion to the tiny group of people who are car sellers who do not fairly represent what they sell. The second sentence makes the unwarranted assertion that all car salespeople lie. In the next several examples, notice the commas surrounding several types of interruptions in the sentences, interruptions of non-essential material.

* Separate examples or contrasts added to independent clauses

In the next example, although the information about the specific subjects is interesting—important, even—its omission would not change the basic meaning of the sentence.

At the Nautical Institute of the Strait Area Campus of the Nova Scotia Community College, you can study marine-related subjects, including industrial rigging, marine emergency duties, and navigation simulation.

The campus in Port Hawkesbury, not Halifax.

* Use a comma to separate a tag (confirmatory) question

Port Hawkesbury is on Cape Breton, isn't it?

* Use commas with speaker tags that interrupt direct quotations

"Do you know," asked Jeff, "where I can study marine safety procedures?"

"You can do that in Port Hawkesbury," said Thewodros.

▶ ACTIVITY 11–8*

Separating Non–essential Language from Independent Clauses

Add commas, where necessary, to correctly punctuate these sentences.

1. "Don't you think Zejnil that there's nothing like a special event such as a festival or a rodeo to add some excitement to everyday life?"

2. "Yes" said Saima "and the people of British Columbia really know how to throw great events."

3. Vancouver's Chinatown second in size only to San Francisco's is the perfect place to be for the Chinese New Year.

4. The Rain Festival which celebrates Vancouver's generous precipitation is held in Gastown the first Sunday in April.

5. The Pacific National Exhibition which is held from late August to Labour Day attracts people from all over the province doesn't it?

6. The Cloverdale Rodeo held on the Victoria Day weekend is a popular event in Surrey.

7. Victoria not unexpectedly has the country's biggest celebration of Victoria Day including the huge Swiftsure Race for sailboats.

8. "Even smaller communities (e.g., New Westminster) make the summers special by hosting concerts in bandshells don't they?"

9. The Country Living Festival held in Chilliwack for three weeks in mid-May gives attendees a chance to celebrate even before summer begins.

10. Nanaimo the sun porch of Canada hosts many special events including the Great International Nanaimo Bathtub Race, Empire Day, the Nanaimo Festival, and the Vancouver Island Exhibition.

11. The Filberg Festival an arts and crafts show and more is held in Comox in the first week in August.

12. It's a bit of a surprise to learn that Mardi Gras held in February each year is one way the people of Dawson Creek add excitement to their lives.

13. The good citizens of Kelowna look after the human desire to feast with among other events the Black Mountain Rodeo and the Wine Festival.

14. You'll feel like it's a festival whenever you visit Barkerville Historic Town a former gold-rush town restored to the way it looked in the 1870's.

▶ ACTIVITY 11–9*

Review of Sections 11.1–11.8

Test your ability to write complete sentences. Make whatever changes are necessary to edit these sentences.

1. Joni Mitchell was born in Fort Macleod, Alberta one of her best songs is "Both Sides Now."

2. William Shatner grew up in Montreal, his most famous acting role was Captain Kirk of the *USS Enterprise*.

3. Once called the most famous Canadian on the planet *Baywatch* star Pamela Lee was born Pamela Anderson in Ladysmith, British Columbia.

4. Leslie Nielsen star of the film comedies *Naked Gun* and *Airplane* was born in Regina.

5. *Reader's Digest* (Canadian English edition) has the largest number of subscribers of any publication in Canada the Canadian French edition also sells well.

6. The English-language edition of *Chatelaine* has the second-largest paid circulation incidentally the French-language edition is also very popular.

7. Although more Canadians subscribe to *Maclean's* than *Time*.

8. Alfred Billies co-founder of Canadian Tire died in 1995.

9. Since *Maclean's* magazine began ranking Canadian universities Mount Allison University has been identified as a top school for undergraduate studies.

10. Because he had helped to discover how to use insulin to treat diabetes Sir Frederick Banting became the best known Canadian from Alliston, Ontario.

11.9 ENSURE AGREEMENT OF SUBJECT AND VERB IN PERSON

In English, subjects of a sentence can be in the first, second, or third person. When we are speaking of ourselves, we use the first person (*I* or *we*). When we are speaking to someone, we use the second person (*you*). When we are speaking about other people, or things, we use the third person (*everyone, he, it, she, they, many, the people,* and so forth). Native speakers of English almost always automatically do something when they begin a sentence in first, second or third person: they adjust the form of the verb to agree with that person. Consider the following:

I run.	We run.
You run.	You run.
He runs.	They run.
She runs.	All of them run.
A dog runs.	Dogs run.

Notice the form of verb used for the sentences in third person (*he, she, a dog*)? It is the base form plus *s*. In regular verbs in the present tense, only the third-person-singular subject requires the verb form to change. Except for the subjunctive mood, person does not affect the verb form in other tenses. (I ran, you ran, he ran, we ran . . . .)

The verb *be* is more problematic. Here are the verb forms for *be* in the present and past tenses.

I am.	We are.	I was.	We were.
You are.	You are.	You were.	You were.
He/She/It is.	They are.	He/She/It was.	They were.

▶ ACTIVITY 11–10★

Ensuring Agreement of the Subject and Verb in Person

Proofread and edit these sentences. Identify a correct sentence with a *C*.

1. A new store, Sgt. Preston's Outpost, sell RCMP mementos.

2. I dislikes that Disney has the marketing rights.

3. You sees Mountie refrigerator magnets for sale in the store.

4. They has RCMP belt buckles.

5. He buy some Li'l Mountie slippers as a gag gift for his boss.

11.10 ENSURE AGREEMENT OF SUBJECT AND VERB IN NUMBER

You've seen that nouns and pronouns can be singular (one thing) or plural (more than one object). A singular subject must be accompanied by a verb in the singular form. To be grammatical, a sentence with a plural subject requires a verb in the plural form.

The biggest <u>campus</u> of Douglas College <u>is</u> in New Westminster, BC.

Other <u>campuses</u> of Douglas College <u>are</u> in Maple Ridge and Coquitlam.

* Find the true subject and make its verb agree in number

You'll have no problem with choosing the verb form that matches your subject if you remember one more point: the subject of a sentence is never found in the prepositional phrase.

One of the CEGEP's is in Hull.

The verb form is *is* because the subject is *one* (not the word *CEGEP's*, which is after the preposition *of*) and *one* is singular.

* Use a plural form of the verb when two or more subjects are joined by *and*

Alvaro <u>is</u> cooking.

Alvaro and Martha <u>are</u> cooking.

* Use a singular verb form with singular indefinite pronouns

Everybody swims.

* Use a singular verb form with collective nouns (and indefinite articles) when they refer to the group as a whole; use the plural form when they refer to individuals.
Collective nouns, such as *class*, *couple*, *family*, and *majority*, can refer to one group or to individuals within a group.

The majority supports the proposed bill.

The majority have voted for it.

To achieve subject–verb agreement, you just need to think about whether you are referring to the group—use the singular—or the individuals—use the plural form of the verb.

Some indefinite pronouns take a plural verb form in some contexts and a singular verb in others (*all, any, most, none, some*). Again, you'll choose the correct verb form if you identify whether the pronoun is representing a group or whole rather than individual items.

All of the pie is gone.

All of the children are gone.

Some of the house is brick.

Some of the houses are brick.

▶ **ACTIVITY 11–11***

Ensuring Agreement of the Subject and Verb in Number

Write a C when the parenthesized verb agrees in number with its subject, and correct any errors inside the parentheses.

1. The Canadian Broadcasting Corporation (CBC) began broadcasting television programs in 1952. The CBC vaults at the Broadcasting Centre in Toronto (holds) some remarkable records of Canadian television's first two decades.

2. One of the finds (are) recordings by French torch singer Edith Piaf.

3. On one of the recordings, Sean Connery (act) in his first Shakespearean play.

4. Hour-long dramas (includes) plays by Alice Munro, Robertson Davies, Mordecai Richler, and Margaret Atwood.

5. Leslie Nielsen and William Shatner (appears) in dramas, too.

6. There (is) cans of film, videotape, and kinescopes (Quill B1+).

11.11 CREATE LOGICAL CONSTRUCTIONS

Consider what's wrong with this sentence.

X By dreaming of a white Christmas nearly made myself sad.

It doesn't sound quite right, does it? And that's probably all you need to know to fix it. But, considering why it's ungrammatical may help you avoid making such constructions, too.

When we read *"by dreaming of a white Christmas"* we expect this adjective phrase to modify a noun or pronoun, but it doesn't. We can supply a pronoun for it to modify:

By dreaming of a white Christmas, I nearly made myself sad.

We could also rewrite the prepositional phrase to be a gerundive phrase; in other words, we could make it the subject of the sentence and fix the construction.

Dreaming of a white Christmas nearly made me sad.

Mixed constructions occur when word groups are combined in ungrammatical or non-meaningful ways. Writers sometimes start a sentence one way and then, partway through, they think of a better way to say it and continue writing the remainder of the sentence without considering whether the newly conceived ending will work with the original beginning. As long as you proofread carefully, you'll catch these illogical constructions and fix them.

A similar problem occurs if writers use, after a linking verb, words that cannot logically follow that verb.

X Reading is when you experience wonderful situations.

The sentence just doesn't make sense. This construction is better writing:

When you read, you experience wonderful situations.

Now you've got a logical construction.

▶ **ACTIVITY 11–12★**

Creating Logical Constructions

Rewrite these sentences to make them logical constructions.

1. We were tired of being unemployed is the main reason we came to the Wascana Institute in Regina.

2. Being uninterested in jobs traditionally filled by women was why we didn't study dental assisting or early childhood education.

3. My reason for studying farm business management was because people will always have to eat.

4. Jan found the Pork Production Technician program, which upon entering it made a good choice.

5. You can choose a program that will lead to work or as one who studies only what is interesting.

11.12 ENSURE PRONOUN–ANTECEDENT AGREEMENT IN PERSON

What is wrong with the following sentence?

X If a person wants to conserve water, you should put mulch around plants to slow evaporation.

If the sentence sounds wrong, that's good: You can probably fix it. Here's the reason it sounds odd. The sentence begins with the third-person point of view (*a person*), and the problem occurs when the writer uses the second-person pronoun *you* to refer to the third-person antecedent *person*—there's a lack of pronoun–antecedent agreement in person. The writer's sudden *shift of person* is disconcerting. Try this activity to see if you can fix this kind of problem when you proofread.

▶ **ACTIVITY 11–13★**

Ensuring Agreement in Person

Rewrite this passage, eliminating the writer's sudden shifts in person or viewpoint. Show a consistent third-person viewpoint.

Water conservation saves money because—to make the water safe for drinking—we must pay to treat every drop of water that comes out of the tap. You should plant drought-resistant trees. We could all water during the cool parts of the day. Citizens should put only one inch of water on lawns. If we cut our grass higher, we will use less water. If everyone conserves a little, we can save a lot of water.

▶ **ACTIVITY 11–14★**

Ensuring Consistent Person

Rewrite this passage to avoid the sudden shifts in perspective the writer has created by changing abruptly from the viewpoint of one person to another.

Cavendish Farms—the PEI company that makes those great frozen french fries—was named after Cavendish Beach. You may know that the original plant was opened in New Annan in 1961. We called it Seabrook Farms. Now we concentrate on potato processing. The company has become one of Canada's largest exporters of french fries. And, as President Robert Irving noted in 1996, "This province is now Canada's largest potato-growing area" ("Growing" 3).

11.13 ENSURE PRONOUN–ANTECEDENT AGREEMENT IN NUMBER

Why is the following sentence incorrect?

X If a person quits smoking, they will improve their health.

Person is the antecedent of two pronouns in this sentence. In other words, two pronouns—*they* and *their*—refer to the word *person*. *Person* is a singular noun, and its accompanying verb must be in the singular form—subject–verb agreement in number—and the pronoun and its antecedent should also agree in number. The pronouns *they* and *their* are plural. The easiest way to make them agree in number is to change the antecedent to a plural noun (*people*); then the pronouns, which are plural, too, are in agreement in number.

If people quit smoking, they improve their health.

In the example above, the plural antecedent *people* agrees in number with the plural pronouns *they* and *their*.

The problem with the lack of agreement could also have been fixed by rewriting so that the pronouns and antecedent were singular, as in this example.

If a person quits smoking, she will improve her health.

The antecedent *person* is singular and its corresponding pronouns—*she* and *her*—are singular, too. This editing creates another problem, though: the new sentence is gender-biased, sexist.

Here are several conventions you should follow to ensure pronoun–antecedent agreement. They are very similar to the conventions for subject–verb agreement.

＊ When antecedents are joined by *and*, use plural pronouns

Kelsey Institute and Palliser Institute are post-secondary schools of the Saskatchewan Institute of Applied Science and Technology; they offer many practical programs.

＊ When the antecedent is a collective noun, use a singular pronoun when referring to the group as a whole

The Humber College faculty is supporting longer library hours; it supports the purchase of more periodicals, too.

＊ When the antecedent is a collective noun, use a plural noun when referring to individuals in the group

The faculty of York University are meeting their new classes today.

＊ Ensure demonstrative pronouns agree with their antecedents

Many job-seeking students are enrolled in engineering programs. These are among the offerings at the University of Waterloo.

Although *these* is in another sentence, it refers to *programs*, which is a plural word. When the antecedent is plural, its corresponding pronoun must also be plural, and consistently so, through the whole paragraph and document. This creates a consistency of pronoun agreement that makes your writing easier to read.

＊ When pronouns and antecedents are joined by *either . . . or*, or *neither . . . nor*, make the pronoun agree with the nearer antecedent.

Either Rona or her brothers will bring their guitars.

Neither the twins nor Rhonda brought her mandolin.

▶ **ACTIVITY 11–15★**

Ensuring Agreement of Pronouns and Their Antecedents

Rewrite these sentences to correct any problems with pronoun–antecedent agreement.

1. Movie reviews are always interesting. It can range from panning to praising a film.

2. Take David Cronenberg's *Crash*, for example. They had reviews that said it was disgusting and reviews that called it a masterpiece.

3. People who are excited by car crashes are the characters, a complex psychological character.

4. The film is based on J.G. Ballard's novel. They are a rich source of material for Cronenberg to work from.

5. Novel and film—it is both highly modern.

11.14 ENSURE PRONOUN–ANTECEDENT AGREEMENT IN GENDER

In the English language, pronouns can be masculine (*he*), feminine (*she*), or neutral (*it*). Here's a sentence in which the writer shows how to ensure the pronoun agrees in gender with its antecedent.

My <u>uncle</u> asked <u>his</u> physician how to quit smoking.

Since *uncle* is a masculine noun, any pronoun referring to the uncle must also be masculine.

In brief sentences, you will probably easily and automatically ensure this kind of agreement, but to ensure consistent gender references, you have to be careful to avoid making shifts in gender in your paragraphs and documents.

X A citizen can take several steps to conserve water (City of Niagara Falls, n.p.). She can eliminate leaks in faucets and hoses. When washing a car, he can use a pail rather than a hose.

The simplest way to write with consistent references to gender is to change all the pronouns to the gender-neutral plural forms.

Citizens can take steps to conserve water. They can eliminate leaks in facets. When washing cars, they can use pails instead of hoses.

▶ **ACTIVITY 11–16★**

Creating Consistency of Gender

Rewrite this passage to avoid sudden, disconcerting shifts of gender.

Harriet Tubman escaped slavery in the United States and came to St. Catharines in 1851. She didn't just thank her lucky stars that in Canada slavery had been outlawed in 1834, and despised before that. He made nineteen dangerous trips back into the United States of America. Her indomitable spirit led him to become a nurse and a spy for the Union throughout the American civil war. Called the Moses of her people, there was a reward of $40,000 on his head. Her efforts helped more than 300 other slaves come to freedom (Ffrench).

11.15 SOME CONCLUDING THOUGHTS

There really are so many conventions of Standard English. How can you learn the most with the least effort and in the least time? Write the very best document you can. Ask your English teacher to identify errors in your writing. Then find and study the relevant material in your text. Observe these conventions, and you will more often get what you want from your writing.

CHAPTER 12

Observing Other Basic Standard English Conventions

"The pen is a formidable weapon, but a man can kill himself with it a great deal more easily than he can other people."
—*George Dennison Prentice*

CHAPTER OBJECTIVE

You will learn to observe more conventions of Standard English, including correct use of pronouns, adjectives, and adverbs, and a preference for the active voice and varied sentence structure.

12.1 USE THE CORRECT PRONOUN CASE

What is wrong with this sentence?

X Me want to attend Champlain Regional College in Lennoxville.

That *me* doesn't sound right? The writer has used the *objective* form of the first-person-singular pronoun, but what's needed is the first-person-singular *subjective* form of the pronoun (*I*).

I want to attend the University of Winnipeg.

This list contrasts the subjective and objective forms of the pronouns.

Subjective Pronouns

Singular	Plural
I	we
you	you
he/it/she/who	they/who

Objective Pronouns

Singular	Plural
me	us
you	you
her/him/it/one/whom	them/whom

* Use the subjective form of the pronoun when it is the subject of the sentence or when it refers to the subject

She and I attended the Dawson Creek campus of Northern Lights College (NLC).

The recipients of some helpful career exploration were we.

The last sentence is correct because the writer knew that both the subject of the sentence (*recipients)* and the pronoun referring to it (*we*) had to be in the subjective form. (But it is so formal a sentence, you are not likely to ever hear it spoken.)

* Use the objective case of the pronoun when the pronoun is an object of a verb, verbal, or preposition

NLC graduated <u>us</u>.

Us is the direct object; you need to choose the objective form for this pronoun, just as in the next sentence in which the pronoun is the object of a preposition.

NLC awarded Associate Arts degrees to <u>us</u>.

Be careful to use the objective form of the pronoun when you have compound objects.

The President told Sara and <u>me</u> that we had done well.

Test yourself. Explain why the next two sentences have pronouns in the correct case.

Who is coming to the party?

Whom shall we ask to make a toast?

The first sentence is correct because the writer made *who* the subject of the sentence, and *who* is the subject form of this pronoun.

The second sentence is correct because the subject of the sentence is *we*. *Whom* is in the objective form because it is the object of the sentence.

▶ **ACTIVITY 12–1***

Using the Correct Pronoun Case

Indicate when an underlined pronoun has been used correctly, and change the pronoun case when necessary.

1. How many of the Acadia students <u>whom</u> did not read the materials passed the test?

2. Give that book to Paula and I.

3. Vinnie and <u>me</u> are going to Heritage College in Hull.

4. Both of <u>we</u> attended Grant MacEwan College.

5. <u>Who</u> shall I say called?

12.2 MAKE CLEAR REFERENCES TO NOUNS

Your readers will more easily understand your writing if you ensure that when you use a pronoun, you make it clear just exactly to whom or to what that pronoun refers.

X I'd like to study computer-aided drafting at Westviking College because it's interesting.

Think about it. Does the writer believe the program is interesting, or is it the college that's interesting? The following sentence is clearer.

At Westviking College, I'd like to study drafting because it is interesting.

Your meaning will be clearer if you keep the pronoun near the word to which it refers, its antecedent. This practice reduces problems such as the one that occurs in the next sentence.

X I chose to study at Westviking College in Corner Brook because of its beautiful setting.

Is the campus in a beautiful locale, or does the writer mean that Corner Brook, Newfoundland, was the scenic attraction? It's a little hard to tell. The situation is clarified in this sentence:

I chose to study at Westviking College in Corner Brook because I can go from classroom to ski slopes in just fifteen minutes.

This rewriting has eliminated a pronoun that had no clear referent. Unless there are two community colleges in Corner Brook, it now seems clear that the student who chose Westviking did so because of the ski slopes.

Take a moment to consider how to fix this sentence so that a reader can easily and quickly understand it.

X Kim told her mother that she was a saint.

Did you imagine the solution of having one speaker quote another?

Kim said, "Mom, you're a saint."

Perhaps you clarified the sentence by rewriting it with indirect speech.

Kim told her mom that her mom was a saint.

▶ ACTIVITY 12–2★

Making Clear References to Nouns

Rewrite the following sentences as directed.

1. He bought a new shirt at the bookstore at the University College of the Fraser Valley in Chilliwack; it was not very nice.

    Rewrite so we know that the *shirt* was ugly.

2. Sally told her mother that she was too easily frustrated.

    Rewrite with an indirect quotation so that we know that the *mother* is frustrated.

3. He told his father that he was a pessimist.

    Use a direct quotation to make it clear that the *father* is the pessimist.

4. Jill told her partner that the head of the firm needed to talk to her.

    Use a direct quotation so that we can tell that the *boss* wants to talk to Jill's *partner*.

5. He put a new engine in his car, but it still didn't run well.

    Make it clear that the *car* is the problem.

12.3 USE THE CORRECT TENSE

There are nine tenses in the English language. Whenever you construct a sentence, you have to choose the tense that will best express your meaning, that will best show when actions occurred.

Each verb tense tells the reader about the time of the action, with reference to when you are telling or writing about the action. The form of the verb changes for the various tenses. Examine how three verbs change in form, and meaning, in the different tenses. You can study a verb that changes in regular, predictable ways (*help*), one that is irregular (*take*), and one that is very common but very irregular (*be*).

★ **Present Tense**: Begin with the present tense. Use it when you are telling about an action occurring now (e.g., I see it!). You also use the present tense for general truths (e.g., Democracy is the most participative governmental system), for actions that are habitual (I like to watch movies on video), or for very near future events (My classes begin tomorrow). In writing reports in which you express your opinion, use the present tense.

The literature <u>shows</u> that people abused as children do not necessarily become abusive adults.

Here are the present-tense forms of these three common verbs:

I help/take/am

You help/take/are

He/she/it helps/takes/is

We help/take/are

You help/take/are

They help/take/are

You might ask: How can I figure out the verb form for a verb as idiosyncratic as *be*? The dictionary will show you the correct form. The *Penguin Canadian Dictionary*, for example, lists the base, simple form of the verb, and if the verb is irregular (e.g., *take*), the -*s* form that we use for the third-person-singular (*takes*), the past tense form (*took*), the past participle (*taken*), and the present participle (*taking*).

★ **Past Tense:** Look at how these verbs are formed in the past tense, which you use for actions that have already been completed (e.g., I worked for my uncle last summer).

Here are the same three verbs in past tense:

I/he/she/it helped/took/was

You/we/you/they helped/took/were

★ **Present Perfect Tense:** Use the present perfect tense to express actions that began in the past and either continued to the time you wrote about them or are still having an effect at the time of writing.

She has studied all night to prepare for her next exam.

To express the present perfect tense, use the present tense of the auxiliary verb *have*, and add the past participle of the main verb, as demonstrated below:

I/we/they/you have helped/taken/been

He/she/it has helped/taken/been

★ **Past Perfect Tense:** Use the past perfect to report actions that were completed before a specified time in the past.

I had paid my bill before the overdue notice arrived.

Form the past perfect with the past-tense auxiliary of *have* (*had*) and the past participle of the main verb, as follows:

I/you/he/she/it/we/you/they had helped/taken/been

★ **Future Tense:** Use the future tense to express actions that will occur in the future. Form it by using the auxiliary verb *will* and the base form of the verb, as follows:

I/you/he/she/it/we/you/they will help/take/be

★ **Future Perfect Tense:** Use the future perfect tense to indicate an action that will have occurred before some specific time in the future.

I will have completed my exams before I begin my summer job.

Form the future perfect tense with the future tense of the auxiliary *have* and the past participle of the main verb, as follows:

I/you/he/she/it/we/you/they will have helped/taken/been

★ **Present Progressive Tense:** Use the present progressive tense to express an action that is progressing even as you report on it.

I am eating a roti as I am talking to you on my cellphone.

Form the present progressive tense by combining the present tense of the auxiliary verb *be* with the present participle of the main verb, as below:

I am helping/taking/being

You are helping/taking/being

He/she/it is helping

We/you/they are helping/taking/being

★ **Past Progressive Tense:** Use the past progressive tense to describe an action that was going on when another event in the past began.

I was eating a calzone and talking on my cellphone when I drove into the ditch.

Form the past progressive tense using the past tense of the auxiliary verb *be* and the present participle, as follows:

I/he/she/it was helping/taking/being

You/we/they were helping/taking/being

★ **Future Progressive Tense:** Use the future progressive tense to report an action that will be happening in the future.

I will be recuperating for awhile.

Form the future progressive tense with the future tense of the verb *be* and the present participle of the main verb, as demonstrated:

I/you/he/she/it/we/you/they will be helping/taking/being

12.4 USE TENSE CONSISTENTLY AND LOGICALLY

Your reader will form a more favourable impression of your writing if you avoid unnecessary shifts of tense. Consider what is wrong with this paragraph.

X I went diving. I wade into the pond to check that it was deep enough. I will not want to hurt myself by hitting an obstacle when I dive (*Safe Diving*).

The shift of tense from the first to the second sentence is particularly distracting. Notice the improvement when the writer uses tense consistently and logically.

I wanted to dive. I waded into the pond to ensure that it was deep enough. I didn't want to hurt myself by hitting an obstacle.

▶ ACTIVITY 12–3★

Using Tense Consistently and Logically

Rewrite this passage to use tense logically. Cast the passage mostly in the past tense.

A fascinating article in the Yarmouth *Vanguard* tell about Eugene Meuse, an inventor who will be born in 1885 in Amirault's Hill ("Program" 5B). By age fourteen he will have made his own camera and begin a lifelong passion for taken photographs. He invent an easy chair, a cranking can opener (patented in 1911), and even a "design for a high speed aircraft with wings which fold back in flight."

12.5 USE THE CORRECT VERB MOOD

Use the *indicative* mood to ask questions or to state facts or opinions:

George Brown College is in Toronto.

Use the *imperative* mood to issue commands:

Go to Selkirk College. Find a part-time job in Castlegar.

You've already studied how to ensure subject–verb agreement for the indicative and imperative moods. The *subjunctive mood*, which you use to express a conjecture or a situation contrary to fact, influences the verb form in two cases.

To form the subjunctive mood in the third-person-singular in the present tense, you drop the -*s* ending of the verb.

I insist my boss *buy* lunch for everyone whenever she schedules noontime meetings.

Notice that *buy* is not in the verb-s form that the third-person pronoun would take in the present tense of the indicative mood. The *-s* has been dropped to express the subjunctive mood.

You may remember that the subjunctive mood is used for verbs in *that* clauses and for clauses beginning with *if* when the clause suggests something contrary to fact, or something that is unlikely.

If you were here with me again, I would be happy.

You can tell that the writer is still alone.

In contrast, when the situation is not against fact, we do not use the subjunctive.

I know that my boss buys lunch every day.

For the verb *be*, form the subjunctive by using *be* for all forms of the present tense, *were* for all forms of the past tense, and *have been* for all forms of the present perfect tense.

Were you there, things would have gone differently.

Be consistent in your choice of mood. See if you can detect a shift in mood in this sentence:

X If he were alone, he would be lonely, and if he was to fall down, there would be no one to help him.

Note that in the second *if* clause, the writer has shifted out of the subjunctive mood.

If he were alone, he would be lonely, and if he *were* to fall down, there would be no one to help him.

▶ **ACTIVITY 12-4★**

Using the Correct Form of the Verb

Write the correct form of the verb for each of these sentences in the subjunctive mood.

1. She demanded that an apology (is, was, be) offered.

2. Someone suggested that the order (be, is, was) dropped.

3. I demand that he (stops, stop) calling me names.

4. Wish you (are, was, were) here.

5. I recommend he (come, comes) to school today.

12.6 FAVOUR THE ACTIVE VOICE

In English, you can express yourself using the active or passive voice. You are using the active voice when you make the subject carry out the action. You are using the passive voice when you create sentences in which the subject is acted *upon*.

Active Voice: Mary wrote the paper.

Passive Voice: The paper was written by Mary.

When you write in the active voice, you make your sentences more direct and succinct. To transform a sentence from the passive to the active voice, determine who does the action. Then write the sentence with the actor as the subject. You almost always make the better choice when you write in the active voice. If the actor (doer) is unknown, as in the next sentence where the writer does not know the robber's identity, you should use the passive voice.

X Someone robbed the variety store.

The variety store was robbed.

When you are proofreading, be careful that you have chosen voice logically; usually you will also maintain a consistent voice. Don't jar your reader by switching to the passive voice unnecessarily.

▶ **ACTIVITY 12-5★**

Favouring the Active Voice

Rewrite this paragraph, favouring the active voice unless there is a good reason for using the passive voice.

Pasta was being cooked by Maureen Brisebois ("Lucky Woman" A4) in Aylmer, Quebec. An old tree was struck by lightning. The clothes line was travelled by the lightning. Brisebois was passed by a huge flash of electricity. A pot was lifted by Brisebois. The water spilled out because part of the pot had been fused to the element. If her other hand had been touched by metal—even the sink—Brisebois would have been killed.

12.7 USE ADJECTIVES TO MODIFY NOUNS

When you use an adjective to modify a noun, you provide additional information about that noun. In the next sentence, *tiny* and *brown*—adjectives—are used correctly to modify your reader's understanding of the noun *mouse*: readers form a different picture of the creature than they would have if those words were different, or omitted.

He was startled by the tiny brown mouse sitting next to his keyboard.

▶ **ACTIVITY 12–6★**

Using Adjectives to Modify Nouns

Put a C beside any sentence that has a correct word inside the parentheses and change any wrong words to appropriate adjectives.

1. Dr. Wilfred Bigelow had a very (cleverly) idea in his sleep (Papp A6).

2. He was recently named to the (Canada) Medical Hall of Fame for the procedure that came from his idea.

3. Dr. Bigelow dreamed that chilling patients before their (majorly) heart surgery could delay the deterioration of body tissue that occurs when a patient's circulation is stopped.

4. His (startling) suggestion stunned the American Surgical Association in 1950.

5. While serving in a surgical unit in the Second World War he had seen (savagely) frostbite.

12.8 USE COMPARATIVE AND SUPERLATIVE ADJECTIVES CORRECTLY

An adjective can be used to provide additional information by a comparison, too.

Positive Form: Montreal is big.

Comparative Form: It is bigger than Quebec City.

Superlative Form: Montreal is the biggest city in the province of Quebec.

★ Form the comparative by

  – adding -*er* to the adjective form

Positive: large

Comparative: larger

  – preceding the adjective—almost all adjectives of two or more syllables—with *more*

Positive: eager

Comparative: more eager

  – preceding the adjective with *less*

Positive: eager

Comparative: less eager

The superlative form is used when we are comparing more than two things. The superlative tells us the one that has the most (or least) of whatever quality we are comparing.

* **Form the superlative by**
    - adding -*est* to the adjective

Positive: odd

Superlative: oddest

    - preceding the adjective with *most* (for most adjectives of two syllables, and all those with more than two syllables)

Positive: eager

Superlative: most eager

    - preceding the adjective with *least* to form the negative superlative form

Positive: eager

Superlative: least eager

Some adjectives form the comparative in irregular ways. You'll have to consult your dictionary. Be careful to find the entry for the part of speech you want to use. Look for the positive form; the comparative and superlative forms will be listed if they are irregular.

* **Some adjectives cannot take the comparative or superlative.** Can a meal be *more perfect*? Can a dress be *most unique*? Several words—*infinite, unanimous, fatal*—do not make sense in comparative and superlative forms.

* **Avoid double comparisons.** What's wrong with this sentence?

X He was her most best friend.

The writer has already expressed the superlative by choosing the word *best*. Don't use two forms of the comparison to refer to the same object.

He was her best friend.

▶ ACTIVITY 12–7*

Using Comparative and Superlative Adjectives Correctly

Indicate correct sentences (C) and correct the instances where the writer made a mistake in using an adjective in the comparative or superlative form.

1.   The lily looks (more sick) than the spider plant.

2.   He is the (eagerer) applicant.

3. About February, I want to go to a (more warmer) place.

4. He is the (less eagerer) applicant.

5. She has the (most best) class notes at Seneca College.

12.9 USE ADVERBS TO MODIFY VERBS, ADJECTIVES, AND ADVERBS

The most common use of an adverb is to modify a verb. In other words, the adverb tells more about the action word in the sentence by providing additional information that answers questions such as *in what way, to what extent, when, where,* and *why* an action occurred.

X He smiled shy at the camera.

He smiled shyly at the camera.

You can form most adverbs by adding *-ly* to an adjective (*clear–clearly*), but some adverbs are irregular (e.g., *too, very, well*).

I played well in the go tournament at Algonquin College.

★ Adverbs can also modify adjectives

I saw a very large painting in Kelowna.

Here the adverb *very* modifies your understanding of the adjective large.

★ Adverbs can modify adverbs, too

It showed the very eerily elegant beast Ogopogo ("Dragon Dodging" D6).

The adverb *eerily* modifies the adjective *elegant*, but the extreme eerieness is emphasized by the adverb *very* modifying the adverb *eerily*.

▶ **ACTIVITY 12–8★**

Using Adverbs

Proofread and edit this paragraph so that the adverbs are used correctly.

Most students want to read <u>good</u>. They know that reading <u>proficient</u> is important to academic success. They try very <u>industrious</u> to read difficult materials. But if they <u>real</u> want to improve, they should read more <u>easy</u> understood materials.

12.10 USE COMPARATIVE AND SUPERLATIVE ADVERBS CORRECTLY

* **You usually create the comparative form of the adverb by preceding it with *more*, and the superlative with *most***

Positive: carefully

Comparative: more carefully

Superlative: most carefully

* **When adverbs do not end in *-ly*, form the comparative and superlative by adding *-er* and *-est***

Positive: fast

Comparative: faster

Superlative: fastest

* **Form the negative comparative form with *less* and the negative superlative form with *least***

Positive: lonely

Comparative: less lonely

Superlative: least lonely

* **Consult your dictionary for the comparative and superlative forms of irregular adverbs**

Positive: well

Comparative: better

Superlative: best

* **Some adverbs cannot logically take comparative or superlative forms.** Remember that some adverbs, such as *chiefly, fatally*, and *perfectly*, can't logically take comparative or superlative forms. Does this sentence make sense?

X He shot himself more fatally.

How can you shoot yourself *more* fatally?

* **Avoid double comparisons.** What's wrong with this sentence?

X He went to the most best restaurant.

The writer has already expressed the superlative with *best*. There can be no restaurant better. It is not Standard English to add another indicator of the superlative. Don't use simultaneously two forms of superlative to refer to the same object.

▶ **ACTIVITY 12-9★**

Using Comparative and Superlative Adverbs Correctly

Proofread and edit these sentences. Write a C beside any correct examples.

1.   I went to a more perfect restaurant.

2.   My most smallest calculator is the thickness of a credit card.

3.   He was a very friend dog.

4.   That is the least friend dog.

5.   My most unique possession is my fur vegetable.

12.11 PLACE MODIFIERS CORRECTLY

Your writing is more interesting when you use modifiers—adjectives, adverbs, phrases, and clauses—that put some flesh on the bare bones of plain sentences. Be careful where you place those modifiers, though, or you can unintentionally puzzle or even amuse your audience.

★ Place modifiers close to what they describe. What is wrong with this sentence?

X My father offered me a slice of homemade pie with a smile.

It sounds as though the pie had a smile, and while that may be how Dad made it, it's more likely Dad was doing the smiling. The modifying phrase *with a smile* is a misplaced modifier. Look how much clearer the meaning is in the following sentence.

Smiling, my father offered me a slice of pie.

Now the modifier has been placed nearer what it describes.

Consider how you could rewrite this sentence to more clearly modify the one idea you want to describe more fully.

X He almost ate a Nanaimo bar every night.

Is your rewrite something like this?

He ate a Nanaimo bar almost every night.

★ When a modifier begins a sentence, ensure that the modifier is followed by the word it modifies. What is wrong with this sentence?

X Crawling up his arm, Tim noticed a blackfly.

It sounds as though Tim is crawling up somebody's arm. Isn't this sentence clearer?

Crawling up his arm, a blackfly startled Tim.

Now *crawling up his arm* clearly modifies blackfly.

What's wrong with this sentence?

X After eating lunch, the train took us to Windsor.

After eating lunch seems to modify the train—to suggest that the train just finished a meal—but that can't be. This is a dangling modifier. Try to give it a clear, logical subject to modify. Isn't this an improvement?

After eating lunch, we took the train to Windsor.

Now the modifying clause does not dangle; it clearly modifies *we*.

▶ **ACTIVITY 12–10★**

Placing Modifiers

Proofread and edit these sentences, placing modifiers so that your reader always knows to what you're referring.

1. The car dealer showed me into the showroom with a smile.

2. Her sister and her brother dropped out of Sheridan College before graduating. Maria only graduated.

3. I left for work in a rush.

4. I saw a bird in my binoculars.

5. He said today he heard a loon.

6. Swimming in the soup, he noticed a fly.

7. To be well cooked, you must poach an egg until the yolk is solid.

8. While still a baby, my mother began to read to me.

9. After searching for days, the keys were found.

10. Muttering to herself, the dog was given an injection by the vet.

12.12 CREATE PARALLELISM

Parallelism: "in writing, balance between parts of a sentence or paragraph, obtained by echoing structure or style" ("Parallelism"). Look at the two sentences below:

X Rohinton Mistry writes with compassion, insight, and he is humorous.

Parallel: Rohinton Mistry writes with compassion, insight, and humour.

The second sentence has a series of balanced nouns. The next sentence also has a parallel structure:

Parallel: Read *Such a Long Journey*, and you will laugh, sigh, and cry.

▶ **ACTIVITY 12–11★**

Creating Parallelism

Rewrite these sentences so that they are better balanced.

1. Keyano College in Northeastern Alberta is a good choice if you wish to study to be an electrician, millwright, or how to do welding.

2. You could also choose to learn nursing, carpentry, or to be a cook.

3. Students can also study physics, sociology, or the life of plants.

4. Business students can study accounting, report writing, or how to market.

5. The Heavy Equipment Training includes how to operate a crawler tractor, motor grader operation, or hydraulic backhoe operation.

12.13 USE MATURE SENTENCE STRUCTURE

The emphasis in chapter 12 has been on creating correct sentences. It is important to write correctly; it helps you make a good impression on your audience. Everyone expects college graduates to write correctly. Sometimes students, in their attempts to be correct, fall into a pattern of writing simple sentence after very simple sentence. Their writing is boring. Your writing will be more interesting if you use mature sentence structures.

Sentences can be described as simple, compound, complex, and compound–complex. Your writing should comprise a mix of such constructions. Here's a suggestion for creating mature sentence structures.

★ **Subordinate some short sentences.** Consider these brief, simple sentences.

X (immature): Dandelions are despised. They are dug up. They are poisoned. They are a nutritious vegetable *(Nutrition-Rich A9)*.

Now see how they can be transformed into a more interesting complex sentence.

Although dandelions are despised, dug up, and poisoned, they are actually a nutritious vegetable.

The whole idea of the bad reputation of dandelions has been reduced in importance by subordinating it. Brevity has been achieved by turning three separate sentences into a list of past participles serving as adjectives. The whole construction is much more interesting. Try it yourself by completing Activity 12–12★.

▶ **ACTIVITY 12-12★**

Creating Mature Sentence Structures

Here are some overly simple sentences. Transform them into more interesting, compound–complex sentences.

1. Chemicals have been dumped on them. You can't use dandelions then. They can be used as salad greens. They can be used to make wine. The roots can be roasted to make a kind of coffee.

2. Dandelions are high in vitamin A. They are high in iron. They are high in calcium, phosphorus and potassium. They also have a lot of copper.

12.14 VARY THE SENTENCE STRUCTURE

Complex and compound sentences are necessary to mature writing, but if those are the only types of sentences you create your writing will have a certain sameness that will not impress your readers. Don't write long sentences just because they seem fancier. Write a sentence just as long as it needs to be to do the job. If a brief sentence will do, write a brief sentence. Some brief sentences add punch to the writing.

12.15 SOME CONCLUDING THOUGHTS

You need to know a lot to write Standard English. You've been studying how to write correct and effective sentences. In the next two chapters, you can turn your attention to some finishing touches, the final mechanical conventions of written English.

CHAPTER 13

Checking Your Punctuation

"Just get it down on paper, and then we'll see what to do with it."
—Maxwell Perkins

CHAPTER OBJECTIVE

After studying this chapter, you be able to proofread and edit your sentences to observe the punctuation conventions of Standard English.

13.1 USING THE APOSTROPHE

* Use the apostrophe to show possession for nouns and indefinite pronouns.
To show possession, add an *'s.* If the result is a double *s,* drop the last *s.* You will occasionally see names with an *'s* after an *s* (e.g., *Charles's*), and this is standard as long as the pronunciation is not awkward; you would not see *Moses's,* for example.

Ontario's trillium symbol

a dollar's worth of candy

someone's children

children's toys

a two-weeks' vacation

X the provinces's responsibilities

the provinces' responsibilities

the Smiths' garden

      In formal usage, use the possessive case for a noun or personal pronoun preceding a gerund

The loon's calling echoed across the lake.

Calling—a gerund; that is, a noun that is derived from an action word—is the subject of the example sentence. Who is the owner of the calling? That's the possession of the loon.

She approved of James's cooking the meal.

When two or more people jointly own something, add an apostrophe to the last name

We sent them to Bill and Liu's bait shop.

★ Use an apostrophe to show the plural of abbreviations, alphabet letters, numbers, and words. You may notice that writers commonly omit an apostrophe in abbreviations or numbers (VCRs, 1990s). Note, though, this would create confusion if done for letters (*is* versus *i's*). You can count on being understood if you consistently use the apostrophe in all these situations.

He has run several BBS's.

Dot your *i's*; cross your *t's*.

★ Add an apostrophe to the last word in hyphenated words

My daughter-in-law's favourite singer is Buffy Sainte-Marie.

★ Add an apostrophe to show contractions. The apostrophe signals the reader that the word is a contraction, that a letter (or letters) has been omitted.

Who's (who is) going to Sault College?

She'll (she will) attend this year.

★ Add an apostrophe to show missing letters or numbers. The apostrophes indicate that the spelling omits one or more letters.

Odds 'n' Ends (and)

The '93 winner (1993)

★ Do not use an apostrophe for possessive pronouns.

X   Its claws are sharp.

We don't mean *it is claws are sharp*, so we do not use an apostrophe. Omit an apostrophe for all possessive pronouns: *his, hers, its, ours, theirs, yours*, and the adjective *whose*.

Whose mouse is this?

Test yourself to see how well you can apply the conventions for using apostrophes.

▶ **ACTIVITY 13-1***

Using the Apostrophe

Examine each sentence. If it is correct, write "C" beside it; correctly use the apostrophe in the rest.

1. Charon seldom took two months vacation.

2. Sir Galahads speech was good, but it had too many *thees*.

3. Those are not Cinderellas photo's in the album.

4. An Indian fast-food restaurant on Yonge Street advertised: Curry at it's best.

5. Ontario licence plates say "Yours to discover."

6. The Fine Kettle-'o'-Fish Restaurant is my sister-in-law's favourite place.

13.2 USING BRACKETS

* **Use brackets to enclose remarks *you add* to a quotation.** In the next sentence, the writer has added the words *of cigarettes*. They were not part of the original quotation.

Health Canada researcher Louise Holt said, "and 50 per cent of smokers [of cigarettes] try to quit each year" ("Doctors" D3).

* **Use brackets around *sic* to indicate you recognize the writer made an error you've left as printed.** The writer below has indicated that Trudy really did say "resemble," not "resent."

"I resemble [sic] that remark," said Trudy angrily.

* **Use brackets when you want to indicate a parenthesis within a parenthesis.** Two artists are indicated within the parentheses, so any additional parenthetical material will be shown inside brackets to avoid confusing the reader with parentheses within parentheses.

Trees painted by the Group of Seven (e.g., Tom Thomson [1877–1917] and James MacDonald [1873–1932]) "look as if they're made of Plasticine," says painter Mary Pratt (Hume B1).

ACTIVITY 13–2★

Using Brackets

1. Add a parenthetical comment to make it clear that you are referring to drinkers of alcohol: "Heavy drinkers have more health difficulties than abstainers."

2. Show that the misspelling in the next sentence was made by the writer you are quoting, not you. "I was filled with angrr toward the bullies."

3. Add birth and death dates (1885–1970) to this sentence: Group of Seven artists (e.g., Lawren Harris) emphasized the ruggedness of the Canadian wilderness.

13.3 USING THE COLON

The colon is a powerful piece of punctuation: it draws the reader's attention to the words following it.

★ **Use the colon to introduce a list following an independent clause.** Ordinarily, you would choose a period to follow a complete statement or independent clause. When you present a list after a complete statement, however, use a colon to introduce that list.

I visited three folk festivals that year: the Winnipeg Folk Festival, the Mariposa Folk Festival, and the Festival of Friends.

X: My favourite cities in Quebec are: Montreal, Quebec City, and Lennoxville.

In the second sentence, the colon is misused. It should not introduce the list because it is not preceded by an independent clause. Here's how it should be done.

My favourite cities in Quebec are Montreal, Quebec City, and Lennoxville.

Here's another correct example:

To make excellent pancakes, choose good ingredients: farm-fresh brown eggs, fresh butter, and real maple syrup.

The colon has been correctly used to introduce the list: the colon is preceded by an independent clause.

★ **Use a colon between independent clauses where the second explains the first.** When two independent clauses—each will express a main idea—are highly related, and the second illustrates the point made in the first clause, use a colon to join them. Here's an example:

You don't have much choice: you can pay me now or pay me later.

The photo caption for a story ("Women Fans" A28) about a popular Toronto Blue Jays player showed an effective example of the colon used between two independent clauses:

"Eva Goodenough [and] daughter Cheryl think alike on Roberto Alomar: Please keep him!" (Unfortunately, the Blue Jays didn't.)

The writer chose to capitalize the second independent clause. Contrast it with this next example from an editorial about how the Niagara Falls firefighters, who had upgraded their rescue equipment and procedures, sometimes need to rescue people who come to the Falls to end their lives ("Gorge Rescue" A6). Note how the editorial writer chose to use a lowercase letter to start the explanation part of the sentence.

"Citizens of this community, though, know the reality of living in the midst of one of the world's most famous attractions: it brings with it the unwanted notoriety of being a place to die."

A survey of recently published writing handbooks shows that the explanatory independent clause can be capitalized—especially in more formal writing—or left in lowercase, but it's best to use your choice consistently within a piece of writing.

Even a very brief independent clause can be followed by a colon if the second independent clause explains the first. Consider this example:

Remember: St. John's is in Newfoundland, and Saint John is in New Brunswick.

Use a colon, too, in the kind of sentence–like writing you might do for a sign or a want ad, as shown here:

For lease: 2-bedroom apartment.

★ **Use a colon to introduce a quotation.** In less formal writing, a comma often precedes a quotation.

Ms. Yang said, "With more than two million people, Toronto is Canada's largest city."

If you want to create a more formal tone, you should choose to introduce the quotes with a colon; for longer quotes from a piece of published writing, a speech or a conversation, you must introduce with a colon.

Frank Zingrone (A27) recently wrote:

As higher-paid electric roles replace lower-paid jobs in our information based society, more and more of total wealth is falling into fewer and fewer hands. We are reversing the gains of the last 50 years by shifting too much money into the top stratum of high-priced information role players who only amuse us in our socio-economic miseries. As Neil Postman observes, we may be *Amusing Ourselves to Death*.

* Do not use a colon to introduce a question, unless the question is the direct object in the sentence. Sometimes we want to ask a question as part of a statement that we are making. Mark Jaffe (B6), in an article about global warming, did this.

X "The question is: What will that heat do?"

But, it is still more common to see such a sentence punctuated this way:

"The question is What will that heat do?"

The reason the second version is more common is that Jaffe's version uses a colon after a construction that is not a complete sentence.

The following example is correct because the question occurs after a complete sentence.

After he retired from Stelco, my father-in-law often queried his friends: Why would the chickens vote for Colonel Sanders?

In less formal writing, we could substitute a comma for a colon.

* Do not use a colon after a question that is the subject of a sentence.

Are they coming? is the question they asked.

* Use a colon to introduce an appositive. We know that the colon draws attention to the words that follow it. We can use it to emphasize information of whole clauses or even shorter constructions, such as words in apposition, words that explain the nouns to which they refer.

Winnipeg is two things my old dog is not: interesting and lively.

* Use a colon to separate parts of time, books. Note the way the colon separates hours and minutes.

When it's 10:00 in Nova Scotia, it's 10:30 in Newfoundland.

In the next example, the colon separates the title of a book from its subtitle.

If you like clever, humorous comic strips, you'll enjoy Lynn Johnston's book *For Better or For Worse: The Tenth Anniversary Collection*.

▶ **ACTIVITY 13-3***

Using the Colon

Proofread these sentences; add a colon or remove one, or indicate that the sentence is punctuated correctly.

1. If you visit central Canada, be sure to see the most striking attraction Niagara Falls.

2. For 9,000 years, people have travelled to see this river system, a natural wonder of the world the rapids upriver, the Falls itself, and the huge gorge.

3. There's only one way to really experience the awesome power of Niagara Falls look up through the spray of the Falls as you stand in the prow of the *Maid of the Mist* ferryboat.

4. From dusk (about 900 p.m. in May), the Falls are illuminated by colourful lights.

5. The question is How high is the Horseshoe Falls?

6. Many people go away never realizing the most intriguing fact about the Falls the depth of the water below the Falls is greater than the height of the Falls itself.

7. Attractions upriver from the Falls include Old Fort Erie, Dufferin Islands Nature Area, and the Niagara Parks Greenhouse.

8. Be sure to see the other interesting attractions downriver the Niagara Spanish Aero Car Ride, the Floral Clock and Lilac Gardens, and Brock's Monument, a tribute to the British hero of the War of 1812.

9. To fully experience the power of the Falls, locals also advise seeing several other attractions Journey Behind the Falls (tunnels), the Gateway Festival Park Viewing Platform, and the Niagara Falls Imax Theatre's film *Niagara Miracles, Myths and Magic*.

10. There's no doubt about it if you're in Ontario, you've got to see Niagara Falls!

13.4 USING THE COMMA

Writers use the comma more frequently than any other piece of punctuation. Gain control of it, and your writing will be well on the way to creating a good impression on your readers.

Writers use the comma often because it has many uses. In chapter 11, you read about the use of commas to avoid run-on sentences. This chapter shows most of the other reasons you use commas.

* **Use commas to separate items in a series.** Some writers leave out the comma just before *and*—the conjunction—but you make it a little easier for your reader to see the separateness of the items on the list when you include a comma before *and*.

Separate a series of words:

That summer they visited Petit-Saguenay, Chicoutimi, and Alma.

They did not visit Tadoussac, Forestville, or Betsiamites.

Separate a series of phrases:

Picking a topic, narrowing the focus, and reviewing the literature are all part of writing a research essay.

Separate a series of clauses:

She considered what she wanted to study, she investigated where she wanted to live, and she chose which school she wanted to attend.

* Use commas to separate two or more coordinate adjectives. When adjectives are of equal importance and could be written in reverse order without sounding odd, put a comma between them. The words *inexpensive* and *durable* are adjectives that modify the noun *umbrellas.* The comma shows the reader that these words each provide separate additional information about the umbrellas.

We sell inexpensive, durable umbrellas at Under the Weather.

Do not use commas between adjectives when they sound natural in just one order:

The little old elf smiled at me.

You can test the need for commas to separate adjectives. If a sentence still sounds natural after you insert the word *and* between the adjectives, you can put commas in place of the *and's*.

"Chrétien declared that without Ottawa's enforcement of standards . . . the country would end up with a two-tier, American-style health-care system" (Laxer, "PM's Words" F3).

* Do not use commas after numbers in a series.

We rented two spacious, bright rooms.

* Use a comma in certain comparisons and contrasts.

The more I know cats, the more I like my dog.

The more I get to know dogs, the less I like them.

* Use a comma to separate multiple elements in addresses, dates, and place names.

We've lived at 6161 Dawlish Avenue since 1985. (The figure and the street name are considered one element of an address; you could hardly find the house without all that information.)

Send it to 15 Brant Street, Hamilton, Ontario L8L 4C5. (Note that you do not put a comma between a province and a postal code, though.)

My birthday is May 28. (May 28 is considered one element.)

She was born on Monday, April 7, 1952, on a sunny day. (There are three elements in this date. However, if you write only the month and year, you do not use a comma.)

The first community colleges in Ontario opened in September 1967.

There are two other oddities about writing dates. Don't use any commas when you express the date in this form: Her birthday is 7 April 1952. When you write dates metric style—which makes the most sense to me—don't use any commas: 2001 04 07. (Notice that the elements are arranged from the largest unit to the smallest.)

* **Use commas to divide numbers of four and more digits.** Use commas to separate the numbers into units of three, counting from the ones column.

Fewer than 80,000 people live in Niagara Falls.

Don't use commas in numbers that refer to addresses, pages, or years, though, even if they exceed three digits.

Come to 6161 Culp Street.

Look on page 2213.

In 1882, Alberta was created from the division of the Northwest Territories.

* **Use one or two commas to separate words that precede or follow a direct quotation.**

"I want to study automotive service technology," she said.

"Then," said the recruiter, "you may want to attend Red Deer College."

"Is Red Deer between Edmonton and Calgary?" asked Lydia.

"Yes," said the recruiter.

In Lydia's last question, the question mark replaces the comma; it is incorrect to include both pieces of punctuation.

* **Use a comma in sentence-like constructions with omitted words.**

George attends Yukon College; his brother, Brock University.

* **Use a comma after the greeting and complimentary close in friendly letters.**

Dear Canan,

Yours truly,

* **Do not place a single comma between a subject and a predicate.**

X Awareness of how students' attitudes and beliefs about their learning develop and what actions facilitate learning, can help educators.

The comma should be omitted. But this next sentence is correct, because the *two* commas surround an interruption, an insertion of some non-essential information.

In Alberta, which was named after Queen Victoria's daughter Louise Alberta, tourism is the third-largest sector of the economy.

▶ **ACTIVITY 13–4★**

Using the Comma

Proofread and correct these sentences. Put a C beside any correct sentences.

1. Newspaper advertisement: "If you're thinking about buying electronics before October 19. You're out of your mind."

2. Student interest this year is particularly heavy in the technology, business and tourism programs.

3. Edit my recent fortune cookie: "You have a friendly heart and are well admired."

4. They are partly correct but mostly wrong.

5. If you're in Surrey, British Columbia visit Kwantlen University College.

6. At Kwantlen University College which has its principal campus in Surrey you can begin to study for a degree.

7. My favourite chewing gum includes several sugars: sorbitol mannitol aspartame and xylitol.

8. Selecting species planting seeds and watering beds are all part of gardening.

9. After she planted the seed watered the plants and harvested the crop the little red hen ate alone.

10. We sold three large luscious watermelons to passing tourists.

13.5 USING THE DASH

A dash—or a pair of dashes—emphasizes an interruption in your thinking. Dashes draw attention to the added information; commas and parentheses de-emphasize the interruption.

When you want to indicate a dash, write or type two hyphens, leaving no spaces before, between, or after. Some word-processing programs will automatically turn double hyphens into dashes, and many will let you select a hyphen from a menu of special marks.

★ Use a dash to show an abrupt change of thought.

I think—now what was I going to say?

★ Use a dash to make a strong parenthetical comment.

Touring the Niagara vineyards—it's best by bicycle—is a popular new activity for tourists and residents.

Note that when you write a complete sentence within dashes, you omit the capitalization of the first word and the period at the end. Should your interruption contain an exclamation point or question mark, include it before the second dash.

★ **Use a dash to emphasize an appositive.** In the sentence below, *the Great Canadian Mine Buster* is simply an equivalent term (an appositive) for the opinion about the best wooden roller coaster. To emphasize this explanatory information, set it off with dashes.

Ontario's best wooden roller coaster—the Great Canadian Mine Buster—is at Paramount Canada's Wonderland.

★ **Use a dash to attribute a direct quotation at the beginning of a document.** Notice the use of the dash for this quotation recorded by Columbo (582).

"The twentieth century belongs to Canada."

—Sir Wilfrid Laurier

Such quotations are common at the start of a variety of documents. In an essay, you would simply enclose a quotation within the paragraph you were writing. You can read more about this in the section on quotation marks.

★ **When a list begins a sentence, use a dash to separate it from the independent clause that follows.**

Stan Rogers, Rita MacNeil, and the Rankins—these are the voices of the Maritimes.

★ **Use dashes when you insert a list in a sentence.**

The Great Lakes near my home—Erie, Ontario, and Huron—are so polluted that people cannot always swim in them.

▶ **ACTIVITY 13–5★**

Using the Dash

Practise using the dash in the following sentences.

1. Draw attention to the nobility of the act in this sentence: His ambitious and noble goal was to take care of them all.

2. Pancakes, French toast, waffles these foods are all best served under maple syrup.

3. I think well, maybe I'm not sure we should go.

4. Studying hard and you should do so every day will help you achieve your goals.

5. That great natural treasure of Vancouver I'm talking about Stanley Park should be carefully protected.

6. Set up this quotation from Agnes Macphail so that it could be the first text in a chapter of a book: "Women's most difficult task since the race began has been to humanize man in order to make a civilized living with him possible."

13.6 USING ELLIPSIS DOTS

The ellipsis mark, or ellipsis dots, is made up of three periods. It's usually suggested that you place spaces before, after, and between them—so do so when handwriting—but when you are using proportionally spaced fonts—which most word processors do—the ellipsis dots look better without intervening spaces.

* Use ellipsis dots to indicate the writer has deliberately omitted words in a quotation. The ellipsis reveals that if you look up the quotation in Columbo (187), you will find that it is longer.

"Canada, having once become the commercial and industrial vassal of the United States, would . . . be absorbed."

—Sir Robert Borden

* Use ellipsis dots in dialogue to suggest the speaker is hesitating and pausing between words.

"Hmm . . . I guess I'll go tonight, but I just don't . . .," her voice trailed off. She seemed to lack the energy to finish the sentence.

The comma that signals the end of the direct quotation and the beginning of the speaker tag follows the ellipsis dots.

* If the ellipsis dots occur at the end of a sentence, complete the sentence with the ending punctuation (a period, a question mark, or an exclamation point).

She seemed to agree, but her voice trailed off into a disquieting silence, "Well, perhaps, I . . . ."

* Do not use ellipsis dots at the beginning of your quotation even if you omit words from the original. Simply indicate that you are quoting by beginning with quotation marks.

▶ **ACTIVITY 13–6★**

Using Ellipsis Dots

Correct the errors in these sentences.

1. Is the sign outside Biggar, Saskatchewan, correctly punctuated? "New York is big...but this is Biggar."

2. Here's how the the Labatt company advertised one of its beers: "Call 1-800-693-2527 to send a gift that can be opened again and again and . . ."

3. Indicate hesitation in this quotation: "Well, I guess hmm maybe I will go tonight."

4. Here's a quotation. Leave out the part about too much masculinity (Columbo 613).

   "The world has suffered long enough from too much masculinity and not enough humanity."

   —Nellie McClung

5. How would you edit this copy (Laxer, "Clark Hangs" F3)? "Conrad Black expressed the sentiments of many executives when he wrote that 'no one in his right mind would invest a cent in Ontario under this regime . . .'"

13.7 USING THE EXCLAMATION POINT

The exclamation point can help your reader feel the strong emotion you wish to convey. Overuse exclamation points, though, and you'll end up like the boy who cried wolf too often: After awhile, no one will pay any attention to you, even when you really do have something worth exclaiming.

★ **Use an exclamation point after an interjection.**

Ow!

★ **Use an exclamation point to end a sentence expressing *strong* emotion.**

What a surprise! I've never eaten pickle pie.

★ **Use exclamation points, sparingly, to give *some* sentences extra emphasis.**

Now that was a night to remember!

▶ **ACTIVITY 13–7★**

Using the Exclamation Point

Insert exclamation points where appropriate. Remove them where necessary.

1. She gouged her finger with the chisel. "Ouch" she cried.

2. What a vacation.

3. Yikes.

4. I went to Maud Island! I dived to explore the sunken destroyer *HMCS Columbia*! British Columbia really knows how to treat divers well ("Ship Scuttled" A3).

13.8 USING THE HYPHEN

The hyphen is used for three distinctly different purposes: it is used to spell some compound words (*gene-splicing, get-up-and-go*), it is used to create compound adjectives that show readers that certain words are tied together to express particular meanings, and it is used—between syllables—to indicate that a word cannot be entirely printed on one line and must be completed on the next.

The challenge in using the hyphen for compound words is that there are two other ways we form compound words in English. Some compound words are spelled out as two separate words (*genetic code, genetic engineering*). Other compound words are spelled as single words (*gentlemen, getaway*). Unless you know them all by heart, you're going to have to use your dictionary to spell compound words.

Here are some rules to help you to make a good impression on your readers when you express yourself with compound words.

★ **Use a hyphen between two or more words used together to modify a noun.** In the next sentences, the hyphens serve their conventional role of assisting the reader in considering the meaning of the combination of words rather than considering them as two separate, independent words.

After slipping his leash, the dog was frightened by his near-death experience.

Do you want a one-, two-, or three-week assignment to Point Pelee?

His eager-to-please attitude warmed the heart of his jaded boss.

You'll like reading my book *Run-on Sentences*.

Note in the last example that if you capitalize the first word in a hyphenated compound word in the title of a work, you only capitalize the other words of the compound if they are important words. Capitalize the first word, even if it is only a prefix, when a hyphenated word is part of a title.

    * Hyphenate two-word numbers and fractions.

thirty-four

The glass was two-thirds full.

sixty-second

    * Hyphenate words preceded by the prefixes *all-*, *ex-* (former), and *self-*.

The Leafs made an all-out effort to win.

As he looked across the crowed room, he saw his ex-wife.

She had become a self-made millionaire.

    * Hyphenate words ending with the suffix *-elect*.

They said they had voted for Premier-elect Kormos.

    * Hyphenate to divide a word that won't fit on a line of print.

    * Don't hyphenate one-syllable words that won't fit on a line of print (e.g., *boost*, *yeast*).

    * Don't hyphenate modifying units that include an adverb that ends in *-ly*.

The Canadian National Exhibition is a widely known attraction.

    * Don't hyphenate compound adjectives that contain a comparative or superlative.

X He was the better-prepared negotiator.

That instructor prefers the more capable students.

    * Don't hyphenate a common fraction when you use it as a noun.

One third of Canada's population lives in Ontario.

    * Don't hyphenate compound adjectives when they follow nouns, unless your dictionary shows them as hyphenated compounds.

The Toronto Symphony played a crowd-pleasing composition by Howard Cable.

The composition was very crowd pleasing.

    * Don't hyphenate a word at the end of a line if doing so will leave a very short element (e.g., *a-way*, *sis-ter*).

    * Don't hyphenate words if they are already hyphenated (e.g., don't write *attention-defi-cit disorder*).

ACTIVITY 13-8 ★

Using the Hyphen

Correct the errors. Put a C beside any already-correct sentences.

1. He has some not-so-fond memories of growing up in Cabbagetown.

2. Miss Vickie wrote her customers: "Let me know how you like my country-style chips."

3. He was a widely-known philanthropist.

4. My mother in law is a gem.

5. Twenty two people came to his funeral.

6. She was very self determined.

13.9 USING PARENTHESES

When you want to indicate that information in a sentence is interesting but not essential, you may choose to parenthesize it.

★ Use parentheses to show incidental information.

The Night the Gods Smiled (the first book Eric Wright wrote about Inspector Charlie Salter) concerns a murder at a fictional community college.

The parentheses suggest that the reader regard the material as an aside. If the parenthetical insertion is an entire grammatical sentence, the writer omits the capital for the first word and the period for the end of the sentence. Include other punctuation within the parentheses if it applies to the material parenthesized.

Jane Urquhart's *The Whirlpool* (it is set in Niagara Falls in the summer of 1889) won France's Best Foreign Book Award in 1992.

When the information is placed as non-essential language within commas, as in the example below, the reader will give it a little more attention.

The Night the Gods Smiled, Eric Wright's first book about Inspector Charlie Salter, concerns a murder at a fictional community college.

The next example shows the way an author can emphasize an interruption—like a shout—by using dashes.

I got my acceptance—what a relief!—to the program I preferred.

* Use parentheses to enclose letters or numerals in lists.

Your jobs are to (1) take the dirty dishes from the busers and the cooks, (2) wash those dishes, and (3) shelve them.

* Use parentheses around directions to the reader.

The map (see page 60) shows campus locations.

Your writing will look cluttered and even disorganized if you overuse parentheses. If you find you've over-parenthesized, try some of these strategies.

* Increase the emphasis of some parenthesized information by using commas to make it non-essential language.

Draft: Mary Pratt (the Maritimes Realist painter) did not become well known until after age 60.

Revised: Mary Pratt, who is an East Coast Realist painter, attained fame after age 60.

* Emphasize some parenthetical material by using dashes.

Few smokers—perhaps only ten per cent—succeed when they try to quit (Doctors D3).

▶ **ACTIVITY 13–9***

Using Parentheses

Put a C beside correct sentences and fix the others by parenthesizing interruptions.

1. "The Premier took a shot at inventing his own crisis last month when he told reporters the province was 'bankrupt' (it's not) and 'going down the tubes' (it's not)" (Walkom B5).

2. "Sadly, Canadian governments even are considering turning the operation of jails over to private U.S. companies (New Brunswick has hired the first one) who run them for profit" ("Keeping" A24).

3. Stanley Park in Vancouver has a commemorative bench program (MacQueen B5).

4. For a modest cost $1,800–$3,000 "you can buy a bench at a city park or beach, and dedicate it to a special person or a worthy cause."

5. An inscription on a small bronze plaque marks each commemorative bench.

6. From one of the benches "The Leader" you can look across the harbour and see the downtown skyscrapers.

7. The inscriptions are varied: "Mildred and George Cutforth are remembered by their family seven sons and one daughter"; Bill Con is commemorated "A man with a spirit as free and a will as strong as these trees"; and Bob Wade is honoured "happiness walking the seawall."

13.10 USING THE PERIOD

* Use a period after sentences that are declarative, mildly imperative, or indirect or polite questions.

The College of New Caledonia has several campuses in the central interior of British Columbia.

Be careful.

He asked what I thought of the pie.

Would you please send me the calendar for the Southern Alberta Institute of Technology.

In the last example, the speaker is politely giving an order rather than making a request.

When you complete a sentence with a period, question mark, or exclamation point, don't add a period.

X They came home at 2:00 a.m..

They came home at 2:00 a.m.

X He asked, "Where is Aurora College?".

He asked, "Where is Trent University?"

* Use a period after a sentence-like construction.

Good evening.

When should you come? By six.

* Use a period between divisions in references to literary works.

Macbeth III.ii.140–54 or 3.2.140–54

Both citations refer to lines 140 through 154 in the second scene in the third act of the play.

* Use periods with most abbreviations and with initialisms.

Abbreviations	Initialisms
Mr.	*B.A.*
Ms.	*R.N.*
Rev.	*Ed.D.*
etc.	*e.g.*

* Don't use periods with initials of well-known organizations.

RCMP

CBC

UN

* **Don't use periods in acronyms (initials that are pronounced as words).**

MADD (Mothers Against Drunk Driving)

* **Don't use periods with some abbreviations (e.g., Canada Post abbreviations for the provinces).**

ON

BC

* **Don't use a period after a title of a report or essay.**

X The Causes of Unemployment.

The Causes of Unemployment

Unemployment: Can We Reduce It?

▶ **ACTIVITY 13-10★**

Using the Period

Correct any errors. Write a C beside correct examples.

1. Would you please pass me the salt?

2. Take care!

3. Mr and Mrs Lapierre work for the C.B.C.

4. I work for C.A.R.E.

5. I work for C.A.R.E..

13.11 USING THE QUESTION MARK

* **Use a question mark after a direct question.**

Would you like to see a film tonight?

* **Do not use a question mark for indirect questions or polite requests.**

She asked what I wanted.

Would you please hand me that flamingo.

* **Use a single question mark after a question in a question.**

X Why did the tourist ask, "Where is the park??"

Why did the tourist ask, "Where is the park?"

* **Use a question mark for a question within a declarative sentence.**

When will the clown get here? is the question the children keep asking.

If the question is a direct object of the sentence, though, remember to place a comma before the question, as in the next example.

She asked herself, Am I happy at St. Lawrence College?

* **Use question marks when you ask a series of questions.**

The author gets us wondering, Why are people like that? Why violence? Can't we all just get along?

In less formal writing, you might begin each question with a lowercase letter:

My diary is full of questions: will she call? do I care? will I be called late to supper?

* **Use a question mark within parentheses to indicate uncertainty about the validity of the information.** If you are unsure of the accuracy of information you are discussing, put a question mark within parentheses immediately after the doubtful point. Do not leave a space.

He painted that in 1957(?).

Carr(?) painted that.

▶ ACTIVITY 13–11 *

Using the Question Mark

Fix any sentences that contain errors. Use a C to show a sentence that is correctly punctuated.

1. They asked what I wanted?

2. When did the children ask, Are we there yet??

3. Will this be on the final exam? they asked.

4. His daydreaming was punctuated with questions: Will the test be too difficult? Will I get through all the questions? Will there be a blizzard overnight?

5. Punctuate the next sentence to indicate that you're not sure if the couple have four children. They lived happily ever after with their four children.

13.12 USING QUOTATION MARKS

★ Use quotation marks around direct quotations.

He said, "Would you like extra sauce on your pizza?"

"You bet!" she said.

"Would you prefer," he continued, "hot sauce, mild sauce, Mexican sauce, or our new curry sauce? Or, you can have a white pizza with no sauce at all."

"My," she said, "you have a lot of choices."

There are several details you must control to use quotation marks in direct quotations:

- Start a new paragraph for each speaker.
- When you quote dialogue that extends uninterrupted over more than a sentence, simply enclose all the speech within quotation marks; place the quotation marks at the beginning and end of the utterance. If the speech takes several paragraphs, put quotation marks at the start of each paragraph but at the end of only the final paragraph.
- Place commas and periods *inside* closing quotation marks, but place colons and semicolons *outside* closing quotation marks.

Cheryl whispered, "It's not over yet"; then she put her finger to her lips.

Next, several students sang "Feelings": Jose, Placido, and Luciano.

But use no comma when you include a very short quotation that is not a complete sentence.

Her exact words were that her date was "a few bricks short of a load."

When they are part of the quotation, place question marks, dashes, and exclamation points *inside the quotation marks*, and *outside* when the punctuation applies to the whole sentence.

Did Cheryl say, "We will stay until they have finished singing"?

"There"—the exterminator shone the flashlight under the stove—"are the rats!"

★ In a paper, if you include a brief quotation, integrate it within your own writing.

As Clymer and Roen noted, quoting an associate professor of nuclear and energy engineering, "An engineer who cannot write is about as useful as a bookkeeper who cannot add (26)."

★ If you quote text or speech longer than four lines, block your quote 2.5 centimetres (one inch) from the left margin by creating a new, temporary margin.

Prime Minister Chrétien's remarks capture the Canadian fondness for our medicare system:

> There is a wide consensus in our country about preserving our distinctive state-funded health-care system called medicare. Under our system, you can go to the doctor of your choice. You are admitted to a hospital if you need to be. Period. Not if you have enough money. Or the right private plan. The fact is that no one in Canada needs to worry about medical bills. It is one of our proudest achievements. Canadians want to keep medicare. And we will. (qtd. in Marleau B2)

★ **Use quotation marks around the titles of parts of works and short works (articles, chapters, episodes, essays, poems, and songs)** We can read text faster if writers have placed quotation marks around and used capitals for the important words in titles of brief works or parts of works. When you give your own work a title, though, don't include quotation marks, but put quotation marks around the title of one of your essays if you refer to it in some other writing that you do.

"Time for Action" was the best essay I wrote this term.

★ **When writing longhand, use quotation marks around language used as a language example or in a special sense, including definitions of words you use.**

The word "modem" means "a 'modulator–demodulator' device for converting computer data for transmission or reception via telephone lines" ("Modem").

When you're word processing, though, use italics or underlining. Note that *modulator–demodulator* was in double quotation marks in the dictionary entry. When you have a quotation within a quotation, use single quotation marks for the inner quotation.

★ **Don't use quotation marks around slang expressions.**

X She was a "good-for-nothing."

He was a good-for-nothing.

If you feel that the expression is too informal, express your thought with other words.

★ **Don't use quotation marks around language used sarcastically.**

X My "best friend" stabbed me in the back.

My so-called best friend stabbed me in the back.

If you're not sure that your audience will be able to tell that you are being sarcastic, rewrite to make your intention clear.

▶ **ACTIVITY 13–12★**

Using Quotation Marks

Write a C beside correct examples. Rewrite any sentences where question marks were omitted or used incorrectly.

1. My "dear friend" stole my car.

2. He had a "heart of gold."

3. She said, "Let's go to a film tonight".

4. "No." he said.

5. "Don't you"—her eyes widened with puzzlement—"like films?"

6. She asked him again if he wanted to go.

7. "I'd rather sing 'Red River Valley,'" he answered.

8. "But isn't Donald Sutherland—oh, I thought this was true—your favourite actor"?

9. "In that case," he said, "I would love to go to the film."

10. Imagine handwriting the next sentence; punctuate it correctly. The word film has many meanings.

13.13 USING THE SEMICOLON

Writers use semicolons for several reasons. Chapter 11 shows how writers avoid creating run-on sentences by using semicolons to separate closely related independent clauses (This is the *Mushroom Gourmet*; I'm ordering the stuffed mushrooms, not the chicken wings) and when joining independent clauses with conjunctive adverbs (She wants to study animal health technology; therefore, she chose Red River Community College in Winnipeg).

★ **Use a semicolon to separate elements in a series that already has internal commas.** Consider how much harder it is to read the first sentence as compared to the second.

X I was introduced to Jan, a chef training student, Anju, an electrical engineering student, and Kim, a precision metal fabricating student.

I was introduced to Jan, a chef training student; Anju, an electrical engineering student; and Kim, a precision metal fabricating student.

Since there are already commas around the added details—the non-essential material—it is easier to read if we place semicolons between the elements in the series.

* Use a semicolon to separate independent clauses that have internal punctuation.

I studied chemistry, which was fascinating; and I also studied accounting, which I didn't enjoy.

Ordinarily, you would only put a comma before the coordinate conjunction *and*, but you need to use the semicolon because you used commas in the first independent clause. Too many commas may confuse the reader.

► **ACTIVITY 13-13 ***

Using the Semicolon

Write C if the example is correct. Use semicolons to fix any errors in these sentences.

1. Sid Adilman (F1) wrote, "Like Raffi; Sharon, Lois, and Bram; and Classical Kids; [Fred] Penner runs his own company."

2. Advertisement in the newspaper: "We thank all applicants for their interest; however, only those granted an interview will be contacted."

3. Average citizens can remain uninformed about issues of importance governments will continue to ignore the interests of average people.

4. I picked lettuce, asparagus, Brussels sprouts, and cabbages and my back never thanked me for the exercise.

5. I would like to introduce Jean, who works in shipping, Hideo, who works in accounting, Tom who works in advertising, and Marge who works in expediting.

13.14 USING THE SLASH

* Use a slash to show alternatives. In the next sentence, the writer doesn't know if the conductor will be a man or woman. The writer's instructions—probably to a child—are to give the ticket to either the man or woman who is the conductor.

When the conductor asks for your ticket, give it to him/her.

But your writing will found less mechanical if you find another way to express yourself.

When the conductor asks for your ticket, show it.

* Use a slash for a fraction if it is not on your keyboard. Notice the space between the whole number and the fraction.

5/8

3 2/3

⋆ When quoting two or three lines from a poem or play, use a slash to indicate the end of a line.

Edgar Allan Poe wasn't always gloomy: "The happiest day, the happiest hour/My sear'd and blighted heart hath known."

⋆ Use a slash to separate two equal choices.

Give the money to the secretary/treasurer.

▶ **ACTIVITY 13–14⋆**

Using the Slash

Proofread these sentences and make any corrections necessary.

1. Send a letter to the presidentsecretary.

2. When the operator answers, order that zirconium ring from himher.

3. Express four-sevenths as a figure. The answer was 4 7.

4. Show that this schoolyard chant is two lines: I hate you, You hate me. We're a dysfunctional family.

13.15 SOME CONCLUDING THOUGHTS

Reading text that is free of punctuation errors is like listening to a clear radio signal: it's more enjoyable. It's easier to pay attention to the message. Don't send your readers static: strive to observe the punctuation conventions of Standard English.

CHAPTER 14

Getting the Details Right: More Conventions to Control Before You Leave College

"The waste basket is the writer's best friend."
—*Isaac Bashevis Singer*

CHAPTER OBJECTIVE

You will proofread and edit your written work to observe these conventions of Standard English: abbreviating, capitalizing, enumerating, italicizing/underlining, spelling, and syllabicating.

14.1 ABBREVIATING

When you are taking notes, you save time by abbreviating. For all but the most informal writing, though, your document will make a better impression if you write words in full. There are a few situations in which using abbreviations is the better choice, and these circumstances are indicated in this section.

You have to proceed carefully to use abbreviations correctly. Some are written in block capitals with no periods (e.g., CBC, NAFTA, CEGEP); others with capitals and periods (e.g., B.A.); while still others are conventionally written in lower case with periods (e.g., a.m.). I checked these in the *ITP Nelson Canadian Dictionary of the English Language*; you may have to look in your dictionary to correctly spell abbreviations you use.

* **Spell out the names of holidays.**

Visit us on Canada Day.

* **Spell out names of the days and months.**

Visit us on August 1, 2100.

The recycling truck will be by again on Friday.

   ★ **Spell out the first names of people.**

X M. Pratt has lived most of her life in Newfoundland.

Mary Pratt has lived most of her life in Newfoundland.

   ★ **Spell out addresses and place names.**

Write to the Niagara Falls Canada Visitor and Convention Bureau, 5433 Victoria Avenue, Niagara Falls, Ontario L2G 3L1.

   ★ **Spell out units of measurement.**

His newly caught tofu weighed 1 pound, 7 ounces or about 650 grams.

He travelled fifty-two kilometres.

   ★ **Spell out names of educational institutions and other organizations, academic courses, departments, and programs.**

Armando is taking the course Child Psychopathology in the Child and Youth Care Program at Lethbridge Community College.

Jilin is studying mechanical engineering technology and enjoys the chemistry courses.

   If a business uses an acronym to describe itself, though, use it, too.

TNT Overland Express

   ★ **Spell out subdivisions of books (chapter, section, page).**

X I liked chap. 12 best.

That's my overview of our next topic. Please read chapter 12 tonight.

   ★ **Use common abbreviations for corporations, countries, government agencies, and well-known organizations.**

CBC

UK

NAFTA

   When you want to use an abbreviation that may not be familiar to your audience, write it out in full the first time you use it. Parenthesize the abbreviation, then use it throughout the remainder of your writing.

Anju Sharma represented her colleague students at the Curriculum Review Committee (CRC). The CRC complimented the professor for choosing *Write of Way*.

   ★ **Use conventional abbreviations in common use.**

15 B.C.

A.D. 1123

7:30 a.m. or 7:30 A.M.

12:17 p.m. or 12:17 P.M.

no. 12 or No. 12

$25

Bring $32 to room no. 15 before 8:00 a.m.

> *** Abbreviate academic titles and titles of polite address.**

Mr. Jim Smith

Ms. Singh

Miss Madeleine Kahn

Mrs. Chin

Dr. Bondar

St. Jude

> *** You may abbreviate academic, governmental, military, and religious titles when they are followed by a person's full, proper name.**

Gov. Gen. Romeo Leblanc

Rev. Ronald Pocklington

Dr. Roberta Bondar

Hon. Joan Ohokannoak

> *** Spell out governmental, military, and religious titles when they are followed only by a person's surname.**

Governor General Leblanc

the Reverend Pocklington

the Honourable Ohokannoak

> Note that when only the surname is used with the titles Reverend and Honourable, *the* precedes the title.

> *** Abbreviate titles (such as *Jr., Sr., D.V.M., L.L.D., Ph.D.*) after surnames.**

Solveiga Miezitis, Ph.D.

Bill Black, Sr.

> Don't use two designations for the same title.

X Dr. Solveiga Miezitis, Ph.D.

> *** Abbreviate Latin phrases, but use them sparingly.** You may use the following abbreviations in academic writing, but use them only within parentheses. (I've shown the English equivalents for several of these common abbreviations.)

e.g. (for example)

et al. (and others)

etc. (and so forth)

i.e. (that is)

N.B. (note well)

p. pp. (page, pages)

Write them out if you can't present them parenthetically.

You can surprise a dinner guest with an easy-to-prepare but unfamiliar dish; for example, you can prepare Thai noodles.

Here are two additional examples of these abbreviations used in sentences. Note that a comma should follow the abbreviation when it begins a list, even if it has only one item.

I enjoy attending special events (e.g., the Dakota Ojibway Winter Tribal Days, in Brandon).

Fans can see rodeos just about anywhere across the West (e.g., the Canadian Finals Rodeo in Edmonton, Medicine Hat's Exhibition and Stampede, two in Moose Jaw, the Saskatoon Exhibition, and so forth).

It is better in all but the most informal writing to write *and so forth* in place of *etc.*, as in the previous example.

* In addressing envelopes, use these abbreviations for the provinces and territories. These are the abbreviations recommended by Canada Post for optimum mail processing (Canada Post Corporation 41).

Alberta	AB
British Columbia	BC
Manitoba	MB
New Brunswick	NB
Newfoundland	NF
Northwest Territories	NT
Nova Scotia	NS
Nunavut	NT
Ontario	ON
Prince Edward Island	PE
Quebec	QC
Saskatchewan	SK
Yukon	YT

ACTIVITY 14–1★

Abbreviating

Correct any errors in these sentences. Write C beside sentences without errors.

1. Visit us at Xmas.

2. Visit us on Mon., Sep. 23, 2014.

3. A. Colville lives down east. (Mr. Colville's first name is Alex.)

4. I visited Ottawa, Ont.

5. That loaf of bread weighs 750 gr.

6. Paul is studying dent. assist. at Vancouver Comm. Coll.

7. For week five, please read ch. 5.

8. Lester works for the CBC.

9. Please come at 6:15 post meridian.

10. Please bring twenty-five dollars to room number twelve before eight ante meridian.

14.2 CAPITALIZING

★ **Capitalize the first word of each sentence.**

The first word of any kind of sentence always begins with a capital.

★ **Capitalize the first, last and main words in titles of works.**

the Vancouver Sun

Who Has Seen the Wind

But don't capitalize articles (*a, an, the*), conjunctions (e.g., *and, yet*), prepositions (e.g., *by, in, on, with, through*), or *to* in infinitives.

★ **Don't capitalize the names of musical compositions when identified by technical information (key or form) rather than by name.**

Swan Lake

Cello Concerto in A minor, opus 129

★ **Capitalize proper nouns (and words derived from nouns).**

academic courses, programs, degrees, institutions: I studied in the Early Childhood Education program at Niagara College. I studied math, including MATH101.

buildings: Calgary Chinese Cultural Centre

businesses: Ordinary People Coffee House

celestial bodies: Mars (but earth—unless treated as a proper noun—moon, sun)

First Nations: Mi'kmaq people, Frog Lake First Nations people, Sunchild First Nation

geographic place names (cities, counties, countries, and so forth): It's the West that's booming. Lethbridge is west of Regina. (The second *west* is in lowercase because the words for directions are common nouns.)

historical events: Battle of Batoche

initials: D.B.R., CBC

languages: Urdu

laws: Section 14 of the Canada Post Act

nationalities: Greek

newspapers: *Times Colonist*

organizations: Canadian Red Cross

people's names: Lucius Wildhaber

races: Black

religious dieties and holy books: Koran

titles before names: Prime Minister Campbell

* **Capitalize the first word of each line of quoted poetry.** But use lowercase if the poet did.

* **Capitalize the first and last words in the salutation of a letter.**

My dearest Aunt,

* **Capitalize the first word in the complimentary close of a personal letter.**

Yours truly,

▶ **ACTIVITY 14–2***

Capitalizing

Write a C beside any correct item, and correctly use capitals in all the sentences.

1. Joan has an atm card.

2. The world council of credit unions (n. pag.) says we should guard these cards just as we do money.

3. I wrote an essay entitled "my plastic pals."

4.   I wonder if an astronaut will take a plastic card to mars.

5.   In peterborough, i used my card to call from sir sandford fleming college to my home in niagara falls.

6.   I once lost my telephone calling card at the cn tower.

7.   I was trying to call the cbc to win free tickets.

8.   After the loss, i had to place an advertisement in the *toronto star*.

14.3 ENUMERATING

★ **Write out a number that starts a sentence, unless it is a date.**

One hundred and ten students signed up for the Law and Security Administration program.

1967 was Canada's centennial.

★ **Write out a number that is only a word or two; use figures for all other numbers.**

two hundred guests

ninety days

$1.46

If you express one number in a sentence as a figure, though, write them all as figures, unless it looks awkward.

In her drawer, she had 132 baseball cards, 76 hockey cards, and 14 lacrosse cards.

For another four days, you may buy one for $19.14.

★ **Use figures for addresses, chapters, dates, decimals, fractions (except less than one), identification numbers, page numbers, percentages, room numbers, scores, time.**

2100 Yonge Street

64 West 58th Street

Bram was related to three-quarters of the people at the cottage.

chapter 4

July 1, 2001

3.12

3 1/2

Verification No. 223-334-552

page 312

32 per cent

no. 6C

The Jays beat the Mets 6–2.

12:01 a.m.

* **Be brief when recording a range of numbers (e.g., references to pages of a book).** Generally, don't reproduce more of the digits of the second number than the reader needs to easily understand the indicated range. Record the second number in full through ninety-nine.

3–4

29–88

99–102

104–05

968–1001

1005–07

1777–1893

1988–89

1988–2001

* **Spell out one number and use a figure for the other when two numbers occur together.**

Give me 4 six-packs.

▶ **ACTIVITY 14–3★**

Enumerating

Indicate any correct sentences, and fix the others.

1. 4 bills came in the mail.

2. Give me two two-packs.

3. I made 5 per cent less money last year.

4. She lives at six Park Street.

5. Read pages 211–01.

14.4 ITALICIZING AND UNDERLINING

Italics draw attention to words; italics emphasize words. In handwriting and type-writing, we achieve this effect by underlining.

⋆ **Italicize titles of works published as separate, whole works (rather than as parts of a larger work).**

Books: *Dictionary of Canadian Quotations*

Brochures: *Your Guide to Protecting Your Plastic Cards*

Comic Strips: *For Better or For Worse*

Compact Discs: *More of the Stompin' Tom Phenomenon*

Films: *Highway 61*

Journals: *The College Quarterly*

Magazines: *Alberta Report*

Musical Compositions, but not if identified by technical information, such as key or format: Mendelssohn's Symphony no. 3 in A minor, opus 56, but Handel's *Messiah*

Musical Productions: *Rent*

But do not italicize or use quotation marks around the titles of legal documents, academic, or business reports.

⋆ **Italicize the names of aircraft, boats, spacecraft, and trains.**

Aircraft: *the Spruce Goose*

Ships: *HMS Bonaventure*

Satellite: *Anik E-1*

Train: *The Canadian*

⋆ **Italicize names of paintings and sculptures.**

Coastal Figure

the Lovers

⋆ **Italicize foreign words not yet anglicized.** Check your dictionary. If it's in there, it's probably been anglicized, and there's no need to italicize it, but watch for an indication that the word is still regarded as foreign, and italicize it.

⋆ **Italicize letters, words, or numbers used as such or used as examples.**

She had an *h* tatooed over her heart.

There are two *o*'s in *Waterloo*.

★ **Italicize for** *occasional* **emphasis.**

Wilno is a *very* small place.

You must use italics sparingly for emphasis, or your reader will stop noticing them.

▶ **ACTIVITY 14–4★**

Italicizing and Underlining

Edit these sentences. If you are handwriting, indicate italics by underlining.

1. Let's try to bounce a signal off Anik E-1.

2. Give a listen to Ron Sexsmith's first CD, Ron Sexsmith.

3. For the next sentence, add emphasis to the idea of smallness. Virgil is a very small community.

4. I like to read the newspaper comic strip Between Friends.

5. Give me that bottle of champagne; I'm going to christen our boat Married and Loving It.

14.5 SPELLING

Poor spelling is an irritant to readers. It distracts them from attending to the meaning of your message. Poor spelling also lowers your readers' judgment about your intelligence. And, readers tend to feel badly treated: they wonder why you cared so little about them that you wouldn't even check your spelling.

Go to the effort of spelling correctly, and you will be more likely to persuade your audience to your point of view.

Some college students have given up trying to improve their spelling. They don't believe that they can still transform themselves into better spellers. But spelling is a skill you can improve throughout your life. This section suggests some practical stategies that are the surest, fastest approach to better spelling.

★ **Proofread with extra-sensitive radar.** The problem with misspellings is that you don't recognize them as misspellings. If you did, you would correct them. The alarm bells signalling a possible misspelling have not gone off. Try thinking of it this way. If you're often misspelling, your spelling radar is set at a level that lets you accept as correct spellings that you would notice if you demanded a higher level of certainty before you identified a word as correctly spelled.

The trick is to adjust your behaviour: check words more often to ensure that they are spelled correctly. Good spellers probably use dictionaries and spell checkers at least as often as poor spellers. Why? Because good spellers want to spell correctly. They became good spellers partly because they more often asked themselves: did I spell this word correctly? They more often check in the dictionary. Often they find they have spelled the word correctly. Sometimes they correct a misspelling, and that gives them an opportunity to study a correct spelling they have yet to memorize.

If you query your spellings more often, you improve as a speller in two ways. First, you fix misspellings on the spot (your reader never knows that you misspelled). Second, you have an opportunity to pay close attention to the correct spelling, an opportunity to add it to the words you spell from memory. Set your spelling radar to be more sensitive and improve your spelling.

* Use the spell-checking capabilities of your word-processing software. When you are using word-processing software, use the spell checker. Microsoft Word has a feature that puts a red wavy line under any word not in its dictionary. That line appears the moment you seem to have misspelled. Then, you can look at a list of suggestions for the correctly spelled word. Not only can you ensure your document is correctly spelled, you have an opportunity to start to memorize another spelling. In many instances, a word you misspelled will reoccur in that piece of writing, so you will have another chance to *practise* the correct spelling, too.

* Compile a list of personal spelling demons. Another way that you can improve as a speller is to compile a personal list of words that you have misspelled. Chances are that if you misspelled the word previously, you'll misspell it again and again until you learn it by heart. Until it's memorized, you can refer to your personal spelling list as you proofread your document.

Keep your personal spelling list handy. If you carry a dictionary with you most places that you write—and you should—keep your personal list in the dictionary. If you roughly alphabetize it, you'll be able to check spellings quite quickly.

* Use an effective spelling study strategy. As you read while you were a child, you probably learned how to spell most of the tens of thousands of words you know. And through reading, you will learn more spellings throughout adulthood. You will find, though, that it takes special effort to learn to spell some words. Try this procedure to learn those more troublesome words.

The most effective way you can learn a new spelling is to use this version of the impression-recall procedure.

1. Look at the word you want to study. (You should have it recorded on your list of personal spelling demons.) It should be printed in lowercase letters; capitalize only if it is a proper noun.

2. As you look at the word, mentally pronounce it.

3. As you pronounce it, briefly remind yourself of the meaning of the word.

4. Continue looking at the word, and pronounce it again.

5. Analyze any distinctive features of the word. Take, for example, the word *debt*. Your thoughts might proceed like this: "*Debt*. That letter *b* is not pronounced. I'm just going to have to remember that the *b* is there. It's funny how the *b* makes *debt* a four-letter word. *D-e-b-t. Debt.*"

6. Now, cover the word, and print out the spelling.

7. Compare your spelling with the correct spelling.

8. If you are correct, you're finished for now. If you've made an error, repeat the study procedure.

You can learn from this highly effective procedure, and it takes very little time.

* Check this list of words college students commonly confuse. Table 14–1 shows words that college students sometimes confuse. They know what they mean, but they sometimes spell a word that looks or sounds like another but is not the correct spelling for the meaning they intend. The spell checker rarely catches the error because you have spelled *a* word correctly, but not the word you intended. Take, for instance, the words *to, two*, and *too*. Each has a unique meaning; your reader will be distracted if you spell a word different in meaning from what you want to express. If your teacher writes a comment indicating you've spelled a sound-alike or look-alike word, it may be on this list. When you find it, add it to your personal spelling list.

TABLE 14–1

Commonly Confused Words

accept/except	I accept that in life there will be exceptions to the rule.
affect/effect	The effects of too much drinking affected my mood.
all ready/already	I was already late by the time my essay was all ready to hand in.
aloud/allowed	During silent reading, you are not allowed to talk aloud.
alright/all right	Alright! My answers are all right.

allude/elude	I would rather that you did not allude to the time in our life when wealth eluded me.
allusion/illusion	He made an allusion to the clever illusion created by the magician.
are/our	Are our families safe?
band/banned	That new Celtic rock band was banned from playing in town.
brake/break	Make sure your brakes are working or you may break something—or someone—with your car.
buy/by/bye	Bye-bye. We're going by car to buy milk.
cents/sense/since	He has more sense than to waste even cents since he became poor.
cites/sights/sites	Oh, the sights he has seen at those historical sites. He cites his earlier articles when he writes about his travels.
close/clothes	My clothes are close fitting.
coarse/course	Of course, I prefer coarse sandpaper. The students in my course sometimes use coarse language.
do/due	I do hope that my books are due tomorrow.
for/fore	For safety's sake, before you swing that golf club, yell, "Fore!"
hear/here	I've placed the speakers here. Can you hear my new CD from where you're sitting?
heard/herd	His ear to the ground, he heard the sound of the hooves of the herd of caribou.
hole/whole	The whole garment was ruined by a giant hole in the collar.
Hungary/hungry	Some recent education graduates who were hungry for a job are teaching English in Hungary.
imply/infer	From her look, he inferred that she was angry. His remark implied that he felt her disappointment was unjustified.
in/inn	They carried a suitcase in each hand as they walked into the inn.
its/it's	It's my new detective novel. Its cover is quite garish, isn't it?
knew/new	When I saw the smoke, I knew he had bought a new barbecue.
know/no	I know that you have no more marbles.
later/latter	I prefer the latter choice to the former. I will have the Brussels sprouts later.
laying/lying	He was lying—plain not telling the truth—when he said he was laying down his guitar for the evening.
loose/lose	They let loose a cheer that they did not lose their shirts at the casino.
muscles/mussels	Keep eating those mussels, and you'll build big muscles.
naval/navel	After gazing at my navel, I decided to join the Navy for a naval career.

oar/or	Either you can use that oar to row the boat or I can.
of/off	One of the students celebrated too loudly and was thrown off the train.
passed/past	He passed the puck, but it went past the receiver's stick.
patience/patients	The physician kept the patients waiting so long that they lost their patience.
peace/piece	After the children agreed to share the last piece of pie, the father felt at peace.
peer/pier	I like to show my peers my boat at the pier.
personal/personnel	The survey from the personnel department certainly asked some personal questions.
plain/plane	He flew the plane to his aunt's and landed it on the plain in front of her ranch.
principal/principle	His principle—always tell the truth—made him popular with the school principal.
right/write	If you choose the right topic, it can be highly enjoyable to write a paper.
scent/sent	He sprayed some scent on the letter and sent it to her.
steal/steel	If that's the correct price for that stainless steel bowl, it's a steal.
suite/sweet	In some hotel suites, you'll find a sweet mint on your pillow.
than/then	They looked in the mirror. Then they knew that he was taller than his dad.
their/there/they're	They're travelling there to see their friends.
threw/through	He threw the ball through the window.
to/too/two	We two fans like to attend away games, too.
waist/waste	If you never waste food, you may have a thick waist.
way/weigh	By the way, how much does that cheese weigh?
weather/whether	Whether you like it or not, we're in for cold weather in January.
we're/where	We're all sure about where we're going.
who's/whose	Who's the person whose keys are locked in his car?

14.6 SYLLABICATING

Sometimes you will not be able to spell out a complete word before you hit the margin of your page. Other educated readers will expect you to use a hyphen to signal that you will complete the word on the next line. Here are some guidelines that your readers expect you to observe in hyphenating words.

* **Hyphenate between the parts of compound words.**

house-break

birth-day

* **Hyphenate between syllables.** Use your dictionary, if necessary, to ensure that you place the hyphen after a pronounceable syllable, ideally at a point where the portion of the incomplete word is large enough that the reader can guess the complete word.

miti-gate

unbreak-able

* **Never divide a one-syllable word (e.g., feared, through).**

* **Don't divide after a single letter.**

X a-fraid

▶ **ACTIVITY 14–5★**

Syllabicating

Correct any errors in these attempts to syllabicate.

1. thir-st

2. a-bout

3. mil-lionnaire

4. m-ighty

5. nerve-dama-ging gas

14.7 SOME CONCLUDING THOUGHTS

As you grow older, you can't perform some skills—gymnastics, for example—as well as when you were younger, but you can improve your writing throughout your life. Just as reading more, reflecting on your writing, and persistently using a dictionary will improve your writing, so you can also ensure progress by referring to a handbook when you wonder about a mechanical convention of Standard English. Keep your copy of *Write of Way* with you when you write. If you look to it to guide you when you wonder how to write correctly, you will steadily transform yourself into a more powerful writer.

CHAPTER 15

Answers to Activities

"Get to the point as directly as you can;
never use a big word if a little one will do."
—*Emily Carr*

▶ **ANSWER FOR ACTIVITY 1–1**

Making a Balloon Outline of a Paragraph

FIGURE 15–1

Balloon Outline of a Paragraph

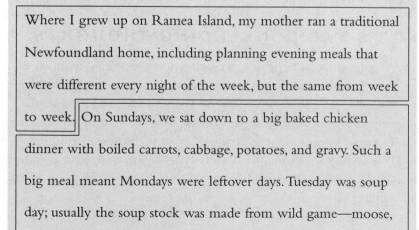

Paragraph One, Draft Two (Classification/Division)

Down-Home Cooking

Topic
sentence

Where I grew up on Ramea Island, my mother ran a traditional Newfoundland home, including planning evening meals that were different every night of the week, but the same from week to week. On Sundays, we sat down to a big baked chicken dinner with boiled carrots, cabbage, potatoes, and gravy. Such a big meal meant Mondays were leftover days. Tuesday was soup day; usually the soup stock was made from wild game—moose,

Support
sentences

Support
sentences

caribou, or rabbit. If it was a Wednesday, we counted on a boiled dinner, maybe veggies and fish or veggies and salt beef. On Thursdays, meat and mashed potatoes with gravy were the centre of our main meal of the day. The meals on Fridays and Saturdays were even more traditionally Newfoundland. Fridays were fish days; the fish was often battered and fried in oil. For religious reasons, there was never any meat on Fridays. On Saturdays we ate pea soup. There was always salt beef in the soup, and Mom often served pork cakes (ground pork and flour—no rising agent—fried).

Concluding
sentence

Although the food changed a little with the seasons—September might mean a partridgeberry pie—there was a reassuring rhythm to these evening meals, which were planned a week in advance, all year long.

▶ **ANSWER FOR ACTIVITY 1–2**

Brainstorming Ideas

FIGURE 15–2

Ideas for How to Enjoy a Blizzard

- be sure to have enough food
- rent good videos
- get out your favourite games, such as Trivial Pursuit or crokinole
- get candles
- buy your favourite snacks
- be sure you're with someone you really like
- buy magazines
- put a blanket in your car
- get a good book
- pay your gas bill
- stock up on firewood
- keep a container of gas in the car
- pay your cable TV bill
- buy a shovel
- buy what you need for a gourmet meal
- get your kids home
- call in sick to work
- get snow tires

▶ **ANSWER FOR ACTIVITY 1–3**

Outlining a Complex Paragraph

FIGURE 15–3

Decimal Outline of 'How to Enjoy a Blizzard'

Topic Sentence:

    With the proper preparations, you can enjoy rather than endure that next winter storm.

Support Sentences

1. Sentence making the first main point:

    The first step to ensuring delight rather than depression is to stock your home with enough good food to outlast the worst winter can throw at you.

    1.1 Additional sentences detailing the support for the first main point:

        Don't forget the most important food group: snack foods.

    1.2. Remember tearing out that newspaper recipe for Thai noodles? Now's the perfect time to make that gourmet meal.

2. Sentence making the second main point:

    Good eats are a necessity, but you'll have more fun if you also have good entertainment.

    2.1 Additional sentences detailing the support for the second main point:

        What better time to take up the Video Shack's offer of five movies for ten bucks for five days?

    2.2 Be sure you've paid the cable TV company.

    2.3. Stock up on magazines, and borrow that Robertson Davies novel you've been meaning to read.

    2.4. Dust off the crokinole board.

3. Sentence making the third main point:

You'll want to share the fruits of your planning with the special people in your life.

    3.1. Additional sentences detailing the support for the third main point:

Call in sick so you don't get stuck at work.

    3.2. Surround yourself with your family.

Concluding Sentence (restatement of topic)

With good food, good entertainment and good company, you're going to hope you're snowed in for weeks.

▶ **ANSWER TO ACTIVITY 1–4**

Writing a Complex Paragraph from an Outline

FIGURE 15–4

Example of a Complex Paragraph, "How to Enjoy a Blizzard"

With the proper preparations, you can enjoy rather than endure that next winter storm. The first step to ensuring delight rather than depression is to stock your home with enough good food to outlast the worst winter can throw at you. Don't forget the most important food group: snack foods. Remember tearing out that newspaper recipe for Thai noodles? Now's the perfect time to make that gourmet meal. Good eats are a necessity, but you'll have more fun if you also have good entertainment. What better time to take up the Video Shack's offer of five movies for ten bucks for five days? Be sure you've paid the cable TV company. Stock up on magazines, and borrow that Robertson Davies novel you've been meaning to read. Dust off the crokinole board. You'll want to share the fruits of your planning with the special people in your life. Call in sick so you don't get stuck at work. Surround yourself with your family. With good food, good entertainment, and good company, you're going to hope you're snowed in for weeks.

▶ **ANSWER TO ACTIVITY 1–5**

Making a Balloon Outline of a Five-Paragraph Essay

FIGURE 15–5

Balloon Version of "Pancakes for Sunday Brunch"

Canuck 1

Gram P. Canuck

Dr. Douglas B. Rogers

ENGL100

April 1, 2001

Pancakes for Sunday Brunch

Para 1: Intro

Lead-in

With time and money scarce in the 1990's, many people satisfy their craving for leisurely gourmet dining by relaxing over inexpensive, homemade meals. Even a busy person can transform a routine Sunday breakfast into an inexpensive, glorious

Thesis

brunch by preparing gourmet pancakes. The secret to wonderful pancakes is to follow three simple steps: select quality ingredi-

Preview main points

ents, cook them carefully, and serve the meal with flair.

Para 2: Support 1

Topic sentence

The successful cook knows that great food begins with great ingredients. Break into a stainless steel bowl two of those

Support sentences

brown eggs you got at the market from the farmer who lets her

Support sentences

chickens run free. Beat the eggs together with a cup of fresh milk. Add a dash of salt, a teaspoon of baking powder, a splash of vanilla, and a mashed banana that has ripened almost to spoiling. Only a wooden spoon will do to stir in the stone-ground whole-wheat flour. Use just enough to turn the mixture from runny to thick but syrupy.

Concluding sentence

You can tell already that these will be great pancakes.

Para 3: Support 2

Topic sentence

The chef must now take care to cook the pancakes to perfection.

Support sentences

Use butter—not oil—to grease the pan. Heat the skillet until it is hot enough to make a test drop of water sizzle but not so hot that the butter smokes. Ladle as many three-inch puddles of the batter as will fit in your frying pan. Don't flip the pancakes until you see bubbles all over the uncooked top; if you turn them only once, they will be lighter.

Concluding sentence

Take care while cooking, and you'll thank yourself when you eat.

Para 4: Support 3

Topic sentence

Your delicious pancakes almost guarantee a good brunch, but you can ensure success by presenting the food with flair.

Support sentences

Pour hot coffee into a carafe. Fill a small pitcher with maple syrup. Find the butter dish. Select your best matching cups and plates. Fetch the Sunday paper. Put a single rose into a bud vase.

Concluding sentences

Now, get out your favourite tray, and carry the whole meal up to your bedroom and your partner. Present the meal with a flourish.

Para 5: Conclusion

Recap

Clincher

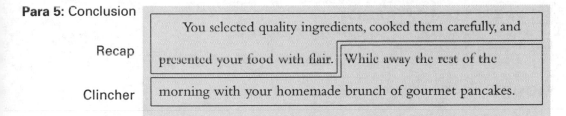

You selected quality ingredients, cooked them carefully, and presented your food with flair. While away the rest of the morning with your homemade brunch of gourmet pancakes.

▶ **ANSWER TO ACTIVITY 1–6**

Brainstorming for an Essay about the Effects of Photo Radar

FIGURE 15–6

Notes about the Effects of Photo Radar

- more tailgating
- ticket doesn't necessarily go to the offender
- slower driving speeds
- more congested highways
- less work for police
- police can concentrate on crime instead of radar
- province makes more money
- maybe insurance prices may be lowered for non-speeders
- invasion of privacy
- fewer accidents
- people will invent devices to fool radar
- engineers will invent better photo radar
- fewer serious accidents
- gas savings from driving at lower speeds
- less cutting in and out of traffic by speeders
- cars will be damaged less in accidents at slower speeds
- people will disguise their plates

▶ **ANSWER TO ACTIVITY 1–7**

Organizing a Five–Paragraph Essay

FIGURE 15–7

Essay Outline for "The Positive Effects of Using Photo Radar to Enforce Speed Limits"

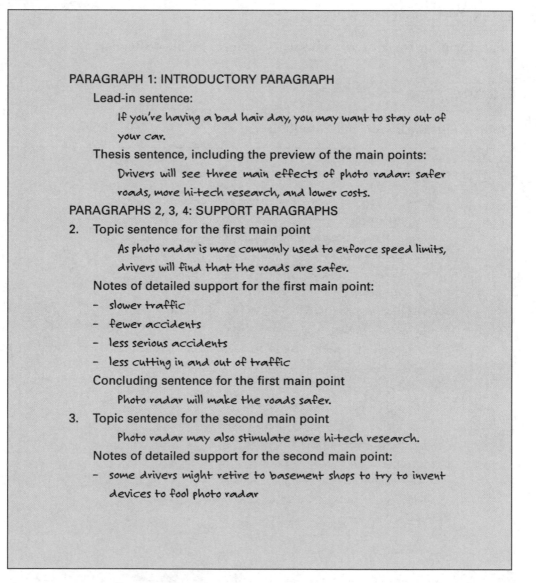

PARAGRAPH 1: INTRODUCTORY PARAGRAPH
  Lead-in sentence:
    If you're having a bad hair day, you may want to stay out of
    your car.
  Thesis sentence, including the preview of the main points:
    Drivers will see three main effects of photo radar: safer
    roads, more hi-tech research, and lower costs.
PARAGRAPHS 2, 3, 4: SUPPORT PARAGRAPHS
  2. Topic sentence for the first main point
        As photo radar is more commonly used to enforce speed limits,
        drivers will find that the roads are safer.
    Notes of detailed support for the first main point:
      – slower traffic
      – fewer accidents
      – less serious accidents
      – less cutting in and out of traffic
    Concluding sentence for the first main point
        Photo radar will make the roads safer.
  3. Topic sentence for the second main point
        Photo radar may also stimulate more hi-tech research.
    Notes of detailed support for the second main point:
      – some drivers might retire to basement shops to try to invent
        devices to fool photo radar

> – engineers might try to research more effective photo radar in
> the hopes of making money by selling this better equipment

Concluding sentence for the second main point

> The best devices will be manufactured, increasing hi-tech
> industrial activity.

4. Topic sentence for the third main point

> Photo radar enforcement of speed limits will also save
> drivers money.

Notes of detailed support for the third main point:

– slower travel would reduce fuel costs

– perhaps insurance premiums would be lowered for owners with
fewer citations

– cars that are run at slower speeds will last longer

– the government might use the fine revenues to reduce taxes

– technicians in photo-radar units might be paid less than police
officers, resulting in savings to taxpayers

Concluding sentence for the third main point

> Perhaps the government will even reduce taxes as it raises
> more revenue from traffic fines, saving us more money.

PARAGRAPH 5: CONCLUDING PARAGRAPH

Summary or recap of the thesis and main points

> Safer roads, more hi-tech research, and lower driving costs
> are all good effects of enforcing speed limits with photo
> radar.

Clincher sentence

> It'll be good for you—even on bad hair days. Oh well, you can
> always wear a hat.

▶ **ANSWER TO ACTIVITY 1–8**

Writing a Brief Essay

FIGURE 15–8

MLA-Style Essay

Composition 1

Group Composition
Professor Kim
ENGL133
January 10, 200x

The Positive Effects of Using Photo Radar to Enforce Speed Limits

If you're having a bad hair day, you may want to stay out of your car. Photo radar enforcement of speed limits has come to our area. As more and more units are put into use, drivers will see three main effects of photo radar: safer roads, more hi-tech research, and lower costs.

As photo radar is more commonly used to enforce speed limits, drivers will find that the roads are safer. To avoid getting tickets, drivers will slow down. Drivers have fewer accidents at lower speeds, and the accidents should cause less serious injuries and fewer deaths. Fear of tickets will discourage riders who recklessly cut in and out of traffic. Photo radar will make the roads safer.

Photo radar may also stimulate more hi-tech research. Our area may become a hotbed of hi-tech industry as some drivers become basement tinkerers trying to invent devices that will prevent photo radar from catching them speeding. Engineers will vie to be the inventor of the 90's better mousetrap—the ultimate photo radar device. The best devices will be manufactured, increasing industrial activity.

Photo radar enforcement of speed limits will also save drivers money. Drivers burn less gas when they travel more slowly. Perhaps insurance rates will be lowered for car owners with fewer tickets. There should be fewer repairs on cars run at slower speeds. Perhaps the government will even reduce taxes as it raises more revenue from traffic fines, saving us more money.

Safer roads, more hi-tech research, and lower driving costs are all good effects of enforcing speed limits with photo radar—even on bad hair days. Oh well, you can always wear a hat.

▶ ANSWER TO ACTIVITY 1–9

Creating an MLA-Style Essay Cover

FIGURE 15–9

MLA-Style Cover/First Page

Labelle 1

Chantal Labelle

Dr. Douglas B. Rogers

COMM 112G

October 14, 2001

Research Essay

Why Canada Should Provide Universal Daycare

Daycare: "the care and training of babies and preschool children

outside the home during the day" ("Daycare"). . . . .

▶ ANSWERS TO ACTIVITY 2–5

Interesting and Uninteresting Topics

___I___   1. Tuition Fees Are Too High

Most students—at least—would be interested in reading a persuasive essay that argued that tuition fees are too high.

___U___   2. It's Best to Eat Maple Sugar with a Fork

___U___   3. Cape Breton Is an Island

This topic seems to be so obvious it is uninteresting.

___I___   4. Nicknames Should Be Banned

Since almost everyone has had a nickname or knows someone who has, this topic is apt to appeal to a wide audience.

___I___   5. Canada Should Provide Universal, Free Daycare

To some audiences—parents, for example—this would be interesting, but childless readers might have no interest in it at all, unless they worked or studied in the child-care field.

___U___   6. Economy cars burn less gas.

___I___   7. Falling snow can make you feel good.

One is at least curious to see what the writer has to say. Since many Canadians hate winter, a wide range of readers might be interested in this topic.

___U___   8. In the spring, the temperature rises.

___U___   9. Politics is about government.

___U___   10. Exercise can make you sweat.

___U___   11. Hockey is popular in Canada.

___I___   12. Beer is the downfall of many first-year students.

(Although some might argue that this makes an obvious point.)

___U___   13. You can ski in the Rockies.

___I___   14. Co-op placements can help students make career choices.

Students will be interested. Older adults may not want to read about this topic.

___I___   15. Medicare should include prescription drugs.

Most Canadians are concerned about health care, and many would be interested because they fear it would raise taxes.

___U___   16. *Per Gradus ad Maius*—steps to the greater—is the motto of Grande Prairie Regional College.

It simply announces a fact.

___U___   17. Dawson College opened in the fall of 1969, the first English-language institution in Quebec's network of CEGEP's (*Colleges de l'enseignment general et professionnel*).

Again, this sentence simply announces a fact.

▶ **ANSWERS TO ACTIVITY 2–7**

Identifying Essays with Single Topics

_____ 1. How to Clean Cars and Fish

__S__ 2. The Two Major Causes of Economic Recessions

The writer may have identified two causes, but the topic is really what causes a recession.

_____ 3. The Causes of Smoking and Drinking

__S__ 4. The Two Major Types of Computer Printers

Again, there is a single topic, types of computer printers.

__S__ 5. How to Sing Duets

It is one topic: how to sing with a partner.

__S__ 6. Hoping and Praying for World Peace

Here, I'd argue that the topic is how to strive for world peace.

__S__ 7. The Best Café in the World

__S__ 8. Electricity or Gas: Which Heats Homes Better?

The single topic is how these two fuels compare for home heating.

_____ 9. Why I Vacation in the Prairies and in the Maritimes

These topics are too dissimilar for one essay.

__S__ 10. Are Twins Really So Similar?

Two people, but one topic: Are twins more similar than other siblings?

▶ **ANSWERS TO ACTIVITY 2–9**

Identifying Theses

_____ 1. Schizophrenia

This is just a word mentioning a broad topic, a topic that is too general for an essay. It does not assert a point.

__T__ 2. Schizophrenia Is Manageable with Drug Treatment

_____ 3. Tourist Attractions in Canada

This is just an announcement or title of a topic. It is not a thesis because it reveals nothing about the writer's contention about tourism in Canada.

___T___   4. Paramount Canada's Wonderland Has the Most Exciting Rides

This is an opinion. Readers will want to see why the writer believes this.

___T___   5. Vancouver Is One of the Great Cities of the World

There is a stong assertion of a proposition here.

_____   6. Juvenile Delinquents and Criminals

Just a mention of a topic, and also too broad to make a good essay.

___T___   7. Child Abuse Is the Major Cause of Juvenile Delinquency

___T___   8. School Failure Is the Major Cause of Juvenile Delinquency

_____   9. The Web site for the College of the Rockies Is www.cotr.bc.ca

Just an announcement of a topic.

_____   10. The Bug Room Is a Permanent Exhibit at the Provincial Museum of Alberta

This is just a statement of a fact. Nothing is contended.

▶ ANSWERS TO ACTIVITY 2–11

Matching Theses and Main Points

(Other answers will also make sense.)

Thesis One: Each school bus should have a driver and a monitor.

1.   Young children will not be picked on.

2.   The driver will not be distracted as often.

3.   Children will be safer boarding and leaving the vehicle.

Thesis Two: Shift work can cause marriages to fail.

1.   It can be depressing to go alone to social events

2.   Going to bed without your partner can make you feel sad.

3.   Eating alone can make a person feel lonely.

Thesis Three: The high cost of attending college is hurting students.

1.   Students are working so much their school work suffers.

2.   Huge debts will create long-term problems.

3.   Trying to do too much causes health problems.

▶ **ANSWERS TO ACTIVITY 2–13**

Creating Main Points

(Here are some suggested answers, but you may think of others that work, too.)

Thesis One: Canada is a great vacation destination because tourists can choose from so many different activities.

3. Tourists can see many different examples of the beauty of nature.

Thesis Two: You can get your family to fire you from your dishwashing chores.

3. Lose your grip on some dishes as you clumsily wash them.

Thesis Three: Babysitting is a great job for college students.

3. The hours are flexible.

Thesis Four: Modern technology is making us lazier.

3. Modern inventions, such as remotes for TV's and CD players, are making us physically lazier.

Thesis Five: Having your wisdom teeth removed is just the beginning of your losses.

3. You will lose your appetite.

Thesis Six: You can boost the odds of having a car accident by making the wrong choices.

3. Disobey traffic laws.

▶ **ANSWERS TO ACTIVITY 2–15**

Creating the Specific Support

Answers will vary for the following exercise. Consider your answer correct as long as your suggested support makes senses and does present evidence that supports the main point.

Thesis One: Each school bus should have a driver and a monitor.

1. Young children will not be picked on.

    – When big kids pick on smaller children, a driver cannot drive the bus and intervene to stop the bullying.

2. The driver will not be distracted as often.

    – Sudden loud noises, for example, will not distract a driver when a monitor is there to look after the children.

3. Children will be safer boarding and leaving the vehicle.

    – It's safer if the driver stays in the driver's seat while a monitor helps the children on and off the bus.

Thesis Two: Shift work can cause marriages to fail.

1. It can be depressing to go alone to social events.

    –   Having acquaintances or family constantly asking, "Where's the better half?" can make you feel lonely.

2. Going to bed without your partner can make you feel sad.

    –   There's probably no time in the day when you more powerfully feel alone than when you shut off the lights and go silently to bed, alone.

3. Eating alone can make a person feel lonely.

    –   Even the pitying look of a restaurant server at a solo diner can make you feel sad.

Thesis Three: The high cost of attending college is hurting students.

1. Students are working so much their school work suffers.

    –   It takes a lot of hours of minimum-wage work to even purchase a textbook, so students sometimes skip classes to get in just a little more paid work.

2. Huge debts will create long-term problems.

    –   Some students are finding that they just can't earn enough money to make the re-payments on their student loans.

    –   If they declare bankruptcy, it will create long-lasting problems in borrowing money, even for a home.

3. Trying to do too much causes health problems.

    –   Between long hours of employment and long hours attending classes and doing homework, students can hurt their health by skipping sleep.

    –   Worrying about money and school work can also cause health-damaging stress.

► ANSWERS TO ACTIVITY 3–1

Meeting Your Audience's Information Needs

1 a.   Ms. Baas, I'm so sorry to be late. My iron broke and ruined the shirt I was going to wear. It took me awhile to find another shirt and borrow an iron. I'll buy another iron today, and I'll make sure I always have enough in the wardrobe to find another shirt if something goes wrong with my first choice.

   b.   Oh, I had such a lousy start today. I hadn't finished the laundry, so I had to iron a shirt before I went to work at that ripoff clothing store. I'd have made it on time, except that my lousy, cheap iron chose today to break. You should have seen the mess after it sprayed this disgusting brown guck all over my shirt! Then I had to give the sniff test to the shirts on my bedroom floor, and wander around the dorm looking for someone who would let me use an iron. By the time I got to work my boss was fit to spit bullets. I have got to get my act together or I'm going to lose this job.

c.   My Sunshine iron broke today.

The iron is still within the warranty period, as you can see from the copy of the sales receipt I've enclosed with the iron. You can see that I bought it at Floor Mart, January 3, 1999.

The iron began to heat up normally, but when I tilted it to iron a shirt, it sprayed dirty brown water all over the garment. The iron began to smell like plastic was burning, and it went cold and would not get hot no matter how I adjusted the heat control dial.

Please repair or replace the iron within a week because I cannot afford a replacement (I'm a student), and I need to look smart for my sales job at a clothing store.

▶ ANSWERS TO ACTIVITY 3–2

Freshening Up Those Clichés

There are many possible answers. Here are some possibilities.

1. as quiet as a sigh (very quietly)
2. as careful as a forensic accountant (carefully or meticulously)
3. as white as a blanched almond (white)
4. between homeless and a hostel (both choices have undesirable consequences)
5. as crazy as a raccoon in a trap (insane or mentally ill)

▶ ANSWERS TO ACTIVITY 3–4

Writing Gender-Inclusive Language

1. weather forecaster or meteorologist (weatherman)
2. humankind, people (mankind)
3. sewer cover, sewer lid (manhole cover)
4. entrepreneur, businessperson (businessman)
5. courier, messenger (delivery boy)

▶ **ANSWERS TO ACTIVITY 3–6**

Creating Messages that Are Gender Neutral

1. Everyone told personal stories; Everyone told a personal story.

2. Visitors to Yarmouth should bring raincoats.

3. Singer-songwriters must be prepared to promote their music by selling their own CD's.

4. Vain people should think less about appearance.

5. A fool is soon parted from money; Fools and money are soon parted.

▶ **ANSWERS TO ACTIVITY 3–8**

Rewriting to Eliminate Wordiness

1. My favourite hobby is . . . .

2. There are several ways to get a tight lid off a glass container.

3. All workers should follow the rules.

4. Some people want us to reverse the vote we took last meeting.

5. Could you please tell me where to find the washroom?

▶ **ANSWERS TO ACTIVITY 3–10**

Rewriting Non-idiomatic Expressions

1. They sold me a pig in a poke.

2. He's not the sharpest pencil in the box.

3. She should pull her own weight.

4. They were helpful: They gave me a hand.

5. At the end of the day, we will have to decide who to vote for.

▶ **ANSWER TO ACTIVITY 4–1**

Detecting Topic Sentences

Maple syrup is the best topping for Red River Cereal. As you begin to taste the sweetness, it radiates to the furthest corners of your mouth. Even after you swallow the last crushed bits of grain, the sweet sensation lingers.

In the spring, I love to go to a sugar bush. The clear plastic tubing transforms the woods. The smell of the sap being boiled down makes me forget the mud oozing round my boots.

Quebec produces the most maple syrup and sugar. In fact, on variety store and grocery shelves all over North America, you can see the words "Made in Quebec" on bags of granulated maple sugar, on small maple leaves made of maple sugar, and on bottles of maple syrup.

▶ ANSWERS TO ACTIVITY 4–3

Practise Creating Topic Sentences

First Topic Sentence:

Handle knives carefully to avoid injuries.

Second Topic Sentence:

Follow sensible procedures to eliminate accidents when you use your stove.

Third Topic Sentence:

To avoid slipping and hurting yourself, immediately clean up any spills on your kitchen floor.

▶ ANSWERS TO ACTIVITY 4–5

Limiting a Paragraph to One Main Idea

1. Follow these easy steps to make yogurt <u>and beer</u> at home.

2. We should make our school buses safer for children <u>and reduce the chance of food poisoning by using bleach on our kitchen dishrags</u>.

3. Gardening <u>and gourmet cooking</u> are engrossing hobbies.

4. Autistic children seldom learn to communicate verbally,<u> nor do they learn how to become independent workers</u>.

5. Many new jobs <u>and regulations</u> are being created in call centres.

▶ ANSWERS TO ACTIVITY 4–7

Ordering Support within Paragraphs

1. Random order is fine; you can do these tasks in any order.

2. Again, these sentences could be arranged in any order.

3. This group of sentences could be arranged emphatically, perhaps in this order:

    1 Pests are becoming resistant to our pesticides.

    2 Pesticides reduce bird and fish populations.

    3 Agricultural aircraft pilots have higher mortality rates.

    4 Pesticides can cause cancer, miscarriages, birth defects.

4. These sentences will make the point more convincingly if they are arranged logically, in this order:

    1 Sleep troubles cause stress.

    2 You drink alcohol to reduce stress.

    3 You sleep poorly because of alcohol.

    4 You feel restless and uneasy because of sleep deprivation.

5. This process writing is best organized chronologically.

    1 At the top of the hill, strap your feet into the board, ninety degrees to the hill.

    2 Slowly shuffle towards the hill until you start your descent.

    3 To help control your speed, carve back and forth across the hill; the wider the turn, the slower you will go.

    4 Once you learn the carve technique, you must learn to stop by turning your body and board ninety degrees while keeping your balance and digging the back edge of your board into the snow as hard as you can.

▶ ANSWER TO ACTIVITY 4–10

Creating Coherence by Repeating Key Words

Rob Deslauriers and Craig Farrish used the word *repeal* five times in this brief but powerful essay urging Canadians to stop spanking children.

▶ ANSWER TO ACTIVITY 4–12

Detecting Cohesion Signals

Several words make it easier to follow the connections among Amy's ideas: *first, next, finally, last.*

▶ **ANSWERS TO ACTIVITY 4–14**

Writing Concluding Sentences

Answers will vary, but here are some examples of effective concluding sentences.

1. None of us could go even a day without doing an activity influenced by our federal level of government.

2. The Shamrock Club has its share of boneheads.

3. I think we have to read between the lines here to create an effective concluding sentence. If the grant writer has indicated that several groups think the Youth Caucus work is important enough to support financially, it's probably because the Trillium Foundation wants assurances that it is funding groups that are winners. It wants to be associated with a success story. That's why I add that thought to the simple summary that several groups are already supporting the organization asking for the grant.

    The Trillium Foundation can join several groups that have recognized that the Youth Caucus is doing important work to improve our environment.

▶ **ANSWERS TO ACTIVITY 4–16**

Organizing Paragraphs

Here's the paragraph in which Jeff Hoogenboom urged video distribution companies to use the letterbox format when releasing films for home viewing.

Video distribution companies should stop releasing films in pan-and-scan formats. When an epic film like Braveheart is panned and scanned for a home-viewing video, viewers miss key visual information, such as the lush scenery and the massive number of revolutionaries, because only the central action survives the reformatting to make a version that fills a television screen. A letterbox version of John Carpenter's Christine captures the director's intent to show you how terribly outnumbered the protagonist is in that high-school hallway, but in the pan-and-scan version, viewers cannot experience the dread because they can't see the whole threat. Send the distribution companies a message: Whenever possible, rent your videos in letterbox versions.

Aaron Smallbone shared these basics for writing a piece of music.

Most people think it's too hard to write music, but if you follow my procedure, you may surprise yourself with a good song. First, pick a style—folk, alternative, blues, or metal—for your song. Then pick up your guitar and strum chords in that style until you start to sense a melody within your chord progressions. Keep playing your chords and humming your melody until you create some lyrics. After a while, you'll feel an urge to ask your friends to listen to a brand-new song.

Like many students, Cheryl Sutch has waited a few tables; the experience led her to recommend the best way to earn good tips.

The right approach can make waiting on tables pleasant—and profitable. Make a good first impression by smiling, making eye contact, introducing yourself, and handing out menus. Your second step is to take beverage orders and enthusiastically describe the specials of the day. When you believe the customers have decided what to order—the menus will probably be resting closed on the table—return with the drinks, and ask if the patrons would like to order. Punch the food order into the restaurant's computer, and check the progress of the cooking so you can serve the food as soon as it is ready. During the meal, ask if everything is okay. When you see the diners have finished eating, clear the table of everything that is no longer needed and find out if anyone would like a dessert, coffee, or tea. Bring the bill with the beverages. Service that is efficient—but not intrusive—almost always leads to a good tip.

▶ **ANSWER TO ACTIVITY 5–1**

Identifying the Components of Brief Essays

FIGURE 15–10

Balloon Version of "Make that a Veggie Burger"

Paragraph 1:
Intro

Make That a Veggie Burger

The rapid expansion of vegetarian items on menus across Canada is a sign that more people are choosing to become vegetarians.

People still eating other animals always ask, "Why did you become a vegetarian?" Many vegetarians hope that as they explain why they chose vegetarianism, the questioner will choose vegetarianism, too, for three reasons: Become a vegetarian because it is good for your health, environment, and conscience.

— lead-in —

— thesis —
Become a vegetarian

— preview of main points —

Paragraph 2:
Support
Paragraph 1

For some, choosing a healthy diet means becoming a vegetarian.
— topic sentence —

Eating less fat—particularly animal fat—reduces the likelihood of developing cancer and heart disease. Dean Ornish, a physician and professor of medicine, recommends a low-fat diet that eliminates meat and dairy products. His studies suggest that this diet can even reverse some symptoms of heart disease. | Choose vegetarianism
— support sentences —

for a lifestyle that leads to better health.
— concluding sentence —

Paragraph 3:
Support
Paragraph 2

The destruction of the rain forests to clear grazing land for beef cattle has led some people to vegetarianism: they want to tread more lightly on the earth, to treat the environment more gently.
— topic sentence —

Others are disturbed to read about how cattle manure runs off the ground and pollutes streams and groundwater. Far more land is needed to feed people meat than to produce enough grains, vegetables, and fruits to sustain human life. | If you care about the
— support sentences —

environment, choose to be a vegetarian: it is an important way to care for our planet.
— concluding sentence

Paragraph 4:
Support
Paragraph 3

Some people become vegetarians because they can't in good conscience kill other animals. If animals have enough consciousness to know their interests—such as preferring to stay alive—their wishes must be considered. | Look at the way we resolve conflicts of
— topic sentence —

interest with other animals with consciousness, human animals. You want to drink alcohol and drive your car. I'm worried you'll hurt me by driving drunk. We consider both interests and decide a limit to the alcohol permitted in the bloodstream: you can still have a beer after work, but I don't have to worry that you'll be driving while impaired. —— support sentences ——

If you have decided not to ignore the interests of non-human animals, choose to become a vegetarian. —— concluding sentence ——

Paragraph 5: Concluding Paragraph

More and more people are becoming vegetarians. If you care about your health, your environment, and your conscience, choose —— re-statement of thesis and main points —— vegetarianism.

▶ ANSWER TO ACTIVITY 5–3

Creating Lead-ins for Essays

Answers will vary, but here's one possible lead-in: Although I liked the people I worked with, I quit my last job and came to college.

▶ ANSWER TO ACTIVITY 5–4

Creating Transitions between Paragraphs

Answers will vary, but here are some examples of topics sentences that also include transition words that remind readers of the point made previously.

They work hard and have a strong desire to win their bouts. These top competitors live totally healthy lifestyles.

But not all of the boxers at the Shamrock Club are as totally committed; some of the fighters participate more casually. These boxers don't have the same dedication as the first type. Boxing is only a secondary activity in their lives. They do the work at a slower pace and don't get the same attention from the coaches. Casual participants don't usually choose as healthy a lifestyle.

In addition to top competitors and casual participants, you will also find a third type of fighters: boneheads.

▶ ANSWERS TO ACTIVITY 5–6

Writing Concluding Paragraphs

Answers will vary for this activity, but here are some that would work.

1. Learning to play a musical instrument benefits you socially, recreationally, and intellectually. When you tune up, you tune up yourself.

2. Taking our children along on our routine chores helps them develop linguistically, intellectually, and socially. It's a wise child that chooses a sociable parent.

3. A voice that draws you into his songs, lyrics that make you feel you know the characters in his songs, and stories about Canadians—these are what make Lenny Gallant a find singer-songwriter. Listen to *The Open Window:* you'll see what I mean.

4. When you write routine classroom assignments in MLA style, you create documents with a pleasing appearance, you save yourself time, and you treat your reader with courtesy. That's a lot of benefit for the small amount of work it takes to learn MLA style.

5. We should reduce financial barriers to college attendance so that workers are better educated, citizens are better informed, and students are less stressed. If we treat students better now, we'll all be better off in the future.

▶ ANSWERS TO ACTIVITY 6–1

Analyzing Narrative Essays

Thinking about the Content

2. The whole of the essay "It Takes a Whole Village to Raise a Child" is cast as a story: It is the story of how a visit to a bookstore led the writer to renew a commitment to trying to help all of our children thrive, but the writer shares four more memories: the story of Karen and Michael and Humpty Dumpty, Roy Ito's basketball players, the shorter children of a daycare centre in an impoverished area of Hamilton, and the illiterate mother, Heather.

4. It's easy and natural, of course, to tell a story from the first-person perspective. It also makes the reader feel included in the event in a way that is rarer when stories are told from other perspectives.

Thinking about the Organization

7. The storytelling is all organized chronologically, just straightforward narrative.

▶ **ANSWERS TO ACTIVITY 6–2**

Analyzing Descriptive Essays

Thinking about the Content

1. The second sentence of the essay could benefit from added descriptive detail: "There is no better way to appreciate the grandeur of this land of lakes and rivers and trees than . . . ." In the fourth paragraph, the cabin's exterior could be described: "Under the shade of the veranda you can see the small log cabin." In the last sentence, the pattern on the sheets could be mentioned: "flannelette sheets showing ships at sea."

3. The rewrite is not as rich in detail. Effective support for descriptive writing is evocative detail.

Thinking about the Organization

6. Here's a decimal outline of the second main point. Chris might have created such an outline as he got ready to draft this paragraph.

2. Plentiful wildlife is another feature of Hidden Bay Resort.

   2.1. Chipmunks beg for food.

   2.2. Raccoons prowl at night.

   2.3. You can see black bears.

   2.4. Moose graze water lillies.

   2.5. Loons trill.

   2.6. Ospreys soar.

   2.7. Yellow warblers sing in the pines.

▶ **ANSWERS TO ACTIVITY 7–1**

Analyzing the Process Essays

Thinking about the Content

1. The original is better. The reviser spoils the unity of the paragraph by making an off-topic remark: "My sister always runs to Mom, just to bug me."

3. Lambert's second main point is that you can get your family to fire you from dishwashing by washing some dishes so poorly that food still sticks to them.

4. The thesis is "Screenwriter/director Anthony Minghella ruined *The English Patient* by radically simplifying the language, the plot, and the characterization."

Thinking about the Organization

6. See figure 15–11, "Balloon Outline of 'How to Appeal a Grade.'"

FIGURE 15–11

Balloon Outline of "How to Appeal a Grade"

Para 1: Intro

How to Appeal a Grade

no lead-in

If you're attending Olds College in Alberta, you can appeal a grade by following the directions in the "Student Rights and Responsibilities" section of the calendar.

— thesis —

If you have a hard-to-resolve disagreement, you may need to go through three steps: discussion with the instructor who assigned the grade, an appeal to the ombud, and an appeal to the Academic Council.

preview of main points

Para 2: Support paragraph 1

The calendar says that if you feel an assigned grade is too low, you should first speak directly to the instructor.

— topic sentence —

Before booking a meeting, you should assemble all relevant assignments.

Support sentences

Look at other students' assignments and the grades they received. Jot an outline of the points you want to make. If you've prepared effectively, and if you listen to your instructor's point of view, you may come to an agreement about the grade.

concluding sentence

Para 3: Support paragraph 2

You may appeal to the ombud if you are unable to come to an

— topic sentence —

agreement about a final grade, but you must do so in writing within

Support sentences

thirty calendar days of becoming aware of the problem. The ombud will facilitate a meeting between you and the instructor. If it is thought to be helpful, the ombud will also invite the appropriate academic dean. The ombud will help you and your teacher discuss the grade. If you and your instructor still disagree about the grade, the ombud will, within fifteen days, convene the Academic Council Appeals Committee.

———— concluding sentence ————

Para 4: Support paragraph 3

The final decision in a grades appeal is made by the Appeals

———— topic sentence ————

Committee. At Olds College, the committee comprises a student representative, a faculty representative, and a Board appointee. As the appellant, you may bring to the appeal one person for support or advocacy. The members of the committee will listen to both points

Support sentences

of view. All three committee members must vote, and the decision must be reported within three days.

———— concluding sentence ————

Para 5: Concluding paragraph

Years go by, and students in class after class agree with their instructors' grades. Still, it's reassuring to know that in case of disagreements, Olds College has created a clear appeals process from the instructor to the ombud to the Academic Appeals Committee.

———— restatement of thesis and main points ————

no clincher

▶ **ANSWERS TO ACTIVITY 7–2**

Analyzing Classification Essays

Thinking about the Content

1. The thesis for "Why Do They Tell Us Not to Spank Our Children?" is Parents who read newspaper and magazine accounts of spanking will learn that child-guidance experts condemn spanking as ineffective and causing bad consequences for both children and their parents.

3. "The third type of fighters are boneheads" is James Marshall's topic sentence for the third point he previewed in his introductory paragraph.

5. Niagara College directs a lot of communication at students, employees, and other residents of the community.

Thinking about the Organization

9. The fourth paragraph has the weakest concluding sentence. It comments on gyms in general, but the essay is really about one gym. That paragraph might be improved with this concluding sentence: Boneheads at the Shamrock Club also show by their lack of interest in a healthy lifesyle that they are not serious about boxing.

▶ **ANSWERS TO ACTIVITY 7–3**

Analyzing Essays Explaining Causes or Effects

Thinking about the Content

1. This is the sentence in which the writer states the thesis and previews the main points: "Plagiarism has terrible effects for both the student plagiarists and the community."

3. The two points made in "Plagiarism's Harvest" are that when students plagiarize, they hurt themselves and their community. This is, of course, a four-paragraph essay because while there is an introductory paragraph and a concluding paragraph, there are only two supporting paragraphs (one for each main point).

Thinking about the Organization

6. This is the clincher for "Plagiarism's Harvest": "Imitation may be the sincerest form of flattery, but when you want to borrow other people's ideas, give them credit by naming the authors and indicating where their work was published."

7. Zacharakes organized her explanation of shift work logically.

▶ **ANSWERS TO ACTIVITY 7–4**

Analyzing Essays that Compare and Contrast

Thinking about the Content

1. We might hear that the sisters are as different as spaniels and greyhounds, or salt and sugar, or folk songs and dance music.

Thinking about the Organization

3. The second paragraph of "Adult and Youth Offenders" lacks a topic sentence. Here's a suggestion: The police followed similar procedures in arresting the youth and the adult.

5. The word *however* draws readers' attention to the contrast of the sisters. You could increase the cohesion of the paragraph on physical differences by adding a word such as "However" or a phrase such as "In contrast" to the beginning of the sentence that starts "My aunt stands . . . ."

7. Point-by-point comparisons of the treatment of adults and children are made in "Adult and Youth Offenders." The sisters are compared point-by-point on three characteristics.

▶ **ANSWERS TO ACTIVITY 7–5**

Analyzing Persuasive Essays

Thinking about the Content

1. The thesis is first stated in the last sentence of the introductory paragraph: "Canada should repeal Section 43 because it contradicts other sections of our criminal code and violates our Charter of Rights and Freedoms and the United Nations convention on the Rights of the Child."

4. Here is a decimal outline that might have been created to make it easier to draft the fourth paragraph in "What's in a Name?"

   3. We should ban nicknames because it is so hard to get rid of them.

      3.1. Steven MacDougall had to use his nickname, *Goose*, to announce his engagement.

      3.2. Imagine introducing your new fiancée to your college friends who all call you by the nickname *Loverboy*.

      3.3. At a reunion—even at age forty—a person might have to introduce himself as *Stinky*.

Thinking about the Organization

6. Rob Deslauriers and Craig Farrish tell interesting stories—case histories, really—to lead into their argument

ANSWERS TO ACTIVITY 8–2

Analyzing the Content of a Research Essay

1. Tommy Hall states his thesis and previews his main points in this sentence:

"Canada's one-tier, publicly supported, health-insurance system is better than two-tier alternatives because it is more economical, efficient and fair."

2. You might state each of the essay's main points in words like these:

Hall first makes the point that Canada's one-tier health-care system is more economical than a two-tier system, such as the one in the United States.

Hall then makes a second point, that a one-tier health-insurance system is more efficient: It delivers more health care to more people for less cost.

Hall makes a third point, that a one-tier health insurance system is fairer because it ensures that all people, regardless of income, receive good quality health insurance.

3. Is your outline similar to this one?

Outline of "Canada's One-Tier Health Care Is the Better System"

Thesis: A one-tier, publicly supported health-insurance system is more economical, efficient, and fair.

1. Canada's one-tier health-care system is more economical than a two-tier system, such as the one in the United States.

    1.1. The United States spends the most on health care (Terrana 14).

    1.2. The existence of so many private insurance plans costs an extra $100-billion annually (Evans B6).

    1.3. Canada spends less of its GNP on health care (Beatty 33).

    1.4. American administrative costs are treble Canadian costs (Beatty 34).

    1.5. "Health care costs Canadians far less" (Bennett xvii).

    1.6. The United States spends more of GDP on health care (Rachlis A20).

▶ **ANSWERS TO ACTIVITY 8–3★**

Summarizing Information

Your summary won't be the same word for word, but compare it to these sugges-tions. The process of comparing will help you refine your ability to summarize.

Before you read the final version of the summary, read through the draft writing that preceded it.

IDENTIFICATION OF THE MAIN POINT OF THE ORIGINAL TEXT:

In the article "Students Can Learn to Read Better," Dr. Douglas B. Rogers says that students can become better readers by extensively reading easy text.

POINT-FORM NOTES OF THE MOST IMPORTANT INFORMATION (MADE AFTER WRITING THE FIRST SENTENCE):

- To find text that is easy for you to read, ask a friend to listen to you orally read
- You've found text that is easy for you to read when a friend listens to you read aloud a 100-word sample and finds that you correctly read at least 97 per cent of the words.
- Easy reading helps you improve your ability to recognize printed words. It helps you figure out the meaning of more words. It expands your knowledge of the world. It helps you understand more complex written discourse.
- Word recognition is reading words on sight. When you can't, you must guess the word or try to recognize it by sounding it out.

TOO-BRIEF VERSION:

If you can correctly read aloud 97 per cent of a 100-word sample, that text is easy reading for you. Extensive easy reading improves all reading skills. You become better at recognizing printed words on sight and guessing or sounding out unfamiliar words. Your comprehension improves as you learn the meanings of more words, better understand complex language structures, and gain more world knowledge. [88 words]

DRAFT VERSION OF SUMMARY:

In the article "Students Can Learn to Read Better," Dr. Douglas B. Rogers says that students can become better readers by extensively reading easy text. To find what you can read easily, ask a friend to listen to you read some materials aloud. If you can correctly pronounce 97 per cent of a 100-word sample, that text is easy reading for you. Extensive easy reading improves all read-ing skills. You become better at recognizing printed words on sight because you begin to recognize them automatically. When you recognize most of the words quickly, you understand what you are reading and this makes it easier to guess unfamiliar words or sound them out. Your comprehension improves as you learn the meanings of more words, better understand complex language struc-tures, and gain more world knowledge. As you know more about more topics, you are more likely to have the background knowledge the writer assumes of you. [153 words]

FINAL VERSION OF SUMMARY:

In "Students Can Learn to Read Better," Dr. Douglas B. Rogers says that you can become a better reader by extensively reading easy text. To find text you can read easily, ask a friend to listen to you read aloud. If you can correctly pronounce 97 per cent of a 100-word sample, that text is easy reading for you. Easy reading improves all reading skills. You begin to recognize automatically many printed words. When you recognize most of the words quickly, you understand what you are reading, and this makes it easier to guess the few unfamiliar words or sound them out. Because you understand the text, you can often surmise the meanings of new words, and that helps you better figure out any complex language structures—and gain more world knowledge. As you learn more, you read better because you know more of the information writers assume of readers. [149 words]

▶ ANSWERS TO ACTIVITY 8–4

Analyzing the Organization of a Sample Research Essay

1. How does your analysis compare to this answer?

INTRODUCTION TO THE ESSAY

Rich or poor . . . . Canada's one-tier, publicly supported, health-insurance system is better than two-tier alternatives because it is more economical, efficient, and fair.

SUPPORT PARAGRAPHS

"Our one-tier health-care system is less expensive than the two-tier system in the United States . . . . Canadians have shown that they are willing to pay the taxes to keep a one-tier health insurance system because it is fairer."

CONCLUSION TO THE ESSAY

Robert Evans' remarks capture the Canadian fondness for our medicare system: ". . . . Not bad, eh?" ("Health Care" 27)

2. Really, all the text from the first line until the end of the assertion of the thesis is designed to get the reader interested in the topic.

3. Hall states his thesis and previews his main points in the last sentence of the second paragraph.

"Despite inequities that remain in our health-care system, Canada's one-tier, publicly supported, health-insurance system is better than two-tier alternatives because it is more economical, efficient, and fair."

4. "There are some people who do not want all Canadians to have equal access to health care, but most Canadians prefer to keep their publicly funded health-insurance system because it is economical, efficient, and fair"

5. Hall makes the final sentence the clincher:

"Not bad, eh?"

▶ **ANSWER TO ACTIVITY 9–2**

Creating a Works-Cited Page

FIGURE 15–12

MLA-Style Works-Cited Page

Epstein 6

Works Cited

Barlow, Maude, and Heather-jane Robertson. *Class Warfare: The Assault on Canada's Schools.* Toronto: Key Porter, 1994.

Fege, Arnold. "Public Education: Can We Keep It?" *Educational Leadership.* Nov. 1992: 86–89.

Nikiforuk, Andrew. "Andrew Nikiforuk Views a Video That Focuses on the Classroom." *Globe and Mail* 12 Mar. 1993: 22.

▶ **ANSWER TO ACTIVITY 10–2**

Creating a References Page

FIGURE 15–13

APA-Style References Page

Making the Grade   7

References

Barlow, M., & Robertson, H. (1994). *Class warfare: The assault on Canada's schools.* Toronto: Key Porter.

Fege, A. (1992, November). Public education: Can we keep it? *Educational Leadership, 50,* 86–89.

Nikiforuk, A. (1993, March 12). Andrew Nikiforuk views a video that focuses on the classroom. *Globe and Mail,* p. 22.

▶ **ANSWER TO ACTIVITY 10–3**

Creating an MLA-Style Cover Sheet for an APA Essay

Kim has created a MLA-style cover with an assignment line. The actual essay title would be on the APA-style cover.

FIGURE 15-14

MLA-STYLE COVER FOR KIM HONSBERGER'S ESSAY

Honsberger   1

Kim Honsberger

Dr. Douglas B. Rogers

ENGL097

April 1, 2013.

Research Essay Assignment

▶ ANSWERS TO ACTIVITY 11-1

Avoiding Fragments

1. Fragment
2. Fragment
3. In the early 1900's, ferruginous hawks soared the skies in most of Alberta.
4. They like to live in open areas, including grasslands and fallow pastures.
5. While they are feeding their young, the parents eat about 480 gophers.
6. In the wild, ferruginous hawks can live for twenty years.
7. The hawks are endangered because cultivation of the land reduces their habitat.
8. Farmers know the hawks control rodent pests, especially gophers.

▶ ANSWERS TO ACTIVITY 11-2

Dividing Fused Sentences

1. Stompin' Tom's famous songs include "Bud the Spud" and "Tillsonburg." "Bud the Spud" is about a renegade potato hauler, and "Tillsonburg" tells about harvesting tobacco.
2. "Sudbury Saturday Night" celebrates the lives of working people. "Lady k.d. lang" praises another singer-songwriter.
3. Tom Connors was born in the Depression in Saint John. He and his single mom were forced on the road when he was three years old.
4. He was abused in St. Patrick's Orphanage. He lived with a foster family, too.

5. By age 13, he had run away. He learned to play guitar and sing for his supper.

6. He travelled Canada. Sometimes the police would jail him for vagrancy.

7. For years, he's worn a black cowboy hat and his stompin' boots. Legend has it that he's used the boots to pound a beat right through a sheet of plywood.

▶ ANSWERS TO ACTIVITY 11–3

Mending Comma Splices

1. Negro Creek Road in Holland Township near Owen Sound, Ontario, has an interesting history. It was named after blacks who settled the area before 1850 (Avery, "Blacks" A10).

2. These early settlers had escaped slavery in the United States. Some other black pioneers had come from England.

3. The 1851 census showed about 50 black families living near Negro Creek and Negro Lake. They arrived before European settlers.

4. The Holland Township Council renamed the road Moggie Road. George Moggie was an early white settler.

5. Howard Sheffield, who can trace his roots back nine generations to the first settlers, wanted the name reinstated. A delegation presented Council with a petition signed by more than 100 black and white citizens.

6. Eventually, five thousand people signed a petition to restore the old name. Late in 1997, the Holland Township council put Negro Creek Road back on the map (Avery, "Negro Creek" A16).

▶ ANSWERS TO ACTIVITY 11–4

Separating Independent Clauses with a Comma and a Coordinating Conjunction

1. Do you like to clean your home and have people over for coffee? (C)

2. Oh, you're not really that fond of the cleaning, but you like chatting over a great cup of coffee.

3. You may have found the main reason for the growing popularity of cafés, and it is not just good coffee.

4. Espresso and cappuccino are the old favourites at cafés, but patrons are more often ordering chococcino and other exotic drinks.

5. Chococcino is prepared like a cappuccino, but you steam chocolate milk into strong espresso coffee.

6. In Niagara Falls, one of my favourite cafés is the Italian Ice Cream Parlour and Café, and I particularly like their cappuccino.

7. When I'm near the University of Toronto, I drop by the Future Bakery Café so that I can drink a bowl of coffee and watch the world pass by. (C)

8. Gathering in a café with a few co-workers lets me dump the stress of work before I go home, yet it doesn't leave me sleepy the way a beer does.

9. I like to combine browsing a bookstore and sipping a coffee, yet I rarely find café bookstores such as the Bookshelf Café in Guelph.

10. The next time I'm in Winnipeg, I'm going to the Roasting House so I can try their espresso. I hear it's excellent. (C)

▶ **ANSWERS TO ACTIVITY 11–5**

Separating Independent Clauses with a Semicolon

1. Nellie McClung showed her concern for women's rights early; in 1890, at age sixteen, she signed a petition for women's suffrage.

2. She became a popular speaker for the Women's Christian Temperance Union; she became a popular writer with the publication of *Sowing Seeds for Danny*.

3. In 1914, suffragette Nellie McClung led Manitoba women in seeking the right to vote; Premier Sir Rodmond Roblin led the opposition.

4. Premier Roblin said, "I don't want a hyena in petticoats talking politics to me"; McClung said, "Never retract, never explain, never apologize—get things done and let them howl."

5. Premier Roblin presided over Manitoba's parliament; Nellie McClung held a mock parliament.

6. Premier Sir Rodmond Roblin said, "Nice women don't want the vote"; suffragette Nellie McClung said, "Politics unsettles men."

▶ ANSWERS TO ACTIVITY 11–6

Separating Independent Clauses with Semicolons and Conjunctive Adverbs (and Transition Phrases)

1. Singer-songwriter Gordon Lightfoot immortalized a Great Lakes shipping disaster; "The Wreck of the Edmund Fitzgerald" told how the ore freighter sank in Lake Superior in 1975.

2. For years, no one knew exactly what had happened to the ship; however, a Michigan entrepreneur videotaped the wreck in 1994.

3. All twenty-nine crew members died during a fierce storm; a gigantic wave probably swamped the *Edmund Fitzgerald*.

4. At a dedication ceremony at the Great Lakes Shipwreck Museum in Whitefish Point, Michigan, the ship's brass bell tolled twenty-nine times; that is, relatives rang the bell once for each lost crew member.

5. The bell then sounded once more that day; appropriately, Gordon Lightfoot stepped forward to ring it in memory of all the sailors lost to the Great Lakes (Sepkowski A28).

▶ ANSWERS TO ACTIVITY 11–7

Separate Introductory Elements from Main Clauses

1. When you try to name Canadian landscape painters, the members of the Group of Seven probably come to mind.

2. Arguably the most famous of the Group of Seven artists, Tom Thomson (1877–1917) changed the way Canadians looked at common objects, such as trees.

3. Peeking out of the woods near Kleinburg, Ontario, the McMichael Canadian Art Collection exhibits many paintings by Tom Thomson, A.J. Casson, and other members of the Group of Seven.

4. Not only can you view their paintings, you can also look at works by contemporary Native American artists. (C)

5. In addition to viewing all this art, you can explore more than 100 acres of the kind of landscape that inspired the artists.

6. Even if you don't go outside, you can still view scenery through the gallery's floor-to-ceiling windows.

7.   If you are interested in purchasing prints or art books, visit the Gallery Shop.

8.   If you stay past lunch, don't worry; you can eat at the McMichael Restaurant.

9.   In the summertime you can even eat your meal on the outdoor terrace. (Or, you could write: In the summertime, you can even eat your meal on the outdoor terrace.)

10. If you are near Toronto, it's worth the forty-minute drive to visit the McMichael Canadian Art Collection.

▶ **ANSWERS TO ACTIVITY 11–8**

Separating Non-essential Language from Independent Clauses

1.   "Don't you think, Zejnil, that there's nothing like a special event, such as a festival or a rodeo, to add some excitement to everyday life?"

2.   "Yes," said Saima, "and the people of British Columbia really know how to throw great events."

3.   Vancouver's Chinatown, second in size only to San Francisco's, is the perfect place to be for the Chinese New Year.

4.   The Rain Festival, which celebrates Vancouver's generous precipitation, is held in Gastown the first Sunday in April.

5.   The Pacific National Exhibition, which is held from late August to Labour Day, attracts people from all over the province, doesn't it?

6.   The Cloverdale Rodeo, held on the Victoria Day weekend, is a popular event in Surrey.

7.   Victoria, not unexpectedly, has the country's biggest celebration of Victoria Day, including the huge Swiftsure Race for sailboats.

8.   "Even smaller communities (e.g., New Westminster) make the summers special by hosting concerts in bandshells, don't they?"

9.   The Country Living Festival, held in Chilliwack for three weeks in mid-May, gives attendees a chance to celebrate even before summer begins.

10. Nanaimo, the sun porch of Canada, hosts many special events, including the Great International Nanaimo Bathtub Race, Empire Day, the Nanaimo Festival, and the Vancouver Island Exhibition.

11. The Filberg Festival, an arts and crafts show and more, is held in Comox in the first week in August.

12. It's a bit of a surprise to learn that Mardi Gras, held in February each year, is one way the people of Dawson Creek add excitement to their lives.

13. The good citizens of Kelowna look after the human desire to feast with, among other events, the Black Mountain Rodeo and the Wine Festival.

14. You'll feel like it's a festival whenever you visit Barkerville Historic Town, a former gold-rush town restored to the way it looked in the 1870's.

▶ **ANSWERS TO ACTIVITY 11–9**

Review of Sections 11.1–11.8

1. Joni Mitchell was born in Fort Macleod, Alberta. One of her best songs is "Both Sides Now."

2. William Shatner grew up in Montreal. His most famous acting role was Captain Kirk of the *USS Enterprise*.

3. Once called the most famous Canadian on the planet, *Baywatch* star Pamela Lee was born Pamela Anderson in Ladysmith, British Columbia.

4. Leslie Nielsen, star of the film comedies *Naked Gun* and *Airplane*, was born in Regina.

5. *Reader's Digest* (Canadian English edition) has the largest number of subscribers of any publication in Canada; the Canadian French edition also sells well.

6. The English-language edition of *Chatelaine* has the second largest paid circulation; incidentally, the French-language edition is also very popular.

7. More Canadians subscribe to *Maclean's* than *Time*.

8. Alfred Billies, co-founder of Canadian Tire, died in 1995.

9. Since *Maclean's* magazine began ranking Canadian universities, Mount Allison University has been identified as a top school for undergraduate studies.

10. Because he had helped to discover how to use insulin to treat diabetes, Sir Frederick Banting became the best known Canadian from Alliston, Ontario.

▶ **ANSWERS TO ACTIVITY 11–10**

Ensuring Agreement of Subject and Verb in Person

1. A new store, Sgt. Preston's Outpost, (sells) RCMP mementos.

2. I (dislike) that Disney has the marketing rights.

3. You (see) Mountie refrigerator magnets for sale in the store.

4. They (have) RCMP belt buckles.

5. He (buys) some Li'l Mountie slippers as a gag gift for his boss.

ANSWERS TO ACTIVITY 11–11

Ensuring Agreement of the Subject and Verb in Number

1. The Canadian Broadcasting Corporation (CBC) began broadcasting television programs in 1952. The CBC vaults at the Broadcasting Centre in Toronto (hold) some remarkable records of Canadian television's first two decades.

2. One of the finds (is) recordings by French torch singer Edith Piaf.

3. On one of the recordings, Sean Connery (acts) in his first Shakespearean play.

4. Hour-long dramas (include) plays by Alice Munro, Robertson Davies, Mordecai Richler, and Margaret Atwood.

5. Leslie Nielsen and William Shatner (appear) in dramas, too.

6. There (are) cans of film, videotape, and kinescopes (Quill B1+).

ANSWERS TO ACTIVITY 11–12

Creating Logical Constructions

(Answers will vary.)

1. We were tired of being unemployed, so we came to the Wascana Institute in Regina.

2. Being uninterested in jobs traditionally filled by women, we didn't study dental assisting or early childhood education.

3. My reason for studying farm business management was that people will always have to eat. (Or, I decided to study farm business management because people will always need to eat.)

4. Jan found the Pork Production Technician program a good choice.

5. You can choose a program that will lead to work or one that is interesting.

▶ **ANSWER TO ACTIVITY 11–13**

Ensuring Agreement in Person

Water conservation saves money because—to make the water safe for drinking—every drop of water that comes out of the tap must be treated. People should plant drought-resistant trees. They should water during the cool parts of the day. Citizens should put only one inch of water on lawns. They should cut their grass higher to use less water. A lot of water can be saved if everyone conserves a little.

▶ **ANSWER TO ACTIVITY 11–14**

Ensuring Consistent Person

Cavendish Farms—the PEI company that makes those great frozen french fries—was named after Cavendish Beach. The original plant was opened in New Annan in 1961. It was called Seabrook Farms. Now the company concentrates on potato processing. The company has become one of Canada's largest exporters of french fries. And, as President Robert Irving noted in 1996, "This province is now Canada's largest potato-growing area" ("Growing" 3).

▶ **ANSWERS TO ACTIVITY 11–15**

Ensuring Agreement of Pronouns and Their Antecedents

1. Movie reviews are always interesting. They can range from panning to praising a film.

2. Take David Cronenberg's *Crash,* for example. It had reviews that said it was disgusting and reviews that called it a masterpiece.

3. People who are excited by car crashes are the characters, complex psychological characters.

4. The film is based on J.G. Ballard's novel. It was a rich source of material for Cronenberg to work from.

5. Novel and film—they are both highly modern.

▶ **ANSWER TO ACTIVITY 11–16**

Creating Consistency of Gender

Harriet Tubman escaped slavery in the United States and came to St. Catharines in 1851. She didn't just thank her lucky stars that in Canada slavery had been outlawed in

1834, and despised before that. She made nineteen dangerous trips back into the United States of America. Her indomitable spirit led her to become a nurse and a spy for the Union throughout the American civil war. Called the Moses of her people, there was a reward of $40,000 on her head. Her efforts helped more than 300 other slaves come to freedom.

ANSWERS TO ACTIVITY 12–1

Using the Correct Pronoun Case

1. How many of the Acadia students <u>who</u> did not read the materials passed the test?
2. Give that book to Paula and <u>me</u>.
3. Vinnie and <u>I</u> are going to Heritage College in Hull.
4. Both of <u>us</u> attended Grant MacEwan College.
5. <u>Whom</u> shall I say called?

ANSWERS TO ACTIVITY 12–2

Making Clear References to Nouns

1. At the bookstore at the University College of the Fraser Valley in Chilliwack, he bought an ugly new shirt.
2. Sally told her mother that her mother was too easily frustrated.
3. He said to his father, "You are a pessimist."
4. Jill said to her partner, "The head of the firm wants to speak to you."
5. Even after he put a new engine in his car, it still didn't work correctly.

ANSWERS TO ACTIVITY 12–3

Using Tense Consistently and Logically

A fascinating article in the Yarmouth *Vanguard* told about Eugene Meuse, an inventor who was born in 1885 in Amirault's Hill. By age fourteen, he had made his own camera and begun a lifelong passion for taking photographs. He invented an easy chair, a cranking can opener (patented in 1911), and even a "design for a high speed aircraft with wings which fold back in flight."

▶ **ANSWERS TO ACTIVITY 12–4**

Using the Correct Form of the Verb

1. She demanded that an apology <u>be</u> offered.
2. Someone suggested that the order <u>be</u> dropped.
3. I demand that he <u>stop</u> calling me names.
4. Wish you <u>were</u> here.
5. I recommend he <u>come</u> to school today.

▶ **ANSWER TO ACTIVITY 12–5**

Favouring the Active Voice

Maureen Brisebois of Aylmer, Quebec, was cooking pasta. Lightning struck an old tree. The lightning travelled along the clothes line. The huge flash of lightning rushed by her. When Brisebois tried to lift a pot, the water spilled out. The pot was fused to the element. If she had been touching metal—even the sink—the lightning would have killed her.

▶ **ANSWERS TO ACTIVITY 12–6**

Using Adjectives to Modify Nouns

1. Dr. Wilfred Bigelow had a very (clever) idea in his sleep.
2. He was recently named to the (Canadian) Medical Hall of Fame for the procedure that came from his idea.
3. Dr. Bigelow dreamed that chilling patients before their (major) heart surgery could delay the deterioration of body tissue that occurs when a patient's circulation is stopped.
4. His (startling) suggestion stunned the American Surgical Association in 1950. (C)
5. While serving in a surgical unit in the Second World War, he had seen (savage) frostbite.

▶ **ANSWERS TO ACTIVITY 12–7**

Using Comparative and Superlative Adjectives Correctly

1. The lily looks (sicker) than the spider plant.
2. He is the (more eager) applicant.

3. About February, I want to go to a (warmer) place.

4. He is the (less eager) applicant.

5. She has the (best) class notes at Seneca College.

ANSWER TO ACTIVITY 12–8

Using Adverbs

Most students want to read <u>well</u>. They know that reading <u>proficiently</u> is important to academic success. They try very <u>industriously</u> to read difficult materials. But if they <u>really</u> want to improve, they should read more <u>easily</u> understood materials.

ANSWERS TO ACTIVITY 12–9

Using Comparative and Superlative Adverbs Correctly

1. I went to a perfect restaurant.

2. My smallest calculator is the thickness of a credit card.

3. He was a very friendly dog.

4. That is the least friendly dog.

5. My unique possession is my fur vegetable.

ANSWERS TO ACTIVITY 12–10

Placing Modifiers

1. With a smile, the car dealer showed me into the showroom.

2. Only Maria graduated from Sheridan College.

3. In a rush, I left for work.

4. While looking through my binoculars, I saw a rare bird.

5. Today he said he heard a loon. (Or, He said he heard a loon today.)

6. He noticed a fly swimming in the soup.

7. To make a well-cooked egg, you must poach it until the yolk is solid.

8. While I was still a baby, my mother began to read to me.

9. After searching for days, I found the keys.

10. Muttering to herself, the vet gave the dog an injection.

▶ **ANSWERS TO ACTIVITY 12–11**

Creating Parallelism

1. Keyano College in Northeastern Alberta is a good choice if you wish to study to be an electrician, millwright, or welder.

2. You could also choose to learn nursing, carpentry, or cooking.

3. Students can also study physics, sociology, or botany.

4. Business students can study accounting, report writing, or marketing.

5. The Heavy Equipment Training includes how to operate a crawler tractor, motor grader, or hydraulic backhoe.

▶ **ANSWERS TO ACTIVITY 12–12**

Creating Mature Sentence Structures

Do your constructions look something like these?

1. As long as chemicals have not been put on dandelions, you can use the leaves to make salads and wine, and you can roast the roots to make a kind of coffee.

2. Dandelions are high in vitamin A, iron, calcium, phosphorus, potassium, and copper.

▶ **ANSWERS TO ACTIVITY 13–1**

Using the Apostrophe

1. Charon seldom took two months' vacation.

2. Sir Galahad's speech was good, but it had too many *thee's*.

3. Those are not Cinderella's photos in the album.

4. An Indian fast-food restaurant on Yonge Street advertised: Curry at its best.

5. Ontario's licence plates say "Yours to discover." (C)

6. The Fine Kettle-o'-Fish Restaurant is my sister-in-law's favourite place.

► **ANSWERS TO ACTIVITY 13–2**

Using Brackets

1. "Heavy drinkers [of alcohol] have more health difficulties than abstainers."

2. "I was filled with angrr [sic] toward the bullies."

3. Group of Seven artists (e.g., Lawren Harrls [1885–1970]) emphasized the ruggedness of the Canadian wilderness.

► **ANSWERS TO ACTIVITY 13–3**

Using the Colon

1. If you visit central Canada, be sure to see the most striking attraction: Niagara Falls.

2. For 9,000 years, people have travelled to see this river system, a natural wonder of the world: the rapids upriver, the Falls itself, and the huge gorge.

3. There's only one way to really experience the awesome power of Niagara Falls: look up through the spray of the Falls as you stand in the prow of the *Maid of the Mist* ferryboat.

4. From dusk (about 9:00 p.m. in May), the Falls are illuminated by colourful lights.

5. The question is How high is the Horseshoe Falls? (C)

6. Many people go away never realizing the most intriguing fact about the Falls: the depth of the water below the Falls is greater than the height of the Falls itself.

7. Attractions upriver from the Falls include Old Fort Erie, Dufferin Islands Nature Area, and the Niagara Parks Greenhouse. (C)

8. Be sure to see the other interesting attractions downriver: the Niagara Spanish Aero Car Ride, the Floral Clock and Lilac Gardens, and Brock's Monument, a tribute to the British hero of the War of 1812.

9. To fully experience the power of the Falls, locals also advise seeing several other attractions: Journey Behind the Falls (tunnels), the Gateway Festival Park viewing platform, and the Niagara Falls Imax Theatre's film *Niagara Miracles, Myths and Magic*.

10. There's no doubt about it: if you're in Ontario, you've got to see Niagara Falls!

▶ **ANSWERS TO ACTIVITY 13-4**

Using the Comma

1. Newspaper advertisement: "If you're thinking about buying electronics before October 19, you're out of your mind."

2. Student interest this year is particularly heavy in the technology, business, and tourism programs.

3. Edit my recent fortune cookie: "You have a friendly heart and are well admired." (C)

4. They are partly correct, but mostly wrong.

5. If you're in Surrey, British Columbia, visit Kwantlen University College.

6. At Kwantlen University College, which has its principal campus in Surrey, you can begin to study for a degree.

7. My favourite chewing gum includes several sugars: sorbitol, mannitol, aspartame, and xylitol.

8. Selecting species, planting seeds, and watering beds are all part of gardening.

9. After she planted the seed, watered the plants, and harvested the crop, the little red hen ate alone.

10. We sold three large, luscious watermelons to passing tourists.

▶ **ANSWERS TO ACTIVITY 13-5**

Using the Dash

1. His ambitious—and noble—goal was to take care of them all.

2. Pancakes, French toast, waffles—these foods are all best served under maple syrup.

3. I think—well, maybe I'm not sure—we should go.

4. Studying hard—and you should do so every day—will help you achieve your goals.

5. That great natural treasure of Vancouver—I'm talking about Stanley Park—should be carefully protected.

6. "Women's most difficult task since the race began has been to humanize man in order to make a civilized living with him possible."

—Agnes Macphail

▶ **ANSWERS TO ACTIVITY 13-6**

Using Ellipsis Dots

1. Well, I love that sign outside Biggar, Saskatchewan, but you would expect it to read: "New York is big, but this is Biggar." However, you could regard the ellipsis as indicating a pause in speech, and then it is correctly punctuated, as long as you put spaces before, between, and after the ellipsis dots: New York is big . . . but this is Biggar.

2. Here's how the the Labatt company should have advertised one of its beers: "Call 1-800-693-2527 to send a gift that can be opened again and again and . . . ."

3. "Well, I guess . . . hmm . . . maybe I will go tonight."

4. Here's the quotation with the part about too much masculinity left out (Columbo 613).

   "The world has suffered long enough from . . . not enough humanity."

   —Nellie McClung

   Many, though, would feel that something crucial has been omitted from McClung's statement.

5. Here's an edited version (Laxer, "Clark Hangs" F3): "Conrad Black expressed the sentiments of many executives when he wrote that 'No one in his right mind would invest a cent in Ontario under this regime . . . .'"

▶ **ANSWERS TO ACTIVITY 13-7**

Using the Exclamation Point

1. She gouged her finger with the chisel. "Ouch!" she cried.

2. What a vacation!

3. Yikes!

4. I went to Maud Island. I dived to explore the sunken destroyer *HMCS Columbia*. British Columbia really knows how to treat divers well ("Ship Scuttled" A3).

▶ **ANSWERS TO ACTIVITY 13–8**

Using the Hyphen

1. He has some not-so-fond memories of growing up in Cabbagetown. (C)

2. Miss Vickie wrote her customers: "Let me know how you like my country-style chips." (C)

3. He was a widely known philanthropist.

4. My mother-in-law is a gem.

5. Twenty-two people came to his funeral.

6. She was very self-determined.

▶ **ANSWERS TO ACTIVITY 13–9**

Using Parentheses

1. "The Premier took a shot at inventing his own crisis last month when he told reporters the province was 'bankrupt' (it's not) and 'going down the tubes' (it's not)" (Walkom B5). (C)

2. "Sadly, Canadian governments even are considering turning the operation of jails over to private U.S. companies (New Brunswick has hired the first one) who run them for profit" ("Keeping" A24). (C)

3. Stanley Park (in Vancouver) has a commemorative bench program (MacQueen B5).

4. For a modest cost ($1,800–$3,000) "you can buy a bench at a city park or beach, and dedicate it to a special person or a worthy cause."

5. An inscription on a small bronze plaque marks each commemorative bench. (C)

6. From one of the benches ("The Leader") you can look across the harbour and see the downtown skyscrapers.

7. The inscriptions are varied: "Mildred and George Cutforth are remembered by their family (seven sons and one daughter)"; Bill Con is commemorated ("A man with a spirit as free and a will as strong as these trees"); and Bob Wade is honoured ("happiness walking the seawall").

▶ **ANSWERS TO ACTIVITY 13–10**

Using the Period

1. Would you please pass me the salt.

2. Take care.

3. Mr. and Mrs. Lapierre work for the CBC.

4. I work for CARE.

5. I work for CARE.

▶ **ANSWERS TO ACTIVITY 13–11**

Using the Question Mark

1. They asked what I wanted.

2. When did the children ask, Are we there yet?

3. Will this be on the final exam? they asked. (C)

4. His daydreaming was punctuated with questions: Will the test be too difficult? Will I get through all the questions? Will there be a blizzard overnight? (C)

5. They lived happily ever after with their four(?) children.

▶ **ANSWERS TO ACTIVITY 13–12**

Using Quotation Marks

1. My so-called dear friend stole my car.

2. He had a heart of gold.

3. She said, "Let's go to a film tonight." (C)

4. "No," he said.

5. "Don't you"—her eyes widened with puzzlement—"like films?" (C)

6. She asked him again if he wanted to go. (C)

7. "I'd rather sing 'Red River Valley,'" he answered. (C)

8. "But isn't Donald Sutherland—oh, I thought this was true—your favourite actor?"

9. "In that case," he said, "I would love to go to the film." (C)

10. The word "film" has many meanings. (Write *film* if you're word processing.)

▶ **ANSWERS TO ACTIVITY 13–13**

Using the Semicolon

1. Sid Adilman (F1) wrote, "Like Raffi; Sharon, Lois, and Bram; and Classical Kids; [Fred] Penner runs his own company." (C)

2. Advertisement in the newspaper: "We thank all applicants for their interest; however, only those granted an interview will be contacted. (C)

3. Average citizens can remain uninformed about issues of importance; governments will continue to ignore the interests of average people.

4. I picked lettuce, asparagus, Brussels sprouts, and cabbages; and my back never thanked me for the exercise.

5. I would like to introduce Jean, who works in shipping; Hideo, who works in accounting; Tom, who works in advertising; and Marge, who works in expediting.

▶ **ANSWERS TO ACTIVITY 13–14**

Using the Slash

1. Send a letter to the president/secretary.

2. When the operator answers, order that zirconium ring from him/her.

3. Express four-sevenths as a figure. The answer was 4/7.

4. Show that this schoolyard chant is two lines: I hate you, You hate me./We're a dysfunctional family.

▶ **ANSWERS TO ACTIVITY 14–1**

Abbreviating

1. Visit us at Christmas.

2. Visit us on Monday, September 23, 2014.

3. Alex Colville lives down east.

4. I visited Ottawa, Ontario.

5. That loaf of bread weighs 750 grams.

6. Paul is studying dental assisting at Vancouver Community College.

7. For week five, please read chapter 5.

8. Lester works for the CBC. (C)

9. Please come at 6:15 p.m.

10. Please bring twenty-five dollars to room number twelve before eight a.m.

▶ ANSWERS TO ACTIVITY 14–2

Capitalizing

1. Joan has an ATM card.

2. The World Council of Credit Unions (n. pag.) says we should guard these cards just as we do money.

3. I wrote an essay entitled "My Plastic Pals."

4. I wonder if an astronaut will take a plastic card to Mars.

5. In Peterborough, I used my card to call from Sir Sandford Fleming College to my home in Niagara Falls.

6. I once lost my telephone calling card at the CN Tower.

7. I was trying to call the CBC to win free tickets.

8. After the loss, I had to place an advertisement in the *Toronto Star*.

▶ ANSWERS TO ACTIVITY 14–3

Enumerating

1. Four bills came in the mail.

2. Give me 2 two-packs.

3. I made 5 per cent less money last year. (C)

4. She lives at 6 Park Street.

5. Read pages 211–301.

▶ ANSWERS TO ACTIVITY 14–4

Italicizing and Underlining

If you were handwriting answers, you would have underlining where the text shows italics.

1. Let's try to bounce a signal off *Anik E-1*.

2. Give a listen to Ron Sexsmith's first CD, *Ron Sexsmith*.

3. Virgil is a *very* small community.

4. I like to read the newspaper comic strip *Between Friends*.

5. Give me that bottle of champagne; I'm going to christen our boat *Married and Loving It*.

▶ **ANSWERS TO ACTIVITY 14–5**

Syllabicating

1. thirst

2. about

3. million-naire

4. mighty

5. nerve-damaging gas

PART 5

Readings

"Most people won't realize that writing is a craft.
You have to take your apprenticeship in it like anything else."
—*Katherine Anne Porter*

You can study the *Write of Way* published essays to improve your writing and read-ing of essays. As you improve your ability to read and write essays, you will begin to use these same skills to write effective business reports, letters to the editor, and grant applications.

If you read more essays, you will learn how to write them better. If you did nothing different this year than read the three or four essays published daily in your local news-paper, you would begin to write better essays more easily. (You can also find good essays in magazines, journals, and trade publications.) Analyze the published essays in chapter 16, and you will improve your writing even faster.

CHAPTER 16

How the Pros Develop Ideas in Essays

"If the pen is mightier than the sword, why isn't it a felony to carry a ball-point in your jacket pocket?"
—*Michael Coren*

CHAPTER OBJECTIVE

By reading and analyzing the published essays, you will improve your ability to write essays—and to read them.

Essays have been an important part of English literature a long time, ever since Francis Bacon's first essays were published in 1597, a scant 17 years after French author Michel de Montaigne invented the essay in 1580 ("Essay"). Since then, powerful essays have changed the way whole societies view the world. Jonathan Swift's "A Modest Proposal" (1729), with its satirical suggestion to ease poverty by encouraging the rich to eat the children of the poor, raised awareness of the starvation of the Irish. Essayist Thomas Paine influenced the Declaration of Independence; pamphlets like his *Common Sense* roused such yearning for freedom that Paine had to flee from England to France after being charged with treason—because of what he wrote!

Essays have evolved from Montaigne's formal and elaborately stylish attempts to express in brief prose pieces his thoughts and feelings about what was important in his life (*Essais*) to today's more succinct explanatory and informative essays. The essays in *Write of Way* represent the diversity of formal and informal essays. Alan Borovoy explores why courts should ignore evidence gathered illegally. "Stopping Sexual Abuse in Sport" and Larry King's "How to Talk to Anyone, Anytime, Anywhere" exemplify the informative and persuasive essays popular today. Ruth Lemke's 1997 "Encounter with a Pirate" reads like a short story, but it is an account and reflection about a real-life event.

Do the activities that follow each essay, and you will clarify and reinforce your under-standing of the principles of essay writing presented in the earlier chapters of *Write of*

Way. The discussion questions prompt you to analyze the content of the essays, to find the authors' theses and to evaluate how well the writers support their contentions. The COSA formula for effective writing says that your writing will be more convincing if you organize your document well. Many of the discussion questions prompt you to critique the organization of the published essays.

If you want to improve your reading ability, begin by reading "You Can Learn to Read Better" (16.1). Discussing the answers to the activities that accompany each essay will also improve your reading comprehension by expanding your vocabulary and background knowledge and your ability to interpret writing.

16.1

Probably the most common mistake made by underdeveloped readers themselves and by teachers who want to help them is the selection of reading materials that are just too difficult. In this process essay, Doug Rogers draws on a background of thirty years of experience to describe how to become a better reader.

You Can Learn to Read Better

Douglas B. Rogers

> *"The labour market economically rewards those with strong literacy skills and penalizes those with low skills, and . . . net employment growth in Canada is largely restricted to jobs that demand high literacy skills."*
> —*J. Douglas Willms,*
> *Atlantic Centre for Policy Research in Education,*
> *University of New Brunswick*

Employers increasingly seek job applicants with strong literacy skills. As *Vancouver Sun* reporter Kim Bolan notes in her analysis of the International Adult Literacy Survey, "Most Canadians can read and write, but more than 40 per cent don't have the literacy skills needed to function effectively at work or at home" (A1). If you don't read well, you would probably like to improve, but you may not know what to do. Weak readers can follow a procedure to increase their reading ability: they must spend more time doing *easy* reading. To understand why, you need to learn a little about the process of reading, which is a combination of recognizing printed words, understanding individual word meanings, comprehending discourse, and remembering new information. Once you understand how people read, you can plan to become a stronger reader.

Reading begins with recognizing words in print. You start by fixing your gaze on the first word of text, whether it's a stop sign or a novel. When you recognize a word on sight, you hear its pronunciation in your mind, and you understand its meaning. If you've been reading for several words, you'll remember the author's last few thoughts; you'll add this new information to your understanding, to your memory. Of course, if you have a problem with word recognition, the process will break down.

You are likely to try one or both of two strategies when you do not recognize a word on sight. You may make a sensible guess about that word. After all, you've been understanding the author's content or message, so you may be able to surmise what she expressed next.

When you don't recognize the word on sight, you might also try to sound it out, to use phonic analysis. If you're lucky—and skilled—you'll pronounce the word closely enough to its correct pronunciation that you will suddenly recognize the word in its printed form. Then you can relate the new information to your memory of what the author was expressing a moment ago. You'll understand a little more of the author's message.

Suppose you determine the word's pronunciation, but you don't know what the word means. That means your reading is bogging down not because of a word recognition problem but because of a limitation in your understanding of a word meaning. If you're a college student, you have probably learned to recognize many words by sight, know so much about the world that you guess efficiently the probable meaning of many unfamiliar words, and are probably proficient at phonic analysis. If you have trouble reading, it is probably because you do not always understand the words the authors have used to express their thoughts and feelings. The smaller your vocabulary, the fewer materials you will be able to read.

When you can recognize the authors' words in print and know the meanings of these words, you may still encounter difficulty interpreting the situations described by *groups* of words, words organized into phrases, clauses, paragraphs, and whole documents. You have trouble understanding because you are puzzled by the complex language structures of the discourse or—more commonly for college students—because your knowledge of the world does not include some of the information the author assumes you know already. Think of this comprehension problem as caused by a mismatch. Imagine trying to understand text about word processing when you do not know the meaning of these terms as they apply to computer software: *function key, menu, mouse click, button.* And, since you have no experience with using a computer, you cannot really picture the situation, the equipment, and the actions of the keyboarder. Can you imagine how difficult it would be for you to read a passage in which the author explained *none* of these terms— in which the author provided no photograph of the equipment—assuming that you know all this? If you're an under-prepared college student, you may frequently experience this kind of problem when you try to read your textbooks.

Even when you do understand the meaning of a passage of text, you may still experience the fourth kind of reading difficulty: You may find it hard to *remember* the new information. To remember some information or procedures, you may have to study-read, to use a strategy such as rehearsing the new information you learned in the passage of text.

Underachieving readers experience difficulties with one or more reading behaviours: recognizing words in print, knowing the meaning of words, interpreting the meaning of a passage of text, and remembering—and applying—what has been read. So, what's an underachieving reader to do?

The process of learning to read better is quite straightforward: To improve, you've got to spend more time engaged in *easy* reading. When researchers look at the behaviour of grade one children who are rapidly learning to read, they see students who are reading easy book after easy book. In a study I did in an elementary school, the proficient readers usually rejected a difficult book. They put it aside, found another that was easy to read—and thus spent more time reading. By contrast, weak readers showed me what they were trying to read in their free time. They had picked books that were too difficult for them. These children knew they were weak readers and tried to catch up to their proficient peers by reading difficult books that just frustrated them and reduced the time they read. Underachieving readers rarely engage in the easy reading that facilitates progress in learning to read better.

When students are given daily practice with "challenging" reading material, they make no progress at all in learning to read, even if they do it for a whole school year!

When William Powell connected children to electronic monitoring equipment (similar to lie detectors), his studies showed that when children try to read difficult material, they experience physiological stress.

There is convincing evidence that a powerful technique for developing reading ability is reading lots of easy-to-read text, and that prolonged experience with frustration-level reading materials actually retards the development of reading prowess.

How easy is easy? How can you determine if you're reading material that is easy enough so that you will improve your reading proficiency? Here's a procedure you can try.

- Select a book or other reading material that you think you can read easily.
- Ask a friend to choose, at random, a passage of one hundred words. Be sure that you have never read it.
- Read the passage aloud while your friend looks on and counts all the word-recognition errors you make. (If you repeat a word as you try to recognize it, that doesn't count as an error as long as you do succeed in reading it.)
- If you can correctly read aloud at least 97% of the words, this material is easy reading for you.
- Read that material and find and read more text at a similar level of difficulty.
- From time to time, have your friend test you on more difficult material.

Think about the power of this procedure to help you improve your word recognition. As you correctly recognize words on sight, you will begin to recognize those words more and more quickly and automatically. You will likely understand the materials so well that when you do not recognize a word on sight (e.g., the word *jigging*), you can probably guess or predict its identity. If you're correct—and the word is important enough to reoccur in the text—you will begin to recognize *that* word on sight. If you must use phonic analysis to read the word—you sound it out—you'll begin to recognize it more quickly as you encounter it a second, a third time.

Easy reading builds your vocabulary, too. If you come to a word for which you do not, yet, know the meaning (e.g., *jigger*), you can probably infer what it means. When you correctly guess the meaning, you begin the process of *remembering* that meaning.

As you learn to read on sight more and more words, as you learn more word meanings, as you comprehend more of the situations described by writers, you will be developing more of the world knowledge that writers assume of readers. You increase your ability to comprehend—to interpret—more complex reading materials (e.g, a newspaper account of the east coast fishery). *And*, every time you learn more about some aspect of the world—including information you learn in conversations or while watching television (e.g., a news report about the Atlantic fishery)—it becomes easier to *read* about this topic. When you know more, your more extensive background knowledge helps you predict the identity of words unfamiliar in their printed form. Knowing what these words *might* be even makes it easier to use phonic analysis just to check the accuracy of your hunch. When you improve in any aspect of reading performance, the whole act of reading grows easier.

Doing extensive easy reading is the most efficient way to become a better reader.

Thinking about the Content

1. What is the thesis of "You Can Learn to Read Better"?

2. How does Rogers support his thesis?

3. If you accept the observation from the study the author conducted in an elementary school, what advice would you give parents who wanted to help their children learn to read better?

4. Summarize in a single sentence the process of determining if a material is an easy read for you.

Thinking about the Organization

5. When does Rogers directly state the essay's thesis? Quote another part of the essay where Rogers restates the thesis. Why does he repeat himself?

6. How does Rogers try to capture the reader's interest in the lead-in to the essay?

7. Why does Rogers include in the Willms citation information about Willms' job?

8. Which of the traditional elements of a conclusion to an essay is missing? Write one for the essay.

Ideas for Your Writing

Some educational researchers study case histories to better understand a learning process. Reflect on the factors that made you the reader you are today. Explain the reasons for your level of reading ability. Your support for the essay will be more helpful to your teacher if you can recount stories of interactions you had with your teachers, parents, or other adults or children important in your learning to write.

16.2

Jay Ingram is one of Canada's best known science writers and broadcasters. He makes his living by studying the scientific literature and explaining new discoveries in clear and entertaining ways. In this essay, Ingram explains the effects of procrastination.

Proof You Procrastinate at Your Peril

Jay Ingram

I'm not exaggerating when I say I've been putting off writing this particular column for weeks. It is of course about procrastination, a practice that I have perfected over the years. And while the research I'm about to describe makes it clear that procrastinating isn't very good for you, I'd bet that it will have little effect on those of you who do procrastinate—like me.

There are two ways of looking at the all-too-prevalent habit of putting things off until the last minute. Critics label it as simple self-indulgence and argue that it cannot be beneficial because it allows you less time than is necessary to do something well. It has even been argued that procrastinators are creating an excuse for themselves in advance of an anticipated poor performance.

However, practitioners like to say that they do their best work under pressure, the pressure that is only truly felt when a deadline looms, or is actually past. And in the meantime they get to laze around while the conscientious ones are working overtime.

Nagged by these unanswered questions, two psychologists at Case Western Reserve University in Cleveland, Dianne Tice and Roy Baumeister, examined the effects of procrastination on university students, a group that elevates the habit to an art form.

They first gave the students an assignment, then identified the procrastinators using something called Lay's Scale of Procrastination. The psychologists also measured the students' levels of stress and illness. Then they simply allowed the semester to pass. Lest you think you are too mature or responsible to indulge in this potentially self-destructive habit, try answering a few of these questions from the Lay's Scale with "not true for me," "true for me" or something in between:

- A letter may sit for days after I write it before I mail it.
- I generally return phone calls promptly.
- When it's time to get up, I most often get right out of bed.
- I usually return an RSVP request shortly after I receive it.
- I always seem to end up shopping for birthday gifts at the last minute.
  These are just a few of the 20 questions on the list.

At the end of the semester the date that each student handed in the assignment was recorded, and the students were asked to complete a questionnaire estimating how relieved they felt that the assignment was done.

And, here are the results. Not surprisingly procrastinators (as determined by Lay's scale) handed in their papers significantly later than nonprocrastinators. A more intriguing finding was that they also received lower grades (the person marking papers had no idea who had handed them in late). In the first version of the experiment, stress levels were only measured at the beginning of the semester, and as you might expect, the procrastinators were feeling just splendid—not a care in the world. They were feeling much better than their colleagues, who were already wrestling with the assignment. They also felt great relief when they finally handed in their work.

This study, if taken alone, seems to support the contention that it all works out in the end for the procrastinators, even if they do sweat it out a little in the final few days. However, a second version of the study was done where stress levels were measured throughout the semester, and in that case a different story unfolded.

At the end of the semester, the procrastinators were suffering much more than their nose-to-the-grindstone friends; they experienced higher stress, more symptoms of ill health and visited health professionals more often. In fact their end-of-term ill health outweighed the health benefits of idleness at the beginning.

So the bottom line is not good for procrastinators. The may feel better early on but those feelings of well-being are erased, and then some, when the deadline is upon them. And to top it all off, they don't perform as well as those disgusting eager beavers who hand in their work early.

Thinking about the Content

1. Ingram wrote an essay based on an article from the research literature. What is his thesis?

2. What are the two main points that Ingram makes in his essay?

3. Quote the sentence in which Ingram states a detail that supports his contention that school work suffers when students procrastinate.

4. In which paragraph does Ingram support his point that procrastination is bad for people because it hurts their health?

Thinking about the Organization

5. Ingram's first two sentences comprise a lead-in to his essay. Which two techniques does he use to try to create a lead-in that will pique your interest so that you will want to read the whole paper?

6. In your own words, write a sentence in which you state Ingram's thesis and preview the main points he makes.

7. Does Ingram recapitulate his thesis and main points in his conclusion? Does he write his clincher in a separate sentence? Which type of clincher did he write?

Ideas for Your Writing

In every field, there is always a ready audience for brief, well-expressed interpretations of important information. Most readers of Ingram's column do not feel they have the time to read all the science journals he reads, but they enjoy his discussions of the most interesting material. You can distinguish yourself if you can write briefly and informatively about information important in your area of expertise.

Browse a few issues of magazines or journals that are important to people doing the job you want to do. Notice how the publications vary in complexity: journals tend to publish longer more technical writing; magazines and newsletters have briefer, simpler writing. Select a lengthy, possibly complex, article and write your briefer interpretation, just as Ingram did. Be sure to indicate the primary source; don't plagiarize. If you're particularly pleased with your essay, send it to a newsletter that includes material similar to the essay you wrote.

16.3

Gwynne Dyer, who did not leave Newfoundland until he was 16, now writes from his London base about the whole world. An independent journalist and historian, his articles are published in more than forty countries.

Ten Thousand Languages

Gwynne Dyer

In a time when English has become the first and only "global language," used regularly by Koreans to communicate with Danes and by Turks to talk to Peruvians (both in the flesh and on the Net), it is reassuring to learn that it is not pushing other languages to the wall. On the contrary, concludes David Dalby of the Observatoire Linguistique; the world contains over 10,000 living languages, 50 per cent more than previously estimated.

The smallest of those languages have only one or two living speakers, and will die with them: Bikya, for example, is now spoken only by one 87-year-old woman living near Furuawa on the Cameroon–Nigerian border. But most of them have enough speakers to carry on forever, and the dominance of English is no threat at all.

This conclusion runs contrary to almost everything that has been said about the subject for decades. As long ago as 1985, "Development Forum," published by the United Nations University, coined the phrase "language death"—and suggested that endangered languages needed active conservation policies in the same way that we protect endangered species of animals.

But Dalby dismisses the common assertion that one-third of spoken tongues are in imminent danger of extinction as "absolute rubbish." The only languages in any danger at all are those spoken by very small groups of hunter-gatherers, and what puts them at risk is not "global English" but any nearby bigger language that comes equipped with books, schools, and television.

Dalby should know, for he is Welsh, and the institute he directs, despite its French name, is in Wales. Welsh was the very first language to come under pressure from English, but half a millennium after the English conquest of Wales, fully one-third of the population can speak Welsh. Almost all Welsh-speakers are bilingual in English, however—and that, Dalby reckons, is the dominant pattern for the future.

Until now, amazingly, nobody had done a full compilation of the world's languages and dialects. The international network of scholars who collaborated in the effort to produce a 1,600-page register of all the world's languages never suspected that so many languages existed, because each expert only knew his own region. So where do all these languages come from?

They come from a past before civilization, when language diversity was so extreme that every little group of a few hundred human beings had its own language (as the people of the Papua New Guinea highlands still do).

There may have been only ten million people on the planet then, but they would have spoken at least 20,000 different languages. And most, like the New Guinea highlanders, would have spoken a bit of the neighbouring groups' languages, too: multilingualism is not the exception but the norm in human history.

Then came civilization and the growth of mass societies in which millions spoke the same language. Mass civilization has been such a successful phenomenon that five millennia later, only eight languages account for fully half of the world's people. (In order of size, they are: Chinese, English, Hindi, Spanish, Russian, Bengali, Arabic, and Portuguese.)

The hundred biggest languages account for 95 percent of the world's people, and in some of the longest civilized places—the Middle East, Europe, East Asia—the surviving minority languages are counted only in the dozens. But in most places many more "little languages" have survived: the United States and Brazil are home to hundreds, India and Indonesia to over a thousand each.

Moreover, new technologies have lowered the cost of providing books, radio, and even television service to the point where languages with only 20,000 speakers can become perfectly viable mediums of communication for modern living, especially if they are geographically isolated.

A good example is Inuktitut, spoken by Canada's Inuit (Eskimo) people. The small Inuit communities scattered across the vast expanse of the eastern Arctic are all being given satellite uplinks and Internet connections, enabling them to talk to each other in Inuktitut, to access the few thousand books that have been written in Inuktitut or translated into it, and (if they are bilingual) to use all the rest of the world's information resources as well.

But that's the rub: "if they are bilingual." And "bilingual" actually means bilingual in English, since 80 percent of what's on the Net is in English. And isn't becoming bilingual in English the first step down the road to "language death."

The French certainly think so, and launch periodic linguistic pogroms to purge their language of English loanwords. But such paranoia is not justified by the evidence: bilingualism or multilingualism was once the natural state of human beings, and doesn't necessarily cause language loss at all.

The 300 million people who speak one of the world's 9,900 "little languages" do not need to worry. Most of them are already bilingual in one of the bigger languages, because it helps when travelling and gives them access to broader sources of information. But their own languages are not in decline. On the contrary, desktop publishing, low-cost newspaper publishing, and cheap broadcasting are dramatically expanding the possibilities for living in languages like Basque, Assyrian and Inuktitut.

What's true of the little languages is also true of the big ones facing the apparent juggernaut of global English. The emergence of English as the first global lingua franca is a remarkable phenomenon, but it doesn't really threaten anybody else.

The native speakers of English number around 450 million: more than any other language except Chinese but less than 7 percent of the world's population. Count those who have learned English as a second language, however, and the total soars to 1.3–1.5 billion, far surpassing any potential rival.

A global lingua franca is needed in this time when everything else is starting to work on a global scale, and English just happened to be the leading candidate (for transient reasons of American economic and military dominance) at the right time. Timing is all, and it may now retain this role for centuries. But there is not a shred of evidence to show that English threatens the position of other languages in their own home markets.

Thinking about the Content

1. Finish this sentence by stating, in your own words, Dyer's thesis: Although English has become the world's first global language, ...

2. Dyer, in discussing David Dalby's inventory of the world's spoken languages, says that Welsh was the first language to come under pressure from English. How convincingly does this example support Dyer's contention that the rise in the use of English will not extinguish other languages?

3. Dyer asserts that "multilingualism is not the exception but the norm in human history." What observation about the highlands of Papua New Guinea does Dyer make to support this point?

4. Discuss how advances in new communication technologies enhance the likelihood of survival of languages with as few as 20,000 speakers.

5. In his first paragraph, Dyer writes "it is not pushing other languages to the wall." Comment on the appropriateness of the tone, given that his intended audience is newspaper readers.

6. Dyer describes English as "the first global lingua franca." He never defines *lingua franca*. Comment on how effectively Dyer has met the information needs of his audience, general newspaper readers.

Thinking about the Organization

7. Quote the sentence in the second paragraph and the sentence in Dyer's final paragraph in which he states his thesis.

8. Does Dyer conclude his essay with a clincher or a restatement of the thesis?

Ideas for Your Writing

Dyer's "Ten Thousand Languages" is a persuasive essay. As Dyer himself notes in his discussion of the efforts of French attempts to eliminate English loan words, people feel strongly about native languages. Use one of the techniques for creating the content of a document (see section 2.1), and write a persuasive essay about a point of view you hold about language learning. Possible topics are that bilingual parents should ensure that their children are also bilingual or that speakers of less common languages should ensure that their language is represented on the Internet.

16.4

Suzanne Ziegler is an educational researcher and consultant. She lives in Toronto. Her essay shows how an expert can share professional insight with a lay audience.

Failing Young Kids Jeopardizes Their Future at School

Suzanne Ziegler

Changes in educational policies, practices and prejudices are often described as pendulum-like in sequence: what is trendy this decade is out-of-fashion the next, and back again thereafter, and so on. Why is this so? Presumably one cause is a lack of solid evidence for what works and what doesn't.

In medical research, by contrast, cures and preventives, once discovered, are not thrown away in favor of something merely new or different. In educational research, however, it is much more difficult to do the kind of experimentation that yields unequivocal results—the double blind studies, controlled to eliminate unwanted bias or extraneous influences.

So it is rare to have overwhelming evidence to support or defeat any educational practice. One of those rare cases concerns the consequences of having young children repeat a grade in school. The evidence is clear and well-documented: The principal effect of having children repeat a grade is to lower their over-all academic achievement level and ultimately to decrease the likelihood they will complete high school. Educational researchers and many teachers have long known this. School and school board policies have been slow to reflect this knowledge. Governments seem to be incapable of digesting it.

No one is happy to promote a child who is clearly lagging behind his peers in essential knowledge or skills. And there certainly should be better alternatives than either "social" promotion or failure. But the bottom line, hard as it is to swallow, is that in the great majority of cases, if failure or promotion are the only two alternatives (and all too often that is apparently the case), then there is only one right choice: promotion.

In studies which track children at comparably low levels of achievement, some of whom are promoted and others of whom are retained in grade, the advantage is always with the first group. The failed students have a much higher dropout or non-completion rate than the low achievers who were promoted.

Those who are promoted do not become high achievers; they remain near the bottom of the class. But those who are failed have the same outcome: they are at or near the bottom of their class, but their classmates are not their peers, but children a year younger. While a very few children who are failed do improve their achievment levels in the longer term, these few cannot be identified in advance. That means every decision to fail a student is much more likely to result in deterioration of achievement and opportunity than the reverse.

Most of the research concerns children in kindergarten and Grade 1. Teachers and parents often think retention will help the child who is small, who is socially immature, who is born late in the year, and/or who is having difficulty with pre-reading or reading skills. The evidence is abundant and crystal clear: it doesn't work.

Is there a middle path? Maybe.

The research is still young, but it appears that intensive tutoring, delivered one-on-one or perhaps in small groups (like pairs) by highly skilled and trained teachers, will enable most children without significant disabilities to catch up and keep up with their peers.

What is obvious about such interventions is their cost. Untrained volunteers or paraprofessionals do not produce the same results. All can be helpful additions to the work of the teacher; but they do not substitute for it.

A characteristic of successful interventions of this type is that they are intense, and move fast, with little time for learning on the job. Catching up with peers means aiming at a moving target. Programs (like *Reading Recovery*), which produce results that eliminate the promote-or-fail dilemma, depend on expensive training and delivery. So are quality preschool and junior kindergarten programs, which have been shown to have remarkable effects on preventing school failure and later social problems.

When programs such as these are provided, promotion is the natural and satisfactory conclusion. Governments which deprive school of the resources to deliver these programs leave them with only one ethical choice: "social" promotion.

Thinking about the Content

1. What is Ziegler's thesis?
2. Quote the sentence in which Ziegler indicates two bad effects of making children repeat a grade in school.

3. When Ziegler wrote her essay, what audience did she imagine? What makes you think so? How might she have written differently if she wanted to be published in a professional educational journal?

Thinking about the Organization

4. It is not until late in the third paragraph that Ziegler states her contention, the thesis of the essay. Write an introduction that begins with a question as the lead-in and then state the thesis and preview the main points.

5. Does Ziegler conclude her essay with a restatement of her thesis or a clincher?

Ideas for Your Writing

Our thoughts about school can motivate us to write. Letters to the editor, memoirs, persuasive essays—thinking about school has led to a lot of different kinds of writing. Think about an essay you might write as you reflect on your schooling. Perhaps you'll write a process essay about how to improve schools, a comparison of high school and college, a description of the effects of a poor schooling experience, or a narrative about some of your days in school.

16.5

Isabel Shessel drew on her extensive experience working with clients with learning disabilities (LD) to write this process essay about how adults with LD can not only cope, but thrive.

Overcoming the Odds: Adults with Learning Disabilities

Isabel Shessel

At 30 years of age, Rob still reads at a grade-three level. He left school after grade 11. Is he another one of the unemployed, disillusioned statistics that we often hear about? Not for a moment! Rob has worked for the same company for 13 years (moving from line-man to supervisor), owns his own home and runs a thriving business of his own.

We are left wondering why some people, despite significant learning disabilities (LD), are able to cope very well, while others experience lifelong failure, disappointment and dissatisfaction.

This article examines some of the strategies people like Rob have mastered to lead productive, self-fulfilled lives.

The concept of risk suggests that individuals exposed to negative circumstances (e.g., poverty, disability, child or sexual abuse) are more likely to experience negative long-term effects than those who have not been exposed to such factors. However, research and clinical reports indicate that "even under the most adverse circumstances, many individuals develop and/or maintain healthy personalities and become successful and satisfied adults." This ability to overcome, or protect oneself against, significant risk factors has been referred to as "resilience."

People with LD have long been known to be at risk for a number of negative outcomes across the lifespan (greater high school drop-out rates, underemployment, workplace difficulties, overdependence on others, social/emotional problems). But research on individuals with LD suggests that many, despite significant learning difficulties, have managed to overcome the risk factors in their lives. Research in the fields of social psychology and learning disabilities has begun to examine and identify these characteristics of success.

The information provided here has its roots in my own research on adults with LD. The study examined what strategies some individuals employed to "survive," despite their LD, and how their beliefs have also sustained their resilience.

The first strategy I would like to discuss is persistence, which can be defined as the ability not to give up in the face of failure. Individuals in my study used many words to describe this quality (determination, perseverance, tenacity, stubbornness, and "stickability"). As one individual said, "If I wasn't a little bit stubborn, I don't think I'd be where I am today." A group of researchers in the U.S. have suggested that persistence is "perhaps the most striking characteristic of the successful adults with LD."

Another strategy which appeared important for people with LD is well-developed self-advocacy skills. For some of the individuals I interviewed, this was crucial. One person said: "If I hadn't been able to stand up for myself, nobody else would have...My life's survival has depended on this."

Another individual mentioned the distinction between "best-interest advocacy" and "self-interest advocacy." He explained that "best-interest advocacy" involves someone other than yourself acting on your behalf for what they think is in your best interest. "Self-interest advocacy" is acting on your own behalf for what *you* want, and having the capacity to make decisions regarding your own future.

Clearly, the ability to act on your own behalf is the optimal situation. One does, however, need the appropriate skills and knowledge to do this effectively.

A third adaptive strategy is the use of humour. This appeared to be a unique strategy (that is, it was not mentioned elsewhere in the literature on LD). The ability to laugh at themselves was a powerful tool in the lives of some of the participants. They indicated that it was an "important catharsis" in relieving stress, anxiety, and frustration for themselves and those around them. One individual explained it this way: "It makes it liveable." Even those individuals who did not use this strategy indicated that humour was valuable, admitting they took life "too seriously."

What people believe about themselves and their environment can have a powerful impact on what they do in life. According to Martin Seligman, noted psychologist at the University of Pennsylvania, the way people respond to setbacks or obstacles—optimistically or pessimistically—is "a fairly accurate indicator of how well they will succeed in school, in sports and in certain kinds of work." This response style has been referred to in the psychology literature as "explanatory style."

In my own research, I found that whether individuals viewed life as a tremendous struggle or as a series of learning experiences seemed to determine their personal sense of well-being, accomplishment and success. Those who viewed life more positively were more successful in using adaptive strategies and in achieving their goals.

Cognitive reframing theory (a term from the field of psychology) suggests that an individual has the capacity to reinterpret negative experience in more positive ways, and this in turn reduces stress, anxiety and negative self-esteem. This positive thinking allows one to focus attention on more proactive tasks (like working towards personal goals).

This reinterpretation of experience was evident in a number of people interviewed. One individual offered the following advice: "You can't internalize failures . . . you have to learn from them." The ability to look at negative experiences in more positive and constructive ways is a valuable adaptive strategy for people with LD.

According to Dr. Seligman and his associates, adaptive strategies for living *can be learned*. It therefore becomes vital for professionals in the field of learning disabilities (teachers, counsellors, psychologists) to assist children and adults with LD to develop appropriate strategies that will empower them to become self-sufficient, productive and self-fulfilled members of society.

Included with this article is advice for people with LD, which I compiled from my research. Individuals with LD willingly shared their ideas, in the hopes that the life experiences of other people with LD would then be less painful and frustrating. I have also included some references. Three of these books are biographies of people who have truly triumphed over their hidden disability.

References

Faking It, by C. Lee and R. Jackson. Personal biography. Published 1992 by Boyton/Cook Publishers, Portsmouth, NH.

Brilliant Idiot, by A. Schmitt and M.L. Clemens. Personal biography. Published 1992 by Good Books, Intercourse, PA.

The Optimistic Child by M.E.P Seligman, K. Reivich, L. Jaycox and J. Gillham. Parent reference. Published 1995 by HarperCollins. New York, NY.

Reversals: A Personal Account of Victory Over Dyslexia, by E. Simpson. Personal biography. Published 1991 by The Noonday Press. New York, NY.

Succeeding Against the Odds, by S.L. Smith. Practical techniques and inspiring stories. Published 1991 by Jeremy P. Tarcher, Inc., Los Angeles, CA.

Advice to Other People with Learning Disabilities

Learn to communicate effectively.

Learn to "speak for yourself" (self-advocacy skills).

Be creative and flexible in problem solving (look at alternatives).

Learn to take risks.

Develop a good support network (including family, friends, professionals).

Take responsibility.

Be "tenacious."

Believe in yourself.

Do not allow your learning disability to consume you.

Disclose your learning disability when and if it is appropriate.

Set goals for yourself.

Learn from failures: do not dwell on them.

Develop personal strategies for daily living and learning.

Understand "who you are," your strengths and your weaknesses.

Understand your rights and how to obtain them within systems.

Do not be afraid to ask for help when you need it.

"Like who you are."

Do not be ashamed of your learning disability.

Develop good stress management strategies.

Learn to work through your strengths.

Never apply for a job that you are not qualified for.

Make the right career match.

Strive for balance in yourself.

Learn to laugh at yourself.

Develop good organizational skills.

Look for the positive in all situations.

Develop self-discipline.

Never say, "I cannot."

Thinking about the Content

1. In your own words, express Shessel's thesis and main points.

2. Find a quotation that provides support for Shessel's assertion that persistence is "perhaps the most striking characteristic of the successful adults with LD."

3. Find a quotation that supports Shessel's point that people with learning disabilities will be more successful if they develop self-advocacy skills.

4. For whom did Shessel write this article? How can you tell? Do you think her readers would feel that their needs were met?

Thinking about the Organization

5. What technique does Shessel use to create an interesting lead-in to her article?

6. Readers expect that writers will conclude essays by recapitulating the thesis and ending with a final thought. How well does Shessel's final paragraph fulfill readers' expectations?

Ideas for Your Writing

"Overcoming the Odds" is an example of a classification essay: it categorizes the strategies used by people who succeed despite learning disabilities. It is also an example of a process essay in that it suggests a procedure people with LD can follow. The essay is also a narrative: Shessel tells the story of her study of the field of learning disabilities. We can also see that the essay explains a phenomenon: Shessel tells us what *causes* success for people who have learning disabilities. Essay writers often use more than one method of developing ideas.

Human-interest stories intrigue us with their accounts of how one individual triumphed over adversity. Think of yourself or someone you know who succeeded against the odds, and write an essay that explains such unexpected success.

16.6

People around the globe tune into CNN's *Larry King Live* to hear him talk to famous and newsworthy guests. King frequently starts conversations with complete strangers—live, on television. As Larry King himself notes, "The vast majority of people would rather jump out of an airplane without a parachute than sit next to someone they've never met. . . ." In this essay, King shares his secrets about how to enjoy meeting strangers.

How to Talk to Anyone, Anytime, Anywhere

Larry King

I never wanted to be anything but a broadcaster, a talker. And for 40 years I've been doing just that. To me, the ability to talk well is one of the great pleasures in life and can bring with it some of life's greatest rewards.

I'm not saying it's always easy. The vast majority of people would rather jump out of an airplane without a parachute than sit next to someone they've never met at a dinner party.

But the more you work at it, the easier it will be. To get you started, here are my six basic ingredients for learning how to talk to anyone, anytime, anywhere.

1. You Don't Have to Be Quotable

If you could have witnessed my first morning in broadcasting, you would have bet the ranch that I was the last guy who'd survive, much less succeed, as a professional talker.

It happened at WAHR, a small radio station in Miami Beach, Fla., on the morning of May 1, 1957. I had been hanging around there hoping to crash into my dream world of radio. The station's manager liked my voice but didn't have any openings.

I lived near the station and went by every day, watching the disc jockeys, the newscasters, the sports announcers. After three weeks the morning deejay quit. The manager told me I had the job starting Monday morning. I didn't sleep that whole weekend. I kept rehashing things to say. By Monday I was a basket case.

Picture me at 9 a.m. sitting in the studio with my new theme song, Les Elgart's "Swingin' Down the Lane," cued up.

I start the song. Then I fade the music down so I can talk. Only nothing comes out. My mouth feels like cotton.

So I bring the music up and fade it again. Still no words coming out of my mouth. It happens a third time. The only thing my listeners are hearing is a record going up and down in volume.

Finally, the exasperated manager kicks open the door to the control room and shouts, "This is a communications business!" Then he turns and leaves, slamming the door behind him.

In that instant, I leaned towards the microphone and said: "Good morning. This is my first day on the radio. I've been practising all weekend. But my mouth is dry. The manager just kicked open the door and said, "This is a communications business."

I wasn't exactly quotable that morning, but I *was* able to get something out by telling my listeners about the predicament I was in, and that gave me the confidence to continue. The rest of the show—as well as my career—went fine.

2. Attitude Counts

After that fiasco in Miami, I made a commitment to keep talking even when it might not be comfortable—in other words, to work at it. The right attitude—the will to talk—is crucial to becoming a better talker.

I think one reason I've had a certain amount of success in broadcasting is that the audience can see I love what I'm doing. You can't fake that. And if you try, you will fail.

Tommy Lasorda, the former manager of the Los Angeles Dodgers, once came on my radio show the night after his team suffered a crushing loss in the National League play-offs. From his enthusiasm, you never would have guessed he was the *losing* manager.

When I asked him how he could be so exuberant, he said: "The best day of my life is when I manage a winning game. The second-best day of my life is when I manage a losing game." That enthusiasm and his willingness to share it have made him a successful manager and, by the way, a very successful talker, too.

3. Remember to Take Turns

Careful listening makes you a better talker. Good follow-up questions are the mark of a good conversationalist. In fact, I have an important rule that I remind myself of every morning: Nothing I say this day will teach me anything. So if I'm going to learn, I have to do it by listening.

4.   Broaden Your Horizons

The best conversationalists are able to talk about issues and experiences beyond their own daily lives. You can expand your world through travel, but you can also do it without leaving your own backyard.

When I was a boy, my widowed mother got an elderly woman to care for us while Mom tried to scrape up money for food, clothing and to keep our little apartment. The helper's father had fought in the Civil War, and as a child she had actually seen Abraham Lincoln. I was able to talk to her, so in a way my childhood was a window on another era in history.

The point is this: People with backgrounds different from your own can help broaden your conversational repertoire and your thinking.

5. Keep it Light

One of my cardinal rules of conversation is never stay too serious too long. Similarly, a key quality I look for in a potential guest is a sense of humour, preferably self-deprecating. Frank Sinatra is one guest who's never been afraid to make fun of himself.

During an interview with me, Sinatra recalled comedian Don Rickles coming over to his table at a Las Vegas restaurant to ask a favour. Rickles was dining with a friend.

"Would you mind saying hi to her, Frank?"

"Of course not," the singer replied. "Bring her over."

Then Rickles said that his friend would be even more impressed if Sinatra could come over to their table. So a short time later Sinatra walked across the restaurant, slapped Rickles on the back, and said how delighted he was to see him.

Whereupon Rickles said: "Beat it, Frank. This is personal."

What's key to the story—and most appealing to the audience—is that Sinatra so obviously enjoys retelling this joke at his own expense.

6. Be the Genuine You

Anybody I've ever talked to for more than a few minutes knows at least two things about me: that I'm from Brooklyn, and that I'm Jewish. That's because I'm deeply proud of both.

You should be as open and honest with your conversational partners as you'd want them to be with you, willing to reveal what your background is and what your likes and dislikes are. That's part of the give-and-take of conversation, part of getting to know people.

Talk-show hosts Regis Philbin and Kathie Lee Gifford come into our homes easily and naturally, and they're not afraid to reveal their tastes or tell stories on themselves. Without making themselves the focus of their talk, they are themselves. If they—or a guest—tell a sad or joyful story, they are not afraid to show their feelings.

Mel Tillis, the successful country-and-western singer, is absolutely charming as an interview guest, even though he stutters. It doesn't show up when he's singing, but it does when he's talking. Instead of letting it bother him, Mel is up-front about the problem, jokes about it, and is so completely at ease with himself that he puts you at ease, too.

As for myself, I learned something critical after surviving that case of "mike fright" on my first day of broadcasting: Be honest and you won't go wrong.

Whether you're talking to one person or a million, the rules are the same. It's all about making a connection. Show empathy, enthusiasm and a willingness to listen, and you can't help becoming a master of talk.

Thinking about the Content

1. What is King's thesis?

2. How does King support his first main point that it's easier to begin speaking if you don't feel that every utterance has to be worthy of inclusion in one of John Robert Columbo's dictionaries of Canadian quotations?

3. What makes King's telling of the story about Tommy Lasorda such effective support for his point that you talk most easily when you are enthusiastic?

4. What does King tell himself every morning to help him remember to take turns when conversing?

5. How does King support his contention that you'll talk more easily if you learn more?

6. Express in your own words King's fifth tip for becoming a good conversationalist. How does he support his advice?

7. What is King's sixth tip for being an expert conversationalist?

8. Reread the final paragraph. Would you change any of the language to ensure all readers feel the writer addressed them with a respectful tone?

Thinking about the Organization

9. Early in an essay, writers often state their thesis and preview the main points they will support. Comment on how King did this in his introduction.

Ideas for Your Writing

You may have found that the hardest part of making a new friend is deciding to start a conversation, to break the ice. You may be more nervous *anticipating* the job interview than talking with your potential new boss. Whether it's asking for directions, asking a question in class, asking for a date, or asking a stranger in class to photocopy notes you've missed, you have probably felt the same cotton in your mouth as Larry King did his first day on the air. Write an essay sharing *your* strategy for successful communication in one of the situations just mentioned.

16.7

I once read that parents are never happier than the least-happy of their children. And few events can make us depressed as fast as a quarrel between parents and children. *Homemaker* staffer Elizabeth Airdrie wrote this process essay to suggest how we can all get along.

Stop Fighting With Your Kids: A 10-Point Plan for Families

Elizabeth Airdrie

Jessica, 3, throws a tantrum in the supermarket. Josh, 14, is late for school—again. Allyson, 16, reels home drunk from a party. If you're like most parents, you turn to the traditional troika of high-handed tactics: shouts, threats, punishment. They don't work, of course. Jess is stubborn and tearful. Josh is surly and uncommunicative. Ally is threatening to run away from home.

What's wrong with this picture? As a parent, you want what's best for your kids. They want to please you. Why, then, with all these good intentions floating around, does your home regularly turn into a battlefield?

"Some of the most damaging interactions in families can be attributed to the very normal desire parents have for their kids to excel," says Nancy Samalin, director of Parent Guidance Workshops in New York City and author of *Love and Anger: The Parental Dilemma* (Penguin Books, 1991). Unfortunately, she says, parents' well-meaning suggestions or offers of help backfire, interpreted by children as criticism or pressure to be different from who they are. Conflicts ensue, which can escalate into all-out warfare.

Whatever the conflict, calm discussion will resolve it more effectively than nagging and yelling. In addition, there are strategies to practise which will help avoid some conflicts before they begin. Samalin, along with other family behavior experts, helped us draw up this 10-point plan to stop fighting with your kids.

1. Encourage Kids to Be Individuals

Parents have a tendency to see kids as reflections of themselves, which can put too much pressure on children and undermine their confidence. Instead, emphasize exactly whose accomplishment or difficulty is at stake, says Toronto psychologist Dr. Harold Minden, author of *Two Hugs for Survival* (McClelland & Stewart, 1983). Rather than saying "Hey, great report card, I'm proud of you, kid," or "I really don't understand your bad mark in French; I was always good at languages," say, "You must be very proud of that report card," or "You seem to be having trouble with French."

2. Recognize Your Kids' Strengths

Samantha, 8, does a lot of things that irritate you, but she also has some wonderful qualities. Instead of nagging her about her messy room and carelessness with money, praise her for being so thoughtful to her grandparents. This kind of approach, says Dr. Minden, both affirms the child's good qualities and gives more weight to criticism when it is warranted.

3. Free Kids from Family "Roles"

Parents are tempted to typecast their children, as in: "Jane's a neat freak; Jonathan's a slob." Says Nancy Samalin, "When kids are repeatedly labelled as bossy or sensitive, smart or mischievous, stubborn or helpful, they feel compelled to live up to the reputation assigned to them." This can lead to trouble.

4. Encourage Kids to Think for Themselves

Kids are often capable of working things out more equitably and satisfactorily than we give them credit for, says Cheryl Picard, a professor at Carleton University in Ottawa who teaches conflict resolution skills to community, family and school groups. "When people come up with their own solutions, they have a much stronger interest in seeing those solutions met." For example, 17-year-old Lauren is more likely to get home on time if she suggests 1 a.m. for her weekend curfew than if you impose it.

5. Deal with Incidents as They Come Up

Caitlin, 6, swipes a candy bar from the corner store, and you're tempted to blurt: "That's stealing! If you keep doing that, you'll wind up in jail!" Prophesying the future based on a single event is a common trap parents fall into, says Samalin. "When kids disappoint or deceive, it's only a short leap in the parental imagination to dire long-term consequences." Far better to focus on the present, address the specific behavior and why it is unacceptable.

6. Let Kids Deal with the Consequences of Their Behavior

You've been late for work twice this week because you had to deliver 11-year-old Kirsten's forgotten lunch to school. You're not happy about this, and you let her know it. "Parents come to a child's rescue with the intention of being helpful," says Samalin, "but if it becomes more than the occasional bailout, they get angry." As a result, kids not only fail to experience the consequences of their mistakes, they don't even appreciate the rescuer. Allow kids to take responsibility that's appropriate for their age. Ask yourself, "What's the worst that can happen if I don't step in?"

7. Practise Problem-Solving

Ben's history teacher has just called to report that Ben, 15, has been skipping class, and he hints that Ben has been occupied in some nefarious activity during that time. You're itching for a showdown with Ben; once you've calmed down, spirit him off to a quiet corner and have him tell—uninterrupted—his side of the story. Ask him to express his feelings about it and suggest ways to solve the problem.

8. Watch Your Timing

You're trying to get dinner on the table, and nine-year-old Sarah is bugging you about getting a puppy. Exasperated, you want to tell her just plain "No!" and get her out of your hair. Instead, say that you'd rather not talk about it now, but you'd like to fix a time for later. According to Caroline Piotrowski, a family studies professor at the University of Manitoba in Winnipeg, the prime time for conflict is after school and before dinner— "when parents are least able to deal with it." Recognize the times when you're feeling tense, and reserve important discussions for times when you're more relaxed.

9. Let Your Kids Know You Love Them

...and that your love is unconditional. You may not always tolerate what they do, but you'll never waver in accepting who they are.

10. Be Patient

Changes won't happen overnight, says Cheryl Picard. "But if you respect your children and trust the process, the number of family fights will drop." Bonus: your children will have an increased sense of responsibility and self-esteem.

Thinking about the Content

1. What is Airdrie's thesis?
2. Note two ways Airdrie created specific support for her thesis.

3. Speculate about how Airdrie learned more about her topic. Suggest how she was able to provide the quotations from experts in parent–child relations.

Thinking about the Organization

4. In which paragraph does Airdrie assert her thesis?

5. In the lead-in to her essay, what is the principal way Airdrie tries to capture the reader's attention?

6. In her introduction, why didn't Airdrie preview the points she made in the essay?

Ideas for Your Writing

Airdrie implies that most parents want what's best for their children and that most kids want to please their parents, yet it is common for parents and children to fight. When we were children we may have thought how unfair parents could be. When we sent our children off to college, we may have thought about how we could have done better as parents. Grandparents rethink how to raise children. Write an essay in which you share your plan for how parents should interact with their children to end the fights.

16.8

Dr. Gifford-Jones is the pseudonym of a surgeon who shares his broad interest in health by writing a medical column published in newspapers across Canada. In this process essay, Dr. Gifford-Jones eschews jargon and shows how a medical journalist can explain complex ideas in language that makes sense to newspaper readers.

Losing Weight Easy as 1, 2, 3

Dr. Gifford-Jones

Are you one of the tens of thousands whose weight has gone up and down like a yo yo? Possibly you've tried a dozen magic diets without success? And finally decided it's a hopeless task trying to beat the battle of the bulge? Well before you toss in the towel there is one final way to attack this universal problem. It requires merely a simple lesson in arithmetic and a willingness to accept a basic law of physics.

The good news is that you don't have to change your eating habits one iota. After all, it only requires a glance to realize that 99% of dieters cannot discipline themselves to a lifetime of saying no to food.

Rather, you can continue to eat as much as you've been eating. No more, no less. In fact to prove this method works, it's essential to eat as much as before.

You must also accept one scientific fact, the First Law of Thermodynamics. This immutable law of nature states that if you consume more calories than you burn up this excess energy is stored as fat. If you consume fewer calories than you burn up, you lose weight. Sounds easy to grasp.

Some of my patients can't accept this law. They say, "But doctor I don't eat anything and still gain weight." Sorry, but unless the laws of this universe change it can't happen.

I remind these sceptics that there were no obese people in the concentration camps of Nazi Germany. These victims were tragically aware of the relationship between caloric intake and energy consumption.

Now a simple arithmetic lesson. Each pound of fat contains about 3,500 calories. So when you consume 3,500 calories it's either used up in energy or stored as one pound of fat.

My weight hadn't changed for years. That's why I was shocked when I stepped on a scale following a ship's cruise. I had stored up nearly a pound a day by eating high caloric foods. But I hadn't burned it up lounging in a deck chair reading for hours.

Some people may burn up all but 100 calories a day. The next day it may be an extra 50 or 300 calories. But it makes no difference whether the time interval is short or long. Once you have collected another 3,500 extra calories the scale goes up one pound. If this depresses you, there is a solution.

To lose weight without dieting you must expend energy by walking, walking, walking. It must be 20 minutes a day more than your usual routine.

Walking 20 minutes a day will burn up about 100 calories and result in losing one pound a month. If you walk an hour more each day you will lose three pounds a month.

But won't you eat more if you walk more? Research shows that if you are overweight, an extra hour a day of walking will not increase your appetite.

Experts claim appetite increases only after you return to your best weight. This is your weight between 21 and 25 years of age. At this weight, appetite increases to stabilize your body.

Several years ago, Martin Katahn, Director of Weight Management Program at Vanderbilt University, admonished obese people never to go on a diet.

He claims that repeated dieting or prolonged dieting makes it easier to gain weight on less food.

Katahn maintains that dieting makes the body more efficient at storing unwanted fat.

He explains that it required thousands of years for our body's metabolism to adjust to a feast or famine existence. And that it's impossible for our natural biological instinct to forget past famines.

Dieting is therefore interpreted as a threat to survival. Faced with less caloric intake, the body turns down its "feast or famine thermostat" and begins burning energy at a slower rate.

Katahn says that in the case of a crash diet (fewer than 500 calories a day) the metabolic rate can drop as much as 45%.

Once the dieting is over and people return to their normal eating habits, our survival instinct again comes into play.

Not knowing when the next famine will occur, the feast or famine thermostat adjusts to store more fat while the going is good.

I think there's an element of truth to Katahn's theory. And I also believe the laws of physics.

If you share this view you could be 36 pounds lighter this time next year.

But before you start more walking buy an appropriate walking shoe, which has a firm counter for the heel, moderate cushioning and a toe box with ample room. And start slowly.

It's also prudent for all patients, particularly the elderly, and those with major obesity or cardiac troubles to check with their doctors.

Happy walking!

Thinking about the Content

1. Quote the sentence in which Gifford-Jones states his thesis.

2. What evidence does Gifford-Jones present to counter the belief that dieting is the way to lose weight?

3. Review figure 5-1, then sketch an outline of the content of "Losing Weight Easy as 1, 2, 3."

4. Why does Gifford-Jones tell the story of his weight gain while on a boat cruise?

5. Gifford-Jones uses some colloquial expressions, even clichés. Why does he do this? Rewrite in more novel language two overworked expressions he includes in his first paragraph.

Thinking about the Organization

6. What technique does Gifford-Jones use to create a lead-in for his column?

7. Leave Gifford-Jones' clincher ("Happy walking!"), but reorder the preceding three paragraphs so that the restatement of the thesis occurs just before the clincher. Rewrite the three paragraphs as much as necessary to create this different conclusion to the essay.

Ideas for Your Writing

Scientists and engineers are creating new knowledge at an accelerating pace. Researchers specialize to gain their leading-edge understanding. Members of the public increasingly look to reports by writers who combine writing ability and specialist training in science or engineering and to researchers who have the ability to explain complex information. You are studying to develop expertise in your subject. Pick a topic from your area of specialty, research it further, and write a brief essay to explain your understanding to newspaper readers.

16.9

Like many Canadians, Rosie DiManno's parents emigrated to Canada. DiManno's narrative essay describes what it was like to grow up in an Italian-Canadian family in Toronto. DiManno is a columnist for the *Toronto Star*, Canada's largest circulation newspaper.

Growing Up on Grace

Rosie DiManno

I was about 6 years old when I discovered that I was a Canadian.

This came as a rude shock.

Insofar as I had a vague image of a huge world with a bunch of different countries in it, I thought I was an American.

My parents are Italian immigrants and I was born in Toronto, grew up on Grace St. downtown, but didn't learn English until I started school. In my household, whenever the adults spoke of leaving their old country for this new one, it was always put in these terms: We came to *America.* They made no distinction between the United States and Canada, or maybe I just didn't grasp it.

America. Sometimes it was said with regret and sadness, other times in terms of a bold adventure, but never with a sense of belonging. It was always this alien place in which they found themselves, and to which they were grateful for whatever comforts they had acquired. But their suspicions and their sense of isolation lingered. It's why they—and every other ethnic group that ventures to this city—clustered in self-contained, unilingual neighborhoods, both to shun and to defend themselves from shunning. They weren't cultural ghettos; they were outposts of the familiar, like pioneer forts in a hostile land. The land of the *Inglese.*

It was the early '60s. I watched American TV beamed from Buffalo: *Captain Kangaroo* and *Commander Tom.* Sitcoms like *Petticoat Junction* and *The Honeymooners*—which had no similarities to our own existence on Grace St. but which I misunderstood as that larger American reality, from which I was excluded only because of my parentage, not by geographic boundaries. And certainly not because these were phony, idealized domestic situations that only existed within a television tube.

This, I thought—flipping between *Leave It To Beaver* and *I Love Lucy*—is how people *really* live, except on my street: The privileged people, not the interlopers (like us), the imposters (like us); the ones who have proprietary first dibs on the country, the ones who drink milk at the dinner table, who have cereal for breakfast, who make sandwiches from pre-sliced white bread, who wear high heels in the house.

There was no Canadian flag, remember, as the most visible national icon. At Clinton Public School, they flew the Union Jack, but I thought that was just a weird variation on the Stars and Stripes. There was a photograph of the Queen at the head of the class, and this got me to thinking about the relationship between the Queen and the president, who was also familiar to me from American TV news. We sang "God Save The Queen" in school, but at night, when the TV stations signed off, it was the American national anthem that accompanied the fade to black. There was no "O Canada."

Perhaps my main problem is that I never watched the CBC.

It dawned on me, somewhere around Grade 1, that I was not American at all, although this growing suspicion was something I kept to myself for awhile. It's not the kind of thing you ask an adult about, lest you appear colossally stupid, and I was not in the habit of asking my parents anything. They were probably more alien to me than the Ricardos.

When I was forced to accept this reality, it was with a sense of loss. Here I had been trying to visualize myself growing up and fitting into this bustling American lifestyle, this energetic and self-confident and purposeful country. But I was stuck with dreary old/young Canada. Second-rate by ancestry, third-rate by an accident of birth.

The dismay wore off, of course. Certainly, it was shed abruptly when I met my bosom friend Barbara Zloty, in Grade 5. She really was an American but had moved to Toronto with her mother to stay with relatives because her father was fighting in Vietnam. I could not imagine having a father fighting a war in a distant country, maybe getting killed, maimed. Eventually, Barbara's father was wounded, and they returned to El Paso.

Barbara made me my first grilled-cheese sandwich, which seemed terribly decadent and decidedly *Inglese*. My mother, who did not believe that we should ever enter the homes of anyone outside the extended family—and rarely were any of us invited—had forbidden me to have lunch at Barbara's. I went anyway. When I got home from school that afternoon, my mother met me halfway up the street and hit me with her shoe.

This is supposed to be a narrative about My Canada, yet I'm not sure what that means. I can tell you only small stories about growing up in a small piece of the country, as insular as any tumbleweed-tossed Prairie town or desolate Maritime hamlet.

I grew up not in a country but on a street. My territory stretched from Bloor to Harbord, with traffic lights at either end, Christie Pits to the north, Bickford Park directly across from the house, Montrose Park to the south. Bickford Park, where I climbed every tree, had no amenities: no playground, no pool, no soccer pitch. Just a weary little softball diamond, one drinking fountain, and a huge sewer grate that was cool against your face when you lay across it on hot summer days.

And yet the park fascinated us, we overprotected young children who were never allowed to roam beyond the busy thoroughfares at either end of Grace. Once I saw a man running through the park with his mangled left arm hanging by just a few strands of sinew. Once I found a gold signature pin that said: Rosalba. That is my real name, abbreviated and Anglicized once I started school, in a desperate attempt to be more English. It fills me with wonder, still, that I should find such a pin, with that odd name, in the grass of Bickford Park.

There were many Italians on that street, some relatives, some merely *paisans*, some with no ancestral connection but part of the cultural fraternity that kept Us separate from Them. There were several Jewish families, too, and I remember feeling a kinship with them, because they were also aliens. (Later on, in my teens, we would move to a predominantly Jewish neighbourhood in Downsview. This resulted in one curious anomaly: My mother now speaks English with a Yiddish accent and is as likely to make a brisket for dinner as lasagna.)

I was mortified, in those days, by our Italian-ness. I begged my mother to shave her legs, to which she finally acquiesced, although she never did understand the fuss. I hated the tomatoes and tangle of vegetables in our backyard and longed for the banality of a grass carpet. I hated the pepper and onions that my mother would string like braids on the front porch.

In late spring, my father—a farmer and shepherd before emigrating—would dump a load of manure on the front lawn because this is the world's best fertilizer. On those occasions, I would walk right past my house lest any classmates realize that I lived in such a Munsters-like place.

My father—and I respect him for this only in retrospect—never attempted to ingratiate himself with the *Inglese* by being less Italian or by altering the rhythms of his life, although he was impeccably hospitable and generous.

He hunted, not for sport, but for food and I can see him now, skinning jackrabbits over the cellar sink. In the fall, he would slaughter a pig; at Easter, a lamb.

My parents made sausages and strung them to dry inside a makeshift smokehouse. Prosciutto would be salted and hung for a year in the wine cellar. My mother would spend weeks slicing fresh tomatoes and bottling them for sauce, sterilizing the bottles in a steel drum of boiling water in the backyard, stoking the fire underneath. She'd pickle cucumbers and artichokes, cauliflower and olives.

I loved all these foods, so common now in Italian restaurants and grocery stores, but I was ashamed of them then. I would throw away my lunch at school and starve rather than expose these peculiar items to my *Inglese* friends. I pined for peanut-butter sandwiches.

Sometimes, I would go grocery shopping with my mother just so I could persuade her to buy all this ostensibly tasty English stuff that I saw advertised on TV: jelly rolls, Cap'n Crunch cereal, Pop Tarts, Wonderbread, SpaghettiOs, Campbell's soup, Kraft macaroni and cheese, marshmallows. It all tasted foul, it made me gag. But if this is what it took to be *Inglese*, I would suffer for my pride.

In autumn, after weeks of consultation and innumerable taste-testing expeditions, the crates of grapes would be delivered to the house: hundreds of them, stacked on the lawn. California grapes for homemade wine. Families would help each other out in the complicated wine-making process, churning and pressing and sifting and decanting. It was, I suppose, a different version of the barn-building efforts in other cultures, a community event.

Invariably, I would step on a nail.

Menstruating women were not allowed near the mulch, lest they spoil the wine. I, still a child, was humiliated on behalf of these women, who would be sent upstairs to make themselves otherwise useful. I only realized later that they considered it a blessing to be so ostracized from such back-breaking work, and the constant curses of the men.

I rebelled against all of it. The religious processions that were the highlight of the calendar year, refusing to parade along the street in my bride-like Communion gown; refusing to attend the Catholic school in which I had been enrolled (hiding out in the sewer pipes at Christie Pits) until my mother threw up her hands in defeat; refusing to kiss the aunts and the uncles (all of whom had chin whiskers); refusing to eat anything that had a hint of tomato in it; refusing to speak Italian.

Education was not valued highly in our family, which possibly made us, our sub-group of Italian immigrants, different from other ethnic groups washing ashore in Canada. Education was feared by these Italians—a fear nurtured and encouraged by the Catholic church. Education would take children away from their parents, the priests said, would make them question authority, would draw them into the outside world, which was a forbidden place.

Yet every week, from the time I was very small, my mother would take me, in a clandestine venture, to the St. George main library, a good 20-block hike from our house. She could barely read Italian but she wanted me to learn something from the ridiculed pleasure of books.

An education, particularly a post-secondary education, was considered a waste on a girl. If I were to have any profession at all, it was decided on my behalf, I would become a teacher: a feminine profession, respectable, akin to mothering. I played along and planned my escape.

So there came a time when the street, and the neighbourhood, became too small and too cramped an existence for me. Symbolically, it was enough for my parents. They finally felt safe and entrenched. They knew nothing about the rest of the country and did not care. They didn't know the difference between a city and a province.

They were clueless about the vastness of Canada, although they had come to Toronto from Halifax by train. They never ventured outside the city, rarely strayed from the neighborhood. The most ambitious foray I can recall is one winter when we took the streetcar to the College St. Eaton's store—the most WASPish of establishments—to buy me a typewriter. I'd never seen an escalator before.

My parents never took a vacation—in 45 years, my father has yet to return to Italy for a visit—never mingled with another ethnic group (save for an Indian friend who was my dad's hunting companion, and the Jewish family in whose coin laundry my mother had once worked), never had any curiousity about politics or social issues or even the most innocent of *Inglese* pleasures. My father has never been to a movie, never gone to a hockey game, never attended a parent night at school.

When I'm being generous, I convince myself that he was merely shy, that he felt ignorant in this English culture. But I'm more inclined to believe that he lived completely within himself, and even his family was an intrusion.

Perhaps I have inherited his discomfort, his diffidence, because I don't feel particularly connected to this country, either, although I have a genuine fondness for it.

Too long an outsider, beseeching entry. Relentlessly *Inglese* in attitude and tastes, irredeemably Italian in my genes. But not hyphenated, never hyphenated. A clumsy hybrid, maybe.

I used to fret so much, in my younger days, about how I could ever reconcile these two cultures, how I could be Rosalba and Rosie and still stay intact. The struggle doesn't seem very important anymore.

But I am constantly astonished by third generation Italian Canadians who seem more proud of their ancestral homeland than the country of their birth, who chatter in Italian on St. Clair Ave., who seem more Italian to me now than my parents did 30 years ago. Cultural pride is one thing, but so much of this overt Italian sensibility seems to me to be a betrayal—of Canada, and to those of us who broke all the rules so that we didn't have to stay insularly Italian, imprisoned by culture, in this country.

I don't wave flags and I find the notion of Canada Day contrived, if sweet. But I have felt moments of intense patriotism. Little moments, like spotting a Maple Leaf on a teenager's backpack in Europe. Grand moments, like when a Canadian wins a gold medal at the Olympics. Aching moments, like when I visit the Canadian war cemetery in Casino, just down the mountain from my parents' village. (As children, they survived the battle of Monte Cassino.) And historical moments, like covering the referendum in Montreal in 1995, and feeling a sudden swell of anxiety, as if we were letting something very precious slip away, through carelessness and self-absorption.

As an adult, when I visit my ancestral village in Italy—which lost half its population to Toronto after the war—they always ask about life in *America*. I have given up trying to make the distinction. It just doesn't seem significant, from the perspective of a mountaintop south of Naples.

It's funny, though. From the first time I set foot on Italian soil, I felt as if I belonged. I looked like everyone else, my name didn't sound foreign. I felt a thousand years of history rushing through my blood. But I couldn't live there.

And every time I come through Canada Customs, travel back across the border, I breathe a sigh of relief. Home.

My parents are Canadian citizens now. Grace St. is long ago and far away. They are living the good, Canadian life: a suburban home, a cottage, two cars, a truck, money in the bank. They take occasional trips, mostly church-organized, and are finally seeing a little more of the country. They vote. And they try very hard to pretend that we are not a fractured, dysfunctional family.

They do not read English. They will not read this story. They have never read a word that I have written.

Thinking about the Content

1. What is DiManno's thesis?

2. DiManno's main points seem to be that she became a Canadian in stages. Briefly sketch those stages in her evolving Canadian identity.

3. DiManno's essay is not only a narrative; it is also a descriptive essay. Her rich description of life on Grace Street in downtown Toronto (not far from Honest Ed's) makes it easy to picture the neighbourhood. Indicate some of the specific, descriptive details that DiManno cites as being embarrassingly Italian and that she rejected when she was young.

4. Storytellers often speak in the first person, as DiManno does in "Growing Up on Grace." She seems to speak directly to each reader. Dialogue is also common in narrative essays, yet in DiManno's story, she never quotes anyone. What is the effect of her always telling the story in her own words?

5. Late in her essay, DiManno writes about her parents, "And they try very hard to pretend that we are not a fractured, dysfunctional family." What is the effect of this detail on the unity of the essay?

Thinking about the Organization

6. Quote DiManno's lead-in. What technique does DiManno use to interest us in reading her column, which was published just before Canada Day?

7. Throughout the essay, DiManno says that she felt estranged from her parents. They "were probably more alien to me than the Ricardos," the family in the 1950's sitcom *I Love Lucy*. She makes the point most poignantly in her clincher. Quote it. What makes the remark so poignant?

Ideas for Your Writing

Whether it's a new book or television program about former prime minister Brian Mulroney or Evelyn Lau telling the story of her life as a prostitute—biographies and autobiographies fascinate most of us. Interview an immigrant to Canada and write an essay describing the process of adapting, or tell your own story.

16.10

Alberta Report, *B.C. Report*, and *Western Report* were founded by Ted Byfield. *Report* is the second-most-widely-read truly indigenous newsmagazine in Canada. When they see Byfield's name in the *Report*—or in other publications—many readers turn eagerly to see what he has written. In a time when many people walk away from a troubled marriage, Byfield makes a controversial argument for a different approach to marital difficulties.

The Next Great Social Controversy Will Be Over a Move to Toughen the Divorce Laws

Ted Byfield

The next great issue that will pit left versus right and liberal against conservative in Canada will probably be a fight over divorce law. The Americans are already well into it. However, unlike its predecessors—the abortion controversy, for instance, or the debate over homosexual rights—the divorce dispute will not arise out of a demand for a more liberal law, but for a less liberal one. The evidence grows that the divorce reforms of a quarter century ago are causing more problems than they solved.

Unsurprisingly, as divorces became easier to get, there were more divorces. Today two U.S. marriages in five fail, and the Canadian rate isn't far behind. The consequences are appalling. Divorce almost always results in "downward mobility" for a mother. It was hard enough for one income to support one home; it must now support two. The data accumulates that children of broken homes are more likely to drop out of school, get pregnant, turn to crime, and fail to find permanent work. Sexual abuse of children is far more likely where the mother finds a live-in boyfriend. The dollar cost of all this is incalculable. So is the cost in terms of human distress and misery.

No one can long remain a stranger to this phenomenon. We either live through it ourselves, or watch others doing so. I have four close friends, all recently divorced, in every instance painfully. In fact, I've never heard of a happy divorce. Always there is a sense of tragedy, defeat, loss, not just to the couple but to the whole community. Moreover, there seems no rule; divorce strikes like a disease. I've known couples who seemed ideally suited and who yet break up. I've known divorced people whom I can't imagine anyone wanting to divorce and others I can't imagine anyone wanting to marry.

One conclusion nevertheless seems obvious: If easy divorce results in more divorces, then tougher divorce laws should result in fewer. This proposal, advanced by conservative family values groups, instantly created an explosive argument. Easy, "no-fault" divorce, in which either party can apply for a divorce and get one without having to prove the other party at fault, is now the law in 40 of the 50 states. The other 10 allow divorce on the application of both parties. Liberals saw such laws 30 or more years ago as a milestone in social advance. They will fight furiously against any threat to them.

Thus the divorce question now ascends upon the American media, providing a cover story for *Esquire* magazine, a combative article in *The Nation* and sequential argument in the publication *Slate*, all informative for Canada because the same proposal will doubtless arise here.

The conservative case is self-evident. In 1960 when getting a divorce meant proving there was a need for one, 16% of marriages failed. The rate is now 40%.

Ah yes, writes Katha Pollitt, voicing the liberal and feminist viewpoint. But many other things have changed—urbanization, increased domestic violence, the economic independence of women. These played a big part. And tougher laws will penalize poorer women, who will be forced to stay longer in physically abusive marriages. As for children, surely they are better off with one parent than with two in a miserable marriage. People do not divorce frivolously; it occurs almost always after prolonged and agonizing struggle. Finally, she concludes, there is no direct evidence that tougher laws will save a marriage.

In response, David Blenkenhorn of the American Institute for Family Values states the obvious: what the law requires certainly affects what people do. To contend that tougher laws will not reduce the number of divorces is simply absurd. As for physical abuse, that itself could become the kind of fault that would justify divorce. In any case, abuse frequently continues even after a divorce, as in the O.J. Simpson affair. As for children, the evidence mounts that they're better off and far more secure with two squabbling parents than with one parent alone. The children themselves often say this.

(I know this to be true. My father was an alcoholic and my parents fought physically and verbally, and we were thrown out of one house after another because he would usually drink the rent. But when they finally broke up, in the first of four separations, I was about 10. It was as though everything I depended on was suddenly coming to an end. Their marriage, however tumultuous, was the only world I knew. Don't worry, said my mother. It will be far better this way. It wasn't.)

In the *Esquire* article, we're given a very different portrayal of divorce. John Taylor tells the story of the downfall of his own marriage with the skill of the master novelist—the idyllic wedding, the beginning of life together, the arrival of a daughter, his wife's sense of abandonment as his work consumed more of his time, his "face mask" as a happy husband, his affair with another woman, how he rationalized it, his wife's increasing disconsolance, their two separate lives under one roof, fruitless counselling, their conclusion that they should end the marriage, the agony of telling their daughter, her alarm and dismay, his life as a single man, his loneliness, his gradual acceptance of it, and his final conclusion that divorce is a good thing. His wife writes an accompanying article that reaches the reverse conclusion. The daughter doesn't write an article. She doesn't need to. Just think how fortunate you are, he tells her, when she complains of the one day a week she spends with her divorced father. You have two houses; other children have only one. "I don't *want* two houses, " she replies in a jagged voice. "I want one house." That says it all.

Mr. Taylor leaves an unmistakable impression I don't believe he intended. In every element of both the marriage and divorce, one consideration always becomes pivotal, namely what he himself wants. Not the wife, not the daughter. He is a product of the "me generation" and it isn't very good at marriage.

Something else emerges in the debate, always from the liberal side. Ms. Pollitt denounces the "male supremacist Christians" of the Promise-Keepers movement, the "religious fanatics, abusers, controllers, revenge seekers and people out of touch with reality" that she sees behind the tougher divorce movement. Even Mr. Taylor can't resist a swipe at "the absolutists blindly adhering to their codes of duty." Who, he demands, "has the right to moralize about these choices, to add the weight of public censure to the private anguish they always entail?" Yet the whole purpose of his article is plainly to defend himself against exactly this censure.

Given such vehemence, it would be easy to conclude that the cause of divorce is the rejection of God. But I've seen too much evidence to the contrary. Divorce has afflicted some of the most saintly people I've ever known.

Thinking about the Content

1. In your own words, express Byfield's thesis.

2. Byfield says divorce causes bad effects for women, children, and society. List the effects he notes to support this contention.

3. What audience is Byfield writing for? How does this influence the content he creates for the essay?

4. Byfield cites many statistics to bolster his contention, but he also recounts two long stories—mini case histories, really. How does including these stories add or detract from Byfield's argument?

5. The last two paragraphs of Byfield's essay introduce the view of divorce held by the Christain right. Comment on the effect this information has on the unity of the essay.

Thinking about the Organization

6. Which technique for capturing the interest of the reader does Byfield use in his first paragraph?

7. Think about the characteristics of an effective clincher. How effective is Byfield's conclusion to the essay?

Ideas for Your Writing

Byfield wrote a process essay about how to reduce the incidence of divorce by urging the government to exert more control over our lives. Other thoughtful people encourage us to take better care of one another. They emphasize how *we* can improve our lives. Act in your own interest: research for *your* life. Survey the relevant literature to write a process essay about how to plan for a successful marriage or how to sustain a marriage.

16.11

Catherine Ford, national columnist with the *Calgary Herald*, describes death as the "last conversational taboo." People refer to death as "passing on," "resting in peace," and "meeting one's Maker." Perhaps you've felt not just sorrow at a death but awkwardness in talking with the surviving family and friends. Ford tells us how we should respond to one another when someone among us dies.

Dealing with the Inevitable

Catherine Ford

For a few years when I was in my early 20s, we were as close as two peas in a pod. So close, we considered marriage.

Why it didn't work out is irrelevant. Suffice it to say after all these years, I choose only to remember the joyful moments. I choose only to remember the man who could be spontaneous, charming and fun; who once, when he discovered my favourite candy was black jelly beans, drove to the factory outside Toronto and bought a 20-pound box. All black.

One year on my birthday, he arrived at the office at noon hour with a complete lobster dinner, served on china, with a split of champagne.

When I jokingly asked for a year's supply of pantihose as a Christmas present—after frantically searching for spares in the dresser—he bought 52 pair, all the same shade and all the right size.

Like every other person who touches a life, he is as much a part of my experience and understanding of others as anyone else. He died at Christmas. I only found out this past week.

Do I grieve? Within myself, only for the man I once knew, not the person he became. But without, for his children and grandchildren, and for the hope they might remember him as a man who laughed easily and well.

That a person would die is inevitable, that any of us would ignore his or her existence is inexcusable. Every death diminishes us all, just as every life replenishes our community. And every death is a community responsibility.

Amazingly, death is the last conversational taboo. Even the word is used with caution. I was told my friend had "passed on," as if the very word "die" is cursed. "Cancer" was only whispered.

I thought this week of all the people in my life who have died—husband, father, grandparents, aunts and uncles, friends and colleagues—and their lives and deaths are as vivid today as they ever were. Exactly 24 years ago Sunday my father died. Not a week goes by that I don't think of him, but on the anniversary of his death, the memories will be especially sharp.

If there is a lesson from such sorrow, it is one that all of us will face and too many will ignore: that death is a community experience, to be shared, and that death brings with it a responsibility of affirmation for the life that was lived.

Yet generations raised isolated from war, with the sterility of hospitals, and the impersonality of funeral homes, finds itself now facing death without having learned what to do. As the baby boomers age, they inevitably lose parents, spouses and siblings. They lose friends and loved ones to disease and accidents and old age.

Years ago, when we were born and died at home, children were not shielded from such inevitabilities. They learned how to handle life's passages.

As adults, they are ill-equipped to handle death and its rituals. Even the ordinary small rituals. What do I do? What do I say?

If there is a worst reaction, it is to do or say nothing.

Few people ever hasten to explain that they don't go to weddings because they just don't believe in them; yet it is common to hear adults say they never go to funerals, as if the purpose of the gathering was their personal comfort.

Yet the same emotion that makes us celebrate with friends and relatives at their marriage, must move us to grieve with them when the inevitable happens.

It is a responsibility too many of us ignore, push away or repudiate. And when we do so, we unwillingly and unwittingly hurt our friends, sometimes our families, and inevitably, we hurt ourselves.

Years ago, walking down the long aisle of the cathedral behind my husband's coffin, flanked by his daughters, I remember looking up at the congregation and being silently comforted by the faces I saw. The cards and letters bolstered us all. Now, all these long years later, I do not remember what people said—only that they said something. And, inevitably, I remember the hurt when friends said nothing, as if this wonderful person had never lived, never been a part of my life.

Don't know what to say? Say anything. Any words at all. Even a simple "sorry" suffices. Because you don't remember the words, you only remember the validation of a life lived.

Thinking about the Content

1. What is Ford's thesis in "Dealing with the Inevitable"?

2. When Ford recalls the funeral for her husband, what technique is she using to support her thesis? (See the discussion in section 2.5 about creating specific support.)

3. When people do not mention in conversation someone who has recently died, they do so because they do not want to cause pain for the survivor. What observation about her father does Ford make that suggests we should not be inhibited in sharing our memories of a friend or relative who has died?

4. Ford puts a twist on a cliché when she says not that she and a friend were as similar as two peas in a pod but that the couple was as "close as two peas in a pod." Is this change sufficient to revivify the cliché? Express the couple's intimacy in another novel way.

5. Ford suggests that adults today are less equipped to deal with "death and its rituals." Why was this easier for adults in the past?

Thinking about the Organization

6. What technique does Ford use to grab our interest in the lead-in to her essay?

7. Which technique for creating cohesion within paragraphs does Ford use in the paragraph beginning "It is a reponsibility . . . ."?

8. Why doesn't Ford write a clincher that is more upbeat, perhaps even humorous?

Ideas for Your Writing

In "Dealing with the Inevitable" Catherine Ford writes a persuasive process essay. She tells us how to respond more responsibly and more helpfully when someone among us dies. Reflect on death and dying. Think about an experience with death when you or people around you were not as helpful as you would have liked. Jot ideas, outline your thesis, main points, and support, and write an essay about your ideas. Experiment with telling stories to support your recommendations.

16.12

Margaret Atwood wrote her first book of poems at age five and found the experience so completely satisfactory that she was not moved to write another until eleven years later. In her final year as an undergraduate, Atwood self-published a book of poems, disassembling the print after each poem because there were not enough *a*'s. Best-sellers *The Edible Woman*, *The Handmaid's Tale*, and *Alias Grace* and film adaptations of some of her novels have made her Canada's best known author. In this narrative essay, Atwood considers the origins of creativity.

Why I Write Poetry

Margaret Atwood

I recently read an account of a study which intends to show how writers of a certain age—my age, roughly—attempt to "seize control" of the stories of their own lives by deviously concocting their own biographies. However, it's a feature of our times that if you write a work of fiction, everyone assumes that the people and events in it are disguised biography—but if you write your biography, it's assumed you're lying your head off.

The latter may be true, at any rate of poets: Plato said that poets should be excluded from the ideal republic because they are such liars. I am a poet, and I affirm that this is true. About no subject are poets tempted to lie so much as about their own lives; I know one of them who has floated at least five versions of his autobiography, none of them real. I, of course, am a much more truthful person than that. But since poets lie, how can you believe me?

Here, then, is the official version:

I was once a snub-nosed blonde. My name was Betty. I had a perky personality and was a cheerleader for the college football team. My favourite colour was pink. Then I became a poet. My hair darkened overnight, my nose lengthened, I gave up football for the cello, my real name disappeared and was replaced by one that had a chance of being taken seriously, and my clothes changed colour in the closet, all by themselves, from pink to black. I stopped humming the songs from *Oklahoma!* and began quoting Kierkegaard. And not only that—all of my high-heeled shoes lost their heels, and were magically transformed into sandals. Needless to say, my many boyfriends took one look at this and ran screaming from the scene as if their toenails were on fire. New ones replaced them; they all had beards.

Believe it or not, there is an element of truth in this story. It's the bit about the name, which was not Betty but something equally non-poetic, and with the same number of letters. It's also the bit about the boyfriends. But meanwhile, here is the real truth: I became a poet at the age of 16. I did not intend to do it. It was not my fault.

Allow me to set the scene for you. The year was 1956. Elvis Presley had just appeared on the *Ed Sullivan Show*, from the waist up. At school dances, which were held in the gymnasium and smelled like armpits, the dance with the most charisma was rock'n'roll. The approved shoes were saddle shoes and white bucks, and the evening gowns were strapless, if you could manage it; they had crinolined skirts that made you look like half a cabbage with a little radish head. Girls were forbidden to wear jeans to school, except on football days, when they sat on the hill to watch and it was feared that the boys would be able to see up their dresses unless they wore pants. TV dinners had just been invented.

None of this—you might think, and rightly so—was conducive to the production of poetry. If someone had told me a year previously that I would suddenly turn into a poet, I would have giggled. (I had a passable giggle, then.) Yet this is what did happen.

I was in my fourth year of high school. The high school was in Toronto, which in the year 1956 was still known as Toronto the Good because of its puritanical liquor laws. It had a population of 650,509 people at the time, and was a synonym for bland propriety. The high school I attended was also a synonym for bland propriety, and although it has produced a steady stream of chartered accountants and one cabinet minister, no other poets have ever emerged from it before or since—or not that I know of.

The day I became a poet was a sunny day of no particular ominousness. I was walking across the football field, not because I was sports-minded or had plans to smoke a cigarette behind the field house—the only other reason for going there—but because this was my normal way home from school. I was scuttling along in my usual furtive way, suspecting no ill, when a large invisible thumb descended from the sky and pressed down on the top of my head. A poem formed. It was quite a gloomy poem: the poems of the young usually are. It was a gift, this poem—a gift from an anonymous donor, and, as such, both exciting and sinister at the same time.

I suspect this is why all poets begin writing poetry, only they don't want to admit it, so they make up explanations that are either more rational or more romantic. But this is the true explanation, and I defy anyone to disprove it.

The poem that I composed on that eventful day, although entirely without merit or even promise, did have some features. It rhymed and scanned, because we had been taught rhyming and scansion at school. It resembled the poetry of Lord Byron and Edgar Allan Poe, with a little Shelley and Keats thrown in. The fact is that at the time I became a poet, I had read very few poems written after the year 1900. I knew nothing of modernism or free verse. These were not the only things I knew nothing of. I had no idea, for instance, that I was about to step into a whole set of preconceptions and social roles that had to do with what poets were like, how they should behave, and what they ought to wear; moreover, I did not know that the rules about these things were different if you were female. I did not know that "poetess" was an insult, and that I myself would some day be called one. I did not know that to be told I had transcended my gender would be considered a compliment. I didn't know yet that black was compulsory. All of that was in the future. When I was 16, it was simple. Poetry existed; therefore it could be written; and nobody had told me—yet—the many, many reasons why it could not be written by me.

At first glance, there was little in my background to account for the descent of the large thumb of poetry onto the top of my head. But let me try to account for my own poetic genesis.

I was born on November 18, 1939, in the Ottawa General Hospital, two and a half months after the beginning of the Second World War. Being born at the beginning of the war gave me a substratum of anxiety and dread to draw on, which is very useful to a poet. It also meant that I was malnourished. This is why I am short. If it hadn't been for food rationing, I would have been six feet tall.

I saw my first balloon in 1946, one that had been saved from before the war. It was inflated for me as a treat when I had the mumps on my sixth birthday, and it broke immediately. This was a major influence on my later work.

As for my birth month, a detail of much interest to poets, obsessed as they are with symbolic systems of all kinds: I was not pleased, during my childhood, to have been born in November, as there wasn't much inspiration for birthday-party motifs. February children got hearts, May ones flowers, but what was there for me? A cake surrounded by withered leaves? November was a drab, dark and wet month, lacking even snow; its only noteworthy festival was Remembrance Day. But in adult life I discovered that November was, astrologically speaking, the month of sex, death and regeneration, and that November first was the Day of the Dead. It still wouldn't have been much good for birthday parties, but it was just fine for poetry, which tends to revolve a good deal around sex and death, with regeneration optional.

Six months after I was born, I was taken in a wooden box to a remote cabin in northwestern Quebec, where my father was doing research as a forest entomologist. I should add here that my parents were unusual for their time. Both of them liked being as far away from civilization as possible, my mother because she hated housework and tea parties, my father because he liked chopping wood. They also weren't much interested in what the sociologists would call rigid sex-role stereotyping. This was beneficial to me in later life, as it helped me to get a job at summer camp teaching small boys to start fires.

My childhood was divided between the forest, in the warmer parts of the year, and various cities, in the colder parts. I was thus able to develop the rudiments of the double personality so necessary for a poet. I also had lots of time for meditation. In the bush, there were no theatres, movies, parades, or very functional radios; there were also not many other people. The result was that I learned to read early—I was lucky enough to have a mother who read out loud, but she couldn't be doing it all the time, and you had to amuse yourself with something or other when it rained. I became a reading addict, and have remained so ever since. "You'll ruin your eyes," I was told when caught at my secret vice under the covers with a flashlight. I did so, and would do it again. Like cigarette addicts who will smoke mattress stuffing if all else fails, I will read anything. As a child I read a good many things I shouldn't have, but this also is useful for poetry.

As the critic Northrop Frye has said, we learn poetry through the seat of our pants, by being bounced up and down to nursery rhymes as children. Poetry is essentially oral, and is close to song; rhythm precedes meaning. My first experiences with poetry were Mother Goose, which contains some of the most surrealistic poems in the English language; and whatever singing commercials could be picked up on the radio, such as: You'll wonder where the yellow went/When you brush your teeth with Pepsodent!

Also surreal. What yellow? I wondered. Thus began my tooth fetish.

I created my first book of poetry at the age of five. To begin with, I made the book itself, cutting the pages out of scribbler paper and sewing them together in what I did not know was the traditional signature fashion. Then I copied into the book all the poems I could remember, and when there were some blank pages left at the end, I added a few of my own to complete it. This book was an entirely satisfying art object for me; so satisfying that I felt I had nothing more to say in that direction, and gave up writing poetry altogether for another 11 years.

My English teacher from 1955, run to ground by some documentary crew trying to explain my life, said that in her class I had showed no particular promise. This was true. Until the descent of the giant thumb, I showed no particular promise. I also showed no particular promise for some time afterwards, but I did not know this. A lot of being a poet consists of willed ignorance. If you woke up from your trance and realized the nature of the life-threatening and dignity-destroying precipice you were walking along, you would switch into actuarial sciences immediately.

If I had not been ignorant in this particular way, I would not have announced to an assortment of my high-school female friends, in the cafeteria one brown-bag lunchtime, that I was going to be a writer. I said "writer," not "poet"; I did have some common sense. But my announcement was certainly a conversation-stopper. Sticks of celery were suspended in mid-crunch, peanut-butter sandwiches paused halfway between table and mouth; nobody said a word. One of those present reminded me of this incident recently— I had repressed it—and said she had been simply astounded. "Why?" I said. "Because I wanted to be a writer?"

"No," she said. "Because you had the guts to say it out loud."

But I was not conscious of having guts, or even of needing them. We obsessed folks, in our youth, are oblivious to the effects of our obsessions; only later do we develop enough cunning to conceal them, or at least to avoid mentioning them at parties. The one good thing to be said about announcing yourself as a writer in the colonial Canadian fifties is that nobody told me I couldn't do it because I was a girl. They simply found the entire proposition ridiculous. Writers were dead and English, or else extremely elderly and American; they were not 16 years old and Canadian. It would have been worse if I'd been a boy, though. Never mind the fact that all the really stirring poems I'd read at that time had been about slaughter, battles, mayhem, sex and death—poetry was thought of as existing in the pastel, female realm, along with embroidery and flower arranging. If I'd been male I would probably have had to roll around in the mud, in some boring skirmish over whether or not I was a sissy.

I'll skip over the embarrassingly bad poems I published in the high school year book (had I no shame? Well, actually, no) mentioning only briefly the word of encouragement I received from my wonderful Grade 12 English teacher, Miss Bessie Billings: "I can't understand a word of this, dear, so it must be good." I will not go into the dismay of my parents, who worried—with good reason—over how I would support myself. I will pass over my flirtation with journalism as a way of making a living, an idea I dropped when I discovered that in the fifties, unlike now, female journalists always ended up writing the obituaries and the ladies' page, and nothing but.

But how was I to make a living? There was not then a roaring market in poetry. I thought of running away and being a waitress, which I later tried but got very tired and thin; there's nothing like clearing away other people's mushed-up dinners to make you lose your appetite. Finally, I went into English literature at university, having decided in a cynical manner that I could always teach to support my writing habit. Once I got past the Anglo-Saxon it was fun, although I did suffer a simulated cardiac arrest the first time I encountered T.S. Eliot and realized that not all poems rhymed any more. "I don't understand a word of this," I thought, "so it must be good."

After a year or two of keeping my head down and trying to pass myself off as a normal person, I made contact with the five other people at my university who were interested in writing; and through them, and some of my teachers, I discovered that there was a whole subterranean wonderland of Canadian writing that was going on just out of general earshot and sight. It was not large—in 1960, you were doing well to sell 200 copies of a book of poems by a Canadian, and a thousand novels was a bestseller; there were only five literary magazines, which ran on the lifeblood of their editors. But while the literary scene wasn't big, it was very integrated. Once in—that is, once published in a magazine—it was as if you'd been given a Masonic handshake or a key to the Underground Railroad. All of a sudden you were part of a conspiracy.

People sometimes ask me about my influences. These were, by and large, the Canadian poets of my own generation and the one just before mine. P.K. Page, Margaret Avison, Jay Macpherson, James Reaney, Irving Layton, Leonard Cohen, Al Purdy, D.G. Jones, Eli Mandel, John Newlove, Gwendolyn MacEwen, Michael Ondaatje, Pat Lane, George Bowering, Milton Acorn, A.M. Klein, Alden Nowlan, Elizabeth Brewster, Anne

Wilkinson—these are some of the poets who were writing and publishing then, whom I encountered, and/or whose poetry I read. People writing about Canadian poetry at that time spoke a lot about the necessity of creating a Canadian literature. There was a good deal of excitement, and the feeling that you were in on the ground floor, so to speak.

So poetry was a vital form, and it quickly acquired a public dimension. Above ground, the bourgeoisie reigned supreme, in their two-piece suits and ties and camel-hair coats and pearl earrings (not all of this worn by the same sex). But at night, the Bohemian world came alive, in various nooks and crannies of Toronto, sporting black turtlenecks, drinking coffee at little tables with red-checked tablecloths and candles stuck in chianti bottles, in coffee houses—well, in the one coffee house in town—listening to jazz and folk singing, reading their poems out loud as if they'd never heard it was stupid, and putting swear words into them. For a twenty-year-old, this was intoxicating stuff.

By this time, I had my black wardrobe more or less together, and had learned not to say, "Well, hi there!" in sprightly tones. I was publishing in little magazines, and shortly thereafter I started to write reviews for them too. I didn't know what I was talking about, but I soon began to find out. Every year for four years, I put together a collection of my poems and submitted it to a publishing house; every year it was—to my dismay then, to my relief now—rejected. Why was I so eager to be published right away? Like all 21-year-old poets, I thought I would be dead by 30, and Sylvia Plath had not set a helpful example. For a while there, you were made to feel that, if a poet and female, you could not really be serious about it unless you'd made at least one suicide attempt. So I felt I was running out of time.

My poems were still not very good, but by now they showed—how shall I put it?—a sort of twisted and febrile glimmer. In my graduating year, a group of them won the main poetry prize at the university. Madness took hold of me, and with the aid of a friend, and another friend's flatbed press, we printed them. A lot of poets published their own work then; unlike novels, poetry was short, and therefore cheap to do. We had to print each poem separately, and then disassemble the type, as there were not enough a's for the whole book; the cover was done with a lino-block. We printed 250 copies, and sold them through bookstores for 50 cents each. They now go in the rare-book trade for $1,800 a pop. Wish I'd kept some.

Three years or so later—after two years at graduate school at the dreaded Harvard University, a year of living in a tiny rooming-house room and working at a market-research company, and the massive rejection of my first novel, as well as several other poetry collections—I ended up in British Columbia, teaching grammar to Engineering students at eight-thirty in the morning in a Quonset hut. It was all right, as none of us were awake. I made them write imitations of Kafka, which I thought might help them in their chosen profession.

In comparison with the few years I had just gone through, this was sort of like going to heaven. I lived in an apartment built on top of somebody's house, and had scant furniture; but not only did I have a 180-degree view of Vancouver harbour, I also had all night to write. I taught in the daytime, ate canned food, did not wash my dishes until all of them were dirty—the biologist in me became very interested in the different varieties of moulds that could be grown on leftover Kraft dinner—and stayed up until four in the morning. I completed, in that one year, my first officially published book of poems and my first published novel, which I wrote on blank exam-booklets, as well as a number of short stories and the beginnings of two other novels, later completed. It was an astonishingly productive year for me. I looked like The Night of the Living Dead. Art has its price.

This first book of poems was called *The Circle Game*. I designed the cover myself, using stick-on dots—we were very cost-effective in those days—and to everyone's surprise, especially mine, it won The Governor General's Award, which in Canada then was the big one to win. Literary prizes are a crapshoot, and I was lucky that year. I was back at Harvard by then, mopping up the uncompleted work for my doctorate—I never did finish it—and living with three roommates named Judy, Sue and Karen. To collect the prize, I had to attend a ceremony at Government House in Ottawa, which meant dress-ups—and it was obvious to all of us, as we went through the two items in my wardrobe, that I had nothing to wear. Sue lent me her dress and earrings, Judy her shoes, and while I was away they all incinerated my clunky, rubbersoled Hush Puppy shoes, having decided that these did not go with my new, poetic image.

This was an act of treachery, but they were right. I was now a recognized poet, and had a thing or two to live up to. It took me a while to get the hair right, but I have finally settled down with a sort of modified Celtic look, which is about the only thing available to me short of baldness. I no longer feel I'll be dead by 30; now it's 60. I suppose these deadlines we set for ourselves are really a way of saying we appreciate time, and want to use all of it. I'm still writing, I'm still writing poetry, I still can't explain why, and I'm still running out of time.

Wordsworth was partly right when he said, "Poets in their youth begin in gladness/But thereof comes in the end despondency and madness." Except that sometimes poets skip the gladness and go straight to the despondency. Why is that? Part of it is the conditions under which poets work—giving all, receiving little in return from an age that by and large ignores them. Part of it is cultural expectation: "The lunatic, the lover and the poet," says Shakespeare, and notice which comes first. My own theory is that poetry is composed with the melancholy side of the brain, and that if you do nothing but, you may find yourself going slowly down a long dark tunnel with no exit. I have avoided this by being ambidextrous: I write novels too.

I go for long periods of time without writing any poems. I don't know why this is; as Margaret Laurence indicates in *The Diviners*, you don't know why you start, and you also don't know why you stop. But when I do find myself writing poetry again, it always has the surprise of that first unexpected and anonymous gift.

Thinking about the Content

1. As Atwood tries to explain how she became a poet, she writes about the influence of reading. Summarize her viewpoint.

2. Speculate about why Atwood wrote this essay.

3. Who is Atwood writing for? What makes you think so? Would most of her intended audience enjoy reading "Why I Write Poetry"?

4. How would you describe the tone Atwood sets in her essay? Quote a sentence to illustrate your opinion. Is her tone appropriate to her subject matter, given her intended audience?

5. It is sometimes said that genius is ten per cent inspiration and ninety per cent perspiration. After reading Atwood's description of how she became a poet, comment on the accuracy of the equation.

Thinking about the Organization

6. Atwood paraphrases Plato in her introduction. How effective is the reference in arousing a desire to read her essay?

7. Atwood's last sentence is a good clincher to her essay. Describe how Atwood uses the clincher to provide a particularly satisfying ending.

Ideas for Your Writing

Almost anyone who aspires to write would be hoping, while reading Atwood's auto-biographical process essay, to learn more about how to write better. Novices of all kinds want to develop the expertise of the elite performers. Think about a skill you have; perhaps you are a skilled volleyball player. Perhaps you are musical. Jot some notes as you reminisce about how you first got interested in that activity. Why did you pursue excellence? How did you acquire your skill? Who was important in your development? Drawing on your experiences, write a process essay that tells how you developed your talent.

16.13

T. Sher Singh practises law in Guelph, Ontario, and often writes about civil society. His writing always reveals his passionate desire to make Canada an ever-better country.

Let's Minimize Our Bigotry and Maximize Our Humanity

T. Sher Singh

We have a choice. We can identify the most bizarre and inhumane practices around the world and then lower our standards in Canada to match their level. Or, we can set high standards and show leadership to the world.

I recall, from my previous life in a faraway land, fundamentalists of various stripes: Hindu, Muslim, Sikh. Each one fervently believed that his or her religion was the only path to salvation, its spiritual leader the Chosen One, its adherents the Chosen People. Their mission: to make the rest of the world subscribe to their brand of truth, and nothing but.

The result, of course, is anarchy, careering toward disaster. That's why my family fled to Canada 25 years ago, almost to this day.

Here, we have the advantage of living in a relatively new society. We haven't had the full time to complicate our lives to the extent that older communities have. And we still have the opportunity to avoid the mistakes of others.

Nevertheless, we need to be vigilant. The seeds of poison are here and are sown every day. Pat Robertson, the TV evangelist, shamelessly insults Jews, Muslims and Hindus while hiding behind the mantle of love for his own faith. He preaches, for example, that Hinduism is "demonic."

Last week, a member of the Reform party reacted to the criticism of its policies in one of my columns by proclaiming in print that since I belong to Sikhism, which he then went on to describe as "a religion that condones terrorists, murderers," I should go back to the "land from whence (I) came."

The saddest example I have come across recently is from London, Ontario. A few weeks ago, 3,000 citizens gathered in Harris Park under the banner of "March of Jesus." While leading them in a public prayer, Rev. Miguel Sanchez of the London Gospel Temple prayed for the deliverance of people "from the darkness and deception of the spirit of Islam."

Darkness? Deception? Were these words uttered by one who professes to be a man of religion and the shepherd of his flock?

What gives him the impression that his love and respect for his own faith is greater or more relevant than the love and respect Muslims feel for theirs? What gives him the right to stand in public and insult the faith of others? Does he really believe it enhances his own faith?

London Mayor Dianne Haskett, who participated in the so-called prayer, turned into an instant apologist: "From what I know of him, I believed Rev. Sanchez and all other participants have a great love for all people." It begs the question: what does she mean by "love?"

I'm not a Muslim but I have studied Islam. And I believe I know Christianity as well as I do my own faith, Sikhism. I've yet to find even a single element in any of these, and other great religions, which would even remotely suggest that any one is lesser in any way than another.

Since the incident, the reverend and the mayor have apologized, albeit half-heartedly, but only after mounting public outrage by the good people of London.

But Rabbi Joel Wittstein of the Temple Israel of London captured the sadness and, in doing so, helped dispel it.

"I feel your pain," he promptly wrote to the Muslim community, "and offer you whatever understanding, sympathy and anger I possess. That someone could lack all insight into his cruel, stupid and hateful words defies belief." He closed his letter: "Shalom, Salam."

Amazing, isn't it? Basic human decency costs nothing. It demeans nobody. And it enhances everything and everybody it touches.

Thinking about the Content

1. What is Singh's thesis?
2. It's easier to write well about topics we know well. What made this topic such a good choice for Singh?
3. Briefly note the examples of religious intolerance Singh includes in his essay.

Thinking about the Organization

4. In strongly structured essays, writers state their theses early, in the introduction. Does Singh *ever* directly state his thesis? When can you infer it? Why does he take so long to reveal his point of view?
5. Does Singh recapitulate his thesis in the final paragraph? Does he conclude his essay with a clincher?

Ideas for Your Writing

We are cautioned to avoid discussing politics or religion at social gatherings because people care so passionately about these topics that discussion may lead to people arguing, yet they are such important concerns that we want to discuss them. The key to successful discussions is to always use the right tone with your audience: you must convey your respect for other people. Mull over how you feel when you hear someone has been harassed because of religious beliefs. Write an essay in which you suggest how members of our society, which is multicultural, ought to behave.

16.14

Reviews of books, films, CD's, and live performances of song, dance, and theatre are among the most popular essays published in magazines and newspapers. If you've ever sought out and read several reviews of the same product or event, you'll know the reviewers do not always agree. It's interesting to compare their critiques, just as it's fun to discuss a book or film with a friend. John Law epitomizes the breezy, cheeky style of reviewing that makes readers look forward to what their favourite reviewer will say about a new film release.

Hard Core Logo: A Punker's Paradise

John Law

Bruce McDonald's *Hard Core Logo* might be the rawest, loudest and most obnoxious rock and roll movie ever made. It's also, hands down, the best Canadian movie of the year. Canadian to the core, you might say.

McDonald's films—and all of them have been dandy—are, in their own way, as patriotic as the national anthem before a Leafs game. They aren't just Canadian-made, they're Canadian snapshots. More than any other director in recent years, Mcdonald revels in the eccentric northern experience, the good and the gritty. You watch his films, and get the impression Americans would have no idea what the hell's going on—now that's something to celebrate.

It's easy to tag *Hard Core Logo* as a *Spinal Tap* of the great white north, but that would be seriously shortchanging it. Rob Reiner's classic heavy metal spoof is here in spirit, and nothing more. McDonald's film is as unsettling as it is funny—a vivid punk rock circus with the warts front and centre. It's a fake documentary so close to the real thing, the line seems to disappear 10 minutes into it.

Green Day? Offspring? They couldn't swim in the spittle of McDonald's punksters. Hard Core Logo are a pack of Vancouver hardasses reuniting after an ugly split for a benefit concert in aid of their idol, Bucky Haight. It seems the legendary Haight was shot in the legs, and the Logo boys have put their differences aside to jam at a Rock Against Guns concert.

The show goes so well, lead singer Joe Dick (Hugh Dillon of the Headstones) talks his three bandmates into a Canadian reunion tour. Five cities, four thousand kilometres, in a decrepit van with a hole in the floor.

It doesn't take long for the band to get on each other's nerves. Dick is resentful of guitarist Billy Talent (Callum Keith Rennie) because he's playing with hot L.A. band Jennifur. Drummer Pipefitter (Bernie Coulson) has lost too many brain cells in the punk trenches, and thinks the reunion is leading to bigger, better things. Bassist John Oxenburger (John Pyper-Ferguson) is a former psychiatric patient who's lost his pills and is slowly going nuts again. The entire tour is a homicide waiting to happen.

Hard Core Logo is full of surprises, the best being a ferocious performance by Dillon as the band's foul-mouthed frontman. For a genuine punker, Dillon can cut it as an actor too. When he lets loose on stage or swigs beer while telling a reporter off, it's like McDonald just turned the camera on and sat back. Rock and roll can't get more authentic in the movies.

And then there's a hilarious visit to the home of Bucky Haight (Julian Richings), whose legs are supposed to be amputated, but seem in fine working order. The grim final scene may seem too dark after all those laughs, but how many punk bands meet happy endings? McDonald knows this and films it all like a freefall into the mosh pit—with the fun comes a lot of pain.

It'll be a cult film, no doubt, but *Hard Core Logo* is no mere midnight thrill. It's Canadian movie-making with one foot over the edge.

Thinking about the Content

1. What is Law's thesis?

2. What does Law particularly like about this film and other Bruce McDonald films?

3. Does Law provide enough detail so that newspaper readers can decide whether to see the film? Why or why not?

4. Law makes a claim about the films of Bruce McDonald. Does he assume too much knowledge on the part of the audience? What should he add to support his point more effectively?

5. Keeping in mind that Law is writing—for an audience of newspaper readers—about a film rated Adult Accompaniment, how do you feel about the tone of the review?

Thinking about the Organization

6. Law wrote this film review for a newspaper. Which elements usually present in the introductions of essays are also evident in this review?

7. Essay writers usually include in their conclusions a reminder of the thesis and a final thoughtful comment. Indicate the extent to which Law does this in his review.

Ideas for Your Writing

Arts reviewers write some of the best essays you'll read in newspapers. Recall a film you've watched. Use information-retrieval tools in the library or on the Internet to find a few reviews of that film. Read the reviews and then write your own.

16.15

Shortly after he became Grand Chief of the Assembly of First Nations, Phil Fontaine wrote about an issue that concerned him, why some Native youth are experiencing such pain and depression. Fontaine did what all good writers do: he wrote from the base of his own experiences in life.

I Know How Our Youngsters Feel

Phil Fontaine

I first left my home at Sagkeeng Ojibway First Nation Manitoba as a young boy in the 1950s. I had no choice. There were no public schools for Indians, and Federal Government policy forced our parents to give up their children to the care of church-operated residential schools. My parents were Roman Catholic, and I was placed in the residential school operated by the Catholic Church.

The school was located on my reserve, but I was segregated in an alien enclave. We were prevented from speaking our own language or practicing our customs. In order to attend high school, I had to live in a residential school in Winnipeg. Most of my contemporaries shared similar, or worse, experiences, including forced adoption into nonaboriginal families. Thus began a cycle of dislocation, cultural dispossession, family breakdown and abuse.

When I left the residential school, I bore emotional and psychological scars. I was confused and angry. I teetered on the edge of an abyss for years, restlessly roaming the country, seeking solace in alcohol, flouting authority, avoiding personal responsibility. On occasion, I thought about suicide. Looking back, I can see how close I came to taking the road followed by many of my peers and their children.

The enticements offered by gangs—companionship, a collective outlet for anger and material rewards from organized criminal activity—did not exist in my youth. I suppose I was fortunate. I still had a loving relationship with my supportive family.

Poverty and alienation have created youth gangs from all segments of urban society. But the root causes and the magnitude of the problems facing First Nations are unique.

What can be done? We need economically self-sufficient communities that provide dignity and self-esteem, opportunity and hope for young people, both on reserves and in urban centers. Communities and individuals also desperately need measures to restore their cultural, spiritual, emotional and physical health. These are the things that provide a sense of self, security, and motivation to believe in and strive for a better tomorrow.

Despite the challenges First Nations young people face in coping with the modern world, only a tiny minority have opted for the gang life, and a smaller number yet have slipped into criminal behavior. But even that need not be so.

Thinking about the Content

1. What is Fontaine's thesis?

2. What fact probably best supports Fontaine's thesis? What is the best proof of his contention?

3. This brief essay was published in the Canadian version of *Time*, a newsmagazine. Who do you think Fontaine was writing for? Who did he visualize reading his essay?

4. Why did Fontaine write this essay? What was his purpose?

5. Fontaine wrote, "Most of my contemporaries shared similar, or worse, experiences." You know that some children in these residential schools were physically and sexually abused. Why doesn't Fontaine include some of those disturbing stories?

Thinking about the Organization

6. Which sentence in the introductory paragraph of "I Know How Our Youngsters Feel" carries the shock value of a swift uppercut to the jaw? Why does it add such punch to the essay's lead-in?

7. In which paragraph does Fontaine state his thesis? Why is it so late in the essay?

8. What does Fontaine achieve in his clincher? How does it help him achieve his goal in writing the essay?

Ideas for Your Writing

Fontaine's essay develops ideas in several ways. He describes the process that needs to be followed to give Native children the chance to make themselves the best they can be. He narrates part of the story of his life. And in "I Know How Our Youngsters Feel," Fontaine also tries to persuade readers to support policies to empower Native Canadians. Develop one of these threads of his essay. Research and

- write a process essay outlining how the Canadian government should work with Native leaders to help Native people achieve their potential, or
- write a longer narrative describing the life of Phil Fontaine from Sagkeeng Ojibway First Nation to becoming Grand Chief of the Assembly of First Nations, or
- write a persuasive essay urging fairer treatment of First Nations people.

16.16

Ruth Lemke's "An Encounter with a Pirate" illustrates the continuing evolution of the essay form. Lemke muses on what is important in life, just as Montaigne did as he invented the essay in the late sixteenth century. Lemke, though, expresses some of her observations between the lines. She uses the indirect approach, perhaps aware that the point she makes may meet resistance from her readers. Lemke also borrows techniques more common to fiction, but increasingly common in essays today: she uses description and quotes dialogue to express her viewpoint.

An Encounter with a Pirate

Ruth Lemke

My daughter, on her day off, put her daughters, six and seven, and her son, three years of age, into her van and drove me to the community hospital.

I had to undergo 25 tests. As I sat watching the nurse extract eight vials of blood from my arm, I heard my daughter continuously scolding her three-year-old.

He wanted to come in and stop the lady from giving his "Nanna" a needle, he said.

When I emerged from the room, I looked for my grandson and saw him in tears in the hall with his mother holding him back.

He spotted me, and running to me cried, "Are you OK?" "Did it hurt?"

I took him by the hand. "Come on. Let's have some lunch, my treat."

We drove to Zellers. Chasing three young forms, we made for the restaurant.

By this time, Sal, my grandson was very tired. We sat down, Sal beside me, and he placed his head on his arm on the table. Three orange juices arrived and the inevitable happened: Sal lifted his head, moved his arm and the table top entertained his juice. Again he was scolded and again, he was crying. I tried to soothe him.

Suddenly, the noisy tears disappeared. He had just spotted his hero.

Sal has watched and loves Treasure Island. Halloween found him going door-to-door in his pirate costume. He carries a black patch with him that will no longer stay in place because of overuse.

Across from us, a little disheveled but majestic, head in hand, sat a bearded gentleman with a black patch over his left eye. His black hair rested on his hunched shoulders as he nursed a cup of coffee.

Pointing to the gentleman, Sal proudly proclaimed, "There he is."

Covering his hand with mine—reminding him not to point—my eyes followed his gaze. Sure enough, it appeared that right there, from Treasure Island, sat Sal's pirate.

"There is my pirate."

His sisters, of course, took up the conversation, and none too quietly, I am embarrassed to say.

They told Sal he was wrong and that it was just a man who had probably lost an eye.

My daughter ushered the girls out; Sal waited for me to stand and then placed his left hand in my right hand. Of course we had to walk past the gentleman.

What happened next brought tears to my eyes. Sal gingerly touched the arm of the gentleman; he had to see if he was real.

Immediately, as grandmothers do, I looked down to apologize for Sal. The gentleman lifted his head; eyes to eyes the two met. A slight grin emerged from the worn face.

"Yes son, I am a pirate!"

Sal's black eyes sparkled, like the stars in a black night. "Told you so, Nan," he said.

"Told you so!" This wee boy met his dream, that day——he was right, his sisters were wrong. The pirate, his pirate, said so!

I wonder if the gentleman received from Sal the same comfort and joy he had deposited on the three-year-old boy who had been having such a rough day?

They had shared a moment in time.

Thinking about the Content

1. What is Lemke's thesis in "An Encounter with a Pirate"?

2. What technique does Lemke use to support her viewpoint? (See section 2.5.)

3. Comment on the effectiveness of Lemke's decision to use the first person in this narrative essay.

4. Lemke's writing is succinct, yet she enables readers to follow the story with mental pictures almost as clearly as if we were watching a film version of events. How does Lemke make this account come alive?

5. Lemke occasionally uses words in novel ways. Find an instance where she uses a verb in an unexpected way and an adjective that surprises readers.

6. In the second-last paragraph, Lemke uses the word *deposited*. Suggest another word choice that might better suit the tone of the essay.

Thinking about the Organization

7. What technique does Lemke use in her lead-in?

8. Writers often write a clincher to complete an essay. What is Lemke trying to achieve in her last sentence?

Ideas for Your Writing

"It Takes a Whole Village to Raise a Child" (see section 6.1) is another example of an author's using narration to make a point. In that essay, though, the writer clearly states the thesis. By contrast, Lemke never directly states her thesis. She leaves it to each reader to infer. Lemke probably reasons that advice, though often offered, is seldom taken. Perhaps you've an insight to share about human relations. It might be an observation about how less-critical supervisors actually draw better performances from employees. It might be about teacher behaviours that really lead students to excel. Express your viewpoint in an essay, but try to do it *implicitly*, as Lemke did.

16.17

Satire is "the use of ridicule, irony, sarcasm," and so forth "to expose folly or vice" ("Satire"). Naomi Klein, who recently wrote a serious book suggesting strategies ordinary citizens could use to influence the behaviour of multinational corporations, sometimes satirizes the targets of her social criticism. Here she uses humour to lament the commercialization of Canada Day.

You, Me, Canada—We All Can Have Sponsors

Naomi Klein

There was something a little tense about our national holiday last weekend. The clearly irreconcilable debate between Canada Day and Dominion Day is getting so heated that, frankly, I'm afraid it will tear the country apart.

Before anybody takes up arms, allow me to put forward this modest proposal for next year. How about if we call it a draw and rename our national holiday Sponsorship Day?

Hear me out. July 1 is supposed to be a celebration of what makes this country great.

A quick glance around makes it clear that, as the government recedes from such silly frills as culture and national holidays, we would be nothing without our sponsors.

By way of example, let's look at the activities of the so-called "Canada Day" weekend.

Perhaps you started by checking out some jazz at the du Maurier Downtown Jazz festival—from the comfort of a patio dressed up as a giant red cigarette pack. Restaurants and bars across the city draped themselves in their sponsor's color and logo in a show of brand loyalty more moving than any half-hearted miniature-flag-waving exercise.

But the du Maurier-sponsored jazz festival couldn't have happened without its own sponsor, Molson Dry. "This could be good," said its slogan—displayed more prominently than the name of any musician—and it was.

Of course, there was that nasty incident in which two guys were thrown out of a concert at Nathan Phillips Square for distributing those ungrateful "du Murderer" pamphlets.

It seems the protesters thought they were on public property, but, as the police informed them, du Maurier controls City Hall now.

When the temperature got too hot, maybe you caught an advertisement down at the waterfront. Perhaps you rode in a bus that was cleverly masquerading as a giant Mr. Big chocolate bar or maybe you hopped in a rickshaw, kindly volunteering your back as a Molson billboard.

Coincidentally, once you got to the water, you headed over to Molson Place to hear Spirit Of The West —part of the Heineken Summer Music series.

Loving Harbourfront (it's our cultural centre, after all), you came back on Saturday, only to be dazzled by the Benson & Hedges symphony of sponsorship. As you watched the sky light up, you thought: "Wow! These sure are better than the lousy firecrackers they set off at Canada Day last year."

And on Sunday, didn't I see you at the Gay Pride Day parade? What a turnout! But when you watched TV that night, you found that the big news wasn't that 700,000 people showed up (more than ever) or that the event was marshalled by the first Ontario lesbians who won the right to adopt their partners' children.

It was that Labatt had gone in as a sponsor. That's so progressive of them. What a victory for gay rights.

On Monday, the big party itself, you were a bit shocked to find out that there were no fireworks downtown—perhaps Benson & Hedges now has exclusive rights to fire.

Oh, well. With six nights of cigarette-sponsored magic, it seems petty to demand a special show just because it's our national holiday.

Not letting it get you down—"Different is good," as the fast-food slogan says—you capped off the weekend's festivities at Harbourfront's "Coca-Cola Music Workshop," featuring some people whose names were printed too small to read.

Canada Day weekend may be over, but do not fret. The joys of sponsorship extend throughout this very sponsorship summer.

All over the city, ads no longer flog anything as prosaic as their product, they advertise their sponsorship: Players car racing, the Molson Indy, Craven A country music.

Molson has even begun to transcend the very idea that there needs to be something external to sponsor.

The beer company, proud sponsor of yesterday's Lollapalooza at Molson Park, is clearly tired of being upstaged by the big-name rock bands it so generously promotes.

This year, Molson is putting on the Blind Date series in which the name of the band is kept "secret" until it gets on stage. It's a Molson event, straight-up.

All of this in the middle of the sponsorship mania leading up to the Olympics. Athletes are sponsored to compete for medals and the stakes are high indeed: If they win, it will lead to many more sponsorships.

But what's really great about this summer is that anyone can have a sponsor. You don't have to be a race-car driver to get free "Pepsi Stuff." And you don't have to be a jazz musician to get freebies from a cigarette company.

In the Benson & Hedges "Stellar Award" (which has 33 sponsors of its own), all you have to do is fill in a form explaining why your friend is "the most unique person you know" and you could "win cool stuff" like hats and T-shirts. If you win, your head and chest could have their very own sponsors.

Last week's Stellar winner was one Beata Kasper. According to the huge ads announcing her momentous victory, she is "as sweet as life would be without taxes." And who needs to pay taxes when our sponsors are just giving stuff away?

We do need to thank our new leaders somehow, though, and what better way than naming a holiday after them?

Some people aren't willing to wait. You could see the spirit of Sponsorship Day catching on Canada Day when hundreds of people turned out with maple leaves painted on their faces—just like the guy in the Molson "I Am. Canadian" ads.

I was moved. It was a sublime moment of convergence between brand and nation, product and patriotism.

For my part, I'm having "We Want Sponsorship Day" T-shirts printed. They're covered in logos and say "Canada: Yours To Sponsor" on the back.

And let me tell you, I'm not having any trouble covering costs.

Thinking about the Content

1. Express Klein's thesis in your own words.

2. Search through the details in Klein's article and identify two main points that she makes to support her thesis.

3. Which detail most convincingly supports Klein's point that the celebration of Canada Day is being overshadowed by corporate self-promotion?

4. Cite the best example Klein notes to support her main point that some of the self-promotional activities of corporations trivialize the idea of Canadian identity.

Thinking about the Organization

5. Review the text section about creating effective lead-ins (section 5.3). What method has Klein used to motivate you to read this essay, a newspaper column?

6. The introduction culminates with Klein suggesting that the government now has such a small role in Canada Day celebrations that the holiday would be nothing

without the sponsors. After the introduction, Klein's column has two distinct parts. Briefly summarize the sections.

7   Klein's clincher is that she is promoting T-shirts supporting the idea that Canada Day should be renamed Sponsorship Day. Do you think that she really printed such shirts? Why does she say she did?

Ideas for Your Writing

"You, Me, Canada—We All Can Have Sponsors" is a persuasive essay, and it is also a narrative essay telling the story of how Klein spent a Canada Day weekend. Briefly sketch a thesis and main points for these other ways of developing ideas in essays about Canada Day:

- a cause/effect essay about the reasons Canadians should celebrate on Canada Day,
- a classification essay showing the types of activites that celebrate Canada Day in your community, and
- a comparison essay contrasting commercial and public events related to Canada Day.

16.18

Who will guard the guardians? is the way the Romans phrased a question that is still debated today: Who will police the police? How can we permit police officers enough latitude to be successful in fighting crime, yet hold officers accountable for their behaviour? Should we permit high-speed chases, for example, or urge officers not to risk the lives of pedestrians and other drivers? As General Counsel for the Canadian Civil Liberties Association, Alan Borovoy often tries to answer these perennial questions.

The Case for Excluding Tainted Evidence

A. Alan Borovoy

The Supreme Court of Canada is confronting a dilemma. In a New Brunswick case involving a 17-year-old boy convicted of murdering a 14-year-old girl, the court is reconsidering how far unconstitutionally obtained evidence may be used in criminal trials.

In this case, the New Brunswick courts allowed the prosecutors to use DNA evidence that the police obtained by exerting coercive pressures upon the boy while they had him in custody. (The trial occurred before the law was amended to provide for judicial warrants to get DNA samples.)

Since the boy and his lawyer had explicitly refused to give the police DNA samples, there likely will be a ruling that the police violated his constitutional rights. According to the Charter of Rights and Freedoms, unconstitutionally obtained evidence must be excluded if its use "would bring the administration of justice into disrepute."

Under what circumstances, then, will the use of improperly obtained evidence damage the justice system? I address here, not the specific results in this case, but the general principles.

On the one hand, some will argue that, when a terrible crime occurs, it's worse, at least in the short term, to exclude than to admit evidence of this kind. Many Canadians will want to ensure that the trial courts hear as much relevant and reliable evidence as possible. Faced with a crime like murder, there will be a powerful temptation to ignore the niceties of how the evidence was gathered. Indeed, many Canadians would be offended by a court ruling that deliberately risked the acquittal of an apparently guilty person.

On the other hand, I believe it's unacceptable for the law enforcement authorities to break the law with apparent impunity. It's one thing if the police violation were merely a technical oversight. But the public should not see serious police transgressions unaccompanied by sanctions. Such an outcome would promote long-term public cynicism about the administration of justice.

If the police are seen as "getting away" with serious misconduct, labor picketers, anti-abortion protesters and aboriginal demonstrators are more likely to insist that they, too, should be treated with comparable solicitude. The upshot would be increasingly diminished public respect for the rule of law. In order to forestall such a development, the courts should do the most practical thing they can do in such situations: exclude the tainted evidence.

It should not be assumed that significantly more guilty people are likely to go free. In the United States, where virtually all improperly obtained evidence is inadmissible, there is usually enough proof to convict the accused without the tainted evidence.

The most serious police misconduct occurs when accused persons are in custody, deprived of normal support. As a result of such special vulnerability, custodial infringements of the Charter should create a strong presumption against using evidence obtained in this manner. Moreover, the greater the indignity to the accused, the stronger the presumption should be.

We should also consider what possible factor might legitimately influence a court to admit contested evidence. The central factor concerns the efforts made by law enforcement authorities to ensure the police observe their legal obligations.

Have those in authority made conscientious efforts to train, instruct and supervise the police? Have the authorities demonstrated a willingness to impose serious discipline on offending officers including those in the case at issue? Such measures would help considerably to offset any public perception of double standards.

If the courts use their power to exclude tainted evidence in this way, they will wind up strengthening public respect for the administration of justice in our society.

Thinking about the Content

1. What is Borovoy's thesis in "The Case for Excluding Tainted Evidence"?

2. Name three bad effects that Borovoy says would occur if courts considered evidence that was illegally obtained.

3. Summarize in one sentence the main idea Borovoy expresses in paragraph 9.

4. At the inquiry into the wrongful conviction of Guy Paul Morin for the murder of Christine Jessop, Jessop's mother and brother testified that the police had pressured them into changing their testimony about the time they had arrived at home. Morin was jailed for a crime he did not commit. If Borovoy had included a case example like this, a case that showed how police misbehaviour resulted in a miscarriage of justice, what would have been the effect on the essay? Why didn't he include case history examples?

Thinking about the Organization

5. What is the technique Borovoy uses to grab your attention in his lead-in to this essay?

6. Writers often use repetition to ensure that readers see the connections among the ideas in an essay. Borovoy knows that most members of the public hate the idea of a person going unpunished when there is evidence of guilt, even if the police gathered the evidence illegally. He wants readers to accept that their lives would be worse if we let the police break laws to gather evidence. Show three places where he uses repetition to make it more likely that readers will accept his contention that our society would be worse off if the police behaved illegally and more people began to think that justice is administered unfairly.

Ideas for Your Writing

Research the prosecution of Donald Marshall, Guy Paul Morin, or David Milgaard. Write a process essay that describes how the investigation would have proceeded if all the police and witnesses had behaved ethically.

16.19

Michael Valpy has spent many years closely watching Canadian society and writing thoughtful observations. Here he considers the evidence that as governments withdraw from funding the arts and social services private enterprise will increase its support.

The Corporate Philanthropists

Michael Valpy

Not long ago, Matthew Barrett, chief executive officer of the Bank of Montreal, wrote an article for *Policy Options* magazine titled "Good Citizenship Is Good Business." You will want to know why Mr. Barrett, on the subject of corporate responsibility, speaks largely hot air.

Mr. Barrett wrote about new winds of social activism blowing through the corporate world, "a deeper, broader sense of philanthropy.

"Today, throughout North America, more and more corporations are tying corporate giving to corporate strategy, seeking out ways to align their own self-interest with the public good.

"The public today expects business to be concerned with its concerns . . . . Companies are responding to expectations such as these . . . . The need to serve the interests of [its] four constituencies—shareholders, customers, employees, and the community—has led the corporation to assume many new obligations." And so on.

Another banker whose words read well, Allan Taylor, former chairman of the Royal Bank of Canada, once said in a speech: "Given the pressures on governments to limit spending growth, the degree to which businesses are able and willing to respond to social issues will increasingly influence the type of society we live in."

Yes, indeed. Here is a report called Profile of a Changing World, a survey of community-service agencies in 1996 in Canada's largest urban area, carried out jointly by the municipal governments of Metropolitan Toronto and the City of Toronto and by the Social Planning Council of Metropolitan Toronto.

More than half the 382 agencies included in the survey experienced funding cuts in 1996. Government funding fell by $11-million ($10-million from the Ontario government alone) and private funding fell by $8-million. Corporate donations alone were down by $1-million, in a year when Canada's banks made record profits and Big Business's economists described the Canadian economic performance in purple superlatives.

The $19-million total reduced the agencies' income by about 4 per cent. That was in a year when the agencies reported a 60-per-cent increase in demand for the programs they offer.

Thirty-three community agencies closed in 1996, in addition to 21 that closed in 1995. In total, 151 programs were cancelled in 1996, on top of 162 programs cancelled in 1995.

Over the two years, 40 per cent of agencies surveyed reported the loss of at least one program. Immigrant services have been the hardest hit—with, of course, no decrease in the number of immigrants and refugee claimants arriving in Toronto—followed by skills training, counselling and crisis services and educational upgrading.

Municipal grants and United Way allocations remained the only constant source of funding. The most significant source of new money was user fees, which provided $5-million more in 1996 than in 1995.

Governments, politicians and newspaper editorial-writers who talk about the social capital of volunteerism replacing tax-dollar support should read the next paragraph carefully:

Agencies reported that volunteers were harder to find, and keep, and were often unemployed because of inadequate co-ordination, training and supervision. (The staff members paid to co-ordinate volunteers are frequently the first to be laid off in the wake of budget reductions.) Only 69 per cent of the agencies' workers were volunteers in 1996, compared with 78 per cent in 1995.

Corporate donations provided just 1 per cent of agency funding in 1996 (the same as in 1995).

Mr. Barrett said his bank in 1995 gave $10-million of its $1-billion profit to charity. That's 1 per cent. It's not impressive. Many individual Canadians give a far greater share of their incomes. The corporate average is less than half of 1 per cent, and falling.

In general, Canada's 75,000 charitable organizations—apart from arts groups—receive only a sliver of their funds from corporations.

The Canadian Centre for Philanthropy reports that the expectation that corporate and individual charitable donations would increase with reductions in government funding has not been realized. The percentage of individual income-tax filers making claims for charitable donations has steadily declined since 1990 (with a slight increase between 1994 and 1995).

By not increasing their donations, corporations are virtually ensuring that community agencies do less. For every $1 donated by corporations to Toronto agencies, governments donate $60. In general, the ratio of government funding to overall non-government funding is about 2 to 1.

According to the survey, Toronto's agencies cannot replace their lost government funding unless they do one of the following: increase user fees by 20 per cent, increase their United Way grants by almost 100 per cent, increase their fund-raising revenues by 50 per cent, or increase their business revenues (the fees governments pay for contracted services) by 150 per cent.

Thinking about the Content

1. Quote the sentence in which Valpy states his thesis. Reword it in the active voice.

2. Valpy's column is largely a comparison/contrast essay. What does he contrast?

3. What kind of specific support does Valpy present to support his thesis?

4. Does Valpy make any recommendations? Why not?

5. Paragraphs 13 and 14 are about volunteerism. Does Valpy—by including this information—spoil the unity of his essay? Why or why not?

Thinking about the Organization

6. In the first paragraph, what strategy did Michael Valpy use to create a lead-in that would motivate you to read his *Globe and Mail* column?

7. Why does Valpy wait so long (paragraph 17) to announce his thesis? Is this article also a persuasive essay?

Ideas for Your Writing

Employers want employees who take charge of their own professional development, people who are lifelong learners, people who continue to grow on the job. Newspaper reading is one of the best ways to find out what you need to learn next. Students in human services programs might want to read the whole report that Valpy discusses. So might business administration students who want to develop fundraising skills and public relations students who want to plot ways to boost the image of corporate clients. Increasingly, such reports are published on Web sites, making it easy and inexpensive to download them for later reading. Conduct a Web search or a search of periodical databases to identify a report that you should read to become more expert in your area of study. After you read the report, use the information you learn to write an essay or to do other writing that helps you express the new ideas you've gained from your self-initiated study.

16.20

Sir Louis-Hippolyte Lafontaine and Robert Baldwin showed in the second coalition government (1847–51) that francophones and anglophones "could work together for the common good" (*Canada* 10). *La Presse* columnist Lysiane Gagnon explains why many prime ministers have come from Quebec.

Why Quebec Is Always Such a Force in Ottawa

Lysiane Gagnon

Last week's column ended with a question: Why has Quebec produced so many prime ministers?

The disproportionate influence of Quebec on the federal political scene is a phenomenon that has struck observers for many years before the Reform Party used it—in a particularly vicious way—in its television ads in the recent election campaign.

The first reason is quite simple: it has to do with numbers. With a population of nearly seven million, Quebec is the most populous province after Ontario; it is more than twice as big as the third-largest province, British Columbia, and accordingly it has more than twice as many seats as B.C. in the House of Commons.

Because of the size of its population, Quebec is a force to be reckoned with in federal politics. Thus any party aiming for national stature must deal with Quebec's agenda and address French people in their own language. In *realpolitik,* numbers weigh more than good feelings. Some minorities can be ignored because they're too tiny or don't have enough clout. Whether the rest of Canada likes it or not, French-Canadian voters, the vast majority of whom live in Quebec, cannot be ignored, because together they form a quarter of the national population.

It is not a coincidence that all the potential contenders for the post-Chrétien Liberal leadership (Paul Martin, Sheila Copps, Allan Rock, Frank McKenna) are bilingual. Nor is it a coincidence that all leaders of the New Democratic Party have tried to learn French. Nor is it a coincidence that the two men who might eventually replace Jean Chrétien as head of government (Paul Martin and Jean Charest) are bicultural Quebeckers.

They come from a long line of Quebeckers who have a foot in the two main cultural communities of Canada. These men, from Louis St. Laurent to Pierre Trudeau to Brian Mulroney, were the natural bridge builders that Canadian political parties needed.

Because of its rich, mixed demographic makeup, Quebec is the natural producer of bilingual, even bicultural, people. Both Mr. Charest and Mr. Trudeau were born in French–English families. Mr. Mulroney's parents were both of Irish origin, but the family lived in the French-speaking part of a small town. Mr. Martin is bilingual down to his name, which, depending on the pronunciation, can be either French or English.

Another reason for the influence that Quebec wields over Canadian politics is that because francophone Quebeckers have an acute sense of being a minority, they tend to vote as a block in federal elections. A diehard "red" in provincial politics might very well find himself voting for the "blues" in a federal election, depending on what he thinks is better for his community. This is standard minority behaviour.

Francophone Quebeckers are by far the largest homogeneous group in Canada that can massively change its vote from one election to the other. This has happened several times, especially since 1984. Quebec is the only province where voting patterns (at the federal level) do not reflect family traditions. (Even though there are many exceptions, it is a general rule that most people end up voting as their parents did. This is especially true in countries or communities where family cohesion is strong.)

But of course numbers are not everything. Tradition and culture are at the heart of the matter. If Quebec produced more than its share of first-rate politicians who ended up playing major roles in Canadian politics, it is because politics has always been a highly valued activity in Quebec, especially during the long period when French Canadians were more or less excluded from the business world. This led many, among them "the best and the brightest," toward politics—in part because the provincial government was something francophones—the majority of Quebeckers—could control.

With law, medicine and the priesthood, politics was a choice career for francophones. Furthermore, it was often seen as a calling, a vocation—the political leader being the lay equivalent of the priest, someone who would express his people's grievances and lead them toward more power and prosperity. The art of speaking in public and the interest in public affairs was cultivated early on in a school system catering to the (male) elite. In the old liberal arts colleges modelled on France's *lycées,* the finishing year was called *philosophie*, and the year before that was *rhetorique*.

This tradition was so strong that it can still be felt today, even though the conditions have completely changed and francophone Quebeckers can now (and increasingly do) opt for careers in private business or fields unrelated to the state. This is why the 21st century might bring a few more Quebec-born leaders to federal politics in Canada.

Thinking about the Content

1. What is Gagnon's thesis in "Why Quebec Is Always Such a Force in Ottawa"?

2. Briefly list the main points that Gagnon, a political columnist for *La Presse*, presents to support her thesis.

3. Cite a specific detail that supports Gagnon's main point that an important reason why so many prime ministers have come from Quebec is that growing up in Quebec increases the probability that one will be bilingual.

4. Which method of developing ideas does Gagnon use in her essay?

Thinking about the Organization

5. Writers can organize their supporting detail chronologically, emphatically, or logically; sometimes the order is not very important. How has Gagnon organized her main points?

6. Quote Gagnon's clincher.

Ideas for Your Writing

When governments make decisions, our lives change. This is why the political columns in newspapers and newsmagazines are so popular with readers. Visit the library and look through several newspapers. Find and read several political columns from different newspapers and from *Maclean's* and *Alberta/Western Reports*. Pick an issue and write your own essay or letter to the editor on a political topic. If you're particularly pleased with it, send it to a paper, along with a note about your being a student: newspapers are often interested in presenting the viewpoints of students.

16.21

Coaching Association of Canada (CAC) president John Bates and Canadian Professional Coaches' Association (CPCA) executive director Tom Kinsman released this position paper on how to discourage sexual abuse in amateur sport. It was published in *Coaches Report* and distributed to Canada's daily newspapers.

Stopping Sexual Abuse in Sport: What Canada's Coaching Leaders Are Doing

John Bales and Tom Kinsman

Even as Canadians try to digest the unsavory and disturbing revelations of sexual abuse sweeping the hockey world in recent weeks, the cry for action swells. While some demand an official inquiry and others say that screening of all coaches is a must, everyone agrees that "something must be done."

Unpalatable though the admission may be, the fact of the matter is that sexual abuse is a significant problem affecting all walks of life. However, the sporting world may be particularly vulnerable because it is an environment characterized by close relationships. That is why CAC [Coaching Association of Canada] and its professional arm, the CPCA [Canadian Professional Coaches' Association], have been working toward creating a system capable of dealing with and, wherever possible, heading off abuse of athletes.

The impetus can be traced back to the Dubin Inquiry and its investigation of Canadian sport on the heels of the revelations of drug use by sprinter Ben Johnson that led to him being stripped of Olympic gold at the 1988 Olympic Games. For many, that incident was Canada's loss of sporting innocence. Certainly the effect was immediate, enormous, nationwide, and enduring.

Out of that scandal came the public's realization of the enormous influence of the coach, influence that if used irresponsibly could cause great harm. We knew that action had to be taken, not only to weed out the "bad apples," but to support Canada's hundreds of thousands of coaches, who use their power appropriately, who understand that the trust they develop with their athletes is an essential element in developing well-rounded, successful human beings. Our challenge was twofold: to provide coaches with appropriate training and to ensure they work within an ethical framework.

At the core of coaching in Canada is a world-recognized education system, the NCCP [National Coaching Certification Program]. However, once school is out, it is essential to complement the training with a system of regulations, complete with standards of membership, a comprehensive ethical code signed by members, and a monitoring mechanism to ensure accountability.

With the formation of the CPCA in 1993, many of those elements were put in place. Coaches who choose to join the CPCA and become entitled to use its professional designation, ChPC [Chartered Professional Coach], must first meet strict educational standards, have a solid and sustained background of experience, sign the Coaching Code of Ethics, and understand that their membership is revocable.

Sadly, it takes more than education and professional standards to halt sexual abuse, which tends to occur secretly and furtively, and now the nation stands at another watershed, one that is at least as grave as the Johnson affair.

As Sheldon Kennedy has so bravely revealed, he endured sexual abuse by his coach, feeling there was nowhere he could go with his story, and his suffering continued for years. Other sexual abuses have occurred. Some have made the headlines. Several coaches have gone to jail. But seldom has a victim spoken out, and never one with such a high profile. His courage must be rewarded; the outcry generated by his experience must be met with action.

Questions and accusations aside, Kennedy's decision to speak out demands a response on the part of everyone who cares about children and sport in this country—parents, sports organizations, the athletes themselves, and, most certainly, coaches. For our part, we must now ensure that the commitment to ethical behaviour is understood, accepted, and adhered to by *all* Canadian coaches. Such an undertaking demands unprecedented cooperation at every level of society.

Traditionally, the majority of coaches in Canada are community, not career, coaches. They are volunteers, often parents, who coach a team for the love of a game or to make a community contribution. Without these people, sport at the local level simply is not possible. The value of their contribution to sport cannot be underestimated. And, because this role is so important, we urge training in the NCCP and a clear ethical framework for career and community coaches alike.

Enormous though the task is, it becomes possible when everyone involved accepts certain responsibilities.

Parents can take several steps. Talk to your children. Get to know your child's coach. Ask about his or her qualifications. Discuss training rules and standards of behavior. Attend practices and games to watch the coach in action. Pay attention to the interaction with the children. Listen to how the children talk about the coach. If selecting a coach, look for more than an enviable win/loss record; expertise is important, but it is not the only factor in what makes a good coach. If concerns arise, take action. Talk to the coach and, if necessary, the convenor, the league, or the sport's governing body.

Because sport involves a public trust, sport organizations, from the national to the provincial and local levels, can insist that each of their coaches be certified and a member of a coaching association with a code of ethics. All sport organizations should also utilize the CPCA as an objective third party, able to hear complaints fairly and without conflict of interest. While not providing a total solution, this is a big step in the right direction.

What about the role of the athlete? Streetproofing has become an accepted and common practice in our society. We suggest that it is a method that parents apply to their children's sport involvement so that youngsters learn to recognize when a coach's behavior is inappropriate and are taught what they can do to protect themselves and where they can safely go for help.

To ensure that sport takes place in a safe and welcoming environment, we believe that coaches, both career and community, must not only commit themselves to gaining certification, but must also take the additional step of membership in a coaching organization that demands adherence to ethical standards appropriate to working with young people. Only then will we have a chance of ridding sport of unacceptable behavior.

Thinking about the Content

1. What is the thesis of "Stopping Sexual Abuse in Sport"?

2. What are the main points Bales and Kinsman make to support this thesis?

3. Note a detail the authors provide to support their main point that children can act to reduce the incidence of sexual abuse.

4. Explaining processes or causes or effects, classifying, comparing, persuading, describing or narrating—which method of developing ideas does this essay exemplify?

5. Who do Bales and Kinsman see as their audience?

6. Part of the way Bales and Kinsman build support for their thesis is to use a case example. Whose story do they tell to influence readers to agree that sexual abuse in sport must cease?

Thinking about the Organization

7. "Enormous though the task is, it becomes possible when everyone involved accepts certain responsibilities," wrote Bales and Kinsman. Rewrite this sentence to announce more clearly the thesis of the essay and to preview the main points.

Ideas for Your Writing

Many Canadians are interested in sports. They like to watch their children play—and the professionals. Adults play Slo-pitch, listen to sports newscasts, and read about sports in the newspapers. For each of the methods of developing ideas in essays (indicated in the table of contents for chapters 6 and 7), create a topic. Select the sports topic you like best and write an essay about it.

16.22

Each year a smaller proportion of Canadians live in the Atlantic provinces. Low birth rates, migration out to look for work, and only a small influx of recent immigrants to Canada have all contributed to a declining representation in the House of Commons. Harry Bruce, in a persuasive essay, gives his reasons for why the Maritime provinces should unite.

Maritime Union: Politicians Must Rise Above Parochialism to Avoid Disaster

Harry Bruce

As the premier of Quebec during a first ministers' conference, you represent seven million people, but among those lined up against you are the premier of New Brunswick, with a population only one-tenth as big, and the premier of Prince Edward Island, whose people number no more than those of the little city of Sherbrooke.

Why should you take such pipsqueak provinces seriously? Why should they have any impact on the fate of Quebec?

Recognizing the absurdity of such face-offs, Prime Minister Jean Chrétien has quietly encouraged MPs George Rideout of Moncton and Ron MacDonald of Dartmouth to promote a union of the four Atlantic provinces, or failing that, the Maritimes.

Even more quietly, Chrétien has assigned Prairie cabinet colleague Lloyd Axworthy to explore the possibility of a marriage between Saskatchewan and Manitoba. Columnist Brian Cole, in the Winnipeg Free Press, has beaten drums for the same cause: Saskatoba.

The chances of keeping Quebec within Confederation would improve if anglophone Canadians were to show enough creative vigor to make the roster of provinces look like this: Columbia-Alberta, population 6 million; Saskatoba, 2.4 million; Ontario, 10 million; Quebec, 7 million; Atlantica, 2.4 million.

The Quebec premier would face not nine anglo premiers, but four, and not one would represent a province that could fit half its people into a baseball stadium.

But forget Quebec for now. The Maritimes must unite for far more pressing reasons.

Directly Dependent

Roughly 70 per cent of Prince Edward Island's economy is directly dependent on the federal government. The island can't even afford a building for its own legislature: its lawmakers meet in a Charlottetown chamber that the feds own.

New Brunswick and Nova Scotia are also heavily dependent on money Ottawa funnels down East from the richer provinces. It amounts to fully 40 per cent of the provincial government revenues in all three of the Maritime provinces.

Now hear this: whether or not Canada survives, the richer provinces WILL TURN OFF THIS TAP.

Consider Greater Toronto. It accounts for 20 per cent of Canada's economic output. "Toronto is the golden goose, not only for Ontario but for all of Canada," Rocco Rossi of the Boston Consulting Group insists. "Toronto drives Ontario's share, and therefore in a great way underpins Canadian Confederation."

It's going to stop doing that. A tariff system that forced Canadians in the boonies to buy goods from Toronto long kept the city content with the feds' subsidizing poorer provinces, but all that's changing.

As long as Toronto benefited from Confederation to the same extent that it shared its wealth, John Barber writes in the *Globe and Mail*, it had no grounds for complaint, "but in a free-trading global economy, Newfoundlanders and Manitobans aren't forced to buy Inglis washers and Massey-Harris combines." And Toronto will refuse to subsidize Maritimers to enable them to buy refrigerators in New England.

Toronto has endured its own fierce recession, experienced a "recovery" that created few jobs, and reeled under the pressures of globalization. "People are saying, 'Hey, we need to take care of our interests, too,'" Rossi says. "'We've always been the nice guy. So who's taking care of us?'"

Depths of Poverty

Whether or not Maritimers feel Hog Town has always been the nice guy, their political leaders must quit ducking a godawful probability. The drying-up of federal subsidies may well plunge the Maritimes into depths of poverty unknown since The Dirty '30s. This may happen even if Quebec does not separate. If Canada falls apart, conditions down here will be even worse.

Whatever the future of Canada, the only way the Maritimes can avoid a brutal immersion in poverty is to become economically self-sufficient, and to do that they must unite. If Newfoundland wants in, so much the better.

To achieve union, our politicians must make a superhuman effort to rise above the province-by-province competition for economic advantage, town-by-town rivalries, and cove-by-cove back-biting that have so long afflicted this corner of Canada.

The *Evening Times Globe*, in Saint John, reported last year that local MP and ex-mayor Elsie Wayne, when asked if she favored Maritime Union, "pointedly warned that the unionists generally assume Halifax or Moncton should be the capital, but she believes Saint John is the more logical choice because of its size and industry."

My town—first, last, and always. That's precisely the kind of thinking that threatens to scuttle the whole idea of Maritime Union, and thereby leave the people of Elsie's beloved Saint John dirt-poor in the fog.

Staunch Unionist

Listen, instead, to Moncton economist Donald J. Savoie. A bold, staunch unionist, Savoie says, "We should launch something equivalent to a war effort.

"Every public and private institution, from our universities to our business leaders and the labor movement, should be asked to contribute to the goal of economic self-sufficiency."

Why aren't more of our down-east politicians talking like that? Where's the ruddy war effort?

Thinking about the Content

1. What is Bruce's thesis?

2. What are the two main reasons Bruce presents to support his thesis?

3. Quote the sentence in which Bruce most forcefully asserts that Maritime union is necessary to avoid poverty.

Thinking about the Organization

4. In the first few paragraphs, Bruce presents details to support his contention that the four Atlantic provinces should form one province of about 2.4 million people. Which sentence startles readers, providing a lead-in that creates the desire to read his essay?

5. Quote the two sentences in which Bruce signals a transition, signals that he is moving from discussing the first major reason to unite the Maritime provinces to his second reason.

6. Bruce's article is organized into three sections. Describe them.

7. Does Bruce recapitulate his argument in his conclusion? Between the final two sentences, add a sentence that restates his contention and his two main points.

Ideas for Your Writing

"Maritime Union: Politicians Must Rise Above Parochialism to Avoid Disaster" is a persuasive essay. Politics is a rich source of topics for persuasive essays. Brainstorm ideas for an essay you might write about a political issue. Jot some notes and create a thesis. Research your topic, and outline an argument. Pretend that you're a political columnist, and write a brief essay to try to persuade readers to your point of view.

16.23

Sometimes the public debates public policy issues a long time before a law is changed or created. Certainly the public has reached no consensus about whether the Criminal Code should be changed to make it illegal for parents to spank their children. In this persuasive essay, veteran writer and social activist Michele Landsberg tries to convince readers that they should repeal Section 43, the law that permits spanking.

Let's Outlaw *Any* Hitting of Children

Michele Landsberg

When I read the welcome news that a major task force will probe the causes of child abuse deaths in Ontario, I reached for the phone and called Corinne Robertshaw.

It has been 15 years since Robertshaw, then a lawyer working in the federal civil service, did her horrific and detailed report on child abuse deaths.

She discovered that up to 200 Canadian children every year were being beaten, kicked, burned and battered to death—while doctors, children's aid workers and coroners looked the other way, listing the deaths as "accidental."

Had the federal government acted on her recommendations—instead, it desperately tried to bury the report—how many tormented infants might have been saved in the decade and a half since then?

Robertshaw now has a trenchant bit of advice for the task force.

What she pointed to was like the murder weapon that lies in full view in detective stories—and is maddeningly overlooked just because it's so obvious and innocent-looking.

It's Section 43 of the Canadian Criminal Code—the law that allows teachers, parents and other adults in authority to use "reasonable force" for the "correction" of a child.

It has been successfully used as a legal defence by parents who bruised, hurt and wounded their children with straps, sticks, belts and fists.

I confess that I balked when Robertshaw insisted, in her calm, factual manner, that Section 43 was "a key factor" in the torment and murder of children. But it turns out that she can back up her argument with powerful research.

Repeal Section 43 and hitting a child becomes an assault to be judged like any other.

Children's aid workers could step in earlier to potentially abusive situations. The federal government—and hundreds of community organizations—could credibly launch a massive education campaign on how to raise children without violence.

Children would quickly learn that no one has a right to hurt them.

And our whole culture would undergo a sea-change. We would live in a climate in which hitting children is no longer acceptable.

Here's one incisive statistic that should zing straight to the hearts of those who so vociferously insist on their right to hit their kids: Parents who approve of physical punishment have a child abuse rate *four times higher* than those who disapprove.

"The majority of child abuse cases are 'disciplinary incidents' in which the parents admit that they just lost it and went too far," said psychologist Dr. Joan Durrant, professor of family studies at the University of Manitoba, who carried out a recent eye-opening study for the federal government.

She particularly remembered the case of a father who, to force his daughter to eat dinner faster, put a knife on the table—and ended up stabbing her with it.

Does hitting a child really work as discipline?

Emphatically not. Quite the opposite.

Among findings cited by Dr. Durrant: there's a clear association between a mother's use of corporal punishment and severe tantrums among pre-schoolers.

There are also strong links between frequent spankings and all forms of children's and teens' theft, aggression, assault and violent behavior against siblings, schoolmates and parents.

One large British study showed that the best predictors of having a criminal record by age 20 were having been hit at least once a week at age 11 and having a mother who strongly believed in corporal punishment.

In fact, even though most Canadian parents admit to swatting their children at least once, almost all say they think physical punishment is ineffective—and they're ashamed of having used it.

When more than a quarter of a million Canadian children experience some form of abuse each year— and when physical punishment is responsible for the majority of child abuse cases—how can the task force not demand the repeal of Section 43, which condones violence against the most defenceless?

Of course, social conservatives will fall back on their tired old excuse for doing nothing: "You can't change human nature." Maybe not, but the point of law is to change human behavior.

We did it with smoking, with drunk driving, with seat belts.

The most dramatic example of the power of law to shape public values is in Sweden, where corporal punishment was banned in 1979.

The Swedish rate of approval of corporal punishment has since tumbled from 53 per cent to 11 per cent—and Sweden has one of the lowest child abuse death rates in the world.

Violence toward children is, sadly, a learned behavior.

Those who have been beaten grow up believing the brutality was justified—and that they have the right to inflict the same pain on their own flesh and blood.

Of course, the causes of child abuse are many and complex. "But this is one specific, obvious piece that we keep missing. If we don't hit them, we can't physically harm them," said Dr. Durrant.

Every member of the task force has a grave duty to examine his or her own past experience and confront the personal legacy of any corporal punishment.

In light of the evidence, it's no longer tolerable for responsible adults to say, "It didn't hurt me any." It did. It does.

There's every reason to believe that unless we change our disgustingly abusive law, we can't even begin to stop the battering, the broken bones—and the murder.

Thinking about the Content

1. What is Landsberg's thesis?

2. Landsberg clearly believes that making spanking illegal would create good effects for our society. What major good result does she predict? What is her argument? What are the principal ways Landsberg supports her contention?

3. Quote the statement by Dr. Joan Durrant that most powerfully supports Landsberg's argument that fewer of Canada's children would be killed by adults if we abolished parents' right to spank them?

4. Landsberg claims that most abuse begins in disciplinary incidents in which parents know they can legally use physical punishment. She cites a case history or anecdote (supplied by Dr. Durrant) to support this claim. Identify that story.

Thinking about the Organization

5. Describe the two techniques Landsberg uses to create an effective lead-in to her essay.

6. Quote Landsberg's clincher, the sentence she wrote to signal that she was concluding the essay and to leave readers with a final thought.

Ideas for Your Writing

Ideas about effective parenting vary widely in our society. If you've ever watched parents discussing their children's recreational sports activities, you'll have seen that parents have different ideas about how to promote excellence in sports. Parents also disagree about how to help children develop musically, morally, and intellectually. Muse about your ideas on how to help children develop. Narrow your focus to one area in which you have strong ideas about how to guide children. You may want to do some research. Using Landsberg's essay as an example, write for parents and tell them your ideas.

16.24

Canadians often note that they know more about the United States than Americans know about Canada. Do Canadians, though, know enough about themselves and their country? Take the quiz, and then read the essay by Gerald Caplan, a public affairs commentator.

The Canada Quiz

The Dominion Institute

1. Which of the following slogans is associated with Canada's constitution?
    Liberty, equality, fraternity
    Peace, order and good government
    Life, liberty and the pursuit of happiness
2. In which province—famous for its deposits of dinosaur bones—would you find Dinosaur Provincial Park?
3. Which Canadian prime minister regularly sought the advice of his dead mother and dog?
4. Which of the following was Canada's only woman prime minister?
    Audrey McLaughlin   Jeanne Sauvé
    Kim Campbell   Flora MacDonald
5. Which river is Canada's longest?
    St. Lawrence   Fraser
    Mackenzie   Saskatchewan
6. Who coined the phrase "the global village" and argued that "the medium is the message"?
7. What is the highest honour that Canada gives to its citizens for outstanding achievement and service to their country or humanity at large?
8. Which hockey team has won more Stanley Cups than any other?
9. Which province was the first to introduce medicare?
10. Which one of the following statements is true?
    Sir Louis-Hippolyte Lafontaine and Robert Baldwin:
        were the first Europeans to see the Rocky Mountains
        were French and British military commanders
        formed an alliance of reformers in Lower Canada and Upper Canada
11. Which of the following Canadian politicians could be called "the last Father of Confederation"?
    Lucien Bouchard   Pierre Trudeau
    Joey Smallwood   Tommy Douglas

12. What major event happened in Winnipeg in 1919?

    General strike   Red River Rebellion

    a great flood   first Stanley Cup game

13. In 1992, Roberta Bondar became

    the first Canadian woman to play in the National Hockey League

    the first Canadian woman to be launched into outer space

    the first Canadian woman to win an Oscar for being best actress

    the first Canadian woman president of General Motors of Canada

14. Who composed our national anthem, *O Canada*?

    Sir John A. Macdonald   Calixa Lavallée

    Robert Charlebois   Gordon Lightfoot

15. Who invented the first practical and commercially successful snowmobile?

16. What famous sail boat or schooner, commemorated on the 10-cent coin, was built in Nova Scotia in 1921?

    Flying Dutchman   *Titanic*

    Bluenose   *La Grande Hermine*

17. Which of the following people are Canadian?

    hockey player Chris Chelios

    country singer Shania Twain

    actor Candace Bergen

    race-car driver Jacques Villeneuve

    actor Michael J. Fox

    actor Catherine Deneuve

18. In 1890, who set out to run across Canada to raise money to fight cancer?

19. What is the name of the new territory that will be created in Canada's north in 1999?

20. On what day do Canadians honour those who served in wartime?

What Difference Does Canadian History Make?

Gerald Caplan

Another Canada Day has come and gone, but not without the usual hysteria about how ignorant we Canucks are about our own country.

Thanks to the Dominion Institute, we once again were called upon to face up to our desperate ignorance about our own geography, history and culture.

The results of a new survey, we were solemnly warned by the institute's executive director, show "a disturbing lack of knowledge about who we are and what we have accomplished together."

Reinforcing this dire conclusion, the *Star's* provincial affairs columnist, Ian Urquhart, grimly noted that the state of Canadian history in our high schools is "abysmal," and invokes no less an authority than Canadian historian Jack Granatstein, author of *Who Killed Canadian History?*

Does it matter, Urquhart asks, that only 44 per cent of Canadians surveyed could associate the phrase "peace, order and good government," with the Canadian Constitution, while the majority selected phrases that were American or French in origin?

Or that only 30 per cent could identify Mackenzie King as the Canadian prime minister who sought the advice of his dead mother and dog?

"Yes," Urquhart assures us, "history is part of the glue that binds us together. Given the decentralized nature of the Canadian state and the constant threat posed by both separatists and continentalists, we need all the glue we can get." Right. Imagine how much better we'd stick together if we all know that Canada's longest-serving prime minister was actually a certifiable nut-case.

Look at another couple of questions reproduced in the *Star*. Only 26 per cent knew which province first introduced medicare, only 25 per cent knew what "major event happened in Winnipeg in 1919."

Here's my question: What difference would it make to our country if everyone correctly answered Saskatchewan and the General Strike? Would it mean they appreciated the efforts of the NDP government in Saskatchewan of introducing medicare in 1961 against the ferocious opposition of the traditional parties and the medical profession?

Would it mean they understood the remarkable solidarity of ordinary working people in Winnipeg after World War I against the combined might of the city's power elite?

In fact, the simple one- or two-word factoids that answer the questions tell us nothing whatsoever about what people know about Canada or its history, except for some names and dates, by themselves completely meaningless. And how come people weren't asked how many Canadians are now denied benefits when they lose their jobs? Now that's important.

May I be personal? As it happens, I have an ancient M.A. in Canadian history and I'm an obsessive collector of useless information. Maybe that accounts for me getting 100 per cent on the 20 questions in the *Star*.

Yet I can name offhand about half a million fellow Canadians who would not agree that makes me a particular stellar citizen. At the same time, I know many wonderful people, dedicated to making Canada a more humane nation, who couldn't have scored very well on these questions but who are a credit to their country.

Look at our southern neighbours. A more ignorant group of earthlings has hardly ever existed. Most know diddlysquat about their own country beyond schoolkid myths. Yet no one doubts their common American-ness. We should be proud that Canadians aren't encumbered with the same national lies and jingoistic legends.

But we're getting closer.

We still see ourselves as a more caring, sharing people than the Americans, even though we haven't acted that way for much of the last decade.

If those who want to keep Canada together helped turn our expressed values into reality, they'd be making a far greater contribution to this country than by asking silly questions.

Thinking about the Content

1. What is Caplan's thesis in "What Difference Does Canadian History Make?"

2. Identify three main points, and a specific supporting detail, that Caplan makes to support his thesis.

3. Caplan is writing for the readers of Canada's largest circulation newspaper. How appropriate is his use of terms such as "certifiable nut-case" and "diddlysquat"? Choose two more formal terms.

4. Reread the last paragraph. Caplan seems to suggest that there is almost no value in studying Canadian history. Sketch an argument in favour of Canada's schools teaching Canadian history.

5. What is the piece of punctuation Caplan uses more often than many essayists? Why does he do this?

Thinking about the Organization

6. In which paragraph does Caplan most clearly express his thesis? Why does he present it so late in the essay?

Ideas for Your Writing

Gerald Caplan asks a question in the title of his essay. Consider how you feel about the teaching of Canadian history. Write a persuasive essay to try to influence newspaper readers to agree with you.

16.25 SOME CONCLUDING THOUGHTS

Reading good essays will help you write better essays. Some of Canada's best writers—Mordecai Richler, for example—write for our daily newspapers. Magazines—*Saturday Night, This Magazine, Maclean's, Canadian Forum,* for example—regularly publish essays.

We cannot have a civil society without informed citizens, and the clash of viewpoints about the good life occur within the pages of these publications. On these pages, men and women debate how we will care for our children and our environment; the quality of our hospitals, libraries, and schools; and the taxes we will pay. I hope to see your name among the writers presenting their thoughts and feelings about these life and death issues.

Fundamentals of Grammar

"The fascinating thing about writing is that it's a way of transforming the things you've experienced; it's like being able to live twice."
—*Jacques Godbout*

OBJECTIVE

When you have trouble understanding chapters 11–14, use the appendix to teach yourself the fundamentals of English grammar.

To really understand the conventions of Standard English (SE), you need to understand the vocabulary and concepts of English grammar. You would make a poor commentator if you discussed a hockey game without knowing what a *goalie* is or the rules for *icing*. You would sound uninformed if you discussed a symphony when you didn't know the names of the instruments. Yet, it might be possible to play hockey—or even the violin—without knowing the vocabulary. Here's the background information you need to understand and discuss the conventions of Standard English.

A.1 PARTS OF SPEECH

Look at these sentences and consider what they have in common:

1. "Car go!"
2. "Me go car!"
3. "Car go store."
4. "The man with the yellow hat likes that curious little monkey."
5. "The I to going am store."

You won't see sentences 1–3 in print, but children two and three years of age speak like this. As different as simple sentence 1 is from complex sentence 4, we construct them both using a small number of types or classes of words and some rules about word order. And there is something familiar and right about sentences 1–4, but sentence 5 is bizarre. It breaks the rules for word order, and we are confused by even subtle deviations from the conventions for word order, as illustrated in sentence 6.

6.   She gave him a present which delighted him.

Was he pleased by her act of generosity, or was the present delightful?

Before you can discuss the kinds of sentence structures that are conventional—or bizarre—you need to learn the parts of speech, the elements you arrange to make sentences.

There are eight parts of speech:

- nouns
- pronouns
- verbs
- adjectives
- adverbs
- conjunctions
- prepositions
- interjections

You use some words as more than one part of speech. For example, you can use *run* as a verb (I run fast) or noun (I have a run in my slacks).

If you feel that these grammatical terms for the parts of speech seem strange and unfamiliar—and, perhaps, too numerous—don't be discouraged about learning them. Think, by comparison, of how many names of vehicles you've learned! As you study this description of written English, you will begin to identify the parts of speech.

A.1.1 Words that Name (Nouns and Pronouns)

Both nouns and pronouns are used as names in sentences, mostly as the names of persons, places, and things.

A noun (N) is a word that names a person (*Seunghoon*); place (*Moose Jaw*); thing (e.g., *cider*) but including an idea, such as *conservation*; a quality (*tolerance*); or an activity (*skating*).

A noun can be singular, naming a single entity (*wolf*), or plural (*seals*).

Some nouns look like another part of speech, verbs (words that describe actions), but they are naming words. Consider this sentence:

Kayaking is my favourite activity.

Kayaking is the naming word, but it is given a special name—*gerund*—because it has the relatively unusual characteristic of being a naming word yet incorporating a verb, a word that indicates doing. It is just a noun based on a form of a verb.

Look at the next sentence where another naming word is also based on a verb form.

To swim is fun.

To swim is the naming word—the noun—in the sentence. This special naming word is called an *infinitive*.

Both gerunds and infinitives can function as nouns, and when they do they are called *verbals*, or verbal nouns.

A pronoun (P) is also a naming word, and it replaces a noun in a sentence: Anna (N) is tall. She (P) is a basketball player. The pronoun refers to Anna. *Anna* is the antecedent of the pronoun *she*. A pronoun can also replace a verbal noun and refer to it: Rafting (N, a gerund) is exciting. It (P) can be dangerous, too.

Like a noun, a pronoun can be singular (*he*) or plural (*they*).

There are several kinds of pronouns:

- These are personal pronouns in the subjective form: *I, you, he, she, it, we, they*.

- These are personal pronouns in the objective form: *me, you, him, her, it, us, them*.

- These are personal pronouns in the possessive form: *mine, yours, his, hers, its, ours, theirs* (e.g., *Ours is the smaller house*).

- These are demonstrative pronouns: *this, that, these, those*.

- These singular indefinite pronouns refer to no specific person or thing: *another, anybody, anyone, anything, each, either, everybody, everyone, everything, neither, nobody, nothing, one, somebody, someone, something*.

- These plural indefinite pronouns refer to no specific persons or things: *both, few, many, others, several, some*.

- These indefinite pronouns can be singular or plural: *all, any, more, most, some, such, which:* Such is life. Such are friends.

- Interrogative pronouns, which are used to ask questions, include the following: *what, which, who* (What is the question?)

- The relative pronouns, which refer to nouns, include: *who, whoever, whose, whom, whomever*—to refer to people—*which, whichever, whatever*—to refer to animals and objects—and *that*—to refer to people, animals, and things: Jewel is a singer that I like.

- Reflexive pronouns are personal pronouns with the word "self" attached: *herself, himself, itself, myself, ourselves, themselves, yourself, yourselves* (Give yourself a valentine.).

Try it and you'll see that all of these pronouns can be used in place of nouns.

A.1.2 Words that Indicate Doing and Being (Verbs)

A verb (V) is a word that tells what a naming word is doing (*sing*) or that links a naming word to a word describing it (*is*). The action verb *wrote* in this next sentence tells what the naming word, *Korman*, did:

Korman wrote.

Verbs can be composed of more than one word. Look at this sentence: Gordon Korman has written more than twenty novels. *Written* is the main verb and *has* is the auxiliary or helping verb (HV). The nine modals—*can, could, may, might, must, shall, should, will,* and *would*—are the most common auxiliary verbs. They indicate ability, necessity, or probability. Consider this sentence: Korman may write more about Bruno and Boots. The modal *may* suggests the possibility that Gordon Korman will write more of the adventures of these mischievous boys.

Linking verbs (LV) join a naming word with a word that describes the naming word. The linking, or copula, verb *are* links the naming word *books* in this sentence to its state of being: His books are humorous.

Are is a form of the verb *be*, the most common linking verb. Other linking verbs tell about states of being that we perceive through our senses, as in this sentence: Children feel happy when they read *This Can't Be Happening at Macdonald Hall*. Common linking verbs include *act, appear, be, become, feel,* and *taste*.

Verbs have three moods. Use the indicative mood to state facts or opinions or to ask questions. Use the imperative mood to issue a command. Use the subjunctive mood to express *if* or *that* clauses that express a wish or request or information that is hypothetical. Verbs such as *ask, demand, insist, recommend, suggest,* and *wish* are often followed by *that*. Then we make the verb subjunctive. We also do this after clauses that begin with *if*, when they express a conjecture or a condition contrary to fact.

If you were here, I would feel better.

A.1.3 Words that Modify Other Words (Adjectives and Adverbs)

The meanings of both naming words and words expressing action can be influenced by accompanying words. An adjective (ADJ) further describes or quantifies a noun or pronoun. Remember this sentence? Korman wrote. Look at the effect of adding a descriptive adjective: Young Korman wrote. We imagine a different picture. Descriptive adjectives can also occur after linking verbs, as in this sentence: Korman is popular. *Popular* is an adjective describing Gordon Korman.

A verbal can also serve as an adjective, as in this sentence with *smiling*, a present participle:

The photo shows a *smiling* Gordon Korman.

In the next sentence, the verbal, in this case in the form of a past participle, also serves as an adjective:

The accomplished author is reading to children.

A verbal in the form of an infinitive can also modify a noun:

The Toilet Paper Tigers is a good book to read.

The infinitive can also serve as an adverb and modify an adjective, as in this sentence where the adjective *easy* is modified:

Fifth-graders find it easy to read.

Adding a limiting adjective can also modify a naming word, as *two* does in this sentence:

Two characters dominate in many of Korman's books.

We change our perception of the Bruno and Boots books when we reflect that these novels have two heroes.

There are several kinds of limiting adjectives or determiners that modify naming words by more specifically identifying or enumerating them. The article *the* indicates a specific noun: The Premier is late. The writer is referring to a specific premier.

Demonstrative adjectives, such as *that, these, this,* and *those* identify particular nouns: This book is funny.

Indefinite adjectives, in contrast, such as *a* or *an*, indicate that the writer is *not* specifying a particular object. In the sentence A premier is powerful, the writer means any or all premiers have a certain characteristic: authority. Here are two more sentences with indefinite adjectives: *Some* jokes are funny. Buy me *a* cat. No specific jokes or cats are indicated.

Interrogative adjectives, such as *which, what,* and *whose*, also modify the meaning of the noun. Which car is funny? *Which* serves as an adjective of the noun *car*.

Numerical adjectives tell us the quantity of the noun in a sentence: Two children sing.

Possessive adjectives, such as *her, my, our,* and *their*, add meaning to the naming words also. The addition of a possessive adjective quite changes the meaning of the last sample sentence: Our two children sing.

An adverb (ADV) usually modifies a word expressing action (V). It usually answers one of the questions where? when? how? or why? It tells us how an action is done (quickly), or when (she swam yesterday), or where it is performed (he stuck out his thumb), or how much it is done (she studies little), to what degree the action is done (she sang enough), or under what condition (they studied together).

An adverb can also modify the meaning of an adjective (Mutt is *extremely* clever) or another adverb (she sniffs her food *very* carefully).

A.1.4 Words that Connect Other Words (Conjunctions and Prepositions)

A conjunction can connect single words (David and Goliath), groups of words (after supper but before bedtime), and whole clauses (We all ate together in the dining room, and then we sang on the veranda).

Coordinate conjunctions join words or groups of words that are the same in kind and significance. When coordinating conjunctions are used in pairs, they are called correlative conjunctions—We sold not only pop but also chips. Here are some common correlatives: *as...as, both...and, either...or, neither...nor, not only...but also, whether...or.*

A subordinate conjunction, such as *after, although, as soon as, because, so that, whereas, while*, begins a subordinate (dependent) clause and joins it to an independent clause: After you give us the money, we will buy the gift.

Here is a list of common subordinating conjunctions: *after, although, as, as if, as soon as, as though, because, before, even if, even though, if, in order that, notwithstanding, otherwise, provided, since, so that, supposing, than, that, though, unless, when, whenever, until, where, whereas, wherever, whether, while.*

Prepositions indicate additional information about the relationships of nouns and pronouns to the other words in the sentence. The result is a prepositional phrase that functions as either an adjective or adverb: He laid his hand on the car. Prepositions may tell spatial relationships (in the box, on the TV), time relationships (after the meal, before the weekend), and conceptual relationships (against all odds). Remember that a preposition is followed by a noun or pronoun, not a whole clause. Here is a list of common prepositions: *about, above, across, after, against, along, at, before, beyond, concerning, during, except, far, from, in, near, of, suspecting, since, to, toward, upon, with.*

A.1.5 Words that Show Emotions (Interjections)

Writers use interjections, such as *no, oops, ouch, well*, to indicate emotion. If the feeling expressed is mild, set off the interjection with a comma. Hmm, I guess you may go to that party. Stronger interjections are followed by an exclamation point: Ouch! That hurt.

A.2 PARTS OF SENTENCES

When you know the parts of speech and the parts of sentences, you will find it easier to write grammatically correct Standard English sentences. When a group of words forms a complete statement, question, exclamation, or demand, it is called a sentence. It has two essential parts, the subject and the predicate. After looking at these essential parts of sentences, you will examine the other parts of sentences. Then it will be time to study how to create Standard English sentences.

A.2.1 The Subject

Take a moment to consider the nature of *subjects*. Who or what a sentence is about is the subject of the sentence. In the examples, a single underline will identify the subject. Consider this sentence: <u>Birds</u> fly. Find the subject by asking who or what is doing the action, the flying. That *who* or *what* is the subject.

Consider this sentence: She runs. What is the subject? Find it by asking, "Who is running?" The subject is an unnamed person referred to as *she*. You can see that the subject can be either of the naming words, a noun or a pronoun, or another form of noun equivalent (e.g., Why I like grammar is a mystery). The specific word that comprises the subject is sometimes referred to as the simple subject.

Sentences can have more than one subject: <u>Birds</u> and <u>bats</u> fly. Search for the subject by asking who is doing the flying. The answer is both birds and bats. The words together are a compound subject.

You can see why, telling as it does who or what a sentence is about, the subject part of a sentence is a major and essential part. The whole subject part, called the complete subject, is shown underlined in the following example: <u>The birds—veterans and fledglings—</u>fly south every winter. The complete subject includes the simple subject and any other words connected to it. The adjectives, *old* and *young*, and the conjunction *and* are part of the complete subject in the sentence above.

All grammatical sentences in English have a subject and a predicate except commands. Stop! is such a command or imperative sentence. The subject *you* is *implied* or understood to be the first word of the sentence: (You) stop.

Look at this interrogative sentence: Are you going? What is the action? Going. Who is doing the going? Someone—*you*—may be going. In this case, the subject is the pronoun *you*, and it's between two parts of the verb *are going*.

What is the subject of this sentence? Many of my friends attend Dawson College. *Many* is the simple subject. *Of my friends* is a prepositional phrase, and you never find the subject of a sentence in a phrase.

A.2.2 The Predicate

The other essential part of a sentence is the predicate. The predicate part of a sentence expresses what the subject does or is; in fact, the predicate includes all the parts of the sentence that are not parts of the complete subject. The simple predicate (shown in the illustrative sentences by double underlining) is the actual verb that expresses the action. Some verbs are more than one word (I am <u>running</u>).

Sentences can have more than one verb, but not all will be the main predicate(s). Consider this sentence:

After he ate the pie, he <u>left</u>.

The main predicate is *left*. It is the word expressing the action of the subject of the main part of the sentence, the independent clause. The idea of eating has been made less important because the verb *ate* is in the subordinate or dependent clause.

Just as a sentence can have more than one subject, it can have a compound verb (Spiders <u>spin</u> webs and <u>catch</u> flies).

The complete predicate consists of the main predicate and the other words related to it, as in this sentence: The man is <u>swimming in a triathlon</u>.

The simple predicate is always a verb. A linking verb is always followed by a subject complement (a noun, pronoun or adjective that renames, describes, or classifies the subject). In the following sentence *the capital* is the complement: Ottawa is the capital of Canada.

If a subject complement is a noun, it is called a predicate noun or predicate nominative, as in the example above. If a subject (or subjective) complement is an adjective, as is *salty* in the next example, it is called a predicate adjective:

The miso tasted salty.

You cannot understand some verbs unless they have complements to complete their meanings. Each linking verb is followed by a subject complement.

Some action verbs are followed by a direct object. A transitive verb needs a direct object (DO) to complete its meaning. The DO names the person or thing affected by the action. Consider this sentence:

Masud threw.

We really can't understand that sentence because it is missing a direct object—whom or what was thrown, in this example. Look how the meaning of *throw* is clarified by including a direct object: Masud threw a javelin. Talat threw a dishrag.

A transitive verb can also be followed by an indirect object (IO):

Nicole threw the ball to her friend.

An intransitive verb, which does not have a direct object, identifies an action that does not directly affect any person or object identified in the predicate. Consider these examples:

The bacon sizzled.

The bread baked in the oven.

Nothing in the predicate is affected by the verbs *sizzled* or *baked*.

English sentences always have a predicate and a subject, although sometimes the subject is only implied.

A.2.3 Phrases

A phrase is a group of meaningful words lacking both a subject and a predicate and, thus, not a complete sentence (e.g., in a box, smiling to herself). A prepositional phrase serves, mostly, as an adjective or adverb and, occasionally, a noun. A verbal phrase—and there are gerund, infinitive, and participial phrases—can serve as a noun, adjective, or adverb.

Prepositional Phrases

A prepositional phrase consists of a group of words beginning with a preposition and including an object (and any words modifying that object). These are prepositional phrases: out of the blue, by the old mill stream, on the Net, in the car. A prepositional phrase can act like a single word as an adjective, adverb, or noun.

* **A prepositional phrase can act as an adjective.** *With the crumpled fender* modifies the noun *car* in this sentence: The car with the crumpled fender is for sale.

* **A prepositional phrase can act as an adverb.**

She sold his Corvette for ten dollars.

For ten dollars serves as an adverb telling how the subject of the sentence sold the Corvette.

* **A prepositional phrase can serve as a noun.**

Within two hours would be better for me.

Within two hours is the subject of the sentence. The phrase acts like a single noun.

Verbal Phrases

A verbal is a word that looks like a verb but does not function as an action word in a sentence. Instead, a verbal functions as a noun or modifier, usually in a verbal phrase.

* A gerund phrase consists of an -ing form of a verb and a complement or modifier. A gerund phrase always serves as a noun in a sentence.

Going to Westviking College is fun.

The gerund phrase serves as the subject. In the next sentence, the gerund phrase serves as a noun again, but this time as a direct object.

You like going to the movies.

In this sentence, the gerund phrase is the object of a preposition:

You are entertained by going to the movies.

The gerund phrase can also act as a noun by being a subjective completion:

Your hobby is going to the movies.

An infinitive phrase is also a group of words without a subject and predicate, and it is constructed from an infinitive and an object and/or modifiers. Infinitive phrases act like single nouns (To hit the ball is thrilling), adjectives (I have a book to lend to you), or adverbs (I play to win).

A participle or participial phrase is a verbal phrase beginning with a participle and followed by a complement or modifier(s), or both. It always functions like a single adjective, as in this example:

Smiling all the while, Kari put out the ant traps.

A past participle can also start a phrase that modifies a noun:

Undeterred by the peril, Onassis saved the cat from the burning car.

A perfect participle can also begin a phrase that acts like an adjective:

Having given his reasons, he resigned.

A.2.4 Clauses

A clause is a meaningful group of words containing a subject and a predicate, so a clause can be a grammatical sentence. There are two main types of clauses: independent (main) and dependent (subordinate).

Independent Clauses

An independent clause sounds like a complete grammatical sentence. It could stand alone as a sentence:

I attend Champaign Regional College.

Independent clauses often appear, though, as parts of longer sentences.

When you visit the Lennoxville Campus, you'll notice that it shares a campus with Bishop's University.

Dependent Clauses

If you read aloud a dependent or subordinate clause, it does not sound like a complete sentence (when you visit the Lennoxville Campus) because a dependent clause does not express a complete thought. There are several types of dependent clauses and they function like single parts of speech—as adjectives, adverbs, or nouns.

An adjective or relative clause modifies a noun or pronoun. It begins with a relative pronoun—*that, which, who, whom*—or a subordinating conjunction—*when, where, why*—and the pronoun or conjunction connects it to the independent clause. Here are two examples:

It was the occasion when we could not come.

The movie that we saw last week is being held over.

The relative pronoun *that* refers to *movie*, its antecedent.

An adverb clause acts like an adverb modifying a verb, another adverb or an adjective. The clause tells how, to what degree, under what condition, why, or with what result. An adverb clause begins with a subordinating conjunction, such as *after, as, because, if, when, where,* or *that.*

He lost so badly that he was discouraged.

To what degree did he lose so badly? To the degree that he was discouraged.

A noun clause serves as a noun: I saw what you did. It can be a subject or subject complement (what you think is untrue) or the object of a preposition (I will give a reward to whomever returns my purse).

A.3 THE STRUCTURE OF SENTENCES

There are four kinds of sentence structures, and they differ because they contain different numbers and types of clauses. Writing is more interesting when writers use a variety of sentence structures.

A.3.1 Simple Sentences

A simple sentence is one independent clause (e.g., I bought a book). It can be longer but still simple: Maria and Jose laughed and sang in the cool woods. Both the subject and verb are compound and there is a prepositional phrase, but the sentence is still one independent clause.

A.3.2 Compound Sentences

A compound sentence is formed from two or more main clauses: I wanted to become a chemist, so I enrolled in the pre-university sciences program.

A.3.3 Complex Sentences

A complex sentence contains an independent clause and one or more dependent clauses. Here the subordinate clause precedes the main clause:

If I obtain my Diploma of Collegial Studies (DEC) at Champlain, I can continue my studies at a university.

A.3.4 Compound–Complex Sentences

A compound–complex sentence has two or more main clauses and one or more subordinate clauses.

From humble beginnings, including being born in a log cabin, Agnes Macphail persevered; she became a teacher and, in 1921, Canada's first female member of parliament.

A.4 THE FUNCTIONS OF SENTENCES

We construct different types of sentences to perform different tasks. Want directions? Ask a question. Use a declarative sentence to tell what you see. Exclaim your surprise. Issue an order.

A.4.1 Declarative Sentences

Write a declarative sentence to make a statement: I bought some tortillas. Most of what you write is expressed in declarative sentences.

A.4.2 Interrogative Sentences

An interrogative sentence asks a question: Did you buy some perogies?

A.4.3 Imperative Sentences

An imperative sentence makes a command or request: Pass the burritos.

A.4.4 Exclamatory Sentences

An exclamatory sentence conveys strong feelings. The exclamation point helps the reader realize the intensity of the emotion expressed. If you ate some really good food at a Caribbean restaurant, you might exclaim, "I loved that roti!"

A.5 SOME CONCLUDING THOUGHTS

Reading about the fundamentals of Standard English can help you improve your writing, perhaps most by helping you learn more as you read. As you understand more about the English language, you'll notice that you sometimes pause while reading and reflect on the way a writer has observed a convention of Standard English. Those moments of introspection will help you to develop a greater command of the conventions of written English.

Works Cited

Adilman, Sid. "Coming of Age." *Toronto Star* 10 Mar. 1996: F1+.

American Psychological Association. (1994). *Publication Manual*. 4th ed. Washington: American Psychological Association.

Avery, Roberta. "Blacks Protest Renaming of Road." *Toronto Star* 3 Dec. 1995: A10.

—. "Negro Creek Road—Placed on Map." *Toronto Star* 2 Dec. 1997: A16.

Bailey, Edward P. and Philip A. Powell. *The Practical Writer*. 4th ed. Fort Worth: Harcourt Brace College Publishers, 1995.

Bergman, Brian. "Conscience of Canada." *Maclean's* 27 Nov. 1995: 24.

Bolan, Kim. "Millions of Canadians Lack Literacy Skills." *Vancouver Sun* 7 Nov. 1997, final ed.: A1.

"Book Contest Winner Was Fluke Entry." *Review* [Niagara Falls] 10 June 1997: A4.

Boulton, Marsha. *Just a Minute: Glimpses of Our Great Canadian Heritage*. Toronto: Little, Brown, 1994.

Canada Post Corporation. *Canadian Addressing Standard*. Ottawa: Canada Post Corporation, 1995.

Canada Quiz. Toronto: The Dominion Institute, 1998.

Canadian Dictionary of the English Language. Toronto: ITP Nelson, 1997.

Canadian Red Cross Society. *Safe Diving*. N.p.: Canadian Red Cross Society, 1989.

City of Niagara Falls. *Water Conservation Program*. Niagara Falls, n.d.

Clymer, D., and D.H. Roen. "Writing Across the Curriculum at the University of Arizona." Ed. M. Fleming. *Writing Across the Curriculum*. Tempe, AZ: Arizona Teachers Association (ERIC Reproduction Service No. ED 274 991), 1984. 17–27.

Columbo, John Robert, ed. *The Dictionary of Canadian Quotations*. Toronto: Stoddart, 1991.

"Crokinole." *Canadian Oxford Dictionary*. Don Mills: Oxford University Press, 1998.

Davies, Robertson. "At My Heart's Core." 1966. *An Anthology of Canadian Literature in English*. 2 vols. Ed. Russell Brown and Donna Bennett. Toronto: Oxford University Press, 1982. 595–641.

"Doctors Feel Inadequate When Smokers Try to Quit." *Standard* [St. Catharines] 28 May 1996: D3.

"Dragon Dodging." *Standard* [St. Catharines] 28 May 1996: D6.

"Essay." *The 1998 Canadian and World Encyclopedia*. CD–ROM.

Evans, Robert. "Canada Should Shun a Two Tier System: The Wealthy Might Gain, But at the Expense of Others." *Gazette* [Montreal] 20 May 1995, Final Weekly Review: B6.

Ffrench, Robert. *Out of the Past Into the Future: An Introductory Learning Guide*. Dartmouth, NS: PRIDE Communications, 1994.

Gibaldi, Joseph. *MLA Handbook for Writers of Research Papers*. 4th ed. New York: Modern Language Association, 1995.

—. *MLA Style Manual and Guide to Scholarly Publishing*. 2nd ed. New York: Modern Language Association, 1998.

"Gorge Rescue a Unique Call." *Niagara Falls Review* 8 Aug. 1995: A6.

Green, Brian and Sarah Norton. *Essay Essentials*. 2nd ed. Toronto: Harcourt Brace, 1995.

"Growing into the Future." Advertisement. *The Guardian* [Charlottetown] 28 Sept. 1996: 1–16.

Hall, Gerry. "Capital Ideas for Discovering Canada." *Toronto Star* 16 Mar. 1996: G13.

Hayman, Robert. "Book 1, No. 117." *Quodlibets Lately Come Over From New Britainiola, Old Newfoun–Land. Epigrams, and Other Small Parcels, both Morall and Divine*. London: N.p., 1628. Rpd. in *Canadian Poetry From the Beginnings Through the First World*. Ed. Carole Gerson and Gwendolyn Davies. Toronto: McClelland & Stewart, 1994. 19.

Hoban, Russell. *Riddley Walker*. 1980. London: Picador–Macmillan, 1982.

Hume, Christopher. "Mary Pratt Lives to Paint." *Toronto Star* 16 June 1996: B1.

"Internet Ethics: Citing Internet Resources." *Classroon Connect* Mar. 1996.

Jaffe, Mark. "Global Warming Treaty 'Can't Do Job.'" *Toronto Star* 18 Mar. 1995: B6.

Jourard, Ron. "Holding the Rod, Sparing the Child." *Globe and Mail* 10 April 1993: D2.

"Keeping Crime on Downward Trend." *Toronto Star* 4 Aug. 1995: A24.

Kusugak, Michael Arvaarluk. *Baseball Bats for Christmas*. Toronto: Annick, 1990.

Laxer, James. "Clark Hangs B.C. Vote on Class Issue." *Toronto Star* 5 May 1996: F3.

—. "PM's Words Can't Stop Assault on Medicare." *Toronto Star* 1 Sep. 1996: F3.

"Lucky Woman Unharmed as Lightning Bolt Melts Her Pot." *Toronto Star* 20 May 1996: A4.

MacQueen, Ken. "Learning a Thing or Two from Park's Magic Benches." *Standard* [St. Catharines] 18 June 1996: B5.

Metcalf, John, and J.R. (Tim) Struthers, eds. *Canadian Classics: An Anthology of Short Stories*. Toronto: McGraw-Hill Ryerson, 1993.

"Modem." *Penguin Canadian Dictionary*. Ed. Thomas M. Paikeday. Markham: Penguin Books Canada; Mississauga: Copp Clark Pitman, 1990.

Murphy, Angela. "Polka King 'A Little Down' As Streak Ends." *The Standard* [St. Catharines] 29 Feb. 1996: A1.

"Nutrition-Rich Dandelions More Than Weeds." *Niagara Falls Review* 5 June 1996: A9.

Papp, Leslie. "A Chilling Idea Wins Honors for Retired Doctor." *Toronto Star* 20 Feb. 1997: A6.

"Parallelism." *Gage Canadian Dictionary*. Rev. Toronto: Gage Educational Publishing–Canada Publishing, 1997.

"Plagiarize." *ITP Nelson Canadian Dictionary*. Scarborough, ON: ITP Nelson, 1997.

Powell, Kerry. "Alberta's At-Risk Wildlife." *Calgary Herald* 27 Jan. 1996: B4.

"Program to Feature Inventor Eugene Meuse." *Vanguard* [Yarmouth, NS] 24 Sept. 1996: 5B.

Quill, Greg. "Discovering Canadian TV Gold." *Toronto Star* 4 May, 1997: B1+.

Rachlis, Michael. "Tax Cut's a Windfall, But at What Cost to Society?" *Toronto Star* 10 May 1996: A29.

"Research." *Gage Canadian Dictionary*. Rev. and Expanded. Toronto: Gage Educational–Canada Publishing, 1997.

"Satire." *Canadian Oxford Dictionary*. Don Mills: Oxford University Press, 1998.

Sepkowski, Karl. "Crew of Edmund Fitzgerald Honored at Bell's Dedication." *Toronto Star* 11 Nov. 1995: A28.

"Ship Scuttled to Begin New Life." *The Standard* [St. Catharines] 24 June 1996: A3.

Slade, Michael. *Headhunter*. New York: Onyx, 1986.

Soros, George. "The Capitalist Threat." *Atlantic Monthly* Feb. 1997: 45–513. 7 Mar. 1997 <http://www.theatlantic.com/atlantic/issues/97feb/capital/capital.htm>.

Urquhart, Jane. 1986. *The Whirlpool*. Toronto: McClelland & Stewart, 1997.

Walkom, Thomas. "Snobelen Speaks Gibberish, But He Speaks the Truth." *Toronto Star* 16 Sep. 1995: B5.

Wingersky, Joy, et al. *Writing Paragraphs and Essays: Integrating Reading, Writing, and Grammar Skills*. Canadian ed. Scarborough, ON: Nelson Canada, 1995.

"Women Fans Go To Bat For Unhappy Alomar." *Toronto Star* 4 Aug. 1995: A21.

World Council of Credit Unions. *Your Guide to Protecting Your Plastic Cards*. N.p.: World Council of Credit Unions, 1991. N. pag.

Zingrone, Frank. "Wired Society Leaves Democracy Twitching." *Toronto Star* 6 Oct. 1994: A27.

Credits

16.16   "An Encounter With a Pirate" by Ruth Lemke. *Spectator* [Hamilton] 9 Sept. 1997: A2. Reprinted with the permission of the Hamilton *Spectator*.

16.17   "You, Me, Canada—We All Can Have Sponsors" by Naomi Klein. *Toronto Star* 6 July 1996, final ed.: J3. Permission courtesy of Naomi Klein.

16.18   "The Case for Excluding Tainted Evidence" by A. Alan Borovoy. *Toronto Star* 5 Dec.1996, final ed.: A33. Permission courtesy of A. Alan Borovoy.

16.19   "The Corporate Philanthropists" by Michael Valpy. *Globe and Mail* 19 June 1997: A9. Reprinted with permission from the *Globe and Mail*.

16.20   "Why Quebec is Always Such a Force in Ottawa" by Lysiane Gagnon. *Globe and Mail* 28 June 1997: D3. Reprinted with the permission of Lysiane Gagnon.

16.21   "Stopping Sexual Abuse in Sport: What Canada's Coaches Are Doing" by John Bales and Tom Kinsman. *Coaches Report* Spring 1997, vol.3, no. 4, pp. 14, 30. Copyright 1997 by Coaching Association of Canada and Canadian Professional Coaches Association. Reprinted by permission.

16.22   "Maritime Union: Politicians Must Rise Above Parochialism to Avoid Disaster" by Harry Bruce. *Ottawa Citizen* 21 Mar. 1996, final ed.: A11. Reprinted by permission of the author.

16.23   "Let's Outlaw Any Hitting of Children" by Michelle Landsberg. *Toronto Star* 22 Sept. 1996: A1, A4. Reprinted with the permission of the Toronto Star Syndicate.

16.24   "The Canada Quiz" is reprinted with the permission of the Dominion Institute. "What Difference Does Canadian History Make?" by Gerald Caplan. Reprinted by permission of the author.